D1488532

THE POETICAL WORKS
OF WILLIAM CULLEN BRYANT

Roslyn Edition

Engraved by S. Hollyer. Guttenburg, N. J.

William Cullen Bryant

From a Photograph by Sarony taken in 1875

THE POETICAL WORKS OF

WILLIAM CULLEN BRYANT

𝕽𝖔𝖘𝖑𝖞𝖓 𝕰𝖉𝖎𝖙𝖎𝖔𝖓

WITH CHRONOLOGIES OF BRYANT'S LIFE AND POEMS
AND A BIBLIOGRAPHY OF HIS WRITINGS
BY HENRY C. STURGES

AND A MEMOIR OF HIS LIFE
BY RICHARD HENRY STODDARD

ILLUSTRATED

AMS PRESS
NEW YORK

811.3
B915po

Reprinted from the edition of 1903, New York
First AMS edition published in 1969
2nd Printing, 1972
Manufactured in the United States of America

International Standard Book Number: 0-404-01143-8

Library of Congress Catalog Card Number: 79-85192

AMS PRESS INC.
NEW YORK, N. Y. 10003

PUBLISHERS' NOTE.

THIS edition of Bryant's poetical writings comprises all the verse that had been collected by the poet before his death, and all that has since been collected by his literary executor. It is the only edition in one volume that does this; the most complete one-volume edition heretofore having been the one called the Household Edition. The present edition, to which the name of Roslyn has been given, contains more than fifty poems that have not heretofore been collected, except in the two-volume quarto edition that was prepared by Mr. Parke Godwin soon after the poet's death.

A further distinction that belongs to the Roslyn Edition lies in the Chronologies of Bryant's Life and Poems, and the Bibliography of his Poetical and Prose Writings, which have been compiled by Mr. Henry C. Sturges. The material embraces, as the reader will observe, about one hundred pages. It is the result of several years of careful research by Mr. Sturges, and will be found an interesting and important contribution to the value of the edition.

NEW YORK, *August 15, 1903.*

CONTENTS.

LIST OF ILLUSTRATIONS.

▼

MEMOIR.

By RICHARD HENRY STODDARD.

MEMOIR.

THE ancestry of William Cullen Bryant might have been inferred from the character of his writings, which reflect whatever is best and noblest in the life and thought of New England. It was a tradition that the first Bryant of whom there is any account in the annals of the New World came over in the Mayflower, but the tradition is not authenticated. What is known of this gentleman, Mr. Stephen Bryant, is that he came over from England, and that he was at Plymouth, Massachusetts, as early as 1632. He married Abigail Shaw, who had emigrated with her father, and who bore him several children between 1650 and 1665, it is to be presumed at Plymouth, of which town he was chosen constable in 1663. Stephen Bryant had a son named Ichabod, who was the father of Philip Bryant, who was born in 1732. Philip Bryant married Silence Howard, the daughter of Dr. Abiel Howard, of West Bridgewater, whose profession he adopted, being a practitioner in medicine in North Bridgewater. He was the father of nine children, one of whom, Peter Bryant, born in 1767, succeeded him in his profession. Young Dr. Bryant became enamored of Miss Sarah Snell, the daughter of Mr. Ebenezer Snell, of Bridgewater, who removed his family to Cummington, whither he was followed by his future son-in-law, who married the lady of his love in 1792. Two years later, on the 3d of November, there was born to him a man-child, who was to win, and to leave,

> " One of the few immortal names
> That were not born to die."

Dr. Bryant was proud of his profession; and in the hope, no doubt, that his son would become a shining light therein, he perpetuated at his christening the name of a great medical authority, who had departed this life four years before—William Cullen. Dr. Bryant was the last of his family to practise the healing art; for Nature, wiser than he, early determined the future course of Master William Cullen Bryant. He was not to be a doctor, but a poet. A poet, that is, if he lived to be anything; for the chances were against his living at all. The lad was exceedingly frail, and had a head the immensity of which troubled his anxious father. How to reduce it to the normal size was a puzzle which Dr. Bryant solved in a spring of clear, cold water, which burst out of the ground on or near his homestead, and into which the child was immersed every morning, head and all, by two of Dr. Bryant's students—kicking lustily, we may be sure, at this matutinal dose of hydropathy.

William Cullen Bryant came of Mayflower stock, his mother being a descendant of John Alden; and the characteristics of his family included some of the sterner qualities of the Puritans. Grandfather Snell was a magistrate, and, without doubt, a severe one, for the period was not one which favored leniency to criminals. The whipping-post was still extant in Massachusetts, and the poet remembered that it stood about a mile from his early home at Cummington, and that he once saw a young fellow of eighteen who had received forty lashes as a punishment for a theft he had committed. It was, he thought, the last example of corporal punishment inflicted by law in that neighborhood, though the whipping-post remained in its place for several years, a possible terror to future evildoers. "Spare the rod, spoil the child," was the Draconian code then; and the rod, in the shape of a little bundle of birchen twigs, bound together with a small cord, was generally suspended on a nail against the wall in the kitchen, and was as much a part of the necessary furniture as the crane that hung in the fireplace or the shovel and tongs.

Magistrate Snell was a disciplinarian of the stricter sort; and as he and his wife resided with Dr. Bryant and his family, the latter stood in awe of him, so much so that young William Cullen was prevented from feeling anything like affection for him. It was an age of repression, not to say oppression, for children, who had few rights that their elders were bound to respect. To the terrors of the secular arm were added the deeper terrors of the spiritual law, for the people of that primitive period were nothing if not religious. The minister was the great man, and his bodily presence was a restraint upon the unruly, and the ruly too, for that matter. The lines of our an-

cestors did not fall in pleasant places as far as recreations were
concerned; for they were few and far between, consisting, for
the most part, of militia musters, "raisings," corn-huskings,
and singing-schools, diversified with the making of maple sugar
and cider. Education was confined to the three R's, though
the children of wealthy parents were sent to colleges as they
now are. It was not a genial social condition, it must be con-
fessed, to which William Cullen Bryant was born, though it
might have been worse but for his good father, who was in
many respects superior to his rustic neighbors. A broad-shoul-
dered, muscular gentleman, proud of his strength, his manners
were gentle and reserved, his disposition was serene, and he
was fond of society. He was not without political distinction,
for he was elected to the Massachusetts House of Representa-
tives for several terms, and afterward to the State Senate, and
he associated with the cultivated circles of Boston both as a
legislator and a physician.

William Cullen Bryant was fortunate in his father, who, if
he was disappointed when he found that his son was born to
be a follower of Apollo and not of Æsculapius, kept his dis-
appointment to himself, and encouraged the lad in his poetical
attempts. We have the authority of the poet himself that his
father taught his youth the art of verse, and that he offered
him to the Muses in the bud of life. His first efforts were
several clever "Enigmas," in imitation of the Latin writers,
a translation from Horace, and a copy of verses which were
written in his twelfth year, to be recited at the close of the
winter school, " in the presence of the Master. the Minister of

the parish, and a number of private gentlemen." They were printed on the 18th of March, 1807, in the *Hampshire Gazette*, from which these particulars are derived, and which was favored with other contributions from the pen of " C. B."

The juvenile poems of William Cullen Bryant are as clever as those of Chatterton, Pope, and Cowley ; but they are in no sense original, and it would have been strange if they had been. There was no original writing in America at the time they were written ; and if there had been, it would hardly have commended itself to the old-fashioned taste of Dr. Bryant, to whom Pope was still a power in poetry, as Addison, no doubt, was in prose. It was natural, therefore, that he should offer his boy to the strait-laced Muses of Queen Anne's time ; that the precocious boy should lisp in heroic couplets, and that he should endeavor to be satirical. Politics were running high in the first decade of the present century, and the favorite bugbear in New England was President Jefferson, who in 1807 had laid an embargo on American shipping, in consequence of the decrees of Napoleon, and the British orders in council in relation thereto. This act was denounced, and by no one more warmly than by Master Bryant, who made it the subject of a satire, which was published in Boston in 1808. It was entitled " The Embargo ; or, Sketches of the Times," and was printed for the purchasers, who were found in sufficient numbers to exhaust the first edition. It is said to have been well received, but doubts were expressed as to whether the author was really a youth of thirteen. His friends came to his rescue in an " Advertisement," which was prefixed to a second edition of

2

his little *brochure*, published in the following year, and certi-
fied to his age from their personal knowledge of himself and
his family. They also certified to his extraordinary talents,
though they should prefer to have him judged by his works,
without favor or affection. They concluded by stating that
the printer was authorized to disclose their names and places
of residence.

The early poetical exercises of William Cullen Bryant, like
those of all young poets, were colored by the books which he
read. Among these were the works of Pope, as I have al-
ready intimated, and, no doubt, the works of Cowper and
Thomson. The latter, if they were in the library of Dr. Bry-
ant, do not appear to have impressed his son at this time; nor,
indeed, does any English poet except Pope, so far as we can
judge from his contributions to the *Hampshire Gazette*, which
were continued from time to time. They were bookish and
patriotic; one, which was written at Cummington on the 8th
of January, 1810, being "The Genius of Columbia;" and
another, "An Ode for the Fourth of July, 1812," to the tune
of "Ye Gentlemen of England." These productions are un-
deniably clever, but they are not characteristic of their writer,
nor of the nature which surrounded his birthplace, with which
he was familiar, and of which he was a close observer, as his
poetry was soon to disclose.

He entered Williams College, in Williamstown, Mass., in his
sixteenth year, and remained there until 1812, distinguishing
himself for aptness and industry in classical learning and polite
literature. At the end of two years he withdrew, and com-

menced the study of law, first with Judge Howe, of Worthington, and afterward with Mr. William Baylies, of Bridgewater. So far he had written nothing but clever amateur
verse ; but now, in his eighteenth year, he wrote an imperishable poem. The circumstances under which it was composed
have been variously stated, but they agree in the main particulars, and are thus given in " The Bryant Homestead Book "
(1870), apparently on authentic information : " It was here at
Cummington, while wandering in the primeval forests, over
the floor of which were scattered the gigantic trunks of fallen
trees, mouldering for long years, and suggesting an indefinitely
remote antiquity, and where silent rivulets crept along through
the carpet of dead leaves, the spoil of thousands of summers,
that the poem entitled ' Thanatopsis ' was composed. The
young poet had read the poems of Kirke White, which, edited
by Southey, were published about that time, and a small volume of Southey's miscellaneous poems ; and some lines of
those authors had kindled his imagination, which, going forth
over the face of the inhabitants of the globe, sought to bring
under one broad and comprehensive view the destinies of the
human race in the present life, and the perpetual rising and
passing away of generation after generation who are nourished
by the fruits of its soil, and find a resting-place in its bosom."
We should like to know what lines in Southey and Kirke
White suggested " Thanatopsis," that they might be printed in
letters of gold hereafter.

When the young poet quitted Cummington to begin his
law studies, he left the manuscript of this incomparable poem

among his papers in the house of his father, who found it
after his departure. " Here are some lines that our William
has been writing," he said to a lady to whom he showed them.
She read them, and, raising her eyes to the face of Dr. Bryant,
burst into tears—a tribute to the genius of his son in which he
was not ashamed to join. Blackstone bade his Muse a long
adieu before he turned to wrangling courts and stubborn law;
and our young lawyer intended to do the same (for poetry was
starvation in America seventy years ago), but habit and nature
were too strong for him. There is no difficulty in tracing the
succession of his poems, and in a few instances the places
where they were written, or with which they concerned them-
selves. " Thanatopsis," for example, was followed by " The
Yellow Violet," which was followed by the " Inscription for
the Entrance to a Wood," and the song beginning " Soon as
the glazed and gleaming snow." The exquisite lines " To a
Waterfowl" were written at Bridgewater, in his twentieth
year, where he was still pursuing the study of law, which ap-
pears to have been distasteful to him. The concluding stanza
sank deeply into a heart that needed its pious lesson:

> " He who, from zone to zone,
> Guides through the boundless sky thy certain flight,
> *In the long way that I must tread alone,*
> *Will lead my steps aright.*"

The lawyer-poet had a long way before him, but he did
not tread it alone; for, after being admitted to the bar in Ply-
mouth, and practising for a time in Plainfield, near Cumming-

ton, he removed to Great Barrington, in Berkshire, where he saw the dwelling of the Genevieve of his chilly little " Song," his Genevieve being Miss Frances Fairchild of that beautiful town, whom he married in his twenty-seventh year, and who was the light of his household for nearly half a century. It was to her, the reader may like to know, that he addressed the ideal poem beginning " O fairest of the rural maids " (circa 1825), " The Future Life " (1837), and " The Life that Is " (1858); and her memory and her loss are tenderly embalmed in one of the most touching of his later poems, " October, 1866."

" Thanatopsis " was sent to the *North American Review* (whether by its author or his father we are not told), and with such a modest, not to say enigmatical, note of introduction, that its authorship was left in doubt. The *Review* was managed by a club of young literary gentlemen, who styled themselves " The North American Club," two of whose members, Mr. Richard Henry Dana and Mr. Edward Tyrrel Channing, were considered its editors. Mr. Dana read the poem carefully, and was so surprised at its excellence that he doubted whether it was the production of an American, an opinion in which his associates are understood to have concurred. While they were hesitating about its acceptance, he was told that the writer was a member of the Massachusetts Senate; and, the Senate being then in session, he started immediately from Cambridge for Boston. He reached the State House, and inquired for Senator Bryant. A tall, middle-aged man, with a business-like look, was pointed out to him. He was satisfied that he could not be the poet he sought, so he posted back to

Cambridge without an introduction. The story ends here, and rather tamely; for the original narrator forgot, or perhaps never knew, that Dr. Bryant was a member of the Senate, and that it was among the possibilities that *he* was the Senator with a similar name. American poetry may be said to have commenced in 1817 with the September number of the *North American Review*, which contained " Thanatopsis " and the " Inscription for the Entrance of a Wood," the last being printed as a " Fragment." Six months later, in March, 1818, the impression which " Thanatopsis " created was strengthened by the appearance of the lines " To a Waterfowl," and the " Version of a Fragment of Simonides."

Mr. Bryant's literary life may now be said to have begun, though he depended upon the practice of his profession for his daily bread. He continued his contributions to the *North American Review* in the shape of prose papers on literary topics, and maintained the most friendly relations with its conductors; notably so with Mr. Dana, who was seven years his elder, and who possessed, like himself, the accomplishment of verse. At the suggestion of this poetical and critical brother, he was invited to deliver a poem before the Phi Beta Kappa Society at Harvard College—an honor which is offered only to those who have already made a reputation, and are likely to reflect credit on the Society as well as on themselves. He accepted, and in 1821 wrote his first poem of any length, " The Ages," which still remains the best poem of the kind that was ever recited before a college society either in this country or in England; grave, stately, thoughtful, presenting in animated,

picturesque stanzas a compact summary of the history of man-
kind. A young Englishman of twenty-one—Thomas Babing-
ton Macaulay—delivered in the same year a poem on " Even-
ing," before the students of Trinity College, Cambridge; and
it is instructive to compare his conventional heroics with the
spirited Spenserian stanzas of William Cullen Bryant.

The lines " To a Waterfowl," which were written at Bridge-
water in 1815, were followed by " Green River," " A Winter
Piece," " The West Wind," " The Burial-Place," " Blessed are
they that mourn," " No man knoweth his Sepulchre," " A
Walk at Sunset," and " The Hymn to Death."

These poems, which cover a period of six busy years, are
interesting to the poetic student as examples of the different
styles of their writer, and of the changing elements of his
thoughts and feelings. " Green River," for example, is a mo-
mentary revealment of his shy temperament and his daily
pursuits. Its glimpses of nature are charming, and his wish
to be beside its waters is the most natural one in the world.
The young lawyer is not complimentary to his clients, whom
he styles " the dregs of men," while his pen, which does its
best to serve them, becomes " a barbarous pen." He is de-
jected, but a visit to the river will restore his spirits; for, as
he gazes upon its lonely and lovely stream,

> " An image of that calm life appears
> That won my heart in my greener years."

" A Winter Piece " is a gallery of woodland pictures which
surpasses anything of the kind in the language. " A Walk at

Sunset " is notable in that it is the first poem in which we see
(faintly, it must be confessed) the aboriginal element, which
was soon to become a prominent one in Mr. Bryant's poetry.
It was inseparable from the primeval forests of the New
World, but he was the first to perceive its poetic value. The
" Hymn to Death "—stately, majestic, consolatory—concludes
with a touching tribute to the worth of his good father, who
died while he was writing it, at the age of fifty-four. The
year 1821 was an important one to Mr. Bryant, for it witnessed
the publication of his first collection of verse, his marriage,
and the death of his father.

The next four years of Mr. Bryant's life were more produc-
tive than any that had preceded them, for he wrote upward of
thirty poems during that time. The aboriginal element was
creative in " The Indian Girl's Lament," " An Indian Story,"
" An Indian at the Burial-Place of his Fathers," and, noblest
of all, " Monument Mountain ; " the Hellenic element pre-
dominated in " The Massacre at Scio " and " The Song of the
Greek Amazon ; " the Hebraic element touched him lightly
in " Rizpah " and the " Song of the Stars ; " and the pure
poetic element was manifest in " March," " The Rivulet "
(which, by the way, ran through the grounds of the old home-
stead at · Cummington), " After a Tempest," " The Murdered
Traveler," " Hymn to the North Star," " A Forest Hymn,"
" O fairest of the rural maids," and the exquisite and now
most pathetic poem, " June." These poems and others not
specified here, if read continuously and in the order in which
they were composed, show a wide range of sympathies, a per-

fect acquaintance with many measures, and a clear, capacious, ever-growing intellect. They are all distinctive of the genius of their author, but neither exhibits the full measure of his powers. We can say of none of them, " The man who wrote this will never write any better."

The publication of Mr. Bryant's little volume of verse was indirectly the cause of his adopting literature as a profession. It was warmly commended, and by no one more so than by Mr. Gulian C. Verplanck, in the columns of the *New York American*. He was something of a literary authority at the time, a man of fortune and college-bred, known in a mild way as the author of an anniversary discourse delivered before the New York Historical Society in 1818, of a political satire entitled " The Bucktail Bards," and later of an " Essay on the Doctrine of Contracts." Among his friends was Mr. Henry D. Sedgwick, a summer neighbor, so to speak, of Mr. Bryant's, having a country-house at Stockbridge, a few miles from Great Barrington, and a house in town, which was frequented by the *literati* of the day, such as Verplanck, Halleck, Perçival, Cooper, and others of less note. An admirer of Mr. Bryant, Mr. Sedgwick set to work, with the assistance of Mr. Verplanck, to procure him literary employment in New York, in order to enable him to escape his hated bondage to the law ; and he was appointed assistant editor of a projected periodical called the *New York Review and Athenæum Magazine.* The at last enfranchised lawyer dropped his barbarous pen, closed his law-books, and in the winter or spring of 1825 removed with his household to New York. The projected periodical was started, as these sanguine ventures always are, with fair hopes of success. It was well edited, and its contributors were men of acknowledged ability. The June number contained two poems which ought to have made a great hit. One was "A Song of Pitcairn's Island;" the other was "Marco Bozzaris." There was no flourish of trumpets over them, as there would be now; the writers merely prefixed their initials, "B." and "H." The reading public of New York were not ready for the *Review*, which had been projected for their mental enlightenment; so, after about a year's struggle, it was merged in the *New York Literary Gazette*, which began its mission about four years before. This magazine shared the fate of its companion in a few months, when it was consolidated with the *United States Literary Gazette*, which in two months was swallowed up in the *United States Review*. The honor of publishing and finishing the last was shared by Boston and New York. Profit in these publications there was none, though Bryant, Halleck, Willis, Dana, Bancroft, and Longfellow wrote for them. Too good, or not good enough, they lived and died prematurely. Mr. Bryant's success as a metropolitan man of letters was not brilliant so far; but there were other walks than those of pure literature open to him, as to others, and into one of the most bustling of these he entered in his thirty-second year. In other words, he became one of the editors of the *Evening Post*. Henceforth he was to live by journalism.

Journalism, though an exacting pursuit, leaves its skillful followers a little leisure in which to cultivate literature. It

was the heyday of those ephemeral trifles, Annuals, and Mr.
Bryant found time to edit one, with the assistance of his friend
Mr. Verplanck, and his acquaintance Mr. Robert C. Sands
(who, by the way, was one of the editors of the *Commercial
Advertiser*), and a very creditable work it was. His contribu-
tions to "The Talisman" included some of his best poems.
Poetry was the natural expression of his genius—a fact which
he could never understand, for it always seemed to him .that
prose was the natural expression of all mankind. His prose
was, and always continued to be, masterly. Its earliest exam-
ples, outside of his critical papers in the *North American
Review* and other periodicals (and outside of the *Evening Post*,
of course), are two stories entitled "Medfield" and "The
Skeleton's Cave," contributed by him to "Tales of the Glauber
Spa" (1832)—a collection of original stories by Mr. James K.
Paulding, Mr. Verplanck, Mr. Sands, Mr. William Leggett,
and Miss Catharine Sedgwick. Three years before (1828) he
had become the chief editor of the *Evening Post*. Associated
with him was Mr. Leggett, who had shown some talent as a
writer of sketches and stories, and who had failed, like himself,
in conducting a critical publication, for which his countrymen
were not ready. He made a second collection of his poems at
this time (1832), a copy of which was sent by Mr. Verplanck
to Mr. Washington Irving, who was then, what he had been
for years, the idol of English readers, and not without weight
with the Trade. Would he see if some English house would
not reprint it? No leading publisher nibbled at it, not even
Murray, who was Mr. Irving's publisher; but an obscure book-

seller named Andrews finally agreed to undertake it, if Mr. Irving would put his valuable name on the title-page as the editor. He was not acquainted with Mr. Bryant, but he was a kind-hearted, large-souled gentleman, who knew good poetry when he saw it, and he consented to "edit" the book. He was not a success in the estimation of Andrews, who came to him one day, by no means a merry Andrew, and declared that the book would ruin him unless one or more changes were made in the text. What was amiss in it? He turned to the "Song of Marion's Men," and stumbled over an obnoxious couplet in the first stanza:

> "The British soldier trembles
> When Marion's name is told."

"That won't do at all, you know." The absurdity of the objection must have struck the humorist comically; but as he wanted the volume republished, he good-naturedly saved the proverbial valor of the British soldier by changing the first line to

> "The foeman trembles in his camp,"

and the tempest in a teapot was over, as far as England was concerned. Not as far as the United States was concerned, however; for when the circumstance became known to Mr. Leggett, he excoriated Mr. Irving for his subserviency to a bloated aristocracy, and so forth. Mr. John Wilson reviewed the book in *Blackwood's Magazine* in a half-hearted way, patronizing the writer with his praise.

The poems that Mr. Bryant wrote during the first seven

years of his residence in New York (some forty in number, not including translations) exhibited the qualities which distinguished his genius from the beginning, and were marked by characteristics which were rather acquired than inherited. In other words, they were somewhat different from those which were written at Great Barrington. The Hellenic element was still visible in "The Greek Partisan" and "The Greek Boy," and the aboriginal element in "The Disinterred Warrior." The large imagination of "The Hymn to the North Star" was radiant in "The Firmament," and in "The Past." Ardent love of nature found expressive utterance in "Lines on Revisiting the Country," "The Gladness of Nature," "A Summer Ramble," "A Scene on the Banks of the Hudson," and "The Evening Wind." The little book of immortal dirges had a fresh leaf added to it in "The Death of the Flowers," which was at once a pastoral of autumn and a monody over a beloved sister. A new element appeared in "The Summer Wind," and was always present afterward in Mr. Bryant's meditative poetry—the association of humanity with nature—a calm but sympathetic recognition of the ways of man and his presence on the earth. The power of suggestion and of rapid generalization, which was the key-note of "The Ages," lived anew in every line of "The Prairies," in which a series of poems present themselves to the imagination as a series of pictures in a gallery—pictures in which breadth and vigor of treatment and exquisite delicacy of detail are everywhere harmoniously blended, and the unity of pure Art is attained. It was worth going to the ends of the world to be able to write "The Prairies."

Confiding in the discretion of his associate Mr. Leggett, and anxious to escape from his daily editorial labors, Mr. Bryant sailed for Europe with his family in the summer of 1834. It was his intention to perfect his literary studies while abroad, and to devote himself to the education of his children; but his intention was frustrated, after a short course of travel in France, Germany, and Italy, by the illness of Mr. Leggett, whose mistaken zeal in the advocacy of unpopular measures had seriously injured the *Evening Post*. He returned in haste early in 1836, and devoted his time and energies to restoring the prosperity of his paper. Nine years passed before he ventured to return to Europe, though he managed to visit certain portions of his own country. His readers tracked his journeys through the letters which he wrote to the *Evening Post*, and which were noticeable for justness of observation and clearness of expression. A selection from Mr. Bryant's foreign and home letters was published in 1852, under the title of "Letters of a Traveler."

The life of a man of letters is seldom eventful. There are, of course, exceptions to the rule; for literature, like other polite professions, is never without its disorderly followers. It is instructive to trace their careers, which are usually short ones : but the contemplation of the calm, well-regulated, self-respecting lives of the elder and wiser masters is much more satisfactory. We pity the Maginns, and Mangans, and Poes, whom we have always with us; but we admire and reverence such writers as Wordsworth, and Thackeray, and Bryant, who dignify their high calling. The last thirty years of the life of

Mr. Bryant were devoid of incidents, though one of them
(1866) was not without the supreme sorrow—death. He de-
voted himself to journalism as conscientiously as if he still had
his spurs to win, discussing all public questions with indepen-
dence and fearlessness; and from time to time, as the spirit
moved him, he added to our treasures of song, contributing to
the popular magazines of the period, and occasionally issuing
these contributions in separate volumes. He published " The
Fountain and Other Poems" in 1842; "The White-Footed
Deer and Other Poems" in 1844; a collected edition of his
poems, with illustrations by Leutze, in 1846; an edition in two
volumes in 1855; "Thirty Poems" in 1866; and in 1876
a complete illustrated edition of his poetical writings. To
the honors which these volumes brought him he added fresh
laurels in 1870 and 1871 by the publication of his translation
of the "Iliad" and the "Odyssey"—a translation which was
highly praised both at home and abroad, and which, if not
the best that the English language is capable of, is, in many
respects, the best which any English-writing poet has yet
produced.

There comes a day in the intellectual lives of most poets
when their powers cease to be progressive and productive, or
are productive only in the forms to which they have accus-
tomed themselves, and which have become mannerisms. It
was not so with Mr. Bryant. He enjoyed the dangerous dis-
tinction of proving himself a great poet at an early age; he
preserved this distinction to the last, for the sixty-four years
which elapsed between the writing of "Thanatopsis" and the

writing of " The Flood of Years" witnessed no decay of his
poetic capacities, but rather the growth and development of
trains of thought and forms of verse of which there was no
evidence in his early writings. His sympathies were enlarged
as the years went on, and the crystal clearness of his mind was
colored with human emotions.

To Bryant, beyond all other modern poets, the earth was a
theatre upon which the great drama of life was everlastingly
played. The remembrance of this fact is his inspiration in
" The Fountain," " An Evening Revery," " The Antiquity of
Freedom," " The Crowded Street," " The Planting of the
Apple-Tree," " The Night Journey of a River," " The Sower,"
and " The Flood of Years." The most poetical of Mr. Bry-
ant's poems are, perhaps, " The Land of Dreams," " The
Burial of Love," " The May Sun sheds an Amber Light," and
" The Voice of Autumn ;" and they were written in a succes-
sion of happy hours, and in the order named. Next to these
pieces, as examples of pure poetry, should be placed " Sella "
and " The Little People of the Snow," which are exquisite
fairy fantasies. The qualities by which Mr. Bryant's poetry
are chiefly distinguished are serenity and gravity of thought ;
an intense though repressed recognition of the mortality of
mankind ; an ardent love for human freedom ; and unrivaled
skill in painting the scenery of his native land. He had no
superior in this walk of poetic art—it might almost be said no
equal, for his descriptions of nature are never inaccurate or
redundant. " The Excursion " is a tiresome poem, which con-
tains several exquisite episodes. Mr. Bryant knew how to

write exquisite episodes, and to omit the platitudes through which we reach them in other poets.

It is not given to many poets to possess as many residences as Mr. Bryant, for he had three—a town-house in New York, a country-house, called "Cedarmere," at Roslyn, Long Island, and the old homestead of the Bryant family at Cummington. He passed the winter months in New York, and the summer and early autumn months at his country-houses. No distinguished man in America was better known by sight than he.

"O good gray head that all men knew"

rose unbidden tc one's lips as he passed his fellow-pedestrians in the streets of the great city, active, alert, with a springing step and a buoyant gait. He was seen in all weathers, walking down to his office in the morning, and back to his house in the afternoon—an observant antiquity, with a majestic white beard, a pair of sharp eyes, and a face which, noticed closely, recalled the line of the poet :

"A million wrinkles carved his skin."

Mr. Bryant had a peculiar talent, in which the French excel—the talent of delivering discourses upon the lives and writings of eminent men ; and he was always in request after the death of his contemporaries.

Beginning with a eulogy on his friend Cole, the painter, who died in 1848, he paid his well-considered tributes to the memory of Cooper and Irving, and assisted at the dedication in the Central Park of the Morse, Shakespeare, Scott, and Hal-

3

leck monuments. His addresses on those occasions, and others that might be named, were models of justice of appreciation and felicity of expression. His last public appearance was at the Central Park, on the afternoon of May 29, 1878, at the unveiling of a statue to Mazzini. It was an unusually hot day, and after delivering his address, which was remarkable for its eloquence, he accompanied General James Grant Wilson, an acquaintance of some years' standing, to his residence in East Seventy-fourth street. General Wilson reached his door with Mr. Bryant leaning on his arm; he took a step in advance to open the inner door, and while his back was turned the poet fell, striking his head on the stone platform of the front steps. It was his death-blow; for, though he recovered his consciousness sufficiently to converse a little, and was able to ride to his own house with General Wilson, his fate was sealed. He lingered until the morning of the 12th of June, when his capacious spirit passed out into the Unknown. Two days later all that was mortal of him was buried beside the grave of his wife at Roslyn.

Such was the life and such the life-work of William Cullen Bryant.

R. H. STODDARD.

CHRONOLOGIES OF BRYANT'S LIFE AND POEMS, A BIBLIOGRAPHY OF HIS POETICAL AND PROSE WRITINGS, ETC.

COMPILED BY HENRY C. STURGES.

CHRONOLOGY OF BRYANT'S LIFE.

FOUNDED ON PARKE GODWIN'S BIOGRAPHY OF BRYANT.

So live, that when thy summons comes to join
The innumerable caravan, that moves
To that mysterious realm, where each shall take
His chamber in the silent halls of death,
Thou go not, like the quarry-slave at night,
Scourged to his dungeon, but, sustained and soothed
By an unfaltering trust, approach thy grave,
Like one who wraps the drapery of his couch
About him, and lies down to pleasant dreams.

1794.

WILLIAM CULLEN BRYANT was born at Cummington, Massachusetts, November 3d of this year. In regard to the exact site of the house in which he was born, Mr. Bryant says, in a statement printed in Parke Godwin's biography of him: "My father and mother then lived in a house, which stands no longer, near the center of the township, amid fields which have a steep slope to the north fork of the Westfield River, a shallow stream brawling over a bed of loose stones in a very narrow valley. A few old apple-trees mark the spot where the house stood, and opposite, on the other side of the way, is a grave-yard in which sleep some of those who came to Cummington while it was yet a forest. It was a small house constructed of square logs, afterward removed and placed near that occu-pied by Daniel Dawes. On my first birthday there is a record that I could already go alone, and on the 28th of March, 1796, when but a few days more than sixteen months old, there is another record that I knew all the letters of the alphabet."

1797.

In September of this year the family moved to Plainfield. "The poet was puny and very delicate in body, and of a pain-

fully nervous temperament," said Senator Dawes in his Cen-
tennial Address, at Cummington, in June, 1879. "In a few
years, when he had become famous, those who had been medi-
cal students with his father when he was struggling for exist-
ence with the odds very much against him, delighted to tell of
the cold baths they were ordered to give the infant poet in a
spring near the house each early morning of the summer
months, continuing the treatment in spite of the outcries and
protestations of their patient, so late into the autumn as some-
times to break the ice which skimmed the surface."

Long years afterward Mr. Bryant wrote: "I have lately
been to look at the site of that house. Nothing is left of it
but the cellar and some portion of the chimney among a thick
growth of brambles."

1798.

"In May," says Mr. Bryant, writing of this year, "our
family moved again to the distance of about two miles, and
occupied a house in Cummington. Not a trace of it now
remains. The plow has passed over its site and leveled the
earth where it stood, but immediately opposite are yet seen the
hollow of an old cellar and the foundation stones of a house
where there lived a neighbor. From my new abode, before I
had completed my fourth year, I was sent to the district
school."

1799.

"In April," continues the poet, "when I was in my fifth
year, our family went to live at the homestead of my grand-
father on the mother's side, Ebenezer Snell, which I now pos-
sess, and which became my father's home for the rest of his
lifetime. While living at the homestead I went with my
elder brother, Austin, to a district school kept in a little
house which then stood near by on the bank of a rivulet that
flows by the dwelling. The education which we received here
was of the humblest elementary kind, stopping at grammar,
unless we include theology, as learned from the Westminster
Catechism, which was our Saturday exercise. I was an excel-
lent, almost infallible speller, and ready in geography, but in

the catechism, not understanding the abstract terms, I made but little progress."

1803.

"In my ninth year," writes Mr. Bryant, "I began to make verses, some of which were utter nonsense. A year or two later my grandfather gave me as an exercise the first chapter of the Book of Job to turn into verse. I put the whole narration into heroic couplets, one of which I remember as the first draft:

> His name was Job, evil he did eschew.
> To him were born seven sons; three daughters too!

I paraphrased afterward the Hundred and Fourth Psalm."

1804–1806.

"In the Spring of 1804," Mr. Bryant says further, in a passage given by Mr. Godwin, "when I was ten years old I composed a little poem, the subject of which was The Description of the School, and which I declaimed on the schoolroom floor. It was afterward printed in the Hampshire Gazette, the county newspaper published at Northampton. Meantime I wrote various lampoons on my schoolfellows and others, and when the great eclipse of the sun took place in June, 1806, I celebrated the event in verse. So my time passed in study, diversified with labor and recreation. In the long winter evenings, in the stormy winter days, I read with my elder brother books from my father's library—not a large one, but well chosen. I remember well the delight with which we welcomed the translation of the Iliad by Pope, when it was brought into the house. My brother and myself, in emulation of the ancient heroes, made for ourselves wooden shields, swords and spears, and fashioned old hats in the shape of helmets with plumes of tow, and in the barn, when nobody observed us, we fought the battles of the Greeks and Trojans over again. I was always, from my earliest years, a delighted observer of external nature; the splendors of a winter daybreak over the wide wastes of snow seen from our windows, the glories of the autumnal woods, the gloomy approaches of the thunder-storm

and its departure amid sunshine and rainbows, the return of
spring with its flowers, and the first snowfall of winter."

1808.

Mr. Bryant further states: "In February, 1808, General Wood-
bridge, of Worthington, a place about four miles distant from
our dwelling, died. He was a promising and popular lawyer,
held in high esteem by the Federal party to which he belonged,
and was much lamented. My father suggested this event as a
subject for a monody. I composed one beginning with these
lines:

> The word is given—the cruel arrow flies
> With death foreboding aim, and Woodbridge dies!
> Lo! Hampshire's genius bending o'er his bier
> In silent sorrow heaves the sigh sincere!

"About this time the animosity with which the two polit-
ical parties—Federalists and Republicans as they called them-
selves—regarded each other was at its height. My father was
a Federalist, and his skill in his profession gave him great
influence in Cummington and the neighboring county. I read
the newspapers of the Federal party, and took a strong interest
in political questions. Under Mr. Jefferson's administration,
in consequence of our disputes with Great Britain, an embargo
was laid in 1807 upon all the ports of our republic, which, by
putting a stop to all foreign commerce, had a disastrous effect
on many private interests, and embittered the hatred with
which the Federalists regarded their political adversaries, and
particularly Mr. Jefferson. I had written some satirical lines
apostrophizing the President, which my father saw, and think-
ing well of them, encouraged me to write others in the same
vein. This I did willingly, until the additions grew into a
poem of several pages. This poem was published in Boston,
1808, in a little pamphlet entitled The Embargo, or Sketches
of the Times—A Satire. By a Youth of Thirteen. I had the
honor of being kindly noticed in the Monthly Anthology, a lit-
erary periodical published in Boston, which quoted from it the
paragraph that had attracted my father's attention. It was
decided that I should receive a college education, and I was

accordingly taken by my father to the house of my mother's brother, the Rev. Dr. Thomas Snell, in North Brookfield, to begin the study of Latin. I began with the Latin grammar, went through the Colloquies of Corderius, in which the words, for the ease of the learner, were arranged according to the English order, and then entered upon the New Testament in Latin. Next the Æneid of Virgil. While I was occupied with the Æneid my father wrote to me advising me to translate some portion of it into English verse. Accordingly I made a rhymed translation of the narrative of A Tempest in the first book. Somebody showed me a piece of paper with the title The Endless Knot, the representation of an intricate knot in parallel lines, between which were written some homely verses. I thought I could write better ones, and my head being full of the ancient mythology, I composed this." (Life, p. 29.)

1809.

" While I was at my uncle's," the poet continues, "another edition of my poem, The Embargo, was published in Boston. It had been revised and somewhat enlarged, and a few shorter poems were added. I went through the Æneid in my Latin studies, and then mastered the Eclogues and the Georgics, after which my uncle put into my hands a volume of the select Orations of Cicero. In the beginning of July, having read through the volume of Cicero's Orations, I left the excellent family of my uncle, where I had been surrounded by the most wholesome influences and examples, and returned to Cummington, after an absence of just eight calendar months. I took my place with the haymakers on the farm, and did, I believe, my part until the 28th of August, when I went to begin my studies in Greek with the Rev. Moses Hallock, in the neighboring township of Plainfield, where he was the minister. I committed to memory the declensions and conjugations of the Greek tongue with the rules of syntax, and then began reading the New Testament in Greek, taking first the Gospel of St. John. At the end of two calendar months I knew the Greek New Testament from end to end, almost as if it had been English, and I returned to my home in Cummington, where a few days afterward I completed my fifteenth year.

1810.

" The next winter I was occupied with studies preparatory to entering college, which, for reasons of economy, it was decided that I should do a year in advance; that is to say, as a member of the sophomore class. At this time I had no help from a tutor, but in the spring I went again for two months to Plainfield and received from Mr. Hallock instructions in mathematics. In the beginning of September, when the annual commencement of Williams College was at that time held, I went with my father to Williamstown, passed an easy examination, and was admitted a member of the sophomore class. After the usual vacation I went again to Williamstown and began my college life. I mastered the daily lessons given out to my class and found much time for miscellaneous reading, for disputations and for literary composition in prose and verse. No attention was then paid to prosody, but I made an attempt to acquaint myself with the prosody of the Latin language and tried some experiments in Latin verse, which were clumsy and uncouth enough. Among my verses was a paraphrastic translation of Anacreon's Ode on Spring:

> So fragrant Spring returns again
> With all the graces in her train!

a version of David's lament over Saul and Jonathan, II Samuel i, 19 (Godwin's Life of Bryant, p. 76); the version of A Fragment of Simonides, a poem recited before my class; also an Indian war-song:

> Ghosts of my wounded brethren, rest;
> Shades of the warrior dead!

(See Godwin's Life of Bryant, p. 90.) Also note by Mr. Arthur Bryant, " I still retain in memory fragments and entire poems written about this period, many of which were never printed." Such as the Œdipus Tyrannus, Elegy on the Death of the Gerrymander, etc. (Godwin's Life of Bryant, p. 94.)

The Gerrymander was a figure representing a monster which the Federal newspapers constructed from outlines made on a map of Massachusetts by a peculiar arrangement of the electoral votes, which Elbridge Gerry was said to have so distributed as to secure a Legislature which would elect him to the United States Senate. To this period in Bryant's life belong the translations of Lucian's Dialogues of the Dead; also several Odes of Anacreon; the lines of Mimnermus of Colophon on The Beauty and Joy of Youth; An Idyl by Bion and choruses from Sophocles. During a school vacation in January, 1810, he wrote a patriotic song called The Genius of Columbia. (For full text of this poem, see Godwin's Life of Bryant, pp. 80–81.) An attempt to declaim before his class a passage from Knickerbocker's History of New York ended in his being compelled to resume his seat under the frowns of the tutor, the humor of it so convulsed him with laughter.

1811.

Under date of May 8th of this year Bryant writes: "Before the third term of my sophomore year was ended, I asked and obtained an honorable dismission from Williams College, and going back to Cummington began to prepare myself for entering the junior class at Yale. I pursued my studies with some diligence and without any guides save my books; but when the time drew near that I should apply for admission at Yale my father told me that his means did not allow him to maintain me at New Haven, and that I must give up the idea of a full course of college education."

At this period he read Cowper, Thomson, Burns, Southey, etc. These studies, however, did not win him from his rambles, during one of which his thoughts took a shape that proved to be of the greatest consequence in his poetic growth. He had been engaged in comparing Blair's poem, The Grave, with another of the same cast by Bishop Porteous, and his mind was also considerably occupied with a recent volume of Kirke White's verses. "It was in the autumn," we are told, "the blue of the summer sky had faded into gray and the brown earth was heaped with sear and withered emblems of the departed glory of the year. As he trod up on the hollow-sounding ground in the loneliness of the woods and among the prostrate trunks of trees that for generations had been moldering into dust, he thought how the vast solitudes about him were filled with the same sad tokens of decay."

In December, 1811, he began the study of law in the office of Mr. Howe, of Worthington, a quiet little village some four or five miles from Cummington. He congratulated himself in a little poem on his escape from the farm. (See p. 103, Godwin's Life of Bryant.) To this period belongs the love-song beginning:

> I knew thee fair and deemed thee free
> From fraud and guile and faithless art;
> Yet had I seen as now I see,
> Thine image ne'er had stained my heart.

1812.

Of this period Parke Godwin says in his Life of Bryant: "Carefully preserved among his papers—and he was for the most part inattentive in keeping what concerned himself only —are several fragments of poems expressive of the joys, the doubts and the disappointments of love." (See Godwin's Life of Bryant, pp. 107–114, for text of these love poems.) He wrote at this time for the Washington Benevolent Society of Boston a Fourth of July ode, in which are these lines:

> Should justice call to battle
> The applauding shout we'd raise!
> A million swords would leave their sheath—
> A million bayonets blaze!

Another series of poems belonging to this period, and never published save in Godwin's Life of Bryant, is called A Chorus of Ghosts. This was published in the New York Review for 1824 over the signature of X, with several stanzas wanting, but since supplied by Mr. Arthur Bryant. (For full text of these poems see Godwin's Life of Bryant, pp. 115–117.)

1814.

In June, 1814, he removed to Bridgewater and resided with his grandfather, Dr. Philip Bryant, and entered the law office of Mr. William Baylies. To this period belong the lines To a Friend on his Marriage, in the North American Review, March, 1818. On the 4th of July he delivered a piece of rhymed declamation, deploring the folly and ravages of war, and rejoicing in the downfall of Napoleon, then sent to Elba. (For text of this Ode see Godwin's Life, p. 121.) On August 9, 1814, he passed his preliminary examination for admission to the bar and received a certificate sprinkled with snuff, instead of sand, for which he paid six dollars. Mr. Bryant was at this time completely possessed with the military fever. A letter dated Cummington, November 16, 1814, Mass. State Archives, reads :

To his Excellency, Caleb Strong, Governor and Commander-in-Chief of the Commonwealth of Mass. :

Humbly representing that William C. Bryant, your petitioner, being desirous to enter the service of the State in the present struggle with a possible enemy, etc., etc.

A severe illness prevented him from enlisting, and after his recovery he penned an Ode to Death, beginning :

Oh, thou whom the world dreadeth—art thou nigh
To thy pale Kingdom Death to summon me ?

1816.

On July 25, 1816, Mr. Bryant was appointed adjutant in the Massachusetts militia, but returned the commission to the adjutant-general February 8, 1817. The treaty of peace signed at Ghent ended the war. To this period belongs the ode written for the Howard Society of Boston.

Oh taught by many a woe and fear
We welcome thy returning wing!
And earth, Oh Peace, is glad to hear,
Thy name among her echoes ring."

(For full text of this poem see Godwin's Life, p. 137.) "On the 15th of August, 1816, he left Bridgewater with his credentials as an Attorney of the Common Pleas in his pocket." He now adopted the poetic form in which he worked for the rest of his life. See poem I cannot forget with what Fervid Devo-

tion. Mr. Godwin says: "All his papers of this period bear
witness to constant and ever renewed attempts in different
forms to paint her (Nature's) varying aspects."

"He hums to himself of flowers, groves, streams, trees, and
especially of winds which abounded in the region in which he
lived. Among other things, he began an Indian story after the
manner of Scott's Highland Poems, but judging by the little of
it that was executed, the descriptive quite overmastered the
narrative parts." (See p. 141 of Godwin's Life for speci-
mens of poems of that period.) "He wrote at this time The
Yellow Violet just before leaving Bridgewater on a visit to
Cummington."

"Another poem, Inscription for the Entrance to a Wood,
published in the North American Review, 1817, under the title
of A Fragment, was composed in an old forest fronting his
father's house."

1817.

On December 15, 1817, he walked over to Plainfield, a town
seven miles from Cummington on the opposite hillside. Mr.
Godwin says in his Life of Bryant: "As he walked up the
hills very forlorn and desolate indeed, not knowing what was
to become of him in the big world which grew bigger as he
ascended and yet darker with the coming on of night. The
sun had already set, leaving behind it one of those brilliant
seas of chrysolite and opal which often flood the New England
skies. While he was looking upon the rosy splendor with rapt
admiration, a solitary bird made wing along the illuminated
horizon. He watched the lone wanderer until it was lost in
the distance, asking himself whither it had come and to what
far home it was flying. When he went to the house where he
was to stop for the night, his mind was still full of what he
had seen and felt, and he wrote those lines, as imperishable as
our language, To A Waterfowl:

> He who from zone to zone
>   Guides through the boundless sky thy certain flight,
> In the long way that I must tread alone
>   Will lead my steps aright!

" He remained in Plainfield eight months, and then entered into a partnership with George H. Ives, of Great Barrington. In June his father wrote to him from Boston that Mr. Willard Philips (an old Hampshire friend) desired him to contribute something to his new Review. The younger Bryant either was not tempted, or was too busy to make reply. The father, while his son was at Bridgewater, discovered the manuscripts of Thanatopsis, The Fragment, and a few other poems carefully hidden away in a desk."

The first number of the North American Review appeared in May, 1815. Mr. Tudor acted as editor until 1817, when it passed entirely into the hands of a club. The chief members were Richard H. Dana, Edward T. Channing, and Willard Philips. Edward T. Channing (brother of William Ellery Channing) afterward became Boylston Professor of Rhetoric at Harvard College. Philips was a tutor at Harvard, but became Judge of Probate and writer of law books. Thanatopsis was carried to Philips. Dana said : " Oh, Philips, you have been imposed upon. No one on this side of the Atlantic is capable of writing such verses." Thanatopsis was published in September. Prefixed were four stanzas on the subject of death, which had no connection with it and were not intended for publication.

1818.

In March, 1818, Mr. Bryant wrote To a Friend on his Marriage, Version of Simonides, and in July an essay on American poetry. The department of original poetry in the North American Review was discontinued in 1818. The essay on the Happy Temperament was published in No. 9, p. 206. In June, 1818, he reviewed Paulding's Backwoodman.

At Mr. Philips's suggestion he wrote an essay on American poetry for the July number, a recent collection of American poetry by Solyman Brown furnishing the subject. On the 29th of January, 1818, he delivered an address before the Bible Society of Great Barrington. This was published in the Berkshire Star of February 6, 1818. In the spring of 1824 the editorship of the North American Review was changed, Mr. Alex.

ander and Edward Everett taking charge. They rejected a critique by Mr. Bryant on The Idleman, and he stopped writing for the magazine.

1819.

Mr. Bryant was interested in the local affairs of the town in which he lived, and on March 9th he was elected Tithingman of his native town, whose duties consisted in keeping order in the churches and enforcing the observance of the Sabbath. He was also elected Town Clerk and appointed Justice of the Peace. (Note.—"An old gentleman still living makes it a boast that he was 'jined' to his first old woman by Squire Bryant.")

1820.

" On the 20th of March, Mr. Bryant's father, who had been ill for a year or more, died at the age of fifty-three. The memory of this loss clung to him for many years."

"Save the fragment called the The Burial-Place, begun and broken off in 1819, Mr. Bryant had written nothing since he entered upon his practise in 1816. The pieces sent to the North American Review were taken from his scrap-book."

"Soon after his father's death, while he was yet full of the sentiment it inspired, an appeal was made to him by the Unitarians in aid of a collection of hymns. Mr. Henry D. Sewall, the editor, applied to Miss Catherine M. Sedgwick, of Stockbridge, to use her efforts in his behalf, and the result was that six hymns were sent for the collections." (See note, p. 163, of Godwin's Life.)

" On the 4th of July he delivered an oration in the Stockbridge church."

1821.

Mr. Godwin says, speaking of this period: " Mr. Dana's project for a periodical to be called The Idleman, and to consist of poetry, essays, criticisms, and historical and biographical sketches, enlisted Mr. Bryant's warmest interest from the beginning. As early as May, 1821, Mr. Channing asked his assistance for it, suggesting 'That a literary frolic now and then is the best restorative for a conscientious but overworked

and jaded attorney.' In reply Mr. Bryant put The Yellow
Violet at Mr. Dana's disposal, and enclosed another piece,
Green River. He also contributed to it A Winter Piece, The
Burial-Place, and a Walk at Sunset."

" Not long after his settlement at Great Barrington, he met
at a village sociable the young lady, Miss Fanny Fairchild,
who afterward became his wife. The depth of his attachment
was not revealed to him until the object of it was temporarily
called away. He began to pity himself very much in rhymes—
Oh Fairest of the Rural Maids is the only one of these poems
the author has cared to print." (See note, p. 167, of Life for
Another.) " On Miss Fairchild's return they became engaged,
and on the 11th of June, 1821, were married at the house of
the bride's sister, Mrs. Henderson." (See letter of Mr. Bryant
to his mother announcing the event, p. 169 of Godwin's Life.)

" A few months after his marriage Mr. Bryant was surprised
by a communication from the secretary of the Phi Beta Kappa
Society of Harvard College, Mr. U. J. Spooner, requesting him
' By a unanimous vote of the Society' to deliver the usual
poetical address at the next commencement." (See letter to
Mr. Spooner dated April 26, 1821, pp. 170–171, of Godwin's
Life ; also letter to his wife dated August 25th, pp. 171–172.)

" His poem called The Ages was delivered August 30th in
the Old Congregational Church of Cambridge. Before leaving
Boston he consented to have it published with his other poet-
ical effusions. The result was a small pamphlet of 44 pages
published in September and containing eight poems : The
Ages, To a Waterfall, The Fragment from Simonides, Inscrip-
tion for the Entrance to a Wood, The Yellow Violet, The
Song, Green River, and Thanatopsis. The October number of
the North American Review contained an elaborate criticism.
The entire collection was copied into a selection of American
Poetry, by Mr. Roscoe, published by Allman, London, 1822.
Blackwood for June contained a favorable criticism."

1823.

" The revolt of the Greeks from Turkish rule excited his
interest. In December, 1823, he delivered an address on the

4

subject in Great Barrington. He also wrote a farce for the stage called The Heroes, but it was a failure."

His friends were very anxious for him to come to New York. Henry J. Anderson at this time had revived the Atlantic Magazine (published for a while by Robert J. Sands). Bliss and White, the publishers, paid him $500 a year and authorized an expenditure of $500 more. (See letter to his wife from New York under date of April 24, 1824. Godwin's Life, p. 189.)

1824.

Theophilus Parsons established the United States Literary Gazette in Boston, publishing the first number April 1st. Mr. Bryant's first contribution was a poem called Rizpah.

A letter written to his friend, Richard H. Dana, at Cambridge, Mass., under date of July 8th, says: "You inquire whether I have written anything except what I have furnished to Parsons (for United States Literary Gazette). Nothing at all. I made an engagement with him with a view in the first place to earn something in addition to the emoluments of my profession, which, as you may suppose, are not very ample; and in the second place to keep my hand in, for I was very near discontinuing entirely the writing of verses." He also mentions in this same letter the narrative poem of the Spectre Ship. This is partly extant in manuscript, but was never published.

His work at this time consisted largely of reviews. See North American Review, No. 11, p. 384; Review of Miss Sedgwick's Redwood. North American Review, No. 19, p. 42; Poems of Henry Pickering. North American Review, No. 20, p. 245; Review of Percy's Masque, by James T. Hillhouse. Besides these the manuscripts of many minor writers were sent to him. He was patient with all, returning often elaborate corrections and advice.

Mr. Bryant fixed two dollars apiece as his compensation for these writings. The publishers, however, offered him $200 a year for an average of 100 lines a month, about 16½ cents a line. Mr. Philips's account, rendered in 1826, shows that of the 1821 edition of his poems, 750 copies were printed and only 270 sold; a profit of $15, minus eight cents, for five years' sale.

A note in General James Grant Wilson's Bryant and his Friends, p. 42, reads : " The writer met Mr. Bryant in a bookstore in the winter of '78, and showed him a copy of this edition he had just purchased for $10. Mr. Bryant remarked, ' Well, that is more than I received for its contents.' "

The poetry of the Gazette was republished under the title of Miscellaneous Poems in 1826. See criticisms in North American Review, vol. xxii, p. 43, 1826. Also Mr. Bryant's own criticism of the poems in New York Review, vol. i, p. 389, mentioning poems by H. W. L. (We know not who he is).

He did not at this time neglect his practise of law. He argued cases at Northampton, New Haven, and before the Supreme Court at Boston. Mr. Trueman Smith, at one time Senator from Connecticut, says that he was associated with Mr. Bryant in the conduct of an important trial at New Haven " in which he evinced the very highest learning, acumen, and assiduity."

For report of his last law case, see Massachusetts Reports, 2d Pickering, p. 320. He alleged the decision was not in accordance with equity, citing in proof one of the last cases in which he was employed. He lost his case on an appeal to the Supreme Court. (Poetical Works, vol. i, p. 99—I broke the spell that held me long.) Interesting data on this period will be found in Godwin's Life, pp. 202–204.

" His solitary brooding habits, his dislike of his occupation (law), his love of the thickets along Green River and the Housatonic, and his reticent, austere manner with strangers contrasted with his cheerful, entertaining, joyous ways among his friends. He had a strange fondness for talking with farmers, woodmen, and stage-drivers. He was a passionate botanist, and knew the name of every tree, flower, and spire of grass. In court he often lost his self-control when provoked by adversaries. He was punctual in going to church, but was terribly prone to pick the sermons all to pieces. A French officer of Napoleon's army, a friend of Lafayette, named Bounton, gave him lessons in French and fencing."

On May 11th of this year Thanatopsis was first published in the Evening Post, with editorial note by Mr. Coleman.

1825.

" Mr. Bryant visited New York in both January and February, 1825—' A literary adventurer' he describes himself. He was three days and nights making the journey by stage. The population of New York was then about 150,000. Broadway extended to Canal Street, the city limit. Then came orchards and fields. Greenwich village, about Twelfth Street, was a summer resort. The fashionable residences were around the Battery and the finest shops were in Maiden Lane.

" Mr. Bryant became joint editor with Mr. Henry J. Anderson of a new publication called The New York Review and Athenæum Magazine, the first number appearing in June. This publication was an amalgamation of the Atlantic Magazine, which had been started in 1824 by Robert C. Sands, edited by him for six months, and sold out to Henry J. Anderson, who was editing The Literary Review. The first number of The New York Review and Athenæum Magazine appeared May 1st, and contained a review of a poem by James A. Hillhouse, entitled Hadad, and an original poem by Bryant called A Song of Pitcairn's Island."

In July he visited Cummington, writing the poems The Skies and Lines on Revisiting the Country. In the autumn he prepared four lectures on poetry, and delivered them before the American Athenæum Society in April, 1826.

1826.

There had been for years in New York an institution called The American Academy of Art, of which Jonathan Trumbull was president, and of which Chancellor Livingston and De Witt Clinton and others were members. This association was managed by laymen, and the artists organized a drawing association, November 8th, which met in the old almshouse building behind the City Hall, January 18, 1826. This became the National Academy of the Arts of Design, with S. F. B. Morse as president. It opened schools and gave exhibitions. Mr. Bryant was appointed one of the professors and read to the classes five lectures on mythology, December, 1827;

repeated in February, 1828; January, 1829; and November, 1831.

Mr. Bryant contributed largely to The New York Review both poetry and prose, but the publication was not a success. It ended with the May number. It was republished from May 13th to August 26th, under the title The New York Literary Gazette and American Athenæum. This too proved a failure. It was then joined with The United States Literary Gazette of Boston, and reissued October 1st with the new title of The United States Review and Literary Gazette, under the joint editorship of James G. Carter in Boston (afterward of Charles Folsom) and William C. Bryant in New York. Mr. Bryant's contributions will be found under their appropriate head later on in this work. This Review ran until October, 1827, and then died a natural death.

Mr. Bryant renewed his license to practise law in the courts of New York in March, and was associated with Mr. Henry Sedgwick in the prosecution of a claim for the recovery of part of the fund raised for the Greeks. He was asked to become temporary editor of The Evening Post.

1827.

" As assistant editor of The Evening Post Mr. Bryant's life from this date became largely that of a journalist, and reference must be made to the columns of the above-mentioned paper for data of this period. In politics he was an ardent free trader, but was never an active politician."

His poetical contributions to The United States Review and Literary Gazette in this year were few. He wrote a review of Dana's poems for The North American. (See No. 26, p. 239, 1827.)

In the latter part of this year the first volume of The Talisman was prepared under the joint editorship of R. C. Sands, G. C. Verplanck, and William C. Bryant. It was published in the name of an imaginary editor, Mr. Francis Herbert. The Talisman was continued in 1829-'30, three volumes in all, and republished in 1832 under the title of Miscellanies by G. C. Verplanck, Robert C. Sands, and

William C. Bryant. The contributions to The Talisman will be found under the proper dates in the Chronology of Bryant's Poems.

1828.

On the 8th of January an Ode was delivered by Mr. Bryant at the Jackson dinner in Masonic Hall, the Democratic meeting place. This was published in the columns of The Evening Post soon after.

1829.

Mr. Bryant became editor-in-chief of The Evening Post on the death of Mr. Coleman in July. For a time his interests were so concentrated on the management of his paper as to leave no time for poetic composition. After a visit to the prairies of the West in 1832 he wrote one poem, but nothing else for three years.

1831.

In this year he prepared a small volume of poems, containing all that he had written since the edition of 1831. This volume was most favorably received, and criticized by William J. Snelling and Henry W. Longfellow in The North American for April, 1832. See also H. W. Prescott in the July number.

1832.

At the suggestion of Mr. Verplanck a copy of the poems was sent to Washington Irving in London, and issued with a dedication to Samuel Rogers. For important letters on this subject, see pp. 264–274, Godwin's Life. To Dana he writes, "I printed a thousand copies, and more than half are disposed of." The reception of the poems in England was favorable. (See Foreign Quarterly Review, 1832, and Retrospective Review, vol. i, p. 311, 1824.) John Wilson in Blackwood's for April, 1832, was loudest in his praise.

In a letter to his brother under date of February 9, 1832, he says: " If it [the volume of poems] brings me two hundred or two hundred and fifty dollars, I shall think myself doing pretty well."

In a letter to Mr. Dana, October 8th, he says concerning his visit to the prairies : " I have seen the great west (Illinois), where I ate corn bread and hominy ; slept in log houses with twenty men and women and children all in the same room. At Jacksonville, where my two brothers live, I got on a horse and traveled a hundred miles to the northward over the immense prairies."

Before leaving for the west Mr. Bryant had arranged a volume of tales called The Sextad, from the number of authors engaged in it. Mr. Verplanck retired from the work, and the title was changed to Tales of the Glauber Spa, and published soon after his return. The five authors were Miss Sedgwick and Messrs. Sands, Leggett, Paulding, and Bryant ; his own contributions consisting of two stories, Medfield and Skeleton's Cave.

Mr. Sands died very suddenly this year, December 17th, and Mr. Bryant wrote a short memoir of his life, which appeared in the first number of The Knickerbocker Magazine, 1833.

1833.

In this year Mr. Bryant wrote no poetry. In the summer he went to Canada, visiting Montreal and Quebec. Just before his departure he was asked to prepare an address on the occasion of a benefit to be given to Mr. William Dunlap. Charles Kemble, Fanny Kemble, and a young actor, Edwin Forrest, had volunteered to appear. Bryant, however, refused. Among his papers was found a prologue for a theater (not named). (See Godwin's Life, p. 293.)

Writing to Dana (p. 295 Godwin's Life), he says : " The edition of my poems by Bliss is sold, all but a handful of copies. . . . I think of publishing another edition soon. . . ." On October 17, 1833, he writes to Dana : " Will you see your booksellers, Russell, Odiorne & Co., and ask whether they will give me $250 for one thousand copies of my book." November 2d he writes : " I have completed the bargain with Mr. Odiorne, and have given him my book with such corrections and additions as I have been able to make." This edition was published at Boston by Russell, Odiorne & Metcalf in 1834, and is nowhere mentioned in any bibliography of American poets.

A poem called The Robber was suppressed, but afterward published by N. P. Willis in the Mirror. (See p. 299 of Godwin's Life for this poem in full. See pp. 300–301 for variations in this poem and The Prairies.)

1834.

On June 24th Mr. Bryant sailed for Europe with his family, thus escaping the abolition riots which took place at this time. He visited France and Italy, spending a month in Rome and Florence, and came back through the Tyrol to Munich. It was during this trip that he met Henry W. Longfellow at Heidelberg, and enjoyed some strolls with him in the pine forests.

1836.

Mr. Bryant was summoned home by the illness of Mr. Leggett, assistant editor of the Post. He arrived in New York March 26th. A testimonial public dinner was offered to him in a letter from Washington Irving, F. G. Halleck, A. B. Durand, and G. C. Verplanck. This dinner Mr. Bryant declined. (See correspondence, pp. 312–313, Godwin's Life.)

On May 23d Mr. Bryant writes : " I have made a bargain with the Harpers for publishing my poems. They are to do it in a neat manner, with a vignette on the title-page. I have written to Weir to furnish the design—' a copy of a little landscape at West Point.' They will pay me twenty-five cents a copy. The work is to be stereotyped, and an impression of twenty-five hundred is to be struck off at first. For these I shall be paid $625."

In September he wrote to his brother John in Illinois : " I think of making some disposition of my interest in The Evening Post, and coming out to the western country with a few thousand dollars to try my fortune. . . . My book is out [the edition of 1836]. It contains some thirty pages more than the last edition, and is better printed. . . . The practise of physic is here undergoing a considerable revolution. The let-alone system is becoming fashionable. I am so far a convert to it that I distrust a physician who is inclined to go to work with large quantities of medicine." This is an allusion to his own conversion to homœopathy, to which he adhered for the rest of his life.

His duties in The Evening Post occupied his full time, writing the leading articles and reviews of books, his office hours being from 7 A. M. to 4 P. M. (See pp. 345–357, Godwin's Life, for data on this period of great agitations on the part of the Abolitionists and Bryant's part in it.)

1838.

In June he writes : " I have no leisure for poetry. To keep myself in health I take long walks in the country. I accustom myself to the greatest simplicity of diet, renouncing tea, coffee, animal food, etc. . . ."

1839.

Mr. Leggett died this year, and Mr. Bryant wrote a memoir for The Democratic Review. The elder Dana sent to Mr. Bryant his son's novel, Two Years before the Mast. (See letter, June 24, 1839, Godwin's Life, p. 373.) It was refused by all the publishers, but finally, through Mr. Bryant's instrumentality, Harper and Bros. published it in 1840.

1840.

In a letter to Mr. Field, Mr. Bryant writes : " We have left the house in Carmine Street, after inhabiting it for two years and a half, and have taken a house in Ninth Street, near the Sixth Avenue, not far from Brevoort's House. . . . The greatest change that I perceive in New York is the introduction of cabs, and mustachios, and in some instances beards as long as those worn by the Dunkers."

1841.

This year he made a trip with Cole, the artist, through the Catskill Mountains. In September he went to Lebanon Springs, and later, with his young friend Samuel J. Tilden, visited ex-President Van Buren at Kinderhook. He also visited R. H. Dana at Rockport, Cape Ann. The Hymn of the Sea was suggested at this time. (See note, p. 391, Godwin's Life.)

1842.

In a letter to the Rev. Orville Dewey he gives a most interesting account of life in New York at this time, and speaks of making an address before the New Homœopathic Society. (See pp. 392–394, Godwin's Life.)

Charles Dickens visited America at this time. It was reported that his first question on landing was, "Where is Bryant?" Mr. Bryant called upon him twice in New York, missing him both times, upon which he received the note printed in Godwin's Life, page 395. They breakfasted together at the appointed time, there being also present Fitz-Green Halleck and Prof. Charles Felton, of Cambridge. Bryant entertained Dickens at his own home, and attended the public banquet and ball given to him. At this time Bryant published, through the Harpers, a new edition of his poems, containing all he had written since the 1836 edition. The title of the new book was The Fountain and other Poems. There were some twenty new poems in all. Dr. Channing's death occurred this year (p. 404, Godwin's Life). Mr. Bryant contributed the hymn sung at the funeral.

1843.

The Evening Post was at this time greatly enlarged in size and usefulness. In March he went south to visit William Gilmore Simms, and traveled as far as Florida. On his return he purchased the property at the place afterward called Roslyn. In July he visited a relative living in the Lake Champlain region.

1844.

The agitation concerning the annexation of Texas brought forth a letter in The Evening Post, August 20, 1844. (See pp. 412–423, Godwin's Life.)

1845.

On the 22d of April Mr. Bryant sailed for Europe with a young friend of his, Charles M. Leupp. During this visit he met Samuel Rogers, Thomas Moore, Leigh Hunt, Miss Joanna Baillie, Mary Howett, Cobden, Bright, Fox, and many other men of mark in literature and art. He returned home in November.

1846.

Though Mr. Bryant had had leisure to write very few new poems since the edition of 1844, he still found time to revise those already written, and a newly illustrated edition of his poems was issued by Messrs. Carey & Hart, of Philadelphia. His old friend Mr. Dana passed criticism upon all those poems. (For a very interesting correspondence between the two, see pp. 13–18, vol. ii, Godwin's Life. For an interesting correspondence at this time between Bryant and Longfellow, see pp. 24–26, vol. ii, Godwin's Life.) He paid his last visit to his mother in the summer. She died May, 1847, aged eighty.

1847.

Mr. Bryant went in the summer to the White Mountains. (See pp. 32–34, Godwin's Life.)

1848.

This year was saddened by the death of Thomas Cole, the artist, and on May 4th Mr. Bryant delivered a eulogy at the Academy of Music before the National Academy of Design.

1849.

Early in this year Mr. John Bigelow became one of the proprietors and editors of The Evening Post. Mr. Bryant was now able to travel extensively. He made a trip to Cuba, being received in the best society. Returning to New York, he sailed June 13th for Europe. He met with a most cordial reception from Samuel Rogers and many others. He visited Scotland, including Abbotsford, going to the Continent in August. He found armed forces everywhere, and France on the brink of revolution. He visited Germany and Switzerland, returning to New York in December, and at the suggestion of Mr. Dana prepared a volume of travels, issued by G. P. Putnam in 1850. He had little time, however, for literary affairs outside of his editorial duties.

1852.

His friend Cooper died in 1851, and on February 25th Mr. Bryant delivered a eulogy before the Historical Society, Daniel

Webster presiding. On the 13th of November Mr. Bryant sailed for the Orient, visiting Egypt, Jerusalem, Damascus, Baalbec, Syria, etc. He returned home in June, 1853.

1854.

In 1854 Messrs. D. Appleton & Co. had become his publishers, and have continued to issue his works from this time on. An illustrated edition of his poems, printed in England, with illustrations by Birket Foster, Dalziel, Pickersgill, and others, was issued at this time, and also an edition without illustrations in two volumes. In regard to this edition Mr. Bryant says, writing to R. H. Dana, under date of May 26, 1854 : " As to my poems with illustrations, that is an idea of my bookseller. . . . But the first thing which my bookseller— it is Appleton—has promised to do is to get out a neat edition in two volumes *without* illustrations. Though I have as great a horror of illustrations as you have, they will, I hope, hurt nobody." The two editions were accordingly issued, one without illustrations in two volumes, printed by D. Appleton & Co., the other in one volume, with illustrations, printed by B. Clay, Broad Street Hill, London.

1855.

Mr. Bryant's life at this period was entirely taken up with politics, especially with the formation of the Republican party, in which he was interested from the first.

1855.

The death of the poet Rogers brought forth a most interesting letter, which will be found on page 84 of Godwin's Life, vol. ii. Mr. Rogers, in an interview with George Bancroft, the historian, said that he " enjoyed reading Bryant's poems more than any other living poet."

The articles of organization of the new political party, drawn up in Wisconsin, were adopted in Ohio, and ratified at Syracuse in September.

1856.

Mr. Bryant attended no political meeting, but at a great gathering held in the New York Tabernacle, April 29th, he sent a letter embodying his views, which was read at the meeting. (See Godwin's Life, vol. ii, p. 89.)   Fremont and Dayton were nominated.   The attack on Charles Sumner by Preston Brooks occurred about this time.   (See contribution of Mr. Bryant to The Evening Post, July 24, 1856, entitled Brooks's Canada Song.)

1857.

On May 2d Mr. Bryant sailed for Europe, accompanied by his wife and daughter.   He traveled through Europe to Spain, where he was offered great facilities through letters of introduction, given him by Archbishop Hughes.   Emilio Castelar was presented to him.   At the age of twenty-four Castelar was already professor of philosophy in the university.

1858.

The early part of this year was spent at Naples, owing to the illness of Mrs. Bryant.   Here he finished his poems The River by Night, The Sick-Bed, and The Life that Is, a pendant to The Future Life.   A letter from the Rev. R. C. Waterston (p. 108 of Godwin's Life) gives an extremely interesting account of a service held in his rooms, at which Mr. Bryant was baptized and partook of the communion.   His own letter (pp. 109–113, vol. ii, Godwin's Life) completes the record of those days.   In Rome he met Crawford, Story, Gibson, Chapman, Page, Terry, Miss Hosmer, Frederika Bremer, and Nathaniel Hawthorne.   (See letter from Hawthorne, Godwin's Life, vol. ii, p. 112.)   At Florence he met Hawthorne at Robert Browning's.   (See Hawthorne's letter, pp. 113, 114, vol. ii, Godwin's Life.)   At Florence also he met Walter Savage Landor, and he speaks with great pleasure of the wise words gathered from his conversations.   He returned to America in August.

1859.

He presided at a lecture given by Abraham Lincoln, and Mr Lincoln said, " It was worth the journey to the east to see such a man."   April 19th he speaks of visiting the new park (Central), " in which thousands of men are at work blasting rocks, making roads, etc."   He also speaks of meeting Mr.

Cobden, who was in New York at this time. They had met in England in 1845. The poems of these times were The Cloud on the Way, Waiting by the Gate, The New and Old, and The Third of November, all reflecting the gloom caused by the death of so many friends: Theodore Sedgwick, Benjamin F. Butler, C. N. Leupp, etc. Washington Irving died in November.

1860.

On the 3d of April Mr. Bryant delivered an address on The Life and Character of Washington Irving before the New York Historical Society. Bryant's poems were translated into French by M. Le Chevalier de Chatelain, and published. (See Bryant's letters to John Bigelow, Godwin's Life, vol. ii, p. 134.) He was elected honorary member of the Boston Historical Society. (See letter from the President, R. C. Winthrop, vol. ii, p. 136, Godwin's Life.) See letter from Rev. Mr. Waterston, giving account of Mr. Bryant's visit to him in Boston, and the celebration of the receipt of the news of Garibaldi's and Victor Emanuel's entry into Rome. November 10th, he wrote to President-elect Lincoln (see pp. 150–152, vol. ii, Godwin's Life), and again January 21 and February 5, 1861.

1861.

His work in the cause of the " Union " occupied the greater part of his time in this year. The poems of this period were, Not Yet, published in July, and Our Country's Call, published in August. Every day was filled with stirring events. A Word to the Chief Magistrate of the Union was published at this time. (See p. 169, vol. ii, Godwin's Life, for full text.)

1862.

Bryant continued his letters to Lincoln. (See p. 175, vol. ii, Godwin's Life. Letter to Dr. Dewey, p. 176.) In September he had an interview of great importance with President Lincoln. (See p. 179, vol. ii, Godwin's Life. See Evening Post, July 1, 1862.) In a letter to the Rev. S. H. Cox, D. D., November 7th, he thanks him for a Latin version of Thanatopsis; and in a letter, December 3d, he thanks Dr. Adolf Laun, of Oldenberg,

Germany, for a translation of his poems in the Sonntagsblatt. In another letter of December 3d, to M. P. Jônain, Epaignes, Charente Inférieure, France, he thanks him for the translation of his poems into French. In the winter of 1862, Sella and The Little People of the Snow were written, and he began a third poem called A Tale of Cloudland, which appears in Poetical Works, vol. ii.

1863.

On June 25th the office of The Evening Post was attacked by rioters during the draft. At this period Bryant wrote The Poet and The Path, and began the translation of the Odyssey, the fifth book being published in the Atlantic Monthly. A collection of his more recent poems was brought out by D. Appleton & Co., under the title of the Thirty Poems, the translation of the fifth book of the Odyssey being included. (See letter, pp. 194–195, vol. ii, Godwin's Life.) In this year he delivered his poem entitled Fifty Years, at the semi-centennial of the class of 1813 at Williamstown. His poems were presented to the Emperor of Brazil, who sent his portrait to Bryant. (See letters, pp. 199–200, vol. ii, Godwin's Life; also Speech on behalf of Missouri Loyalist, p. 201.)

1864.

The volume of Thirty Poems brought forth letters from H. W. Longfellow and R. H. Dana. (See pp. 206–208, Godwin's Life.) October 13th, writing to J. T. Fields, of Boston, he says : "I send you a poem, My Autumn Walk, for the Atlantic Monthly. Ask me for no more verses. A septuagenarian has passed the time when it is becoming for him to occupy himself with The Rhymes and Rattles of the Man and Boy." November 15th, the Century Club celebrated his seventieth birthday with the greatest enthusiasm. (See pp. 214–220, vol. ii, Godwin's Life.) He delivered an address at the laying of the corner-stone of the new Academy of Design building.

1865.

At the beginning of this year he wrote a letter To the Union Army. (See pp. 221–223, vol. ii, Godwin's Life.) He was pushing a petition to abolish slavery throughout the United States, and wrote to Mr. Everett for assistance. (See p. 224, vol. ii, Godwin's Life.) At the opening of the new building of the Academy of Design he delivered the inaugural address. He wrote an Ode on the Death of Lincoln, but refused to write a memoir of him. One of the mammoth trees of California was named for him this year. (See Bryant's letter, p. 233, vol. ii, Godwin's Life.) His poem on The Death of Slavery, written at this time, was brought forth by the passage of the Constitutional Amendment. (See pp. 235, 236, vol. ii, Godwin's Life.) He purchased his old homestead at Cummington.

1866.

He says, February 19th, writing to his friend Dr. Samuel Osgood, in reply to his request for a hymn : " I have written an occasional poem at your suggestion, which is more than I have done for any man for long years, etc. . . . In the winter of life the fountain of Hippocrene crystallizes into ice ; and if I were ever so young, occasional verses would be a dangerous experiment. . . . I have more requests to write than perhaps you would imagine, and am forced to give them all the same answer." (See p. 240, vol. ii, Godwin's Life, for important letter to Dr. Samuel Osgood.) The poet's wife died on July 27th of this year. (See Letters, pp. 244–250, vol. ii, Godwin's Life.) In the fall Mr. Bryant wrote the poem October, 1866. (See letter to J. T. Fields, who asked for verses for Atlantic Monthly, p. 250, vol. ii, Godwin's Life.) He continued his translation of the Odyssey, writing forty lines a day, and carrying a pocket edition of Homer with him wherever he went. In October Mr. Bryant sailed for Europe, visited Spain and Italy, and met Garibaldi, whom he had known in America. He was invited to go with him to Naples, but could not accept. He returned home in August. (See pp. 252–263, vol. ii, Godwin's Life.)

1868.

He retired from his office as President of the American Free Trade League, a farewell dinner being given to him on January 30th.

1869.

In February he delivered an address before the New York Historical Society on the life and character of Fitz-Greene Halleck, who died November 19, 1867. Although engaged with his translations of Homer, Bryant wrote several poems at this period—A Brighter Day, Among the Trees, A May Evening. Also a volume of Travels, Letters from the East, brief after-dinner speeches, and an address at the founding of the Metropolitan Museum of Art.

1870.

Vol. i of the Iliad was issued in February, and vol. ii in June. Vol. i of the Odyssey, September, 1871; vol. ii, March, 1872. (See North American Review, April, 1871, and London Saturday Review, April 23, 1870.) Mr. G. C. Verplanck died in March, and Bryant delivered a memorial address on May 17th before the Historical Society. He also delivered a speech on Translators of Homer at the Williams College alumni dinner; on the Franco-Prussian War at a German fair; on Women and Peace at a woman's convention; and on Free Trade at a Cooper Union meeting. He made the poetical translations for Mrs. Theresa Robinson's Fifteen Years, besides writing the reminiscences referred to of Miss C. M. Sedgwick for her Memoirs, prepared by Miss Mary Dewey. The Library of Poetry and Song engaged his attention at this time. His work consisted of revising, rejecting, and suggesting other poems, and in writing a general introduction. (See p. 94, vol. ii, Godwin's Life.)

1871.

He passed the early summer of this year at Roslyn, the later part at Cummington, and the winters in New York. In a letter to Joseph H. Richards he says, March 30th: "I rise early at this time of the year—about half-past five; in summer half an hour or even an hour earlier. Immediately, with very little encumbrance of clothing, I begin a series of exercises for the most part designed to expand the chest and at the same time call into action all the muscles and articulations of the body." (See pp. 297–299, vol. ii, Godwin's Life.) The first volume of the

5

Odyssey, in twelve books, was finished in April. In January he delivered an address on Italian Unity in the Academy of Music. In May he spoke at the dinner of the Joint High Commissioners, who had just completed a trade treaty between England and America. He also delivered an address on the Progress of German Literature at a dinner to the German ambassador. He addressed an open-air meeting at the unveiling of a statue to Professor Morse in Central Park in June, and later on spoke on the Darwinian Theory to the Williams College alumni. (See letter, p. 299, vol. ii, Godwin's Life.)   On December 7th he sent the last of the Odyssey to his publishers, Messrs. J. R. Osgood & Co. (See pp. 311–317, vol. ii, Godwin's Life, for details of the completion of this work.)

1872.

After the completion of the Odyssey Mr. Bryant went to the Bahamas, Cuba, and Mexico. (See poem, A Memory, p. 318, vol. ii, Godwin's Life.)   In Mexico a formal reception was given to him, and he was made an honorary member of the Geographical Society. He was treated with the highest honors by President Juarez and all Mexico. (See Bryant's letter of acknowledgment, p. 322, vol. ii, Godwin's Life.)   He returned to New York in April. He presented a library to his native town of Cummington.   1873.

During these years he made about a dozen speeches or more in behalf of the Home for Incurables of the Children's Aid Society, on municipal reform at a great meeting in Cooper Institute, for the opening of the new Princeton library, at the unveiling of the statue of Shakespeare in Central Park for his English friends, and at the erection of a statue to Sir Walter Scott for his Scotch friends, besides remarks at the Burns dinner, the dinner to Salvini the actor, and elsewhere. He prepared a volume for G. P. Putnam containing his orations and speeches. He addressed the people of Roslyn on the subject of Mexico, and went on a southern tour. He was elected to the Russian Academy, Baron Tolsteneff presenting his name in an eloquent oration. In July his address at the opening of the Princeton Library was delivered.

1874.

He began his eightieth year with an address on Franklin before the Typographical Society on January 17th. On February 24th he made a speech at a free-trade mass meeting at Cooper Union. He wrote an introduction to a work on Picturesque America. On November 3d he was presented with an address, signed by thousands, congratulating him on reaching his eightieth year. (See pp. 348, 349, vol. ii, Godwin's Life.)

1875.

A new edition of the Library of Poetry and Song was projected at this time, and Mr. Bryant gave it his hearty assistance, writing an introduction to it. (See pp. 353–356, vol. ii, Godwin's Life.) Bryant at this time interested himself in a new edition of Shakespeare, writing a preface for it when finished. This was never published owing to delay about the illustrations. He was entertained by Governor Tilden at Albany, both branches of the Legislature adjourning in his honor. He addressed both Houses (See pp. 357–359, vol. ii, Godwin's Life.) He began a poem on the growth of New York, but never finished it. (See p. 365, vol. ii, Godwin's Life.) In September he delivered an address before the Goethe Society, and later presided at the breakfast given to Lord Houghton by the Century Club.

1876.

He was asked to write a Centennial Ode, but sent only a hymn to be sung by the choir His poem The Flood of Years was composed at this time, and on the 20th of June the commemorative vase of bronze was presented to him at Chickering Hall, Dr. Samuel Osgood making the presentation address. The Emperor of Brazil visited New York at this time, and greeted Mr. Bryant as an old friend, sending him a letter, the text of which will be found on p. 373, vol. ii, Godwin's Life.

1877.

He delivered an address at the unveiling of the statue to Fitz-Greene Halleck in Central Park and on November 3d attended a complimentary reception at the Goethe Club, making an address.   Our Fellow-Worshippers was the closing poem of this year.

1878.

In this the last year of his life Mr. Bryant walked daily to his office and back, a distance of three miles.   He spoke at a reception to Lord Dufferin given by the Geographical Society; at a dinner given to Bayard Taylor, recently appointed minister to Germany ; before the Society for the Suppression of Cruelty to Children; and at a breakfast of clergymen of all denominations.   On February 2d he attended the meeting of the Geographical Society, at which Lord Dufferin was elected an honorary member on motion of Bayard Taylor.   On April 10th he attended a " Commers " given by the German Social Science Association to Bayard Taylor.   He says of this " Commers " : " There were five hundred people at fifteen tables in an immense dining hall, besides the Arion singers in the gallery, who, in the clouds of tobacco smoke which ascended from the beer-drinkers below, looked like the gods on Olympus as they are sometimes seen in pictures.   Beer and cigars composed the bill of fare, and the exercises consisted of songs and speeches," etc.   He attended a breakfast at the Clergymen's Club and made a speech. (See p. 393, vol. ii, Godwin's Life.)   May 27th he wrote his last letter—a criticism of a poem sent to him by R. H. Stoddard.

On May 29th he came to the city, spent the morning working at his desk, and in the afternoon drove to Central Park, where he delivered an oration at the unveiling of a statue to the Italian patriot Mazzini.   His last words in public were an apostrophe to civil and religious liberty :

Image of the Illustrious Champion of Civil and Religious Liberty, cast in enduring bronze to typify the imperishable renown of thy original!   Remain for ages yet to come where we place thee in this resort of millions; remain till the day shall dawn—far distant though it may be—when the rights and duties of human brotherhood shall be acknowledged by all the races of mankind.

He went to the house of General James Grant Wilson after the ceremonies were over and fell on the doorstep, receiving

injuries from which he died on the 12th of June, after an ill-
ness of several weeks. His funeral occurred on the 14th of
June at All Souls' Church, and the interment took place at
Roslyn. Thus as he had wished the old poet was laid at rest.

> I gazed upon the glorious sky
>   And the green mountains round ;
> And thought, that when I came to lie
>   Within the silent ground,
> 'Twere pleasant, that in flowery June,
> When brooks sent up a cheerful tune,
>   And groves a joyous sound,
> The sexton's hand, my grave to make,
> The rich, green mountain turf should break.

CHRONOLOGY OF BRYANT'S POEMS.

1803.

In my ninth year I began to make verses, some of which were utter nonsense. See pp. 22-23, Godwin's Life, for extracts from the poems.

1804.

Description of School, declaimed on schoolroom floor.

1807.

Above poem first published in the Hampshire Gazette of March 18th, under the signature of C. B., Northampton, Mass., March 18, 1807. Other pieces of verse were sent anonymously to the paper about the same time, but they can not now be identified.

1808.

The Embargo, printed in Boston, 1808.

1809.

The Embargo, reprinted 1809, together with The Spanish Revolution, Connecticut River, Reward of Literary Merit, The Contented Ploughman, Drought, Translation from Horace, Carmen 22d, Book I.

1810-1813.

On pp. 76-82 of Godwin's Life will be found extracts from poems of this period, which were never published in full or recognized by Mr. Bryant in collected editions of his poems.

1811.

Thanatopsis was written at this time. See pp. 98-101, Godwin's Life. Pp. 90-118, Godwin's Life, contain still further extracts from the unpublished poems of this period.

1814.

The Yellow Violet.

1815.

I Cannot Forget with what Fervid Devotion, and The Hunter of the West. To a Waterfowl.

1817.

Thanatopsis, published in the North American Review for September 17th. Agricultural Ode, delivered before the Berkshire Agricultural Society. The Fragment (afterward known as The Inscription for the Entrance to a Wood). Love's Power.

1818.

Agricultural Ode, published. To a Waterfowl, published in the North American Review for March. A Friend on his Marriage, published in the North American Review for March. Version of Simonides, Danaë, published in the North American Review for March. Essay on American Poetry, published in the North American Review for July. Happy Temperament, published in the North American Review for July. The Burial-place, composed at Great Barrington, first published in Dana's Idleman, 1821.

1819.

Green River, written in Great Barrington, published in Dana's Idleman, 1821.

1820.

A Winter Piece, written in Great Barrington, published in Dana's Idleman, 1821. A Hymn to Death, Great Barrington, published in the New York Review, October, 1825. Oh Fairest of the Rural Maids, written at Stockbridge, published in the edition of 1832.

1821.

The West Wind, published in Dana's Idleman. A Walk at Sunset, published in Dana's Idleman.

1822.

Spain, written at Great Barrington. The Ages, Phi Beta Kappa, Poem, August 30th.

1823.

The Indian Girl's Lament.   Ode for an Agricultural Cele-
bration, written at Great Barrington, p. 71, edition 1883.

1824.

Massacre at Scio, written at Great Barrington.   March,
written at Great Barrington on March 24th, published in the
United States Literary Gazette, June 1st.   Rizpah, published
in the United States Literary Gazette, April 12th.   The Old
Man's Funeral, published in the United States Literary Gazette,
May 1st.   The Rivulet, written at Cummington in 1823, pub-
lished in the United States Literary Gazette, May 15th.   To
——, written at Cummington in 1824, published in the Uni-
ted States Literary Gazette, June 15th.   An Indian Story,
written at Great Barrington, published in the United States
Literary Gazette, July 1st.   Summer Wind, written at Great
Barrington, published in the United States Literary Gazette,
July 15th.   An Indian at the Burial-place of his Fathers,
written at Great Barrington, published in the United States
Literary Gazette, August 1st.   Love's Seasons, written at Great
Barrington in 1824, published in the United States Literary
Gazette, August 15th.   I Broke the Spell that Held Me Long,
written at Great Barrington in 1824, published in the Atlantic
Souvenir, 1825.   Hymn of the Waldenses, published in the
United States Literary Gazette, September 1, 1824.   Monu-
ment Mountain, published in the United States Literary Ga-
zette, September 15th.   After a Tempest, published in the United
States Literary Gazette, October 1st.   Autumn Woods, pub-
lished in the United States Literary Gazette, October 15th.
Mutation, published in the United States Literary Gazette,
November 15th.   November, published in the United States Lit-
erary Gazette, November 15th.   Song of the Greek Amazon, pub-
lished in the United States Literary Gazette, December 1st.
To a Cloud, published in the United States Literary Gazette,
December 15th.

1825.

The Murdered Traveller, published in the United States
Literary Gazette, January 14th.   Hymn to the North Star,

published in the United States Literary Gazette, January 15th. The Lapse of Time, published in the United States Literary Gazette, February 15th. The Song of the Stars, published in the United States Literary Gazette, March 1st. A Forest Hymn, published in the United States Literary Gazette, April 1st. June, written at Great Barrington in 1825, published in the Atlantic Souvenir, 1826. The African Chief, written in New York, 1825, published in the United States Review and Literary Gazette, December, 1826. The Greek Partisan, published in the United States Literary Gazette, May, 1825. A Song of Pitcairn's Island, published in the New York Review, June, 1825. The Firmament, published in the New York Review, July, 1825. Lines on Revisiting the Country, published in the New York Review, August, 1825. To a Mosquito, published in the New York Review, October, 1825. The Death of the Flowers, published in the New York Review, 1825.

1826.

Springtime, published in the United States Literary Gazette, July, 1826. Mary Magdalen, published in the United States Review, October, 1826. Meditation on Rhode Island Coal, published in the New York Review, April. I Cannot Forget with what Fervid Devotion, written at Cummington, 1815, published in the New York Review, February, 1826. The New Moon, published in the New York Review, March, 1826. The Life of the Blessed, written in New York, 1826, published in the New York Review, May, 1827. The Journey of Life, written in New York, 1826, edition of 1832. The Gladness of Nature, published in the United States Literary Gazette. Midsummer, published in the United States Literary Gazette, July. A Summer Ramble, published in the New York Mirror, August. The Two Graves, published in the United States Literary Gazette, August. The Conjunction of Jupiter and Venus, published in the United States Literary Gazette, September. October, published in the United States Review and Literary Gazette, October. The Damsel of Peru, published in the United States Review and Literary Gazette, November.

1827.

Spring in Town, published in the United States Review, April. A Scene on the Bank of the Hudson, published in the Talisman, 1828. The Hurricane, written in New York, 1827, published in the Talisman, 1828. William Tell, written in New York, 1827, published in the Talisman, 1828.

1828.

The Past, written in New York, 1828, published in the Talisman, 1829. Upon the Mountain's Distant Head, written in New York, 1828, published in the Talisman, 1829. The Lament of Romero, published in the New York Review, February, 1826, and Talisman, 1829. The Greek Boy, written in New York, 1828, published in the Talisman, 1829. The Hunter's Serenade, written in New York, 1828, published in the Talisman, 1829.

1829.

The Evening Wind, written in New York, 1829, published in the Talisman, 1830. Love and Folly, written in New York, 1829, published in the Talisman, 1830. When the Firmament Quivers, written in New York, 1829, published in the Talisman, 1830. The Siesta, written in New York, 1829, published in the Talisman, 1830. Innocent Child and Snow White Flower, written in New York, 1829, published in the Talisman, 1830. The Alcayde of Molina, written in New York, 1829, published in the Talisman, 1830. To the River Arve, written in New York, 1829, published in the Talisman, 1830. The Death of Aliatar, written in New York, 1829, published in the Talisman, 1830. To Cole, the Painter, Departing for Europe, written in New York, 1829, published in the Talisman, 1830. The Twenty-second of December, written for the New England Dinner in New York, published in the Talisman, 1829. To the Fringed Gentian, written in New York in 1829. Edition of 1832.

1830.

Hymn of the City, published in the Christian Examiner.

1831.

Song of Marion's Men, published in the New York Mirror, November.

1832.

The Prairies, written in Illinois in 1832, published in the Knickerbocker Magazine, December, 1833. The Arctic Lover, written in New York in 1832, published in the Knickerbocker Magazine, January, 1833. The Hunter of the Prairies, written in Illinois in 1832, published in the New York Mirror, 1834.

1834.

Earth, written in Pisa in 1834, published in the New York Mirror, March, 1835. The Serenade, published in the New York Mirror, February, 1834.

1835.

Seventy-Six, published in the New York Mirror, May, 1835. Song, published in the New York Mirror, July, 1835. To the Apennines, written in Italy in 1835, published in the New York Mirror, August, 1835. The Knight's Epitaph, written in Pisa in 1835, published in the New York Mirror, September, 1835. The Child's Funeral, written in Sorrento in 1835, published in the Democratic Review, 1835. The Living Lost, published in the New York Mirror, September, 1836. The Hunter's Vision, published in the New York Mirror, November, 1835. The Strange Lady, written in Heidelberg in 1835, published in the New York Mirror, May, 1836. Life, written in Munich in 1835. Edition of 1842.

1836.

The Sharpening of the Sabre, written in New York in 1836, published in the Evening Post, July, 1836. Earth's Children Cleave to Earth, published in the New York Mirror, July, 1836. The Count of Griers, published in the New York Mirror, January, 1836. The Green Mountain Boys, published in the New York Mirror, November, 1836. Catterskill Falls, published in the New York Mirror, November, 1836. A Presentiment, written in New York in 1836, published in the New York Mirror, April, 1837.

1837.

The Battlefield, published in the Democratic Review, October, 1837.

1838.

The Death of Schiller, published in the Democratic Review, August, 1838.

1839.

The Future Life, published in the Democratic Review, March, 1839, reprinted in the Cypress Wreath, 1844. The Fountain, published in the Democratic Review, April, 1839. The Winds, published in the Knickerbocker Magazine, April, 1839. In Memory of William Leggett, published in the Democratic Review, November, 1839.

1840.

I Think of Thee, written in New York in 1840, published in Godey's Lady's Book, January, 1844. The Old Man's Counsel, published in the Democratic Review, February, 1840. An Evening Revery, written in New York, 1840, published in the Knickerbocker Magazine, January, 1841. A Dream, published in the Democratic Review, December, 1841.

1842.

A Northern Legend, written in New York in 1842, published in Graham's Magazine, January, 1843. The Painted Cup, written in Illinois in 1842, published in the Democratic Review. The Antiquity of Freedom, published in the Knickerbocker Magazine, May, 1842. The Maiden's Sorrow, written in New York in 1842, published in the Home Library, 1844. A Hymn to the Sea, written in Cape Ann, Mass., in 1842, published in the Christian Examiner, September, 1842. The Return of Youth, published in Graham's Magazine, October, 1842. Noon, written in Weehawken in 1842, published in the Home Library, 1844.

1843.

The Crowded Street, published in Graham's Magazine, January, 1843. Paradise of Tears, published in Graham's Magazine, January, 1843. The White-footed Deer, published in the Home Library, 1844.

1844.

The Waning Moon, published in Graham's Magazine, July, 1844.

1845.

The Stream of Life, published in Graham's Magazine, July, 1845. The Unknown Way, written at Roslyn in 1845, published in Graham's Magazine, December, 1846.

1846.

The Land of Dreams, written in New York in 1846, published in Graham's Magazine, January, 1847. Oh Mother of a Mighty Race, written in New York in 1846, published in Graham's Magazine, July, 1847.

1849.

The Planting of the Apple-Tree, written in Roslyn in 1849, published in the Atlantic Monthly, January, 1864. The May Sun Sheds an Amber Light, written in Roslyn in 1849, published in the Knickerbocker Magazine, May, 1852.

1850.

The Lady of Castle Windeck. The Saw Mill, published in Graham's Magazine, February, 1850.

1853.

The Burial of Love, written in New York, 1853, published in Graham's Magazine, 1854. The Conqueror's Grave, written in New York, 1853, published in Putnam's Magazine, January, 1854. The Voice of Autumn, written in Roslyn in 1853, published in Graham's Magazine, January, 1854.

1854.

The Snow Shower, written in Roslyn, published in the Knickerbocker Gallery, 1855. A Rain-Dream, written in Roslyn, published in the Crayon, January, 1855.

1855.

Robert of Lincoln, written in Roslyn, published in Putnam's Magazine, June, 1855. The Twenty-seventh of March, written in Roslyn, March, 1855.

1857.

The Lost Bird, written in Madrid in 1857, published in the New York Ledger, 1858. Ruins of Italica, written in Madrid in 1857, published in Thirty Poems, 1863. An Invitation to the Country, published in Harper's Weekly, May, 1857. A Song for New Year's Eve, written in New York, published in Harper's Magazine, January, 1859. The River by Night, written in Naples, 1857, published in Harper's Magazine, June, 1858.

1858.

The Swallow, written in Naples, February 8, 1858. A Sick-Bed, written in Naples, May, 1858, published in the New York Ledger, July 23, 1859. A Day-Dream, written in Naples, published in the New York Ledger, January 5, 1860. The Life That Is, written in Castellamare, May, 1858, published in Thirty Poems, 1864. The Prairies Glow with Flowers, written in Princeton, Ill., 1858.

1859.

The Old World Sparrow, written in Roslyn in 1859. The Song of the Sower, written in Roslyn in 1859, published in Thirty Poems, 1864. The New and the Old, written in Roslyn in 1859.

1860.

The Cloud on the Way, written in New York in 1860, published in the New York Ledger, February, 1860. The Tides, written in Roslyn in 1860, published in the New York Ledger, July 28, 1860. Italy, written in Roslyn in 1860, published in the New York Ledger, October 20, 1860. Waiting by the Gate, written in New York in 1860, published in Thirty Poems, 1864.

1861.

The Constellations, written in Roslyn, published in Thirty Poems, 1864. Not Yet, written in Roslyn in July, published in the New York Ledger, August 17, 1861. Our Country's Call, written in Cummington in September, published in the New York Ledger, November, 1861. The Third of November, written in Roslyn, published in Thirty Poems, 1864. Civil War, written in New York, 1861. The Song Sparrow, written in Roslyn, August, 1861, published in the Williams Magazine.

1862.

The Better Age, written in Roslyn in 1862. A Tale of Cloudland, written in Roslyn in 1862. Castles in the Air, written in Roslyn in 1862, published in the Atlantic Magazine, January, 1866. Sella, written in Roslyn in 1862.

1863.

Fifty Years, written in Roslyn in 1863, published at Williams College. The Little People of the Snow, written in Roslyn in 1863, published in Thirty Poems, 1864. The Poet, written in Roslyn in 1863, published in Thirty Poems, 1864. The Path.

1864.

To the Nightingale, 1864. The Return of the Birds, written in Roslyn, March, 1864, published in the Atlantic Monthly, July, 1864. My Autumn Walk, written in Roslyn, October, 1864, published in the Atlantic Monthly, January, 1865.

1865.

Dante, written in New York, published in the Atlantic Monthly, January, 1866. Abraham Lincoln, Poetical Tribute to the Memory of Abraham Lincoln, written in New York April, 1865, published in the Atlantic Monthly, January, 1866. A Legend of St. Martin, written in Roslyn in 1865. The Words of the Koran, written in Roslyn, November, 1865.

1866.

The Order of Nature, written in Roslyn in 1866 ; edition of 1871. The Death of Slavery, written in Roslyn, May, 1866, published in the Atlantic Monthly, July, 1866.

1867.

A Brighter Day, written in Roslyn, October, 1867, published in the New York Ledger, January 4, 1868.

1868.

Among the Trees, written in Roslyn, published in Putnam's Magazine, January, 1869.

1869.

May Evening, written in Roslyn, published in Appleton's Journal, May, 1869.

1872.

Tree-Burial, written in Roslyn, published in the New York Ledger, August 17, 1872. A Legend of the Delaware, written in Roslyn, published in the New York Ledger, November 9, 1872.

1873.

The Poet's First Song, written in Roslyn, November, 1873, published in The Mayflower, April, 1876. The Two Travellers, written in Roslyn, published in the Atlantic Monthly, January, 1874.

1875.

The Ascension, written in New York, December, 1875, published in the Independent. The Mystery of Flowers, written in Roslyn in 187£. Christmas in 1875, written in New York, published in the New York Evening Post, December, 1875. Our Fellow-Worshippers, written in Roslyn.

1876.

The Dead Patriarch, written in Roslyn in 1876. To ——, written in Roslyn in 1876. The Flood of Years, written in Roslyn, published in Scribner's Monthly, July, 1876. A Lifetime, written in Cummington in 1876.

1877.

The Battle of Bennington, written August 16, 1877. In Memory of John Lothrop Motley, written September, 1877, published·in the International Review.

1878.

The Twenty-second of February, written in New York in February, published in the Sunday-School Times. Cervantes, written April 23, 1878.

PRINCIPAL EDITIONS OF THE POEMS.

1808.

The | Embargo, | or | Sketches of the Times; | A | Satire. |
By a Youth of Thirteen. | Boston : Printed for the Purchasers.
| 1808.

Title and pp. 3–12.

1809.

The | Embargo; | or | Sketches of the Times. | A Satire. |
The second edition corrected and enlarged. | Together with
the | Spanish Revolution | and | Other Poems. | By William
Cullen Bryant. | Boston : | Printed for the author, by E. G.
House, | No. 5, Court Street. | 1809.

Collation : Title as above. Certificate of Copyright on verso,
p. 2, viz. :

District of Massachusetts. Be it remembered, that on the eighth day
of February, in the thirty-third year of the independence of the
United States of America, Peter Bryant, of the said district, has
deposited in this office the title of a book, the right whereof he
claims as proprietor, in the words following, *to wit*, The Embargo, or
Sketches of the Times; a Satire. The second edition corrected and
enlarged; together with The Spanish Revolution; and other Poems,
by William Cullen Bryant, etc.

Advertisement, p. 3, viz. :

A DOUBT having been intimated in the Monthly Anthology of June
last, whether a youth of thirteen years could have been the author of
this poem—in justice to his merits the friends of the writer feel obliged
to certify the fact from their personal knowledge of himself and his
family, as well as his literary improvement and extraordinary talents.
They would premise, that they do not come uncalled before the public,
to bear this testimony—they would prefer that he should be judged by
his works, without favour or affection. As the doubt has been sug-
gested, they deem it merely an act of justice to remove it—after which
they leave him a candidate for favour in common with other literary
adventurers. They, therefore, assure the public, that Mr. Bryant, the

author, is a native of Cummington, in the County of Hampshire, and in the month of November last arrived at the age of fourteen years. The facts can be authenticated by many of the inhabitants of that place, as well as by several of his friends who give this notice; and if it be deemed worthy of further inquiry, the printer is enabled to disclose their names and places of residence.   *February, 1809.*

Preface, pp. 5–6, viz. :

> The first sketch of the following poem was written, when the *terrapin policy* of our Administration, in imposing the Embargo, exhibited undeniable evidence of its hostility to Commerce, and proof positive, that its political character was deeply tinctured with an unwarrantable partiality for *France.* &c., &c.

Text, pp. 7–36.   The Embargo, pp. 7–20.   The Spanish Revolution, pp. 21–26.   Ode to Connecticut River, pp. 27–29. The Reward of Literary Merit, pp. 29–31.   Enigmas, pp. 31–33.   The Contented Ploughman, pp. 33–35. Drought, p. 35.   Translation from Horace, Lib. 1, Car. xxii, p. 36.

1821.

Poems | by | William Cullen Bryant. | Cambridge : | Printed by Hilliard and Metcalf. | 1821.

Collation :   12mo, pp. 44.   Brown paper boards with title as above.   Title as above.   Verso blank.   Advertisement.

> The first poem in this collection was delivered before a literary association.   Some of the others have appeared before, in different periodical publications, and are now by permission, inserted in this volume.

Text, pp. 7–44.   Sub-title, The Ages.   Poem, The Ages, pp. 7–24.   Sub-title, To a Waterfowl.   Poem, To a Waterfowl, pp. 27–28.   Translation of a Fragment of Simonides, pp. 29–30.   Inscription for the Entrance into a Wood, pp. 31–32.   The Yellow Violet, pp. 33–34.   Song, p. 35. Green River, pp. 36–38.   Sub-title, Thanatopsis.   Poem, Thanatopsis, pp. 41–44.

Mr. Godwin, in the two-volume edition of the poems, published in 1883, says of the date when Thanatopsis was written :

Mr. Bryant was himself for a while somewhat uncertain as to the precise time in which this poem was written.   In answer to a gentleman, Mr. S. N. Holliday, who put the question to him, he wrote, under date of New York, March 15, 1855, as follows :

I cannot give you any information of the occasion which suggested to my mind the idea of my poem Thanatopsis. It was written when I was seventeen or eighteen years old—I have not now at hand the memorandums which would enable me to be precise—and I believe it was composed in my solitary rambles in the woods. As it was first committed to paper, it began with the half-line—" Yet a few days, and thee "—and ended with the beginning of another line with the words—" And make their bed with thee." The rest of the poem—the introduction and the close—was added some years afterward, in 1821, when I published a little collection of my poems at Cambridge."

He was seventeen years old November 3, 1811, and he wrote the poem shortly after he left Williams College, in the summer of that year. It was put away with others for revision, when his father found it, and procured it to be published in The North American Review of 1817. As this poem occupies so prominent a position in the history of American literature, I reproduce it here as it was originally written and printed. The reader will easily discover the changes made in it by the author between that time and 1821, when it was first given to the public in its present shape. It is needless to say that the four rhymed stanzas prefixed to it were not intended to accompany it, but, as they were found in the same package with Thanatopsis, they were mistakenly supposed to be an introduction.—EDITOR.

THANATOPSIS.

Not that from life and all its woes
　The hand of death shall set me free;
Not that this head shall then repose
　In the low vale most peacefully.

Ah, when I touch time's farthest brink,
　A kinder solace· must attend;
It chills my very soul to think
　On that dread hour when life must end.

In vain the flattering verse may breathe
　Of ease from pain and rest from strife,

There is a sacred dread of death
Inwoven with the strings of life.

This bitter cup at first was given
    When angry Justice frowned severe;
And 'tis the eternal doom of heaven
    That man must view the grave with fear.

            —Yet a few days, and thee
The all-beholding sun shall see no more
In all his course; nor yet in the cold ground,
Where thy pale form was laid, with many tears,
Nor in the embrace of ocean, shall exist
Thy image.   Earth, that nourished thee, shall claim
Thy growth, to be resolv'd to earth again;
And, lost each human trace, surrend'ring up
Thine individual being, shalt thou go
To mix forever with the elements,
To be a brother to th' insensible rock
And to the sluggish clod, which the rude swain
Turns with his share, and treads upon.   The oak
Shall send its roots abroad, and pierce thy mould.

Yet not to thy eternal resting-place
Shalt thou retire alone—nor couldst thou wish
Couch more magnificent.   Thou shalt lie down
With patriarchs of the infant world—with kings,
The powerful of the earth, the wise, the good,
Fair forms, and hoary seers of ages past,
All in one mighty sepulchre.   The hills
Rock-ribb'd and ancient as the sun, the vales
Stretching in pensive quietness between,
The venerable woods, the floods that move
In majesty, and the complaining brooks
That wind among the meads and make them green,
Are but the solemn decorations all
Of the great tomb of man.   The golden sun,
The planets, all the infinite host of heaven,
Are glowing on the sad abodes of death
Through the still lapse of ages.   All that tread
The globe are but a handful to the tribes
That slumber in its bosom.   Take the wings
Of morning, and the Borean desert pierce,

Or lose thyself in the continuous woods
That veil the Oregon, where he hears no sound
Save his own dashings—yet the dead are there,
And millions in those solitudes, since first
The flight of years began, have laid them down
In their last sleep.   The dead reign there alone.
So shalt thou rest; and what if thou shalt fall
Unnoticed by the living, and no friend
Take note of thy departure ?   Thousands more
Will share thy destiny.   The tittering world
Dance to the grave.   The busy brood of care
Plod on, and each one chases as before
His favorite phantom; yet all these shall leave
Their mirth and their employments, and shall come,
And make their bed with thee!

Since the edition of 1821, certain lines have been further changed. Thus, page 15, line 7 :

—The Barcan desert pierce,

has been written :

—traverse Barca's desert sands,

and then :

—pierce the Barcan wilderness.

Page 15, line 14, was originally :

—and what if thou shouldst fall,
Unnoticed, by the living—

Page 15, lines 25 and 26, stood in 1821 :

The bowed with age, the infant in the smile
And beauty of its innocent age cut off.

Page 16, line 3 :

To that mysterious realm—

read in 1821 :

To the pale realms of shade—   EDITOR.

1832.

Poems | by | William Cullen Bryant. | An American. | Edited by | Washington Irving. | London : | J. Andrews, 167, New Bond Street. | MDCCCXXXII.

Collation : 8vo, pp. xii–235. Title as above. Verso ; London :
J. Moyes, Castle Street, Leicester Square. Dedication

to Samuel Rogers, Esq., pp. iii–vi, signed Washington
Irving, London, March, 1832. Author's Preface, pp. vii–
viii, viz. :

Most of the following poems have been already printed. The longest,
entitled The Ages, was published in 1821, in a thin volume, along
with about half a dozen others now included in this collection. With
a few exceptions, the remainder have since appeared in different publi-
cations, mostly of the periodical kind. The favour with which the
public have regarded them, and of which their republication in various
compilations seemed to the author a proof, has induced him to collect
them into a volume. In preparing them for the press, he has made such
corrections as occurred to him on subjecting them to a careful revi-
sion. Sensible as he is that no author had ever more cause of grati-
tude to his countrymen for the indulgent estimate placed by them on
his literary attempts, he yet cannot let this volume go forth to the
public without a feeling of apprehension, both that it may contain
things which did not deserve admission, and that the entire collection
may not be thought worthy of the generous and partial judgment
which has been passed upon some of the separate poems.

N. Y., January, 1832.

Contents, pp. ix–xii, as follows :

Text, pp. 1–228. Notes, pp. 229–235.

1832.

Poems | by | William Cullen Bryant. | New York : | Published by E. Bliss, 111 Broadway, | And sold by the principal booksellers. | MDCCCXXXII.

Collation : 12mo, pp. 240. Title as above. Verso, Certificate of Copyright and printer's imprint, as follows :

Entered according to an act of Congress, in the year one thousand eight hundred and thirty-one, by W. C. Bryant, in the Clerk's Office of the Court of the United States, for the southern district of New York.
{ New York: Ludwig & Tolefree, Printers. Corner Vesey & Greenwich Streets.

Preface, p. 3. Text, pp. 5–234. Notes, pp. 235–238. Contents,
pp. 239–240.

An edition similar to the above was also printed in Boston
in the same year, 1832. The two were in all respects similar.

1834.

Poems | by | William   Cullen   Bryant. | Boston : | Russell,
Odiorne & Metcalf. | 1834.

Collation : 12mo, pp. xii–240. False Title, Bryant's Poems.
Full title as above. Verso, Certificate of Copyright,
dated 1831, and printer's imprint. Advertisement, p. v,
as follows :

The present edition contains a few poems which were not in the first,
and of which two or three have never before appeared in print   The
author has also made a few corrections, some of which were suggested
by the criticisms which have fallen in his way.

Preface to the First Edition, pp. vii–viii, dated New York,
January, 1832. Table of Contents, pp. ix–xi. Three
poems which were not in the previous editions of 1832
are : The Prairies ; Sonnet, from the Portuguese of
Somedo ; and The Journey of Life. Text, pp. 1–234.
Notes, pp. 235–240.

1836.

First Title-Page :

Poems | by | William   Cullen   Bryant. | Vignette, A view
near West Point, by R. W. Weir.

> ". . . enter this wild wood,
> And view the haunts of nature."
>
> P. 180.

New York : | Harper & Brothers | 1836.

Second Title-Page :

Poems | by | William   Cullen   Bryant. | Fourth   Edition. |
New York : | Harper & Brothers, Cliff St. | 1836.

Collation : 12mo, pp. xii–274. Title as above. Verso, Copy-
right, 1835. Sub-title, p. iii. Advertisement to the
Second Edition, p. v, as follows :

The present edition contains a few poems which were not in the first, and of which two or three have never before appeared in print. The author has also made a few corrections, some of which were suggested by the criticisms which have fallen in his way.

Preface to the First Edition, New York, January, 1832, pp. vii–viii. Contents, pp. ix–xii. Text, pp. 13–267. Notes, pp. 269–274.

The following poems appear in this edition for the first time: Earth, To the Apennines, The Knight's Epitaph, Seventy-six, The Living Lost, The Strange Lady, The Hunter's Vision, Catterskill Falls, The Hunter of the Prairies, The Count of Greiers—From the German, Earth's Children Cleave to Earth.

Four editions of the above collection of poems were made previous to 1839, numbered consecutively from the first to the fifth.

1839.

Poems | by | William Cullen Bryant. | Fifth Edition. | New York : | Harper & Brothers, Cliff St. | 1839.

Collation : 12mo, pp. xii–276. Title as above. Verso, Copyright, 1836. Sub-title, p. iii. Advertisement to the Fifth Edition, p. v, as follows :

The present edition, by the advice of the publishers, is somewhat enlarged. A few corrections have also been made in the text of the poems which were published in the other editions.

Preface to the First Edition, New York, January, 1832, pp. vii–viii. Contents, pp. ix–xii. Text, pp. 13–269. Notes, pp. 271–276.

The only new poem in this edition is The Battlefield, p. 268. There seem to have been at least five reprints of this edition; the last, which is called the tenth edition, having been published in 1843. The destruction by fire of the records of Harper Bros. makes it difficult to be more accurate on this point.

1842.

The Fountain | and | other Poems. | By | William Cullen Bryant. | New York and London : | Wiley and Putnam. | 1842.

Collation : 12mo, pp. 100. False Title. Title as above. Verso, Copyright, 1842, and printer's imprint. Contents, p. v. To the Reader, p. vii :

The poems which compose this little volume have been written within the last five or six years—some of them merely as parts of a longer one planned by the author, which may possibly be finished hereafter. In the meantime he has been tempted to publish them in this form by the reception which another collection of his verses has already met with among his countrymen. NEW YORK, *July, 1842.*

Sub-title, The Fountain. | Text, pp. 11–96. | Notes, pp. 97–100.

The following poems appear in this edition for the first time : The Fountain, The Winds, The Green Mountain Boys, The Death of Schiller, A Presentiment, The Future Life, The Old Man's Counsel, The Child's Funeral, A Serenade, To the Memory of William Leggett, An Evening Revery, The Painted Cup, A Dream, The Antiquity of Freedom.

1844.

Outside Cover Title : The Home Library. | Poetical Series, No. 1. | The White Footed Deer | and other Poems. | By William Cullen Bryant. | New York : | I. S. Platt, 111, Fulton Street. | Press of the Home Library, 1844.

Collation : 16mo, pp. vi–24. Notes, p. 1.

This little volume has yellow paper covers, with title as above. The back cover contains an advertisement of the Home Library, edited by Evert A., Duyckinck, in which the statement is made that the poetical series will commence with The White Footed Deer.

False Title, The White Footed Deer and Other Poems. Title, p. iv, The White Footed Deer & Other Poems, by William Cullen Bryant. Copyright on verso, dated 1844, with printers' and stereotyper's names. S. W. Benedict & Co., 128, Fulton St.

Contents, p. vi.

	PAGE
Advertisement	vii
The White-Footed Deer	1
Noon	5
Washington	8

Advertisement.

All the following trifles in verse except one have been written since the last collection of the author's poems was published.

NEW YORK, *March, 1844.*

Notes, p. 1.

During the stay of Long's expedition at Engineer Cantonment, three specimens of a variety of the common deer were brought in, having all the feet white near the hoofs, and extending to those on the hind feet from a little above the spurious hoofs, etc.

P. 5.

At noon the Hebrew bowed the knee and worshipped. Evening and morn and at noon will I pray and cry aloud, and he shall hear my voice.

1847.

Poems | by | William Cullen Bryant | with Illustrations by E. Leutze. | Engraved by American Artists. | Philadelphia : | Carey and Hart, | 1847. |

Collation : Royal 8vo, pp. 378. Frontispiece, Greek Amazon. Sub-title, Poems by William Cullen Bryant, with vignette portrait, Philadelphia, Carey & Hart. Title as above. Copyright on verso, 1847.

To the Reader, p. 3 :

Perhaps it would have been well if the author had followed his original intention, which was to leave out of this volume, as unworthy of republication, several of the poems which made a part of his previous collections. He asks leave to plead the judgment of a literary friend, whose opinion in such matters he highly values, as his apology for having retained them. With the exception of the first and longest poem in the collection, The Ages, they are all arranged according to the order of time in which they were written, as far as it can be ascertained.

NEW YORK, *1846.*

Contents, pp. 5–9.   List of illustrations, pp. 11–16.   Portrait of
   Bryant, preceding text.   Text, pp. 17–361.   Notes, false
   title, p. 363.   Notes, pp. 365–378.

This edition was reprinted complete in one volume without
illustrations.   Philadelphia, Carey & Hart, 1849.

1854.

Poems | by | William Cullen Bryant. | Collected and ar-
ranged | by the Author. | In Two Volumes. | Vol. I. | New
York, | D. Appleton and Company, | 346 and 348, Broadway. |
London : 16 Little Britain. | MDCCCLIV.

Collation : 12mo, 2 vols.   Vol. I, pp. x–296.   Vol. II, pp. vi–
   286.   Title as above.   Copyright on verso, 1854.

To the Reader.   (Prefixed to the Edition of 1846.)   P. 3 :
Advertisement, p. 5.

> The present edition has been carefully revised by the author, and
> some faults of diction and versification corrected.   A few poems not
> in the previous editions have been added.
>
> NEW YORK, *August, 1854.*

Contents of Vol. I, pp. 7–10.   Sub-title, Poems.   Text, pp.
   1–286.   Notes, pp. 287–296.

Vol. II.   Title as above.   Contents, pp. 3–6.   Sub-title, Poems.
   Text, pp. 1–268.   Notes, 269–286.

> This edition was reprinted in 1855, 1856, 1857, 1859, 1860, 1862, 1864,
> 1864, 1865, 1866, 1869, 1870.
> An edition of the above collection of poems was published in one 36mo
> volume, September, 1854.
> A reprint of the Carey & Hart illustrated edition of 1847 was made in
> this year with the imprint of D. Appleton and Company on the title-
> page.

Poems | by | William Cullen Bryant. | Collected and ar-
ranged by the Author. | Illustrated with seventy-one engrav-
ings. | From drawings by eminent artists. | New York : | D.
Appleton and Company, 346–348, Broadway.

Collation : Sm. 4to, pp. xvi–344.   Title as above.   Copy-
   right on verso, 1854.   Contents, pp. v–ix.   List of illus-
   trations, x–xii.   To the Reader, prefixed to the edition

of 1846, p. xiii. Advertisement, prefixed to the edition of 1854, p. xiv. Sub-title, Poems, p. xv. Text, 1–332. Sub-title, Notes, p. 333. Notes, pp. 335–344.

This edition was printed in England, by R. Clay, Bread Street, Hill. The following poems appear in this edition for the first time: The Unknown Way, Oh Mother of a Mighty Race, The Land of Dreams, The Burial of Love, The May Sun Sheds an Amber Light, The Voice of Autumn, The Conqueror's Grave, The Snow-shower,* A Rain-Dream,* Robert of Lincoln.*

1864.

Thirty Poems. | William Cullen Bryant. | New York : | D. Appleton and Company, | 443 and 445 Broadway. | London : 16 Little Britain. | MDCCCLXIV.

Collation: 12mo, pp. 222. Title as above. Copyright on verso, 1863. Pp. 3–4.

To the Reader:

> The author has attempted no other classification of the poems in this volume than that of allowing them to follow each other according to the order of time in which they were written. It has seemed to him that this arrangement is as satisfactory as any other, since, at different periods of life, an author's style and habits of thought may be supposed to undergo very considerable modifications. One poem forms an exception to this order of succession, and should have appeared in an earlier collection. Three others have already appeared in an illustrated edition of the author's poems.
>
> NEW YORK, *December, 1863.*

Contents, pp. 5–6. Sub-title, Poems, p. 7. Text, pp. 9–210. Sub-title, Notes, p. 211. Notes, pp. 213–222.

The following poems appear in this edition for the first time: The Planting of the Apple-Tree, The Twenty-seventh of March, An Invitation to the Country, Song for New Year's Eve, The Wind and Stream, The Lost Bird—from the Spanish of Carolina Coronado, The Night Journey of a River, The Life that Is, Song, "These Prairies Glow with Flowers," A Sick-

---

* The last three poems do not appear in the American edition of this date.

Bed, The Song of the Sower, The New and the Old, The Cloud on the Way, The Tides, Italy, A Day-Dream, The Ruins of Italica—from the Spanish of Rioja, Waiting by the Gate, Not Yet, Our Country's Call, The Constellations, The Third of November, 1861, The Mother's Hymn, Sella, The Fifth Book of Homer's Odyssey—translated, The Little People of the Snow, The Poet.

1871.

Poems | by | William Cullen Bryant. | Collected and arranged | by the Author. | New York : | D. Appleton and Company, 549 and 551 Broadway. | London : 16 Little Britain. | 1871.

Collation: 12mo, pp. 390. Frontispiece, portrait of Bryant. Title as above. Copyright on verso, 1871. To the Reader, p. iii, New York, June, 1871. Contents, pp. v–ix. Text, pp. 11–375. Notes, pp. 376–390.

This is known as the "Red-line" Edition, and has been frequently reprinted.

1876.

Poetical Works | of | William Cullen Bryant. | Collected and arranged | by the Author. | Illustrated by one hundred engravings. | From drawings by Birket Foster, Harry Fenn, Alfred Fredericks, and others. | New York : | D. Appleton and Company, | 549 and 551 Broadway.

Collation: Sq. 8vo, pp. x–501. Frontispiece, portrait of Bryant. Title as above. Copyright on verso, 1876. To the Reader, p. iii, dated New York, August, 1876. Contents, pp. v–x. Sub-title, Poems. Text, pp. 3–486. Notes, 487–501.

The illustrations in this edition are the same as those used in the English edition of 1854, with the addition of a new illustration to Thanatopsis, p. 21.

The following poems appear in this edition for the first time : October, 1866, The Order of Nature, Tree-Burial, A Legend of the Delawares, A Lifetime.

1883.

The | Poetical Works | of | William Cullen Bryant, | edited by | Parke Godwin. | In Two Volumes. | Volume First. | New York : | D. Appleton and Company. | 1, 3, and 5 Bond Street. | 1883.

Collation : I, 8vo, pp. 358. False Title, The Life and Works of William Cullen Bryant. Vol. III. Title as above. Copyright on verso, 1883. Preface, pp. v–vi. Original Prefaces, vii–x. Contents, xi–xiv. Sub-title, p. 15. Text, pp. 17–326. Notes, pp. 327–358. Vol. II, pp. 372.

SEPARATE PUBLICATIONS.

1820.

An Oration, | delivered at Stockbridge, July 4, 1820. | By William C. Bryant, Esq. | Stockbridge: Printed by Charles Webster, 1820.

12mo. Title, p. 1 (verso blank). Oration, pp. 3–11 (verso blank.)

1841.

Popular Considerations on Homœopathia : | By William Cullen Bryant, Esq., | delivered before the New York Homœopathic Society, | December 23, 1841. New York [1841].

8vo, pp. 24.

1843.

An Address | to the | People of the United States | in behalf of the American Copyright Club. | Adopted at New York, October 18, 1843. New York: Published by the Club, 1843.

12mo, pp. 20.

1848.

A | Funeral Oration | occasioned by the Death of | Thomas Cole. | Delivered before the | National Academy of Design, | New York, May 4, 1848, | by | William Cullen Bryant. | Published by order of | the Council of the Academy. | New York.

8vo, pp. 42.

1850.

Letters of a Traveller, | or | Notes of Things | Seen in | Europe and America. | By William Cullen Bryant. | New York, | George P. Putnam, 155, Broadway. | London : Richard Bentley, | 1850.

12mo, pp. 442.

This edition was reprinted in 1851, under the title of The Picturesque Souvenir, Letters of a Traveller, published by Putnam, with thirteen steel engravings.

7   xciii

1851.

Reminiscences | of the | Evening Post. | Extracted from
the Evening Post | of | November 15, 1851. | With additions
and corrections by the Writer. | New York : | William C.
Bryant & Co., Printers, 18 Nassau Street, N. Y. | 1851.

12mo, pp. 22.

1859.

Letters of a Traveller. | Second series. | By | William Cullen
Bryant. | New York : | D. Appleton and Company | 346 and 348
Broadway. | 1859. |

12mo, pp. 277.

1860.

" How Amiable are Thy Tabernacles, Oh Lord of Hosts." |
A | Forest Hymn | by | William Cullen Bryant, | with | Illus-
trations | by | John A. Nums. | New York : | W. A. Towns-
end & Co. | [1860].

4to, pp. 32, printed on one side only.

There are two variations of this title-page, one with the
imprint " New York, Hurd & Houghton," with plates some-
what worn ; the other, " New York, James G. Gregory."

1863.

Class Ode, Fiftieth Anniversary of the Class of 1813 |
1863. | Fifty years, | for the Fiftieth Anniversary of the Class
of Williams College, which was graduated in 1813.

4to, 2 pp., printed on one side only, signed W. C. B.

1864.

Hymns | by | William Cullen Bryant.

8vo, pp. iv–40.

Nineteen hymns are included in this collection, which was printed for
private circulation only.   Bound in black boards.   Title in gilt
letters on cover.

Book of Hymns, 1864.

" Soon after his father's death (March 20, 1820), while he was yet full
of the sentiment it inspired, an appeal was made to him by the Uni-
tarians in aid of a Collection of Hymns they projected.   Mr. Henry

D. Sewall, the editor, applied to Miss Catherine M. Sedgwick, of Stockbridge, to use her efforts in his behalf."

In a letter to her brother Robert, of New York, dated May 17, 1820, she writes :

"I wish you would give my best regards to Mr. Sewall, and tell him I have had great success in my agency. I sent for Mr. Bryant last week, and he called to see me on my return from Court. I told him Mr. Sewall had commissioned me to request some contributions from him to a collection of hymns, and he said, without any hesitation, that he was obliged to Mr. Sewall, and would with great pleasure comply with his request," etc.

The following is Miss Sedgwick's reply to Mr. Bryant, written more than forty years afterward, on receipt of a copy of hymns published at that time :

" MY DEAR MR. BRYANT:

" But for your prohibition I should at once, on the receipt of my precious little Hymns, have sent to you my earnest thanks, and told you how vividly they recall the day when the young poet, one of the first objects of my hero-worship, offered me in my dear home the six hymns, etc."

Extract from letter—W. C. B. to Rev. A. P. Putnam, November 15, 1873.

Hymns.

Nos. 1 and 2. Composed for some Ordination. Nos. 3, 4, 5, 6, 7, 8. Composed for collection made by Henry D. Sewall. No. 9. Ordination in England. No. 10. After a lapse of thirty years, for Mr. Waterston, Boston. No. 11. For dedication of the Church of the Pilgrims. No. 12. Composed for anniversary of Foreign Missionary Society. No. 13. Written for Mr. Lombard, of Utica, included in a collection at the end of a School Liturgy, compiled in 1859. No. 14. Written at Dr. Osgood's suggestion in 1861-'62, and included by him in his Liturgy. The remaining five, written to complete collection.

1869.

Letters from the East, | by | William Cullen Bryant. | New York : | G. P. Putnam & Son. | 1869.

8vo, pp. 256.

1869.

Some Notices | of the | Life and Writings | of | Fitz-Greene Halleck. | Read before the New York Historical Society on the 3d of February, 1869. | By William Cullen Bryant. | New

York : | Evening Post Steam Presses, 41 Nassau, Cor. Liberty. | 1869.

8vo, pp. 35.

1870.

The | Iliad of Homer. | Translated into English Blank Verse. | By | William Cullen Bryant. | Volume I. | Monogram of Publishers. | Boston : | Fields, Osgood & Co. | 1870.

Royal 8vo.   I. pp. 398, with rubricated title.   II. pp. 426.

1871.

The | Odyssey of Homer. | Translated into English blank verse. | By | William Cullen Bryant. | Vol. I (and II). | Monogram of publishers. | Boston : | James R. Osgood & Company, | late Ticknor & Fields, and Fields, Osgood & Co. | 1871.

8vo, I, pp. xii–324 ; II, pp. vi–311.

Electrotyped and printed at Cambridge, Mass., by Welch, Bigelow & Co.   Reprinted by James R. Osgood & Co., Boston, 1873, 2 vols., 8vo.

1871.

The | Song of the Sower, | by | William Cullen Bryant. | Illustrated with Forty-two Engravings on Wood. | New York : | D. Appleton and Company. | MDCCCLXXI.

4to, pp. 48.

Bound in heavy embossed brown morocco boards.   Illuminated title on back and sides, with vignettes of a harp and plow in gilt, top and bottom.

1873.

The Little | People of the Snow | by | William Cullen Bryant. | Illustrated | from designs by Alfred Fredericks, engraved by A. Bobbett. | New York : | D. Appleton and Company, | 549 and 551, Broadway. | 1873.

4to, pp. 40.

1874.

Among the Trees, | by | William Cullen Bryant. | Illustrated. | From designs by Jervis McEntee, Engraved by Harley. | New York : | G. P. Putnam's Sons, | Fourth Avenue and Twenty-third Street. | [1874].

Sq. 12mo.   Printed on one side only.   Pp. 39.

Thanatopsis, | by | William Cullen Bryant. | G. P. Putnam's Sons. | New York.

4to, pp. 1–18.   Printed on one side only.   Illustrations, proofs on India paper.

The | Flood of Years, | by | William Cullen Bryant. | The Illustrations by | W. J. Linton.

4to, pp. 19–46.   Printed on one side only.   Proofs on India paper.

1878.

The | Flood of Years. | New York : | G. P. Putnam's Sons. | 1878.

4to, pp. 32.

ORATIONS AND ADDRESSES.

1818.

Address on the Bible, Berkshire Star (Stockbridge), February 6th.

This address was delivered before the Bible Society at Great Barrington on the 29th of January, 1818.

1852.

Memorial | of | James Fenimore Cooper. | New York : | G. P. Putnam. | [1852]. | Bryant's Discourse on the Life, Character, and Genius of Cooper, pp. 39–73.

1852.

Report of the Special Committee appointed by the Common Council of the City of New York to make Arrangements for the Reception of Gov. Louis Kossuth, the Distinguished Hungarian Patriot. New York : Published by order of the Common Council, 1852.

8vo, pp. iv–756, with portrait.

Bryant's address as President of the Press Banquet at the Astor House, Monday evening, December 15th, pp. 228–231. (See Orations and Addresses, New York, 1873, p. 261.)

1856.

An address delivered at the fiftieth anniversary of the New York Historical Society.

Address delivered before the New York Horticultural Society at the Exhibition, September 26th. (Orations and Addresses, p. 269, New York, 1873.)

Music in the Public Schools. An address delivered at the close of a series of lectures by Richard Storrs Willis, December 29, 1856. (Orations and Addresses, p. 285, New York, 1873.)

1858.

The Newspaper Press. New England Society Dinner, December 22d. (Prose Writings, p. 208, New York, 1884.)

1859.

Schiller. An address delivered at the Cooper Institute on the occasion of the Schiller Festival, November 11, 1859. (Orations and Addresses, p. 295, New York, 1873.)

1860.

The | Centennial Birthday | of | Robert Burns | as celebrated by the | 1759 (engraved medallion portrait of Burns) 1859 | Burns Club of the City of New York, | Tuesday, January 25, 1859. | Edited by J. Cunningham. | New York, 1860.

8vo, pp. 136, with colored frontispiece.

Mr. Bryant acted as honorary chairman, p. 47.

His speech, pp. 53–57.

1863.

Banquet given in New York on the 16th day of December, 1863, by the Mexican Legation.

8vo, pp. 16.

P. 4, Bryant is mentioned as one of the guests; pp. 14–15, his toast.

1864.

The | Bryant Festival | at | "The Century" | November 5, MDCCCLXIV | New York, | D. Appleton and Company, | 443 & 445 Broadway. | MDCCCLXV.

4to, pp. 88.

Bryant's reply to Mr. Bancroft, pp. 9–13.

1865.

The | Bryant Festival | at | "The Century." | Illustrated Edition. | New York. | Published by the Century Association. | MDCCCLXV.

Collation : 4to, pp. 88. Printed on one side only.

Frontispiece—Photograph of the Century Club House.

Title as above.

Copyright on verso—by the Century Association, 1864.
Only 150 copies printed.   No. 36.
Photograph of Bryant.
Text, pp. 3–88.
Mr. Bryant's reply to Mr. Huntington, p. 42.

The | National Academy of Design. | Ceremonies on the
occasion of | Laying the cornerstone, | October 21, 1863, | and
the | Inauguration of the Building, | April 27, 1865. | New
York, | MDCCCLXV.
Royal 8vo, pp. 92.
200 copies printed.   July, 1865.
Bryant's address, pp. 20–22.

1865.

Address to the Soldiers of the Union Army, January 1,
1865 (p. 221, Godwin's Life, vol. ii).

1866.

Dinner to Señor Matias Romero, Envoy Extraordinary and
Minister Plenipotentiary from Mexico, on the 29th of March,
1864.   New York, 1866.

1867.

Banquet | to | Señor Matias Romero, | Envoy Extraordinary
and Minister | Plenipotentiary from Mexico | to the United
States, | by the | Citizens of New York, | October 2, 1867.
Royal 8vo, 46 pp.
Printed for private distribution.   On pp. 3 and 4 Bryant is
mentioned as member of the committee, and was the toast-
master, pp. 27–30, 36, 38, 40–42, 46.

1868.

Complimentary Dinner to Jonathan Sturges.
8vo, pp. 28.
Bryant was one of the guests (p. 3); his toast, " Literature,
the Fine Arts, and Commerce," pp. 22–25.

1868.

Freedom of Exchange. Speech at a dinner given to Mr. Bryant in New York, January 30, 1868. (Orations and Addresses, p. 313, New York, 1873.)

The Electric Telegraph. Speech at a dinner given to Samuel Breese Morse, December 29, 1868. (Orations and Addresses, p. 325, New York, 1873.)

1869.

A History | of the | Celebration of Robert Burns' | 110th Natal Day, | at the Metropolitan Hotel, | New York. | Jersey City, | 1869.

8vo, pp. 99.

Pp. 31–33, Mr. Bryant's toast on Minstrelsy.

1869.

A Metropolitan Art Museum | in the City of New York. | Proceedings of a Meeting | Held at the Theatre of the | Union League Club, Tuesday Evening, November 23, 1869. | Including | Addresses, Remarks, and Letters | by | Mr. Wm. C. Bryant, Prof. Comfort, Mr. R. M. Hunt, Mr. Henry G. Stebbins, Mr. William J. Hoppin, Mr. Russell Sturgis, Rev. Dr. Thompson, Rev. Dr. Bellows, Mr. Marshall O. Roberts, Mr. Geo. Wm. Curtis, and others. | New York. | Printed for the Committee, | 1869.

Pamphlet of 40 pages.

Mr. Bryant's address as president will be found on p. 8.

1870.

Celebration of the 111th Anniversary of Robert Burns' Natal Day, at Delmonico's Hotel, New York, January 25, 1870. New York, 1870.

8vo, pp. 52.

Bryant's toast, "The Memory of Robert Burns," pp. 12–14. (See Prose Writings, New York, 1884, p. 322.)

1870.

Translators of Homer. Speech to the Williams College Alumni, February 22, 1870. (Prose Writings, p. 267. New York, 1884.)

1870.

A Discourse | on the | Life, Character, and Writings | of | Gulian Crommelin Verplanck. | Delivered before the New York Historical Society, | May 17, 1870, | by William Cullen Bryant. | New York. | Printed for the Society. | MDCCCLXX. 60 pages.

1870.

The Mercantile Library. Address delivered on the Fiftieth Anniversary of the Founding of the New York Mercantile Library, November 9, 1870. (Orations and Addresses, p. 345. New York, 1873.)

1871.

The Struggle for Neutrality in America. An address delivered before the New York Historical Society, at their sixty-sixth anniversary, December 13, 1870, by Charles Francis Adams. New York, 1871.

8vo, pp. 52.

Bryant's remarks as foreign corresponding secretary of the Society, pp. 51, 52.

1871.

The Unity of Italy. The American Celebration of the Unity of Italy, at the Academy of Music, New York, January 12, 1871, with the addresses, letters, and comments of the press. New York, 1871.

Royal 8vo, pp. 197.

Bryant's address, pp. 172–175. (See Orations and Addresses, New York, 1873, p. 353.)

1871.

The Settlement of the Alabama Question. The Banquet given at New York [May 23d] to Her Britannic Majesty's High Commissioners by Mr. Cyrus W. Field. A report edited with a short introduction by Justin McCarthy. London, 1871.

8vo, pp. 72, with two group photographs.

Bryant's speech, pp. 62–66.

Negotiation *vs.* War. Remarks made at the dinner given to the High Commissioners who negotiated the Treaty of Washington. New York, May, 1871. (Prose Writings, p. 284. New York, 1884.)

German Literature. Remarks at a dinner given to Baron Gerolt, German Ambassador, May 17, 1871. (Prose Writings, p. 287. New York, 1884.)

The Morse Statue. Address delivered on the unveiling of the statue of Samuel Finlay Breese Morse, June 10, 1871. (Orations and Addresses, p. 361. New York, 1873.)

1871.

Myles Standish, with an Account of the Exercises of Consecration of the Monument Ground on Captain's Hill, Duxbury, August 17, 1871. Prepared by Stephen M. Allen. Boston, 1871.

8vo, pp. 76.

Letter from Bryant on p. 76.

1871.

Darwin's Theory. Remarks at Williams College Alumni Dinner, December 28, 1871. (Prose Writings, p. 291. New York, 1884.)

1872.

Literary Missionaries. Remarks at a lecture of George Macdonald on Hamlet, introducing the lecturer. New York, 1872. (Prose Writings, p. 298. New York, 1884.)

1872.

Reform. Address delivered at a meeting held in the Cooper Institute, September 23, 1872. (Orations and Addresses, p. 381. New York, 1873.)

Sir Walter Scott. Address on the unveiling of the statue of Sir Walter Scott, in Central Park, November 4, 1872. (Orations and Addresses, p. 389. New York, 1873.)

1872.

Sixty-seventh | Anniversary Celebration | of the | New England Society | in the City of New York | at Delmonico's, | December 23, 1872.

8vo, pp. 106.

Bryant's speech, The Press, is on pp. 42–45.

1873.

An address before the Geographical and Statistical Society of Mexico, February, 1773.

(P. 320, Godwin's Life, vol. ii.)

1873.

Shakespeare. Ward's Statue in the Central Park, New York [May 22, 1872]. New York, 1873.

Royal 8vo, pp. 72. Only fifty copies printed.

Bryant's oration is on pp. 15–22. (See Orations and Addresses, New York, 1873, p. 371.)

1873.

The Princeton Library. Address at Princeton, N. J., June 24, 1873, on the opening of the new building for the College Library. (Prose Writings, p. 324. New York, 1884.)

1874.

Franklin as a Poet. Speech at the celebration of Franklin's birthday by the New York Typographical Society, January 17, 1874. (Prose Writings, p. 329. New York, 1884.)

1874.

The Reception of Peter Cooper by the Arcadian Club, on his eighty-fourth birthday, Feb. 12, 1874. Printed for private distribution. New York, 1774.

8vo, pp. 105.

Bryant's speech, pp. 52–54.

1874.

Proceedings at the Mass Meeting of Citizens in the Cooper Institute, New York, Tuesday evening, March 24, 1874, on National Finances. New York, 1874.

8vo, pp. 63.

Speech of Bryant as one of the executive committee, pp. 12–14.

1874.

National Honesty. Address at a mass meeting held in Cooper Institute, March 25, 1874. (Prose Writings, p. 332. New York, 1884.)

1874.

Eightieth Birthday Address, November 3, 1874.
(P. 349, vol. ii, Godwin's Life.)

1875.

Proceedings at the Complimentary Dinner given to Hon. Simeon B. Chittenden by his friends on the occasion of his retirement from business, March 9, 1875. New York. Printed for private distribution. 1875.

8vo, pp. 47.
Bryant's remarks, pp. 18–19.

1875.

Goethe. Address delivered at the Centennial Festival given by the Goethe Club, of New York, in honor of Goethe, August 27, 1875. (Prose Writings, p. 335. New York, 1884.)

Addresses delivered before the Senate and Assembly, State of New York.
(Pp. 358–360, vol. ii, Godwin's Life.)

1876.

Speech at the Burns Dinner, January 25, 1876. (Prose Writings, p. 320. New York, 1884.)

1876.

To | William Cullen Bryant | at Eighty Years. | From his | Friends and Countrymen. | New York : | Scribner, Armstrong & Co., | 743–745, Broadway, | 1876.

Picture of Bryant vase, frontispiece. Sm. 4to, pp. 64.
With full title, both inside and out, pp. 127.

1877.

The | Halleck Memorial. | Edited by | Evart A. Duyckinck. | Privately printed | ———' A Memorial | of | Fitz-Greene Halleck. | A Description of the | Dedication of the Monument. | Erected to his Memory | at | Guilford, Connecticut, | and | of the Proceedings connected with the unveiling of the Poet's Statue in the Central Park. | No poet had died and received such tribute in America. | Printed for the Committee | by Ammerman and Wilson, | 1 Park Place, New York. | 1877.

Collation: Pp. 72. | Frontispiece. | Portrait of Halleck, Monument, and Guilford, Conn., and Central Park.

1878.

Address delivered at Clergyman's Breakfast, May 1, 1878.

(Vol. ii, Parke Godwin's Life of Bryant, p. 393. New York, 1883.)

Mazzini. Address delivered at the unveiling of the bust of Mazzini, in Central Park, New York city, May 20, 1878. (Prose Writings, p. 343. New York, 1884.)

1879.

Bulletin of the American Geographical Society, November 5, 1878. New York : printed for the Society, 1879.

8vo, pp. 197–298.

On pp. 288–289 are Bryant's remarks at the Arctic Meeting at Chickering Hall, January 31, 1878, at the reception of the Earl of Dufferin.

ESSAYS AND REVIEWS.

1818.

An Essay on American Poetry, with several miscellaneous pieces on a variety of subjects, sentimental, descriptive, moral, and patriotic. By Solyman Brown, A. M. New Haven: Flagg & Gray, 1818. North American Review, July, 1818, pp. 198-211.

Bryant's first review of a book now very rare.

1819.

Trisyllabic Feet in Iambic Measure, North American Review, September, 1819.

1824.

The Ruins of Pæstum, North American Review, No. 19, p. 42. Percy's Masque, North American Review, No. 20, p. 245.

1825.

Hillhouse's Hadad, New York Review, p. 1. Jehan de Nostre Dame's Lives of the Provencal Poets, New York Review, p. 107. Memoirs of Count Segur, New York Review, p. 291. Lives of Provençal Poets, New York Review, p. 104. Rammohun Roy's Precepts of Jesus, New York Review, p. 442. Scott's Lives of the Novelists, New York Review, p. 413. United States Literary Gazette, New York Review, p. 219. Wayland's Two Discourses, New York Review, p. 142. Webster's Address, New York Review, p. 214. Wheaton's Reports, New York Review, p. 203. Memoir of the Life of Richard Henry Lee, etc., New York Review, p. 23. A Pennsylvania Legend, New York Review, The Atheneum Magazine, December, p. 49.

1826.

Memoirs of the Life of the Right Honorable Richard Brinsley Sheridan, New York Review, February, p. 165. Recent

Poetry, New York Review, p. 181. Percival's Poem, New York Review, March, p. 245. Sketches of Corsica, New York Review, April, p. 348. Wheaton's Life of Pinkney, New York Review, May, p. 435.

1872.

Oldham's Poems, Old and New, September. vol. vi, iii, pp. 329–335.

1877.

Abraham Cowley, North American Review, No. 256, May–June, pp. 368–382.

WORKS EDITED BY BRYANT OR CON-TAINING ORIGINAL CONTRIBUTIONS AND INTRODUCTIONS.

1817.

North American Review | and | Miscellaneous Journal. | Vol. Fifth. | Boston. | Published by Cummings & Hilliard, | No. 1 Cornhill. | University Press, Hilliard & Metcalf. | 1817.

Thanatopsis is on p. 338.

A Fragment, afterward known as The Inscription to the Entrance of a Wood, is on p. 340.

1818.

North American Review and Miscellaneous Journal, March, To a Friend on his Marriage. March, Version of Simonides. March, The Waterfowl. July, Essay on American Poetry. No. 9, p. 206, Essay on The Happy Temperament.

1821–'22.

The Idleman, by R. H. Dana. Issued in parts. Part I, dated New York, 1821.

Collation: Part I, Vol. I. Title, The Idleman. Inscription, "How various his employments whom the world calls idle." New York, Wiley & Halsted, No. 3 Wall Street, 1821–'22. Certificate of Copyright on verso, dated May 18, 1821. Preface, pp. 3–14. Letter-press, pp. 15–57.

Volume I consists of four parts, with titles as follow: Part I, pp. 15–57, Domestic Life. Part II, pp. 3–63, The Son. Part III, pp. 3–76, Edward and Mary. Part IV, pp. 5–106, Thomas Thornton.

This last part of Vol. I is a double number, with an address to the public on p. 3, signed "The Author."

Volume II. Title and inscription as above, with the date of

8   cix

1822, and No. 1, Vol. II, in centre of page. Part I, letter-press, pp. 3–156. Paul Felton. Part II. Part III. Part IV, title-page, etc. ; letter-press, pp. 3–64. Men and Books.

Mr. Bryant's contributions are as follows : Green River, Part II, p. 61, vol. i. The West Wind, Part I, p. 155, vol. ii. The Burial-Place, Part II, vol. ii. Walk at Sunset, Part III, vol. ii. Winter Scenes, Part IV, p. 61, vol. ii.

This work was published in eight parts, royal 8vo, with brown paper covers, having title in full as above and numbered consecutively, Vol. I : I, II, III, IV, 1821; Vol. II : I, II, III, IV, 1822.

1825.

The | United States | Literary Gazette. | Vol. I. | From April, 1824, to April, 1825. | Boston : | Published by Cummings, Hilliard & Co. | 1825.

Vol. II, April, 1825–October, 1825. Vol. III, October, 1825–April, 1826. Vol. IV, April, 1826–October, 1826.

1826.

The | New York Review and Atheneum Magazine. | Vol. I. | May to November, 1825. | New York : | E. Bliss & E. White, 128 Broadway. | Clayton & Van Norden, Printers. | 1825.

Vol. II, December, 1825–May, 1826.

New York Literary Gazette and American Atheneum, May 13, 1826, to August 26, 1826.

In May, 1826, the New York Review and the American Atheneum were united with the Literary Gazette under the above title. October 1, 1826, these two were united under the new title of United States Review and Literary Gazette.

The Atlantic Souvenir; a Christmas and New Year's Offering, 1826. Philadelphia : H. C. Carey & I. Lea.

Bryant's two contributions are—June, pp. 64–66, and Oh Fairest of the Rural Maids, p. 135.

1827.

The | United States | Review and Literary Gazette. | Vol. I. | From October 1, 1826, to April 1, 1827. | New York : | G.

and C. Carvill, 108 Broadway. | Boston : | Bowles and Dearborn, 72 Washington Street, | 1827.

Vol. II, April, 1827, to October, 1827.

The above series form such an important page in the history of magazine literature that a few words of explanation are appended with the hope of throwing some light upon the origin of these various publications, and Mr. Bryant's connection with them.

The first one of the series was The United States Literary Gazette of Boston, the first number being issued in April, 1824, under the editorship of Theophilus Parsons, afterward so well known as professor in the Cambridge Law School.

There was at this same time established in New York a monthly periodical under the title of The Atlantic Magazine, edited by Robert C. Sands, the first number appearing in May. The editorship was assumed by Henry J. Anderson, afterward Professor of Mathematics in Columbia College. This periodical was continued through two volumes until April, 1825, when its name was changed to The New York Review and Atheneum Magazine. This periodical ran through two volumes until May, 1826, when it was joined with another publication known under the title of the New York Literary Gazette and Phi Beta Kappa Repository. The title of the new periodical was The New York Literary Gazette and American Atheneum.

The New York Literary Gazette was first known under the title of The Minerva or Literary Entertaining and Scientific Journal, and was edited by George Houston and James G. Brooks. This periodical ran through three volumes, the first number appearing April 10, 1824, the last, September, 1825.

In March, 1825, Mr. Brooks became sole editor, and in September he started a new publication under the title of The New York Literary Gazette and Phi Beta Kappa Repository. This ran from September 10, 1825, to March 4, 1826, in May of the same year its title being again changed as stated above to The New York Literary Gazette and American Atheneum.

Bryant became joint-editor with Mr. Anderson of The New York Review and Atheneum Magazine, and when in October, 1826, the periodical mentioned above was merged with the

United States Gazette of Boston under the title of The United
States Review and Literary Gazette, Mr. Bryant still continued
as the New York editor of the new publication, Mr. James G.
Carter being the Boston editor.

Bryant's contributions to these periodicals will be found in
the Chronology of his Poems.

1826.

Miscellaneous Poems | Selected from the | United States
Literary Gazette. | Boston : | Cummings, Hilliard & Company, |
and Harrison Gray. | 1826.

Collation : 18mo, pp. 172. Title as above. Copyright on verso,
    January 2, 1826. Advertisement, unpaged, verso blank.
    Contents, pp. i–iv. Text, pp. 1–172.

1828.

The Talisman for 1828, 1829, 1830. Published by Elam
Bliss, Broadway, New York.

This work was published as an Annual in three 12mo vols.,
with numerous illustrations by prominent American artists.

Collation : The Talisman, 1828. 12mo, pp. 288. Engraved
    frontispiece. False title-page engraved. Title - page.
    Certificate of copyright on verso, dated 1827. Preface,
    pp. iii–x, signed Francis Herbert, a *nom de guerre* for R.
    C. Sands, dated New York, December 1, 1827. Contents,
    unpaged. List of embellishments, unpaged. Two em-
    bellishments, unpaged. Etruscan antiquities, vase of
    flowers. Text, pp. 1–288.

This publication was the joint production of G. C. Ver-
planck, W. C. Bryant, and Robert C. Sands. Bryant's contribu-
tions for 1828 were : A Scene on the Banks of the Hudson, The
Hurricane, sonnet—William Tell, The Legend of the Devil's
Pulpit, The Close of Autumn, and The Cascade of Melsingah.

1829.

The Talisman, 1829, 12mo, pp. 342. Bryant's contributions
for 1829 were : Recollections of the South of Spain, Moriscan
Romance, To the Past, Lament of Romero, Story of the Island

of Cubá, The Greek Boy, The Hunter's Serenade, Reminiscences of New York.

1830.

The Talisman, 1830, 12mo, pp. 358.

Bryant's contributions for 1830 were: To the Evening Wind, The Indian Spring, Love and Folly, The Whirlwind, song—When the Firmament quivers with Daylight's Young Beam, The Siesta, song—Innocent Child and Snow-white Flower, To the River Arve, Early Spanish Poetry, Eva, The Alcayde of Molina, The Death of Aliatar, Phanette des Gantelmes, The Marriage Blunder, To Cole the Painter, on his departure for Europe, Reminiscences of New York, No. 11.

1830.

The American Landscape. No. 1. Containing the following views: Weehawken, Catskill Mountains, Fort Putnam, Delaware Water Gap, Falls of the Sawkill, Winnipisiogee Lake. Engraved from original and accurate drawings, executed from Nature expressly for this work from well-authenticated pictures, with historical and topographical illustrations. New York, published by Elam Bliss, 1830.

Collation: 4to. Title as above. Engraved cover by J. Smillie, subject, Mambrino's Helmet. Letter-press, pp. 16, including title-page. Prospectus, pp. 2. The American Landscape, signed by A. B. Durand and E. Waite, Jr., dated New York, December 23, 1830. Preface, pp. 2, signed by William Cullen Bryant. Illustrations (six); proof impressions on India paper. No. 1. All published.

The letter-press of this publication was to have been entirely by Mr. Bryant, and the work was to have consisted of views of well-known American scenery by eminent artists. It proved a failure, and ceased with the first number.

1832.

Tales of the Glauber Spa, by several American authors. [Catherine Sedgwick, J. K. Paulding, W. C. Bryant, R. C.

Sands, and William Leggett.] In two volumes. New York: J. and J. Harper, 1832.

12mo, I, ·· . 276; II, pp. 263.

Bryant's two contributions are both in Vol. I, The Skeleton's Cave, pp. 193–227, and Medfield, pp. 243–276.

This compilation was to have been called The Sextad, from the number of authors engaged upon it, but Verplanck withdrew, leaving only five.

1833.

Miscellanies. | First published under the name of The | Talisman. | By | G. C. Verplanck, | W. C. Bryant, | and | Robert C. Sands. | In three volumes. | Illustrated with fine engravings. | Vol. I. | Elam Bliss, New York. | MDCCCXXXIII.

Collation: Vol. I.   12mo, pp. 288.   Illustrated frontispiece.
 Title as above. Copyright on verso. Advertisement of the publishers. Verso, blank. Preface, pp. iii–x, dated New York, December 1, 1827, signed Francis Herbert. Contents, unpaged. List of embellishments, unpaged. Two embellishments, unpaged. Etruscan antiquities. Vase, flowers. Text, pp. 1–288.

Identical in size and contents with The Talisman.

Volume II, 12mo, pp. 342.

Volume III, 12mo, pp. 358.

All the original illustrations, prefaces, etc., reproduced from Talisman.

1834.

The | Atlantic Club-Book, | being | Sketches in Prose and Verse, | by | various Authors. | In two volumes. | New York : | 1834.

8vo, I, pp. 312.   II, pp. 312.

These volumes are composed of a number of pieces compiled from the columns of the New York Mirror.

Bryant's contributions occur on p. 49, vol. i, Song of Marion's Men; p. 217, vol. i, The Robber; p. 92, vol. ii, August.

1839.

The Jubilee of the Constitution. A discourse delivered at the request of the New York Historical Society. New York,

Tuesday, April 30, 1839; being the fiftieth anniversary of the inauguration of George Washington as President of the United States. By John Quincy Adams. New York, 1839.

8vo, pp. 136.

On p. 124 is an Ode, by Mr. Bryant, in four stanzas, Great were the Hearts, and Strong the Minds, written for the occasion.

1840.

Harper's | Family Library. | No. CXI. | Selections | from | American Poets. | By | William Cullen Bryant. | New York: | [1840.]

18mo, pp. 136.

1842.

A Discourse occasioned by the Death of William Ellery Channing, D. D., pronounced before the Unitarian Societies of New York and Brooklyn, in the Church of the Messiah, October 13, 1842. By Henry W. Bellows. New York, 1842.

8vo, pp. 28.

On p. 27 is an original hymn of three stanzas by Bryant, While yet the Harvest Fields are White.

1847.

The True Position of the Church in Relation to the Age. A discourse delivered at the dedication of the Church of the Saviour, Wednesday, November 10, 1847. By R. C. Waterston. Boston, 1847.

8vo, pp. 40.

On p. 40 is a Dedication Hymn by Mr. Bryant in four stanzas, Ancient of Days! except Thou Deign.

1852.

The Home Book of the Picturesque; or, American Scenery, Art, and Literature. Thirteen steel engravings. New York: Putnam, 1852.

4to, pp. 188.

Bryant's contribution is The Valley of the Housatonic, pp. 155–160, with engraving.

1853.

Homes | of | American Authors. | New York: G. Putnam
& Co. | 10 Park Place, 1853.

Sq. 8vo, pp. viii–267.

Bryant's contribution is a sketch of William Gilmore Simms,
p. 257.

1855.

The | Knickerbocker Gallery. | A Testimonial | to the Editor
of the | Knickerbocker Magazine. | From its Contributors. |
With forty-eight portraits on steel. | From original pictures. |
Engraved expressly for this work. | New York, 1855.

4to, pp. xiv + 505.

Bryant's contribution is the Snow Shower, p. 81.

1856.

Celebration of the Two-hundredth Anniversary of the In-
corporation of Bridgewater, Mass., at West Bridgewater, June
3, 1856., etc. Frontispiece and portrait. Boston, 1856.

8vo, pp. 167.

On pp. 18–19 is an ode by Mr. Bryant of seven stanzas, Two
Hundred Times has June Renewed.

[This Ode occurs again on pp. 70–71 of Celebration of the
Two Hundredth Anniversary of the Settlement of Hadley,
Mass., at Hadley, June 8, 1859, etc., Northampton, 1859.

8vo, pp. 98.]

1858.

Memorial of Jessie Willis: prepared for her Little Daughters,
Annie, Blanche, and Jessie, by their Father. New York:
April, 1858. [For private circulation.]

12mo, pp. 75.

On pp. 14–15 is a letter from Bryant to Mr. Willis.

1859.

Gifts of Genius: | A Miscellany | of | Prose and Poetry |
by | American Authors, | New York: | Printed for C. A. Daven-
port. | [1859.]

8vo, pp. xii+264.

Bryant's contributions are To the Public, pp. vii–viii, dated

N. Y., June, 1859, and Bocage's Penitential Sonnet, from the Portuguese, p. 264.

1860.

Helen Ruthven Waterston. [A memorial.] Printed, not published. Boston, 1860.

8vo, pp. 76.

Two extracts from Bryant's Letters are given on pp. 12–13 and 31.

1862.

Only Once. Original Papers, by various contributors. Portraits of Bryant, Lowell, and Catherine Sedgwick. New York, 1862.

4to, pp. 16.

On p. 5 is a poem by Mr. Bryant, The Better Age.

1863.

Imperial Courts | of | France, England, Russia, Prussia, | Sardinia, Austria. | Richly illustrated with | Portraits of Imperial Sovereigns | and their | Cabinet Ministers, | with | Biographical Sketches | and | an Introduction by William Cullen Bryant. | Edited by W. H. Bidwell. | New York, | 1863.

Royal 8vo, pp. xiv–411.

1863.

Songs of the War. Part I. Albany, J. Munsell, 1863.

16mo, pp. 96.

Bryant's contribution is Our Country's Call, pp. 12–13.

1864.

The Spirit of the Fair. Tuesday, April 5, 1864. New York.

4to, pp. 206.

Bryant's contribution is A Morceau from Metastasio, p. 9.

1864.

A Year in China; and a narrative of capture and imprisonment, when homeward bound, on board the rebel pirate Florida. By Mrs. H. Dwight Williams. With an introductory note by William Cullen Bryant. New York, 1864.

12mo, pp. xvi+362.

The Introductory Note is on pp. xiii–xvi.

1865.

Poetical Tributes | to the | Memory of | Abraham Lincoln. | Philadelphia, | 1865.

8vo, pp. 306.

Bryant's contribution is the first, an Ode, on p. 13.

1865.

The Lincoln Memorial: A Record of the Life, Assassination, and Obsequies of the Martyred President. New York, 1865. Portrait and woodcut title-page.

8vo, pp. 288.

On p. 205 is Bryant's Ode for the Funeral of Abraham Lincoln, and on pp. 205–206 three stanzas of A New National Hymn, composed by Mr. Bryant at the request of the reader [Dr. Samuel Osgood], and circulated among a few personal friends, and beginning, Oh, North, with all thy Vales of Green.

1866.

Obsequies of Abraham Lincoln, in the City of New York. Under the Auspices of the Common Council. By David T. Valentine. Portrait and illustrations. New York, 1866.

Royal 8vo, pp. 254.

Bryant's Ode, which had appeared in Poetical Tributes, 1865, is on p. 191.

1868.

The League [Published for American Free Trade League]. No. 10. New York, 1868.

4to, pp. 105–116.

On p. 105 is a letter dated January 18, 1868, accepting the invitation to a dinner, given by the American Free Trade League, in his honor, January 30th.

1868.

A Landscape Book, by American Artists and American Authors. Sixteen steel engravings. New York: Putnam, 1868.

8vo, pp. [4] + 108.

Bryant's contributions are three: Catterskill Falls (pp. 30–

33), with engraving ; The Valley of the Housatonic (pp. 38–43), originally published in the Home Book of the Picturesque, 1852 ; and A Summer Ramble (pp. 63–65).

1868.

Banquet to His Excellency Anson Burlingame, and his Associates of the Chinese Embassy, by the Citizens of New York, on Tuesday, June 23, 1868. New York, 1868.

8vo, pp. 65.

On p. 64 is a letter from Bryant dated Roslyn, June 9, 1868, to Elliot C. Cowdin, declining his invitation to the banquet.

1868.

The Atlantic Almanac, 1868. Edited by O. W. Holmes and Donald G. Mitchell. Illustrated. Boston.

Royal 8vo, pp. 76.

On p. 47 is The Planting of the Apple-tree.

1870.

The Atlantic Almanac. 1870.

Royal 8vo, pp. 72.

On pp. 53–56 is The Breaking of the Truce. (From the Fourth Book of the Iliad.)

1871.

Memorial Record in Memory of Hon. Increase Sumner, of Great Barrington, Mass. Portrait. Bridgeport, 1871.

8vo, pp. 74.

On p. 28 is a letter from Bryant, dated December 14, 1870, declining an invitation to a banquet of the Berkshire Bar, the last meeting of Judge Sumner with his professional colleagues.

1871.

Workday Christianity ; or, the Gospel in the Trades. By Alexander Clark. With an introductory note by William Cullen Bryant. Philadelphia, 1871.

12mo, pp. x + 300.

The Introductory Note, dated New York, March 16, 1870, is on pp. vii–viii.

1871.

A Library | of Poetry and Song. | Being | Choice Selections from the Best Poets. | With an introduction by William Cullen Bryant. New York : | J. B. Ford & Co., 1871.

Royal 8vo, pp. xxxii–789, with Frontispiece—portrait of Bryant. Introduction, pp. xxiii–xxxi.

1871.

II. Proceedings of the Massachusetts Historical Society for May, June, July, and August, 1871.

8vo, pp. 81–156.

On p. 155 is a letter dated Cummington, August 9, 1871, to the Rev. R. C. Waterston, declining an invitation to the celebration of the hundredth anniversary of Scott's birth.

1872–'74.

Picturesque America | or | The Land we live in. | A Delineation by Pen and Pencil | of | The Mountains, Rivers, Lakes, Forests, Waterfalls, Shores, Cañons, Valleys, Cities and other Picturesque Features of our Country. | With illustrations on steel and wood | by Eminent American Artists. | Edited by William Cullen Bryant. | Issued in Nos. | New York : | D. Appleton and Company. | 1872 and 1874.

2 vols., 4to.

1873.

St. Nicholas, Vol. I, No. 1.   November, 1873.   New York.

8vo, pp. 48.

On p. 2 is Bryant's translation from the Spanish, The Woodman and the Sandal Tree.

1875.

The Bryant Celebration by the Chicago Literary Club, November 3, 1874.   Chicago, 1875.

8vo, 33 pages.

On p. 11, Letter from Bryant dated Roslyn, October 27, 1874, to the Rev. Robert Collyer, President of the Chicago Literary Club.   On pp. 18–19, 24 lines of A Poem addressed to Mr A. Bryant, Brookfield, May, 1809, written in the poet's

fifteenth year, and beginning, Once more the Bard, with Eager
Eye, Reviews.

1876.

Laurel Leaves. Original Poems, Stories, and Essays. Illus-
trated. Boston, 1876.

4to, pp. xv + 446.

Bryant's contributions are two poems from the Spanish, The
Price of a Pleasure (p. 53) and The Woodman and the Sandal
Tree (p. 54; see preceding item), besides a prose selection,
The Poet Goethe (pp. 177–186), an address delivered at the
Goethe Celebration, New York, September, 1875.

1876.

Custer's Immortality. A poem, with biographical sketches
of the chief actors in the late Tragedy of the Wilderness. By
Laura S. Webb. New York, Evening Post Press, [1876].

12mo, pp. 72.

With facsimile letter of one page from Bryant to the author.

1876.

New York Tribune. Extra No. 33. Independence Day
Orations, July 4, 1876.

8vo, pp. 64.

On p. 64 is a Centennial Ode by Mr. Bryant of four stanzas,
Through Storm and Calm the Years have Led, sung at New
York, July 4, 1876.

1876.

The Centennial Celebration of American Independence, at
the Academy of Music, New York, July 4, 1876. Hon. John
A. Dix, presiding, with the Oration and the other exercises.

8vo, pp. 81.

Centennial Ode on fourth leaf, unpaged.

1876.

Memoir of Dr. Samuel Gridley Howe. By Julia Ward Howe:
with other memorial tributes. Published by the Howe Memo-
rial Committee. Portrait. Boston, 1876.

8vo, pp. 128.

On pp. 123, 124 is a letter from Bryant to the Hon. F. W. Bird, Chairman of the Committee.

1876.

St. Nicholas, Vol. IV, No. 2, December, 1876.   New York. 8vo, pp. 65–152.
The Boys of my Boyhood, pp. 99–103.

1877.

Studies in Bryant. | A Text-Book | by | Joseph Alden, D. D., | of the State Normal School at Albany. | With an Introduction | by | William Cullen Bryant. | New York : | D. Appleton and Company, 1, 3, and 5 Bond Street. | 1877.
12mo, pp. 127.   Introduction, pp. 5–10.

1877.

A New | Library of Poetry and Song. | Edited by | William Cullen Bryant. | Published in parts.   New York, 1877.
4to, 2 vols.
Portrait frontispiece. | Introduction, pp. 7–14.

1878.

A Popular History | of | The United States | From the | First Discovery of the Western Hemisphere | By the Northmen, To the end of the | First Century of the Union | of the States. | Preceded by a sketch of the Pre-Historic Period and the | Age of the Mound Builders. | By William Cullen Bryant | and | Sydney Howard Gay. | Fully Illustrated. | New York : | Charles Scribner's Sons, | Successors to | Scribner, Armstrong & Co. | 1878.

Collation : 4 vols., royal 8vo, with complete index.   Published in monthly parts.   Frontispiece, Portrait of Bryant, and Preface by Wm. C. Bryant, pp. vii–xxiv.

1878.

The Sunday School Times, Vol. XX, No. 8.   Philadelphia, February 22, 1878.
4to, pp. 113–128.

On p. 113 is a poem by Bryant, his last contribution to any newspaper or magazine, The Twenty-second of February, six stanzas beginning, Pale is the February Sky.

This was a special number of The Sunday School Times. The editorial is followed in the second column by Bryant's poem, and two paragraphs, Religious Patriotism, by Edward Eggleston, D. D., and The Face of Washington, by Joseph Cook. Then follow contributions by President Hayes and the Governors of thirteen States.

1879.

Thoughts | on | The Religious Life | by | Joseph Alden, D. D., LL. D. | Author of The Science of Government, Studies in Bryant, etc. | With an introduction | by | William Cullen Bryant. | New York : | G. P. Putnam's Sons, | 182 Fifth Avenue, | 1879.

12mo, 129 pp., brown covers with outside title. Introduction, pp. 7–12.

1886.

Complete Works of Shakespeare. Edited by W. C. Bryant, assisted by E. A. Duyckinck. Illustrated.

3 volumes, 4to, New York, 1886.

Bryant wrote the Preface to this edition, the actual work of editing having been done by Mr. Duyckinck.

BIOGRAPHIES OF MR. BRYANT

1828.

The | Critic. | A Weekly Review of Literature, Fine Arts, | and the Drama. | Edited by William Leggett.

Volume I, from November 1, 1828, to May 2, 1829.

Biography of William Cullen Bryant, pp. 105–107, December 13, 1828.

The present copy contains Vol. I, through May 2, 1829, and the beginning of a second volume, pp. 1–96, seven numbers, May 9, May 16, May 23, May 30, June 6, June 13, June 20. On p. 89 is a notice signed by the editor, announcing the suspension of publication.

1846.

Thoughts on the Poets. By Henry T. Tuckerman. New York, 1846.

12mo, pp. 318.

Biography, pp. 303–318.

1854.

Off-hand Takings; or, Crayon Sketches of the Noticeable Men of our Age. By George W. Bungay. Illustrated. New York, 1854.

12mo, pp. 408.

Biography of Bryant, pp. 309–315, with steel portrait.

1877.

Men of Mark. By Edwin P. Whipple. Atlas Series, No. 2. New York, 1877.

8vo, pp. 270.

Biography of Bryant by Ray Palmer, pp. 102–126.

1883.

A Biography | of | William Cullen Bryant, | with | Extracts from his private Correspondence | by | Parke Godwin. | In two volumes. | New York : | D. Appleton and Company, 1883. 8vo.

1886.

Bryant and his Friends. Some Reminiscences of the Knickerbocker Writers. By James Grant Wilson. New York, 1886. Bryant and his Friends, pp. 11–127.

1890.

William Cullen Bryant. By John Bigelow. American Men of Letters Series. Boston, 1890.

MEMORIAL ADDRESSES, ETC.

1878.

Bryant Memorial Meeting of the Century, Tuesday Evening, November 12, 1878. Century Rooms, New York.

8vo, 74 pages, including title, and a portrait of Bryant engraved by H. B. Hall, Jr.

1878.

The Life, Character, and Writings of William Cullen Bryant. A Commemorative Address delivered before the New York Historical Society, at the Academy of Music, December 30, 1878. By George William Curtis. New York: Charles Scribner's Sons, 743 and 745 Broadway.

8vo, false title, title, pp. 8–64.

1878.

Tribute to William Cullen Bryant. By Robert C. Waterston, at the meeting of the Massachusetts Historical Society, June 13, 1878. With an Appendix. Boston: Press of John Wilson & Son, 1878.

8vo, 54 pages, including title.

Contains the ancestry of Bryant, several pieces by Bryant, and an account of the circumstances under which they were written and published, numerous anecdotes, and a verbatim reprint of Bryant's last address on unveiling the Bust of Mazzini in Central Park.

1878.

In Memoriam, William Cullen Bryant. Funeral Oration, June 14, 1878. By H. W. Bellows, D. D. New York, 1878.

8vo, pp. 11.

1879.

The Bryant Memorial Meeting of the Goethe Club of the City of New York, Wednesday, October 30, 1878. New York: G. P. Putnam's Sons, 182 Fifth Avenue, 1879.

8vo, 56 pages, including title, portrait of Bryant, coat with "frogs" prefixed.

As originally published, this Memorial had a paper cover, with a list of Members of the Goethe Club on p. 3. The Oration, Bryant among his Countrymen, the Poet, the Patriot, the Man, by Dr. Samuel Osgood, was published separately, 1879, 8vo, pp. 34.

MR. BRYANT'S ORIGINAL PREFACES.

TO THE EDITION OF 1821.

THE first poem in this collection was delivered before a literary association. Some of the others have appeared before in different periodical publications, and are now by permission inserted in this volume.

TO THE EDITION OF 1832.

Most of the following poems have been already printed. The longest, entitled The Ages, was published in 1821, in a thin volume, along with about half a dozen others now included in this collection. With a few exceptions, the remainder have since appeared in different publications, mostly of the periodical kind. The favor with which the public have regarded them, and of which their republication in various compilations seemed to the author a proof, has induced him to collect them in a volume. In preparing them for the press, he has made such corrections as occurred to him on subjecting them to a careful revision. Sensible as he is that no author had ever more cause of gratitude to his countrymen for the indulgent estimate placed by them on his literary attempts, he yet can not let this volume go forth to the public without a feeling of apprehension that it may contain things which did not deserve admission, and that the entire collection may not be thought worthy of the generous and partial judgment which has been passed upon some of the separate poems.

NEW YORK, *January, 1832.*

TO THE EDITION OF 1839.

The present edition, by the advice of the publishers, is somewhat enlarged. A few corrections have also been made in the text of the poems which were published in the other edition (that of 1836).

TO THE EDITION OF 1842.

The poems which compose this little volume have been written within the last five or six years—some of them merely as parts of a longer one planned by the author, which may possibly be finished hereafter.   In the mean time he has been tempted to publish them in this form, by the reception which another collection of his verses has already met with among his countrymen.

NEW YORK, *July, 1842.*

TO THE EDITION OF 1846.

Perhaps it would have been well if the author had followed his original intention, which was to leave out of this edition, as unworthy of publication, several of the poems which made a part of his previous collections.   He asks leave to plead the judgment of a literary friend,* whose opinion in such matters he highly values, as his apology for having retained them. With the exception of the first and longest poem in the collection, The Ages, they are all arranged according to the order of time in which they were written, as far as it can be ascertained.†

NEW YORK, *1846.*

TO THE EDITION OF 1854.

The present edition has been carefully revised by the author, and some faults of diction and versification corrected.   A few poems not in the previous editions have been added.

NEW YORK, *August, 1854.*

---

* Mr. Richard H. Dana, of Boston.—*Ed.*

† Mistakes were made, however, in this respect, which the editor has tried to correct.

TO THE EDITION OF 1863.

The author has attempted no other classification of the poems in this volume than that of allowing them to follow each other according to the order of time in which they were written. It has seemed to him that this arrangement is as satisfactory as any other, since, at different periods of life, an author's style and habits of thought may be supposed to undergo very considerable modifications. One poem forms an exception to this order of succession, and should have appeared in an earlier collection. Three others have already appeared in an illustrated edition of the author's poems.

NEW YORK, *December, 1863.*

TO THE READER.

THE poems in this volume, down to and including the one on page 348, follow each other in the order in which they were written. Those beyond page 348 follow the arrangement adopted by Mr. Parke Godwin in the two-volume edition of Mr. Bryant's Poems.

MR. BRYANT'S POETICAL WORKS.

3

POEMS.

POEMS.

THE AGES

I.

WHEN to the common rest that crowns our days,
Called in the noon of life, the good man goes,
Or full of years, and ripe in wisdom, lays
His silver temples in their last repose ;
When, o'er the buds of youth, the death-wind blows
And blights the fairest ; when our bitter tears
Stream, as the eyes of those that love us close,
We think on what they were, with many fears
Lest goodness die with them, and leave the coming years

II.

And therefore, to our hearts, the days gone by,
When lived the honored sage whose death we wept,
And the soft virtues beamed from many an eye,
And beat in many a heart that long has slept—
Like spots of earth where angel-feet have stepped,
Are holy ; and high-dreaming bards have told
Of times when worth was crowned, and faith was kept,
Ere friendship grew a snare, or love waxed cold—
Those pure and happy times—the golden days of old.

III.

Peace to the just man's memory ; let it grow
Greener with years, and blossom through the flight
Of ages ; let the mimic canvas show
His calm benevolent features ; let the light

Stream on his deeds of love, that shunned the sight
Of all but heaven, and in the book of fame
The glorious record of his virtues write
And hold it up to men, and bid them claim
A palm like his, and catch from him the hallowed flame.

IV.

But oh, despair not of their fate who rise
To dwell upon the earth when we withdraw !
Lo ! the same shaft by which the righteous dies,
Strikes through the wretch that scoffed at mercy's law
And trode his brethren down, and felt no awe
Of Him who will avenge them.   Stainless worth,
Such as the sternest age of virtue saw,
Ripens, meanwhile, till time shall call it forth
From the low modest shade, to light and bless the earth.

V.

Has Nature, in her calm, majestic march,
Faltered with age at last ? does the bright sun
Grow dim in heaven ? or, in their far blue arch,
Sparkle the crowd of stars, when day is done,
Less brightly ? when the dew-lipped Spring comes on,
Breathes she with airs less soft, or scents the sky
With flowers less fair than when her reign begun ?
Does prodigal Autumn, to our age, deny
The plenty that once swelled beneath his sober eye ?

VI.

Look on this beautiful world, and read the truth
In her fair page ; see, every season brings
New change, to her, of everlasting youth ;
Still the green soil, with joyous living things,
Swarms, the wide air is full of joyous wings,
And myriads, still, are happy in the sleep
Of ocean's azure gulfs, and where he flings
The restless surge.   Eternal Love doth keep,
In his complacent arms, the earth, the air, the deep.

"Nature, in her calm, majestic march."

VII.

Will then the merciful One, who stamped our race
With his own image, and who gave them sway
O'er earth, and the glad dwellers on her face,
Now that our swarming nations far away
Are spread, where'er the moist earth drinks the day,
Forget the ancient care that taught and nursed
His latest offspring? will he quench the ray
Infused by his own forming smile at first,
And leave a work so fair all blighted and accursed?

VIII.

Oh, no! a thousand cheerful omens give
Hope of yet happier days, whose dawn is nigh.
He who has tamed the elements, shall not live
The slave of his own passions; he whose eye
Unwinds the eternal dances of the sky,
And in the abyss of brightness dares to span
The sun's broad circle, rising yet more high,
In God's magnificent works his will shall scan—
And love and peace shall make their paradise with man.

IX.

Sit at the feet of History—through the night
Of years the steps of virtue she shall trace,
And show the earlier ages, where her sight
Can pierce the eternal shadows o'er their face;—
When, from the genial cradle of our race,
Went forth the tribes of men, their pleasant lot
To choose, where palm-groves cooled their dwelling-place,
Or freshening rivers ran; and there forgot
The truth of heaven, and kneeled to gods that heard them not.

X.

Then waited not the murderer for the night,
But smote his brother down in the bright day,
And he who felt the wrong, and had the might,
His own avenger, girt himself to slay;

Beside the path the unburied carcass lay ;
The shepherd, by the fountains of the glen,
Fled, while the robber swept his flock away,
And slew his babes.   The sick, untended then,
Languished in the damp shade, and died afar from men.

XI.

But misery brought in love ; in passion's strife
Man gave his heart to mercy, pleading long,
And sought out gentle deeds to gladden life ;
The weak, against the sons of spoil and wrong,
Banded, and watched their hamlets, and grew strong ;
States rose, and, in the shadow of their might,
The timid rested.   To the reverent throng,
Grave and time-wrinkled men, with locks all white,
Gave laws, and judged their strifes, and taught the way of right ;

XII.

Till bolder spirits seized the rule, and nailed
On men the yoke that man should never bear,
And drave them forth to battle.   Lo ! unveiled
The scene of those stern ages !   What is there ?
A boundless sea of blood, and the wild air
Moans with the crimsoned surges that entomb
Cities and bannered armies ; forms that wear
The kingly circlet rise, amid the gloom,
O'er the dark wave, and straight are swallowed in its womb.

XIII.

Those ages have no memory, but they left
A record in the desert—columns strown
On the waste sands, and statues fallen and cleft,
Heaped like a host in battle overthrown ;
Vast ruins, where the mountain's ribs of stone
Were hewn into a city ; streets that spread
In the dark earth, where never breath has blown
Of heaven's sweet air, nor foot of man dares tread
The long and perilous ways—the Cities of the Dead !

XIV.

And tombs of monarchs to the clouds up-piled—
They perished, but the eternal tombs remain—
And the black precipice, abrupt and wild,
Pierced by long toil and hollowed to a fane ;—
Huge piers and frowning forms of gods sustain
The everlasting arches, dark and wide,
Like the night-heaven, when clouds are black with rain.
But idly skill was tasked, and strength was plied,
All was the work of slaves to swell a despot's pride.

XV.

And Virtue cannot dwell with slaves, nor reign
O'er those who cower to take a tyrant's yoke ;
She left the down-trod nations in disdain,
And flew to Greece, when Liberty awoke,
New-born, amid those glorious vales, and broke
Sceptre and chain with her fair youthful hands :
As rocks are shivered in the thunder-stroke.
And lo ! in full-grown strength, an empire stands
Of leagued and rival states, the wonder of the lands.

XVI.

Oh, Greece ! thy flourishing cities were a spoil
Unto each other ; thy hard hand oppressed
And crushed the helpless ; thou didst make thy soil
Drunk with the blood of those that loved thee best ;
And thou didst drive, from thy unnatural breast,
Thy just and brave to die in distant climes ;
Earth shuddered at thy deeds, and sighed for rest
From thine abominations ; after-times,
That yet shall read thy tale, will tremble at thy crimes !

XVII.

Yet there was that within thee which has saved
Thy glory, and redeemed thy blotted name ;
The story of thy better deeds, engraved
On fame's unmouldering pillar, puts to shame

Our chiller virtue ; the high art to tame
The whirlwind of the passions was thy own ;
And the pure ray, that from thy bosom came,
Far over many a land and age has shone,
And mingles with the light that beams from God's own throne

XVIII.

And Rome—thy sterner, younger sister, she
Who awed the world with her imperial frown—
Rome drew the spirit of her race from thee,
The rival of thy shame and thy renown.
Yet her degenerate children sold the crown
Of earth's wide kingdoms to a line of slaves ;
Guilt reigned, and woe with guilt, and plagues came down,
Till the North broke its floodgates, and the waves
Whelmed the degraded race, and weltered o'er their graves.

XIX.

Vainly that ray of brightness from above,
That shone around the Galilean lake,
The light of hope, the leading star of love,
Struggled, the darkness of that day to break ;
Even its own faithless guardians strove to slake,
In fogs of earth, the pure ethereal flame ;
And priestly hands, for Jesus' blessed sake,
Were red with blood, and charity became,
In that stern war of forms, a mockery and a name.

XX.

They triumphed, and less bloody rites were kept
Within the quiet of the convent-cell ;
The well-fed inmates pattered prayer, and slept,
And sinned, and liked their easy penance well.
Where pleasant was the spot for men to dwell,
Amid its fair broad lands the abbey lay,
Sheltering dark orgies that were shame to tell,
And cowled and barefoot beggars swarmed the way,
All in their convent weeds, of black, and white, and gray

XXI.

Oh, sweetly the returning muses' strain
Swelled over that famed stream, whose gentle tide
In their bright lap the Etrurian vales detain,
Sweet, as when winter storms have ceased to chide
And all the new-leaved woods, resounding wide,
Send out wild hymns upon the scented air.
Lo ! to the smiling Arno's classic side
The emulous nations of the West repair,
And kindle their quenched urns, and drink fresh spirit there.

XXII.

Still, Heaven deferred the hour ordained to rend
From saintly rottenness the sacred stole ;
And cowl and worshipped shrine could still defend
The wretch with felon stains upon his soul ;
And crimes were set to sale, and hard his dole
Who could not bribe a passage to the skies ;
And vice, beneath the mitre's kind control,
Sinned gayly on, and grew to giant size,
Shielded by priestly power, and watched by priestly eyes.

XXIII.

At last the earthquake came—the shock, that hurled
To dust, in many fragments dashed and strown,
The throne, whose roots were in another world,
And whose far-stretching shadow awed our own.
From many a proud monastic pile, o'erthrown,
Fear-struck, the hooded inmates rushed and fled ;
The web, that for a thousand years had grown
O'er prostrate Europe, in that day of dread
Crumbled and fell, as fire dissolves the flaxen thread.

XXIV.

The spirit of that day is still awake,
And spreads himself, and shall not sleep again ;
But through the idle mesh of power shall break
Like billows o'er the Asian monarch's chain ;

Till men are filled with him, and feel how vain,
Instead of the pure heart and innocent hands,
Are all the proud and pompous modes to gain
The smile of Heaven ;—till a new age expands
Its white and holy wings above the peaceful lands.

XXV.

For look again on the past years ;—behold,
How like the nightmare's dreams have flown away
Horrible forms of worship, that, of old,
Held, o'er the shuddering realms, unquestioned sway :
See crimes, that feared not once the eye of day,
Rooted from men, without a name or place :
See nations blotted out from earth, to pay
The forfeit of deep guilt ;—with glad embrace
The fair disburdened lands welcome a nobler race.

XXVI.

Thus error's monstrous shapes from earth are driven ;
They fade, they fly—but Truth survives their flight ;
Earth has no shades to quench that beam of heaven ;
Each ray that shone, in early time, to light
The faltering footstep in the path of right,
Each gleam of clearer brightness shed to aid
In man's maturer day his bolder sight,
All blended, like the rainbow's radiant braid,
Pour yet, and still shall pour, the blaze that cannot fade.

XXVII.

Late, from this Western shore, that morning chased
The deep and ancient night, which threw its shroud
O'er the green land of groves, the beautiful waste,
Nurse of full streams, and lifter-up of proud
Sky-mingling mountains that o'erlook the cloud.
Erewhile, where yon gay spires their brightness rear,
Trees waved, and the brown hunter's shouts were loud
Amid the forest ; and the bounding deer
Fled at the glancing plume, and the gaunt wolf yelled near.

XXVIII.

And where his willing waves yon bright blue bay
Sends up, to kiss his decorated brim,
And cradles, in his soft embrace, the gay
Young group of grassy islands born of him,
And crowding nigh, or in the distance dim,
Lifts the white throng of sails, that bear or bring
The commerce of the world ;—with tawny limb,
And belt and beads in sunlight glistening,
The savage urged his skiff like wild bird on the wing.

XXIX.

Then all this youthful paradise around,
And all the broad and boundless mainland, lay
Cooled by the interminable wood, that frowned
O'er mount and vale, where never summer ray
Glanced, till the strong tornado broke his way
Through the gray giants of the sylvan wild ;
Yet many a sheltered glade, with blossoms gay
Beneath the showery sky and sunshine mild,
Within the shaggy arms of that dark forest smiled.

XXX.

There stood the Indian hamlet, there the lake
Spread its blue sheet that flashed with many an oar,
Where the brown otter plunged him from the brake,
And the deer drank : as the light gale flew o'er,
The twinkling maize-field rustled on the shore ;
And while that spot, so wild, and lone, and fair,
A look of glad and guiltless beauty wore,
And peace was on the earth and in the air,
The warrior lit the pile, and bound his captive there.

XXXI.

Not unavenged—the foeman, from the wood,
Beheld the deed, and, when the midnight shade
Was stillest, gorged his battle-axe with blood ;
All died—the wailing babe—the shrinking maid—

And in the flood of fire that scathed the glade,
The roofs went down ; but deep the silence grew,
When on the dewy woods the day-beam played ;
No more the cabin-smokes rose wreathed and blue,
And ever, by their lake, lay moored the bark canoe.

XXXII.

Look now abroad—another race has filled
These populous borders—wide the wood recedes,
And towns shoot up, and fertile realms are tilled ;
The land is full of harvests and green meads ;
Streams numberless, that many a fountain feeds,
Shine, disembowered, and give to sun and breeze
Their virgin waters ; the full region leads
New colonies forth, that toward the western seas
Spread, like a rapid flame among the autumnal trees.

XXXIII.

Here the free spirit of mankind, at length,
Throws its last fetters off ; and who shall place
A limit to the giant's unchained strength,
Or curb his swiftness in the forward race ?
On, like the comet's way through infinite space,
Stretches the long untravelled path of light,
Into the depths of ages ; we may trace,
Afar, the brightening glory of its flight,
Till the receding rays are lost to human sight.

XXXIV.

Europe is given a prey to sterner fates,
And writhes in shackles ; strong the arms that chain
To earth her struggling multitude of states ;
She too is strong, and might not chafe in vain
Against them, but might cast to earth the train
That trample her, and break their iron net.
Yes, she shall look on brighter days and gain
The meed of worthier deeds ; the moment set
To rescue and raise up, draws near—but is not yet.

"*Go forth, under the open sky, and list
To Nature's teachings.*"

XXXV.

But thou, my country, thou shalt never fall,
Save with thy children—thy maternal care,
Thy lavish love, thy blessings showered on all—
These are thy fetters—seas and stormy air
Are the wide barrier of thy borders, where,
Among thy gallant sons who guard thee well,
Thou laugh'st at enemies : who shall then declare
The date of thy deep-founded strength, or tell
How happy, in thy lap, the sons of men shall dwell?

THANATOPSIS.

To him who in the love of Nature holds
Communion with her visible forms, she speaks
A various language ; for his gayer hours
She has a voice of gladness, and a smile
And eloquence of beauty, and she glides
Into his darker musings, with a mild
And healing sympathy, that steals away
Their sharpness, ere he is aware.   When thoughts
Of the last bitter hour come like a blight
Over thy spirit, and sad images
Of the stern agony, and shroud, and pall,
And breathless darkness, and the narrow house,
Make thee to shudder, and grow sick at heart ;—
Go forth, under the open sky, and list
To Nature's teachings, while from all around—
Earth and her waters, and the depths of air---
Comes a still voice—Yet a few days, and thee
The all-beholding sun shall see no more
In all his course ; nor yet in the cold ground,
Where thy pale form was laid, with many tears,
Nor in the embrace of ocean, shall exist
Thy image.   Earth, that nourished thee, shall claim
Thy growth, to be resolved to earth again,

And, lost each human trace, surrendering up
Thine individual being, shalt thou go
To mix for ever with the elements,
To be a brother to the insensible rock
And to the sluggish clod, which the rude swain
Turns with his share, and treads upon.   The oak
Shall send his roots abroad, and pierce thy mould.

    Yet not to thine eternal resting-place
Shalt thou retire alone, nor couldst thou wish
Couch more magnificent.   Thou shalt lie down
With patriarchs of the infant world—with kings,
The powerful of the earth—the wise, the good,
Fair forms, and hoary seers of ages past,
All in one mighty sepulchre.   The hills
Rock-ribbed and ancient as the sun,—the vales
Stretching in pensive quietness between ;
The venerable woods—rivers that move
In majesty, and the complaining brooks
That make the meadows green ; and, poured round all,
Old Ocean's gray and melancholy waste,—
Are but the solemn decorations all
Of the great tomb of man.   The golden sun,
The planets, all the infinite host of heaven,
Are shining on the sad abodes of death,
Through the still lapse of ages.   All that tread
The globe are but a handful to the tribes
That slumber in its bosom.—Take the wings
Of morning, pierce the Barcan wilderness,
Or lose thyself in the continuous woods
Where rolls the Oregon, and hears no sound,
Save his own dashings—yet the dead are there :
And millions in those solitudes, since first
The flight of years began, have laid them down
In their last sleep—the dead reign there alone.
So shalt thou rest, and what if thou withdraw
In silence from the living, and no friend
Take note of thy departure ?   All that breathe
Will share thy destiny.   The gay will laugh

"Beside the snow-bank's edges cold."

When thou art gone, the solemn brood of care
Plod on, and each one as before will chase
His favorite phantom ; yet all these shall leave
Their mirth and their employments, and shall come
And make their bed with thee.　As the long train
Of ages glide away, the sons of men,
The youth in life's green spring, and he who goes
In the full strength of years, matron and maid,
The speechless babe, and the gray-headed man—
Shall one by one be gathered to thy side,
By those, who in their turn shall follow them.

　So live, that when thy summons comes to join
The innumerable caravan, which moves
To that mysterious realm, where each shall take
His chamber in the silent halls of death,
Thou go not, like the quarry-slave at night,
Scourged to his dungeon, but, sustained and soothed
By an unfaltering trust, approach thy grave,
Like one who wraps the drapery of his couch
About him, and lies down to pleasant dreams.

THE YELLOW VIOLET.

When beechen buds begin to swell,
　And woods the blue-bird's warble know,
The yellow violet's modest bell
　Peeps from the last year's leaves below.

Ere russet fields their green resume,
　Sweet flower, I love, in forest bare,
To meet thee, when thy faint perfume
　Alone is in the virgin air.

Of all her train, the hands of Spring
　First plant thee in the watery mould,
And I have seen thee blossoming
　Beside the snow-bank's edges cold.

Thy parent sun, who bade thee view
   Pale skies, and chilling moisture sip,
Has bathed thee in his own bright hue,
   And streaked with jet thy glowing lip.

Yet slight thy form, and low thy seat,
   And earthward bent thy gentle eye,
Unapt the passing view to meet,
   When loftier flowers are flaunting nigh.

Oft, in the sunless April day,
   Thy early smile has stayed my walk ;
But midst the gorgeous blooms of May,
   I passed thee on thy humble stalk.

So they, who climb to wealth, forget
   The friends in darker fortunes tried.
I copied them—but I regret
   That I should ape the ways of pride.

And when again the genial hour
   Awakes the painted tribes of light,
I'll not o'erlook the modest flower
   That made the woods of April bright.

INSCRIPTION FOR THE ENTRANCE TO A WOOD

STRANGER, if thou hast learned a truth which needs
No school of long experience, that the world
Is full of guilt and misery, and hast seen
Enough of all its sorrows, crimes, and cares,
To tire thee of it, enter this wild wood
And view the haunts of Nature. The calm shade
Shall bring a kindred calm, and the sweet breeze
That makes the green leaves dance, shall waft a balm
To thy sick heart. Thou wilt find nothing here

Of all that pained thee in the haunts of men,
And made thee loathe thy life. The primal curse
Fell, it is true, upon the unsinning earth,
But not in vengeance. God hath yoked to guilt
Her pale tormentor, misery. Hence, these shades
Are still the abodes of gladness ; the thick roof
Of green and stirring branches is alive
And musical with birds, that sing and sport
In wantonness of spirit ; while below
The squirrel, with raised paws and form erect,
Chirps merrily. Throngs of insects in the shade
Try their thin wings and dance in the warm beam
That waked them into life. Even the green trees
Partake the deep contentment ; as they bend
To the soft winds, the sun from the blue sky
Looks in and sheds a blessing on the scene.
Scarce less the cleft-born wild-flower seems to enjoy
Existence, than the wingèd plunderer
That sucks its sweets. The mossy rocks themselves,
And the old and ponderous trunks of prostrate trees
That lead from knoll to knoll a causey rude
Or bridge the sunken brook, and their dark roots,
With all their earth upon them, twisting high,
Breathe fixed tranquillity. The rivulet
Sends forth glad sounds, and tripping o'er its bed
Of pebbly sands, or leaping down the rocks,
Seems, with continuous laughter, to rejoice
In its own being. Softly tread the marge,
Lest from her midway perch thou scare the wren
That dips her bill in water. The cool wind,
That stirs the stream in play, shall come to thee.
Like one that loves thee nor will let thee pass
Ungreeted, and shall give its light embrace.

SONG.

Soon as the glazed and gleaming snow
  Reflects the day-dawn cold and clear,
The hunter of the West must go
  In depth of woods to seek the deer.

His rifle on his shoulder placed,
  His stores of death arranged with skill,
His moccasins and snow-shoes laced—
  Why lingers he beside the hill ?

Far, in the dim and doubtful light,
  Where woody slopes a valley leave,
He sees what none but lover might,
  The dwelling of his Genevieve.

And oft he turns his truant eye,
  And pauses oft, and lingers near ;
But when he marks the reddening sky,
  He bounds away to hunt the deer.

TO A WATERFOWL.

Whither, midst falling dew,
While glow the heavens with the last steps of day
Far, through their rosy depths, dost thou pursue
  Thy solitary way ?

Vainly the fowler's eye
Might mark thy distant flight to do thee wrong
As, darkly seen against the crimson sky,
  Thy figure floats along.

Seek'st thou the plashy brink
Of weedy lake, or marge of river wide,
Or where the rocking billows rise and sink
  On the chafed ocean-side ?

There is a Power whose care
Teaches thy way along that pathless coast—
The desert and illimitable air—
    Lone wandering, but not lost.

All day thy wings have fanned,
At that far height, the cold, thin atmosphere,
Yet stoop not, weary, to the welcome land,
    Though the dark night is near.

And soon that toil shall end ;
Soon shalt thou find a summer home, and rest,
And scream among thy fellows ; reeds shall bend,
    Soon, o'er thy sheltered nest.

Thou'rt gone, the abyss of heaven
Hath swallowed up thy form ; yet, on my heart   '
Deeply has sunk the lesson thou hast given,
    And shall not soon depart.

He who, from zone to zone,
Guides through the boundless sky thy certain flight,
In the long way that I must tread alone,
    Will lead my steps aright.

GREEN RIVER.

When breezes are soft and skies are fair,
I steal an hour from study and care,
And hie me away to the woodland scene,
Where wanders the stream with waters of green,
As if the bright fringe of herbs on its brink
Had given their stain to the waves they drink ;
And they, whose meadows it murmurs through,
Have named the stream from its own fair hue.
  11

Yet pure its waters—its shallows are bright
With colored pebbles and sparkles of light,
And clear the depths where its eddies play,
And dimples deepen and whirl away,
And the plane-tree's speckled arms o'ershoot
The swifter current that mines its root,
Through whose shifting leaves, as you walk the hill,
The quivering glimmer of sun and rill
With a sudden flash on the eye is thrown,
Like the ray that streams from the diamond-stone.
Oh, loveliest there the spring days come,
With blossoms, and birds, and wild-bees' hum ;
The flowers of summer are fairest there,
And freshest the breath of the summer air ;
And sweetest the golden autumn day
In silence and sunshine glides away.

Yet, fair as thou art, thou shunnest to glide,
Beautiful stream ! by the village side ;
But windest away from haunts of men,
To quiet valley and shaded glen ;
And forest, and meadow, and slope of hill,
Around thee, are lonely, lovely, and still,
Lonely—save when, by thy rippling tides,
From thicket to thicket the angler glides ;
Or the simpler comes, with basket and book,
For herbs of power on thy banks to look ;
Or haply, some idle dreamer, like me,
To wander, and muse, and gaze on thee,
Still—save the chirp of birds that feed
On the river cherry and seedy reed,
And thy own wild music gushing out
With mellow murmur of fairy shout,
From dawn to the blush of another day,
Like traveller singing along his way.

That fairy music I never hear,
Nor gaze on those waters so green and clear,

And mark them winding away from sight,
Darkened with shade or flashing with light,
While o'er them the vine to its thicket clings,
And the zephyr stoops to freshen his wings,
But I wish that fate had left me free
To wander these quiet haunts with thee,
Till the eating cares of earth should depart,
And the peace of the scene pass into my heart ;
And I envy thy stream, as it glides along
Through its beautiful banks in a trance of song.

Though forced to drudge for the dregs of men,
And scrawl strange words with the barbarous pen,
And mingle among the jostling crowd,
Where the sons of strife are subtle and loud—
I often come to this quiet place,
To breathe the airs that ruffle thy face,
And gaze upon thee in silent dream,
For in thy lonely and lovely stream
An image of that calm life appears
That won my heart in my greener years.

A WINTER PIECE.

THE time has been that these wild solitudes,
Yet beautiful as wild, were trod by me
Oftener than now ; and when the ills of life
Had chafed my spirit—when the unsteady pulse
Beat with strange flutterings—I would wander forth
And seek the woods. The sunshine on my path
Was to me as a friend. The swelling hills,
The quiet dells retiring far between,
With gentle invitation to explore
Their windings, were a calm society
That talked with me and soothed me. Then the chant
Of birds, and chime of brooks, and soft caress

Of the fresh sylvan air, made me forget
The thoughts that broke my peace, and I began
To gather simples by the fountain's brink,
And lose myself in day-dreams.   While I stood
In Nature's loneliness, I was with one
With whom I early grew familiar, one
Who never had a frown for me, whose voice
Never rebuked me for the hours I stole
From cares I loved not, but of which the world
Deems highest, to converse with her.   When shrieked
The bleak November winds, and smote the woods,
And the brown fields were herbless, and the shades,
That met above the merry rivulet,
Were spoiled, I sought, I loved them still; they seemed
Like old companions in adversity.
Still there was beauty in my walks ; the brook,
Bordered with sparkling frost-work, was as gay
As with its fringe of summer flowers.   Afar,
The village with its spires, the path of streams
And dim receding valleys, hid before
By interposing trees, lay visible
Through the bare grove, and my familiar haunts
Seemed new to me.   Nor was I slow to come
Among them, when the clouds, from their still skirts,
Had shaken down on earth the feathery snow,
And all was white.   The pure keen air abroad,
Albeit it breathed no scent of herb, nor heard
Love-call of bird nor merry hum of bee,
Was not the air of death.   Bright mosses crept
Over the spotted trunks, and the close buds,
That lay along the boughs, instinct with life,
Patient, and waiting the soft breath of Spring,
Feared not the piercing spirit of the North.
The snow-bird twittered on the beechen bough,
And 'neath the hemlock, whose thick branches bent
Beneath its bright cold burden. and kept dry
A circle, on the earth, of withered leaves,
The partridge found a shelter.   Through the snow
The rabbit sprang away.   The lighter track

"*Had shaken down on earth the feathery snow,
And all was white.*"

Of fox, and the raccoon's broad path, were there,
Crossing each other. From his hollow tree
The squirrel was abroad, gathering the nuts
Just fallen, that asked the winter cold and sway
Of winter blast, to shake them from their hold.

But Winter has yet brighter scenes—he boasts
Splendors beyond what gorgeous Summer knows ;
Or Autumn with his many fruits, and woods
All flushed with many hues. Come when the rains
Have glazed the snow and clothed the trees with ice,
While the slant sun of February pours
Into the bowers a flood of light. Approach !
The incrusted surface shall upbear thy steps,
And the broad arching portals of the grove
Welcome thy entering. Look ! the massy trunks
Are cased in the pure crystal ; each light spray,
Nodding and tinkling in the breath of heaven,
Is studded with its trembling water-drops,
That glimmer with an amethystine light.
But round the parent-stem the long low boughs
Bend, in a glittering ring, and arbors hide
The glassy floor. Oh ! you might deem the spot
The spacious cavern of some virgin mine,
Deep in the womb of earth—where the gems grow,
And diamonds put forth radiant rods and bud
With amethyst and topaz—and the place
Lit up, most royally, with the pure beam
That dwells in them. Or haply the vast hall
Of fairy palace, that outlasts the night,
And fades not in the glory of the sun ;—
Where crystal columns send forth slender shafts
And crossing arches ; and fantastic aisles
Wind from the sight in brightness, and are lost
Among the crowded pillars. Raise thine eye ;
Thou seest no cavern roof, no palace vault ;
There the blue sky and the white drifting cloud
Look in. Again the wildered fancy dreams
Of spouting fountains, frozen as they rose,

And fixed, with all their branching jets, in air,
And all their sluices sealed.   All, all is light ;
Light without shade.   But all shall pass away
With the next sun.   From numberless vast trunks
Loosened, the crashing ice shall make a sound
Like the far roar of rivers, and the eve
Shall close o'er the brown woods as it was wont.

   And it is pleasant, when the noisy streams
Are just set free, and milder suns melt off
The plashy snow, save only the firm drift
In the deep glen or the close shade of pines—
'Tis pleasant to behold the wreaths of smoke
Roll up among the maples of the hill,
Where the shrill sound of youthful voices wakes
The shriller echo, as the clear pure lymph,
That from the wounded trees, in twinkling drops,
Falls, mid the golden brightness of the morn,
Is gathered in with brimming pails, and oft,
Wielded by sturdy hands, the stroke of axe
Makes the woods ring.   Along the quiet air,
Come and float calmly off the soft light clouds,
Such as you see in summer, and the winds
Scarce stir the branches.   Lodged in sunny cleft,
Where the cold breezes come not, blooms alone
The little wind-flower, whose just opened eye
Is blue as the spring heaven it gazes at—
Startling the loiterer in the naked groves
With unexpected beauty, for the time
Of blossoms and green leaves is yet afar.
And ere it comes, the encountering winds shall oft
Muster their wrath again, and rapid clouds
Shade heaven, and bounding on the frozen earth
Shall fall their volleyed stores, rounded like hail
And white like snow, and the loud North again
Shall buffet the vexed forest in his rage.

THE WEST WIND.

BENEATH the forest's skirt I rest,
  Whose branching pines rise dark and high,
And hear the breezes of the West
  Among the thread-like foliage sigh.

Sweet Zephyr! why that sound of woe?
  Is not thy home among the flowers?
Do not the bright June roses blow,
  To meet thy kiss at morning hours?

And lo! thy glorious realm outspread—
  Yon stretching valleys, green and gay,
And yon free hill-tops, o'er whose head
  The loose white clouds are borne away.

And there the full broad river runs,
  And many a fount wells fresh and sweet
To cool thee when the mid-day suns
  Have made thee faint beneath their heat

Thou wind of joy, and youth, and love ;
  Spirit of the new-wakened year!
The sun in his blue realm above
  Smooths a bright path when thou art here.

In lawns the murmuring bee is heard,
  The wooing ring-dove in the shade ;
On thy soft breath, the new-fledged bird
  Takes wing, half happy, half afraid.

Ah! thou art like our wayward race ;—
  When not a shade of pain or ill
Dims the bright smile of Nature's face,
  Thou lov'st to sigh and murmur still.

THE BURIAL-PLACE.

A FRAGMENT.

EREWHILE, on England's pleasant shores, our sires
Left not their churchyards unadorned with shades
Or blossoms, but indulgent to the strong
And natural dread of man's last home, the grave,
Its frost and silence—they disposed around,
To soothe the melancholy spirit that dwelt
Too sadly on life's close, the forms and hues
Of vegetable beauty.   There the yew,
Green ever amid the snows of winter, told
Of immortality, and gracefully
The willow, a perpetual mourner, drooped ;
And there the gadding woodbine crept about,
And there the ancient ivy.   From the spot
Where the sweet maiden, in her blossoming years
Cut off, was laid with streaming eyes, and hands
That trembled as they placed her there, the rose
Sprung modest, on bowed stalk, and better spoke
Her graces, than the proudest monument
There children set about their playmate's grave
The pansy.   On the infant's little bed,
Wet at its planting with maternal tears,
Emblem of early sweetness, early death,
Nestled the lowly primrose.   Childless dames,
And maids that would not raise the reddened eye—
Orphans, from whose young lids the light of joy
Fled early—silent lovers, who had given
All that they lived for to the arms of earth,
Came often, o'er the recent graves to strew
Their offerings, rue, and rosemary, and flowers.

The pilgrim bands who passed the sea to keep
Their Sabbaths in the eye of God alone,
In his wide temple of the wilderness,
Brought not these simple customs of the heart

With them.   It might be, while they laid their dead
By the vast solemn skirts of the old groves,
And the fresh virgin soil poured forth strange flowers
About their graves ; and the familiar shades
Of their own native isle, and wonted blooms,
And herbs were wanting, which the pious hand
Might plant or scatter there, these gentle rites
Passed out of use.   Now they are scarcely known,
And rarely in our borders may you meet
The tall larch, sighing in the burial-place,
Or willow, trailing low its boughs to hide
The gleaming marble.   Naked rows of graves
And melancholy ranks of monuments
Are seen instead, where the coarse grass, between,
Shoots up its dull green spikes, and in the wind
Hisses, and the neglected bramble nigh,
Offers its berries to the schoolboy's hand,
In vain--they grow too near the dead.   Yet here,
Nature, rebuking the neglect of man,
Plants often, by the ancient mossy stone,
The brier-rose, and upon the broken turf
That clothes the fresher grave, the strawberry plant
Sprinkles its swell with blossoms, and lays forth
Her ruddy, pouting fruit.   .   .   .   .   .   .

"BLESSED ARE THEY THAT MOURN."

Oh, deem not they are blest alone
   Whose lives a peaceful tenor keep ;
The Power who pities man, hath shown
   A blessing for the eyes that weep.

The light of smiles shall fill again
   The lids that overflow with tears ;
And weary hours of woe and pain
   Are promises of happier years.

There is a day of sunny rest
    For every dark and troubled night :
And grief may bide an evening guest,
    But joy shall come with early light.

And thou, who, o'er thy friend's low bier,
    Dost shed the bitter drops like rain,
Hope that a brighter, happier sphere
    Will give him to thy arms again.

Nor let the good man's trust depart,
    Though life its common gifts deny,—
Though with a pierced and bleeding heart
    And spurned of men, he goes to die.

For God hath marked each sorrowing day
    And numbered every secret tear,
And heaven's long age of bliss shall pay
    For all his children suffer here.

"NO MAN KNOWETH HIS SEPULCHRE."

When he, who, from the scourge of wrong,
    Aroused the Hebrew tribes to fly,
Saw the fair region, promised long,
    And bowed him on the hills to die ;

God made his grave, to men unknown,
    Where Moab's rocks a vale infold,
And laid the aged seer alone
    To slumber while the world grows old.

Thus still, whene'er the good and just
    Close the dim eye on life and pain,
Heaven watches o'er their sleeping dust
    Till the pure spirit comes again.

Though nameless, trampled, and forgot,
His servant's humble ashes lie,
Yet God hath marked and sealed the spot,
To call its inmate to the sky.

A WALK AT SUNSET.

WHEN insect wings are glistening in the beam
Of the low sun, and mountain-tops are bright,
Oh, let me, by the crystal valley-stream,
Wander amid the mild and mellow light ;
And while the wood-thrush pipes his evening lay,
Give me one lonely hour to hymn the setting day.

Oh, sun ! that o'er the western mountains now
Go'st down in glory ! ever beautiful
And blessed is thy radiance, whether thou
Colorest the eastern heaven and night-mist coo.,
Till the bright day-star vanish, or on high
Climbest and streamest thy white splendors from mid-sky.

Yet, loveliest are thy setting smiles, and fair,
Fairest of all that earth beholds, the hues,
That live among the clouds, and flush the air,
Lingering and deepening at the hour of dews.
Then softest gales are breathed, and softest heard
The plaining voice of streams, and pensive note of bird.

They who here roamed, of yore, the forest wide,
Felt, by such charm, their simple bosoms won ;
They deemed their quivered warrior, when he died,
Went to bright isles beneath the setting sun ;
Where winds are aye at peace, and skies are fair,
And purple-skirted clouds curtain the crimson air.

So, with the glories of the dying day,
　　Its thousand trembling lights and changing hues,
The memory of the brave who passed away
　　Tenderly mingled ;—fitting hour to muse
On such grave theme, and sweet the dream that shed
Brightness and beauty round the destiny of the dead.

For ages, on the silent forests here,
　　Thy beams did fall before the red man came
Ťo dwell beneath them ; in their shade the deer
　　Fed, and feared not the arrow's deadly aim.
Nor tree was felled, in all that world of woods,
Save by the beaver's tootb, or winds, or rush of floods.

Then came the hunter tribes, and thou didst looк,
　　For ages, on their deeds in the hard chase,
And well-fought wars ; green sod and silver brook
　　Took the first stain of blood ; before thy face
The warrior generations came and passed,
And glory was laid up for many an age to last.

Now they are gone, gone as thy setting blaze
　　Goes down the west, while night is pressing on,
And with them the old tale of better days,
　　And trophies of remembered power, are gone.
Yon field that gives the harvest, where the plough
Strikes the white bone, is all that tells their story now.

I stand upon their ashes in thy beam,
　　The offspring of another race, I stand,
Beside a stream they loved, this valley-stream ;
　　And where the night-fire of the quivered band
Showed the gray oak by fits, and war-song rung,
I teach the quiet shades the strains of this new tongue.

Farewell ! but thou shalt come again—thy light
　　Must shine on other changes, and behold
The place of the thronged city still as night—
　　States fallen—new empires built upon the old—
But never shalt thou see these realms again
Darkened by boundless groves, and roamed by savage men.

HYMN TO DEATH.

OH ! could I hope the wise and pure in heart
Might hear my song without a frown, nor deem
My voice unworthy of the theme it tries,—
I would take up the hymn to Death, and say
To the grim power, The world hath slandered thee
And mocked thee. On thy dim and shadowy brow
They place an iron crown, and call thee king
Of terrors, and the spoiler of the world,
Deadly assassin, that strik'st down the fair,
The loved, the good—that breathest on the lights
Of virtue set along the vale of life,
And they go out in darkness. I am come,
Not with reproaches, not with cries and prayers,
Such as have stormed thy stern, insensible ear
From the beginning ; I am come to speak
Thy praises. True it is, that I have wept
Thy conquests, and may weep them yet again,
And thou from some I love wilt take a life
Dear to me as my own. Yet while the spell
Is on my spirit, and I talk with thee
In sight of all thy trophies, face to face,
Meet is it that my voice should utter forth
Thy nobler triumphs ; I will teach the world
To thank thee. Who are thine accusers ?—Who?
The living !—they who never felt thy power,
And know thee not. The curses of the wretch
Whose crimes are ripe, his sufferings when thy hand
Is on him, and the hour he dreads is come,
Are writ among thy praises. But the good—
Does he whom thy kind hand dismissed to peace,
Upbraid the gentle violence that took off
His fetters, and unbarred his prison-cell?

Raise then the hymn to Death. Deliverer !
God hath anointed thee to free the oppressed

And crush the oppressor.   When the armed chief,
The conqueror of nations, walks the world,
And it is changed beneath his feet, and all
Its kingdoms melt into one mighty realm—
Thou, while his head is loftiest and his heart
Blasphemes, imagining his own right hand
Almighty, thou dost set thy sudden grasp
Upon him, and the links of that strong chain
Which bound mankind are crumbled ; thou dost break
Sceptre and crown, and beat his throne to dust.
Then the earth shouts with gladness, and her tribes
Gather within their ancient bounds again.
Else had the mighty of the olden time,
Nimrod, Sesostris, or the youth who feigned
His birth from Libyan Ammon, smitten yet
The nations with a rod of iron, and driven
Their chariot o'er our necks.   Thou dost avenge,
In thy good time, the wrongs of those who know
No other friend.   Nor dost thou interpose
Only to lay the sufferer asleep,
Where he who made him wretched troubles not
His rest—thou dost strike down his tyrant too.
Oh, there is joy when hands that held the scourge
Drop lifeless, and the pitiless heart is cold.
Thou too dost purge from earth its horrible
And old idolatries ;—from the proud fanes
Each to his grave their priests go out, till none
Is left to teach their worship ; then the fires
Of sacrifice are chilled, and the green moss
O'ercreeps their altars ; the fallen images
Cumber the weedy courts, and for loud hymns,
Chanted by kneeling multitudes, the wind
Shrieks in the solitary aisles.   When he
Who gives his life to guilt, and laughs at all
The laws that God or man has made, and round
Hedges his seat with power, and shines in wealth,—
Lifts up his atheist front to scoff at Heaven,
And celebrates his shame in open day,
Thou, in the pride of all his crimes, cutt'st off

The horrible example. Touched by thine,
The extortioner's hard hand foregoes the gold
Wrung from the o'er-worn poor. The perjurer,
Whose tongue was lithe, e'en now, and voluble
Against his neighbor's life, and he who laughed
And leaped for joy to see a spotless fame
Blasted before his own foul calumnies,
Are smit with deadly silence. He, who sold
His conscience to preserve a worthless life,
Even while he hugs himself on his escape,
Trembles, as, doubly terrible, at length,
Thy steps o'ertake him, and there is no time
For parley, nor will bribes unclench thy grasp.
Oft, too, dost thou reform thy victim, long
Ere his last hour. And when the reveller,
Mad in the chase of pleasure, stretches on,
And strains each nerve, and clears the path of life
Like wind, thou point'st him to the dreadful goal,
And shak'st thy hour-glass in his reeling eye,
And check'st him in mid course. Thy skeleton hand
Shows to the faint of spirit the right path,
And he is warned, and fears to step aside.
Thou sett'st between the ruffian and his crime
Thy ghastly countenance, and his slack hand
Drops the drawn knife. But, oh, most fearfully
Dost thou show forth Heaven's justice, when thy shafts
Drink up the ebbing spirit—then the hard
Of heart and violent of hand restores
The treasure to the friendless wretch he wronged.
Then from the writhing bosom thou dost pluck
The guilty secret ; lips, for ages sealed,
Are faithless to their dreadful trust at length,
And give it up ; the felon's latest breath
Absolves the innocent man who bears his crime ;
The slanderer, horror-smitten, and in tears,
Recalls the deadly obloquy he forged
To work his brother's ruin. Thou dost make
Thy penitent victim utter to the air
The dark conspiracy that strikes at life,

And aims to whelm the laws ; ere yet the hour
Is come, and the dread sign of murder given.

Thus, from the first of time, hast thou been found
On virtue's side ; the wicked, but for thee,
Had been too strong for the good ; the great of earth
Had crushed the weak for ever.   Schooled in guile
For ages, while each passing year had brought
Its baneful lesson, they had filled the world
With their abominations ; while its tribes,
Trodden to earth, imbruted, and despoiled,
Had knelt to them in worship ; sacrifice
Had smoked on many an altar, temple-roofs
Had echoed with the blasphemous prayer and hymn :
But thou, the great reformer of the world,
Tak'st off the sons of violence and fraud
In their green pupilage, their lore half learned—
Ere guilt had quite o'errun the simple heart
God gave them at their birth, and blotted out
His image.   Thou dost mark them flushed with hope,
As on the threshold of their vast designs
Doubtful and loose they stand, and strik'st them down.
  .   .   .   .

Alas ! I little thought that the stern power,
Whose fearful praise I sang, would try me thus
Before the strain was ended.   It must cease—
For he is in his grave who taught my youth
The art of verse, and in the bud of life
Offered me to the Muses.   Oh, cut off
Untimely ! when thy reason in its strength,
Ripened by years of toil and studious search,
And watch of Nature's silent lessons, taught
Thy hand to practise best the lenient art
To which thou gavest thy laborious days,
And, last, thy life.   And, therefore, when the earth
Received thee, tears were in unyielding eyes
And on hard cheeks, and they who deemed thy skill
Delayed their death-hour, shuddered and turned pale
When thou wert gone.   This faltering verse, which thou

Shalt not, as wont, o'erlook, is all I have
To offer at thy grave—this—and the hope
To copy thy example, and to leave
A name of which the wretched shall not think
As of an enemy's, whom they forgive
As all forgive the dead. Rest, therefore, thou
Whose early guidance trained my infant steps—
Rest, in the bosom of God, till the brief sleep
Of death is over, and a happier life
Shall dawn to waken thine insensible dust.

    Now thou art not—and yet the men whose guilt
Has wearied Heaven for vengeance—he who bears
False witness—he who takes the orphan's bread,
And robs the widow—he who spreads abroad
Polluted hands in mockery of prayer,
Are left to cumber earth. Shuddering I look
On what is written, yet I blot not out
The desultory numbers ; let them stand,
The record of an idle revery.

THE MASSACRE AT SCIO.

WEEP not for Scio's children slain ;
    Their blood, by Turkish falchions shed,
Sends not its cry to Heaven in vain
    For vengeance on the murderer's head.

Though high the warm red torrent ran
    Between the flames that lit the sky,
Yet, for each drop, an armèd man
    Shall rise, to free the land, or die.

And for each corpse, that in the sea
    Was thrown, to feast the scaly herds,
A hundred of the foe shall be
    A banquet for the mountain-birds.
12

Stern rites and sad shall Greece ordain
  To keep that day along her shore,
Till the last link of slavery's chain
  Is shattered, to be worn no more.

THE INDIAN GIRL'S LAMENT.

An Indian girl was sitting where
  Her lover, slain in battle, slept;
Her maiden veil, her own black hair,
  Came down o'er eyes that wept;
And wildly, in her woodland tongue,
This sad and simple lay she sung:

"I've pulled away the shrubs that grew
  Too close above thy sleeping head,
And broke the forest-boughs that threw
  Their shadows o'er thy bed,
That, shining from the sweet southwest,
The sunbeams might rejoice thy rest.

"It was a weary, weary road
  That led thee to the pleasant coast,
Where thou, in his serene abode,
  Hast met thy father's ghost;
Where everlasting autumn lies
On yellow woods and sunny skies.

"'Twas I the broidered mocsen made,
  That shod thee for that distant land;
'Twas I thy bow and arrows laid
  Beside thy still cold hand;
Thy bow in many a battle bent,
Thy arrows never vainly sent.

"With wampum-belts I crossed thy breast,
  And wrapped thee in the bison's hide,

And laid the food that pleased thee best,
In plenty, by thy side,
And decked thee bravely, as became
A warrior of illustrious name.

"Thou'rt happy now, for thou hast passed
The long dark journey of the grave,
And in the land of light, at last,
Hast joined the good and brave ;
Amid the flushed and balmy air,
The bravest and the loveliest there.

"Yet, oft to thine own Indian maid
Even there thy thoughts will earthward stray—
To her who sits where thou wert laid,
And weeps the hours away,
Yet almost can her grief forget,
To think that thou dost love her yet.

"And thou, by one of those still lakes
That in a shining cluster lie,
On which the south wind scarcely breaks
The image of the sky,
A bower for thee and me hast made
Beneath the many-colored shade.

"And thou dost wait and watch to meet
My spirit sent to join the blessed,
And, wondering what detains my feet
From that bright land of rest,
Dost seem, in every sound, to hear
The rustling of my footsteps near."

ODE FOR AN AGRICULTURAL CELEBRATION.

FAR back in the ages,
  The plough with wreaths was crowned ;
The hands of kings and sages
  Entwined the chaplet round ;
Till men of spoil disdained the toil
  By which the world was nourished,
And dews of blood enriched the soil
  Where green their laurels flourished.
—Now the world her fault repairs—
  The guilt that stains her story ;
And weeps her crimes amid the cares
  That formed her earliest glory.

The proud throne shall crumble,
  The diadem shall wane,
The tribes of earth shall humble
  The pride of those who reign ;
And War shall lay his pomp away ;—
  The fame that heroes cherish,
The glory earned in deadly fray
  Shall fade, decay, and perish.
Honor waits, o'er all the earth,
  Through endless generations,
The art that calls her harvest forth,
  And feeds th' expectant nations.

RIZPAH.

And he delivered them into the hands of the Gibeonites, and they hanged them in the hill before the Lord; and they fell all seven together, and were put to death in the days of the harvest, in the first days, in the beginning of barley-harvest.

And Rizpah, the daughter of Aiah, took sackcloth, and spread it for her upon the rock, from the beginning of harvest until the water dropped upon them out of heaven, and suffered neither the birds of the air to rest upon them by day, nor the beasts of the field by night.   2 SAMUEL, xxi. 10.

HEAR what the desolate Rizpah said,
As on Gibeah's rocks she watched the dead.
The sons of Michal before her lay,
And her own fair children, dearer than they :
By a death of shame they all had died,
And were stretched on the bare rock, side by side.
And Rizpah, once the loveliest of all
That bloomed and smiled in the court of Saul,
All wasted with watching and famine now,
And scorched by the sun her haggard brow,
Sat mournfully guarding their corpses there,
And murmured a strange and solemn air
The low, heart-broken, and wailing strain
Of a mother that mourns her children slain :

"I have made the crags my home, and spread
On their desert backs my sackcloth bed ;
I have eaten the bitter herb of the rocks,
And drunk the midnight dew in my locks ;
I have wept till I could not weep, and the pain
Of the burning eyeballs went to my brain.
Seven blackened corpses before me lie,
In the blaze of the sun and the winds of the sky.
I have watched them through the burning day,
And driven the vulture and raven away ;
And the cormorant wheeled in circles round,
Yet feared to alight on the guarded ground.

And when the shadows of twilight came,
I have seen the hyena's eyes of flame,
And heard at my side his stealthy tread,
But aye at my shout the savage fled :
And I threw the lighted brand to fright
The jackal and wolf that yelled in the night.

"Ye were foully murdered, my hapless sons,
By the hands of wicked and cruel ones ;
Ye fell, in your fresh and blooming prime,
All innocent, for your father's crime.
He sinned—but he paid the price of his guilt
When his blood by a nameless hand was spilt ;
When he strove with the heathen host in vain,
And fell with the flower of his people slain,
And the sceptre his children's hands should sway
From his injured lineage passed away.

"But I hoped that the cottage-roof would be
A safe retreat for my sons and me ;
And that while they ripened to manhood fast,
They should wean my thoughts from the woes of the past ;
And my bosom swelled with a mother's pride,
As they stood in their beauty and strength by my side,
Tall like their sire, with the princely grace
Of his stately form, and the bloom of his face.

"Oh, what an hour for a mother's heart,
When the pitiless ruffians tore us apart !
When I clasped their knees and wept and prayed,
And struggled and shrieked to Heaven for aid,
And clung to my sons with desperate strength,
Till the murderers loosed my hold at length,
And bore me breathless and faint aside,
In their iron arms, while my children died.
They died—and the mother that gave them birth
Is forbid to cover their bones with earth.

"The barley-harvest was nodding white,
When my children died on the rocky height,

And the reapers were singing on hill and plain,
When I came to my task of sorrow and pain.
But now the season of rain is nigh,
The sun is dim in the thickening sky,
And the clouds in sullen darkness rest
Where he hides his light at the doors of the west
I hear the howl of the wind that brings
The long drear storm on its heavy wings ;
But the howling wind and the driving rain
Will beat on my houseless head in vain :
I shall stay, from my murdered sons to scare
The beasts of the desert, and fowls of air."

THE OLD MAN'S FUNERAL.

I saw an aged man upon his bier,
  His hair was thin and white, and on his brow
A record of the cares of many a year ;—
  Cares that were ended and forgotten now.
And there was sadness round, and faces bowed,
And woman's tears fell fast, and children wailed aloud.

Then rose another hoary man and said,
  In faltering accents, to that weeping train :
  Why mourn ye that our aged friend is dead ?
  Ye are not sad to see the gathered grain,
Nor when their mellow fruit the orchards cast,
Nor when the yellow woods let fall the ripened mast.

' Ye sigh not when the sun, his course fulfilled,
  His glorious course, rejoicing earth and sky,
In the soft evening, when the winds are stilled,
  Sinks where his islands of refreshment lie,
And leaves the smile of his departure, spread
O'er the warm-colored heaven and ruddy mountain head.

" Why weep ye then for him, who, having won
     The bound of man's appointed years, at last,
Life's blessings all enjoyed, life's labors done,
     Serenely to his final rest has passed ;
While the soft memory of his virtues, yet,
Lingers like twilight hues, when the bright sun is set ?

" His youth was innocent ; his riper age
     Marked with some act of goodness every day ;
And watched by eyes that loved him, calm and sage,
     Faded his late declining years away.
Meekly he gave his being up, and went
To share the holy rest that waits a life well spent.

" That life was happy ; every day he gave
     Thanks for the fair existence that was his ;
For a sick fancy made him not her slave,
     To mock him with her phantom miseries.
No chronic tortures racked his aged limb,
For luxury and sloth had nourished none for him.

" And I am glad that he has lived thus long,
     And glad that he has gone to his reward ;
Nor can I deem that Nature did him wrong,
     Softly to disengage the vital cord.
For when his hand grew palsied, and his eye
Dark with the mists of age, it was his time to die."

THE RIVULET.

     THIS little rill, that from the springs
     Of yonder grove its current brings,
     Plays on the slope awhile, and then
     Goes prattling into groves again,
     Oft to its warbling waters drew
     My little feet, when life was new.

When woods in early green were dressed,
And from the chambers of the west
The warm breezes, travelling out,
Breathed the new scent of flowers about,
My truant steps from home would stray,
Upon its grassy side to play,
List the brown thrasher's vernal hymn,
And crop the violet on its brim,
With blooming cheek and open brow,
As young and gay, sweet rill, as thou.

And when the days of boyhood came,
And I had grown in love with fame,
Duly I sought thy banks, and tried
My first rude numbers by thy side.
Words cannot tell how bright and gay
The scenes of life before me lay.
Then glorious hopes, that now to speak
Would bring the blood into my cheek,
Passed o'er me ; and I wrote, on high,
A name I deemed should never die.

Years change thee not.   Upon yon hill
The tall old maples, verdant still,
Yet tell, in grandeur of decay,
How swift the years have passed away,
Since first, a child, and half afraid,
I wandered in the forest shade.
Thou, ever-joyous rivulet,
Dost dimple, leap, and prattle yet ;
And sporting with the sands that pave
The windings of thy silver wave,
And dancing to thy own wild chime,
Thou laughest at the lapse of time.
The same sweet sounds are in my ear
My early childhood loved to hear ;
As pure thy limpid waters run ;
As bright they sparkle to the sun ;

As fresh and thick the bending ranks
Of herbs that line thy oozy banks ;
The violet there, in soft May dew,
Comes up, as modest and as blue ;
As green amid thy current's stress,
Floats the scarce-rooted watercress ;
And the brown ground-bird, in thy glen,
Still chirps as merrily as then.

Thou changest not—but I am changed
Since first thy pleasant banks I ranged ;
And the grave stranger, come to see
The play-place of his infancy,
Has scarce a single trace of him
Who sported once upon thy brim.
The visions of my youth are past—
Too bright, too beautiful to last.
I've tried the world—it wears no more
The coloring of romance it wore.
Yet well has Nature kept the truth
She promised in my earliest youth.
The radiant beauty shed abroad
On all the glorious works of God,
Shows freshly, to my sobered eye,
Each charm it wore in days gone by.

Yet a few years shall pass away,
And I, all trembling, weak, and gray,
Bowed to the earth, which waits to fold
My ashes in the embracing mould,
(If haply the dark will of Fate
Indulge my life so long a date),
May come for the last time to look
Upon my childhood's favorite brook.
Then dimly on my eye shall gleam
The sparkle of thy dancing stream ;
And faintly on my ear shall fall
Thy prattling current's merry call ;
Yet shalt thou flow as glad and bright
As when thou met'st my infant sight.

And I shall sleep—and on thy side,
As ages after ages glide,
Children their early sports shall try,
And pass to hoary age and die.
But thou, unchanged from year to year,
Gayly shalt play and glitter here ;
Amid young flowers and tender grass
Thy endless infancy shall pass ;
And, singing down thy narrow glen,
Shalt mock the fading race of men.

MARCH.

THE stormy March is come at last,
  With wind, and cloud, and changing skies ;
I hear the rushing of the blast,
  That through the snowy valley flies

Ah, passing few are they who speak,
  Wild, stormy month ! in praise of thee ,
Yet though thy winds are loud and bleak,
  Thou art a welcome month to me.

For thou, to northern lands, again
  The glad and glorious sun dost bring,
And thou hast joined the gentle train
  And wear'st the gentle name of Spring.

And, in thy reign of blast and storm,
  Smiles many a long, bright, sunny day,
When the changed winds are soft and warm,
  And heaven puts on the blue of May.

Then sing aloud the gushing rills
  In joy that they again are free,
And, brightly leaping down the hills,
  Renew their journey to the sea.

The year's departing beauty hides
    Of wintry storms the sullen threat ;
But in thy sternest frown abides
    A look of kindly promise yet.

Thou bring'st the hope of those calm skies,
    And that soft time of sunny showers,
When the wide bloom, on earth that lies,
    Seems of a brighter world than ours.

CONSUMPTION.

Ay, thou art for the grave ; thy glances shine
    Too brightly to shine long ; another Spring
Shall deck her for men's eyes—but not for thine—
    Sealed in a sleep which knows no wakening.
The fields for thee have no medicinal leaf,
    And the vexed ore no mineral of power ;
And they who love thee wait in anxious grief
    Till the slow plague shall bring the fatal hour.
Glide softly to thy rest then ; Death should come
    Gently, to one of gentle mould like thee,
As light winds wandering through groves of bloom
    Detach the delicate blossom from the tree.
Close thy sweet eyes, calmly, and without pain ;
And we will trust in God to see thee yet again.

AN INDIAN STORY.

" I know where the timid fawn abides
    In the depths of the shaded dell,
Where the leaves are broad and the thicket hides,
With its many stems and its tangled sides,
    From the eye of the hunter well.

"I know where the young May violet grows,
　In its lone and lowly nook,
On the mossy bank, where the larch-tree throws
Its broad dark bough, in solemn repose,
　Far over the silent brook.

"And that timid fawn starts not with fear
　When I steal to her secret bower ;
And that young May violet to me is dear,
And I visit the silent streamlet near,
　To look on the lovely flower."

Thus Maquon sings as he lightly walks
　To the hunting-ground on the hills ;
'Tis a song of his maid of the woods and rocks,
With her bright black eyes and long black locks,
　And voice like the music of rills.

He goes to the chase—but evil eyes
　Are at watch in the thicker shades ;
For she was lovely that smiled on his sighs,
And he bore, from a hundred lovers, his prize,
　The flower of the forest maids.

The boughs in the morning wind are stirred,
　And the woods their song renew,
With the early carol of many a bird,
And the quickened tune of the streamlet heard
　Where the hazels trickle with dew.

And Maquon has promised his dark-haired maid,
　Ere eve shall redden the sky,
A good red deer from the forest shade,
That bounds with the herd through grove and glade,
　At her cabin-door shall lie.

The hollow woods, in the setting sun,
　Ring shrill with the fire-bird's lay ;
And Maquon's sylvan labors are done,
And his shafts are spent, but the spoil they won
　He bears on his homeward way.

He stops near his bower—his eye perceives
  Strange traces along the ground—
At once to the earth his burden he heaves ;
He breaks through the veil of boughs and leaves ;
  And gains its door with a bound.

But the vines are torn on its walls that leant,
  And all from the young shrubs there
By struggling hands have the leaves been rent,
And there hangs on the sassafras, broken and bent,
  One tress of the well-known hair.

But where is she who, at this calm hour,
  Ever watched his coming to see ?
She is not at the door, nor yet in the bower ;
He calls—but he only hears on the flower
  The hum of the laden bee.

It is not a time for idle grief,
  Nor a time for tears to flow ;
The horror that freezes his limbs is brief—
He grasps his war-axe and bow, and a sheaf
  Of darts made sharp for the foe.

And he looks for the print of the ruffian's feet
  Where he bore the maiden away ;
And he darts on the fatal path more fleet
Than the blast hurries the vapor and sleet
  O'er the wild November day.

'Twas early summer when Maquon's bride
  Was stolen away from his door ;
But at length the maples in crimson are dyed,
And the grape is black on the cabin-side—
  And she smiles at his hearth once more.

But far in the pine-grove, dark and cold,
  Where the yellow leaf falls not,
Nor the autumn shines in scarlet and gold,
There lies a hillock of fresh dark mould,
  In the deepest gloom of the spot.

And the Indian girls, that pass that way,
  Point out the ravisher's grave ;
" And how soon to the bower she loved," they say,
" Returned the maid that was borne away
  From Maquon, the fond and the brave."

SUMMER WIND.

  IT is a sultry day ; the sun has drunk
The dew that lay upon the morning grass ;
There is no rustling in the lofty elm
That canopies my dwelling, and its shade
Scarce cools me.   All is silent, save the faint
And interrupted murmur of the bee,
Settling on the sick flowers, and then again
Instantly on the wing.   The plants around
Feel the too potent fervors : the tall maize
Rolls up its long green leaves ; the clover droops
Its tender foliage, and declines its blooms.
But far in the fierce sunshine tower the hills,
With all their growth of woods, silent and stern,
As if the scorching heat and dazzling light
Were but an element they loved.   Bright clouds,
Motionless pillars of the brazen heaven—
Their bases on the mountains—their white tops
Shining in the far ether—fire the air
With a reflected radiance, and make turn
The gazer's eye away.   For me, I lie
Languidly in the shade, where the thick turf,
Yet virgin from the kisses of the sun,
Retains some freshness, and I woo the wind
That still delays his coming.   Why so slow,
Gentle and voluble spirit of the air ?
Oh, come and breathe upon the fainting earth
Coolness and life.   Is it that in his caves
He hears me ?   See, on yonder woody ridge,

The pine is bending his proud top, and now
Among the nearer groves, chestnut and oak
Are tossing their green boughs about.   He comes ;
Lo, where the grassy meadow runs in waves !
The deep distressful silence of the scene
Breaks up with mingling of unnumbered sounds
And universal motion.   He is come,
Shaking a shower of blossoms from the shrubs,
And bearing on their fragrance ; and he brings
Music of birds, and rustling of young boughs,
And sound of swaying branches, and the voice
Of distant waterfalls.   All the green herbs
Are stirring in his breath ; a thousand flowers,
By the road-side and the borders of the brook,
Nod gayly to each other ; glossy leaves
Are twinkling in the sun, as if the dew
Were on them yet, and silver waters break
Into small waves and sparkle as he comes.

AN INDIAN AT THE BURIAL–PLACE OF HIS FATHERS.

It is the spot I came to seek—
  My father's ancient burial-place,
Ere from these vales, ashamed and weak,
  Withdrew our wasted race.
It is the spot—I know it well—
Of which our old traditions tell.

For here the upland bank sends out
  A ridge toward the river-side ;
I know the shaggy hills about,
  The meadows smooth and wide,
The plains, that, toward the southern sky,
Fenced east and west by mountains lie.

A white man, gazing on the scene,
  Would say a lovely spot was here,
And praise the lawns, so fresh and green,
  Between the hills so sheer.
I like it not—I would the plain
Lay in its tall old groves again.

The sheep are on the slopes around,
  The cattle in the meadows feed,
And laborers turn the crumbling ground,
  Or drop the yellow seed,
And prancing steeds, in trappings gay,
Whirl the bright chariot o'er the way.

Methinks it were a nobler sight
  To see these vales in woods arrayed,
Their summits in the golden light,
  Their trunks in grateful shade,
And herds of deer that bounding go
O'er hills and prostrate trees below.

And then to mark the lord of all,
  The forest hero, trained to wars,
Quivered and plumed, and lithe and tall,
  And seamed with glorious scars,
Walk forth, amid his reign, to dare
The wolf, and grapple with the bear.

This bank, in which the dead were laid,
  Was sacred when its soil was ours;
Hither the silent Indian maid
  Brought wreaths of beads and flowers,
And the gray chief and gifted seer
Worshipped the god of thunders here.

But now the wheat is green and high
  On clods that hid the warrior's breast,
And scattered in the furrows lie
  The weapons of his rest;
13

And there, in the loose sand, is thrown
Of his large arm the mouldering bone.

Ah, little thought the strong and brave
    Who bore their lifeless chieftain forth—
Or the young wife that weeping gave
    Her first-born to the earth,
That the pale race, who waste us now,
Among their bones should guide the plough.

They waste us—ay—like April snow
    In the warm noon, we shrink away ;
And fast they follow, as we go
    Toward the setting day—
Till they shall fill the land, and we
Are driven into the Western sea.

But I behold a fearful sign,
    To which the white men's eyes are blind ;
Their race may vanish hence, like mine,
    And leave no trace behind,
Save ruins o'er the region spread,
And the white stones above the dead.

Before these fields were shorn and tilled,
    Full to the brim our rivers flowed ;
The melody of waters filled
    The fresh and boundless wood ;
And torrents dashed and rivulets played,
And fountains spouted in the shade.

Those grateful sounds are heard no more,
    The springs are silent in the sun ;
The rivers, by the blackened shore,
    With lessening current run ;
The realm our tribes are crushed to get
May be a barren desert yet.

SONG.

Dost thou idly ask to hear
　　At what gentle seasons
Nymphs relent, when lovers near
　　Press the tenderest reasons?
Ah, they give their faith too oft
　　To the careless wooer;
Maidens' hearts are always soft:
　　Would that men's were truer!

Woo the fair one when around
　　Early birds are singing;
When, o'er all the fragrant ground,
　　Early herbs are springing:
When the brookside, bank, and grove,
　　All with blossoms laden,
Shine with beauty, breathe of love,—
　　Woo the timid maiden.

Woo her when, with rosy blush,
　　Summer eve is sinking;
When, on rills that softly gush,
　　Stars are softly winking;
When through boughs that knit the bower
　　Moonlight gleams are stealing;
Woo her, till the gentle hour
　　Wake a gentler feeling.

Woo her when autumnal dyes
　　Tinge the woody mountain;
When the dropping foliage lies
　　In the weedy fountain;
Let the scene, that tells how fast
　　Youth is passing over,
Warn her, ere her bloom is past,
　　To secure her lover.

Woo her when the north winds call
　At the lattice nightly ;
When, within the cheerful hall,
　Blaze the fagots brightly ;
While the wintry tempest round
　Sweeps the landscape hoary,
Sweeter in her ear shall sound
　Love's delightful story.

HYMN OF THE WALDENSES.

Hear, Father, hear thy faint afflicted flock
Cry to thee, from the desert and the rock ;
While those, who seek to slay thy children, hold
Blasphemous worship under roofs of gold ;
And the broad goodly lands, with pleasant airs
That nurse the grape and wave the grain, are theirs.

Yet better were this mountain wilderness,
And this wild life of danger and distress—
Watchings by night and perilous flight by day,
And meetings in the depths of earth to pray—
Better, far better, than to kneel with them,
And pay the impious rite thy laws condemn.

Thou, Lord, dost hold the thunder ; the firm land
Tosses in billows when it feels thy hand ;
Thou dashest nation against nation, then
Stillest the angry world to peace again.
Oh, touch their stony hearts who hunt thy sons—
The murderers of our wives and little ones.

Yet, mighty God, yet shall thy frown look forth
Unveiled, and terribly shall shake the earth.
Then the foul power of priestly sin and all
Its long-upheld idolatries shall fall.
Thou shalt raise up the trampled and oppressed,
And thy delivered saints shall dwell in rest.

MONUMENT MOUNTAIN.

THOU who wouldst see the lovely and the wild
Mingled in harmony on Nature's face,
Ascend our rocky mountains. Let thy foot
Fail not with weariness, for on their tops
The beauty and the majesty of earth,
Spread wide beneath, shall make thee to forget
The steep and toilsome way. There, as thou stand'st,
The haunts of men below thee, and around
The mountain-summits, thy expanding heart
Shall feel a kindred with that loftier world
To which thou art translated, and partake
The enlargement of thy vision. Thou shalt look
Upon the green and rolling forest-tops,
And down into the secrets of the glens,
And streams that with their bordering thickets strive
To hide their windings. Thou shalt gaze, at once,
Here on white villages, and tilth, and herds,
And swarming roads, and there on solitudes
That only hear the torrent, and the wind,
And eagle's shriek. There is a precipice
That seems a fragment of some mighty wall,
Built by the hand that fashioned the old world,
To separate its nations, and thrown down
When the flood drowned them. To the north, a path
Conducts you up the narrow battlement.
Steep is the western side, shaggy and wild
With mossy trees, and pinnacles of flint,
And many a hanging crag. But, to the east,
Sheer to the vale go down the bare old cliffs—
Huge pillars, that in middle heaven upbear
Their weather-beaten capitals, here dark
With moss, the growth of centuries, and there
Of chalky whiteness where the thunderbolt
Has splintered them. It is a fearful thing
To stand upon the beetling verge, and see
Where storm and lightning, from that huge gray wall,

Have tumbled down vast blocks, and at the base
Dashed them in fragments, and to lay thine ear
Over the dizzy depth, and hear the sound
Of winds, that struggle with the woods below,
Come up like ocean murmurs.   But the scene
Is lovely round ; a beautiful river there
Wanders amid the fresh and fertile meads,
The paradise he made unto himself,
Mining the soil for ages.   On each side
The fields swell upward to the hills ; beyond,
Above the hills, in the blue distance, rise
The mountain-columns with which earth props heaven.

　　There is a tale about these reverend rocks,
A sad tradition of unhappy love,
And sorrows borne and ended, long ago,
When over these fair vales the savage sought
His game in the thick woods.   There was a maid,
The fairest of the Indian maids, bright-eyed,
With wealth of raven tresses, a light form,
And a gay heart.   About her cabin-door
The wide old woods resounded with her song
And fairy laughter all the summer day.
She loved her cousin ; such a love was deemed,
By the morality of those stern tribes,
Incestuous, and she struggled hard and long
Against her love, and reasoned with her heart,
As simple Indian maiden might.   In vain.
Then her eye lost its lustre, and her step
Its lightness, and the gray-haired men that passed
Her dwelling, wondered that they heard no more
The accustomed song and laugh of her, whose looks
Were like the cheerful smile of Spring, they said,
Upon the Winter of their age.   She went
To weep where no eye saw, and was not found
Where all the merry girls were met to dance,
And all the hunters of the tribe were out ;
Nor when they gathered from the rustling husk
The shining ear ; nor when, by the river's side,

They pulled the grape and startled the wild shades
With sounds of mirth.   The keen-eyed Indian dames
Would whisper to each other, as they saw
Her wasting form, and say, *The girl will die.*

   One day into the bosom of a friend,
A playmate of her young and innocent years,
She poured her griefs.   " Thou know'st, and thou alone,"
She said, "for I have told thee, all my love,
And guilt, and sorrow.   I am sick of life.
All night I weep in darkness, and the morn
Glares on me, as upon a thing accursed,
That has no business on the earth.   I hate
The pastimes and the pleasant toils that once
I loved ; the cheerful voices of my friends
Sound in my ear like mockings, and, at night,
In dreams, my mother, from the land of souls,
Calls me and chides me.   All that look on me
Do seem to know my shame ; I cannot bear
Their eyes ; I cannot from my heart root out
The love that wrings it so, and I must die."

   It was a summer morning, and they went
To this old precipice.   About the cliffs
Lay garlands, ears of maize, and shaggy skins
Of wolf and bear, the offerings of the tribe
Here made to the Great Spirit, for they deemed,
Like worshippers of the elder time, that God
Doth walk on the high places and affect
The earth-o'erlooking mountains.   She had on
The ornaments with which her father loved
To deck the beauty of his bright-eyed girl,
And bade her wear when stranger warriors came
To be his guests.   Here the friends sat them down,
And sang, all day, old songs of love and death,
And decked the poor wan victim's hair with flowers,
And prayed that safe and swift might be her way
To the calm world of sunshine, where no grief
Makes the heart heavy and the eyelids red.

Beautiful lay the region of her tribe
Below her—waters resting in the embrace
Of the wide forest, and maize-planted glades
Opening amid the leafy wilderness.
She gazed upon it long, and at the sight
Of her own village peeping through the trees,
And her own dwelling, and the cabin roof
Of him she loved with an unlawful love,
And came to die for, a warm gush of tears
Ran from her eyes.   But when the sun grew low
And the hill shadows long, she threw herself
From the steep rock and perished.   There was scooped,
Upon the mountain's southern slope, a grave ;
And there they laid her, in the very garb
With which the maiden decked herself for death,
With the same withering wild-flowers in her hair.
And o'er the mould that covered her, the tribe
Built up a simple monument, a cone
Of small loose stones.   Thenceforward all who passed,
Hunter, and dame, and virgin, laid a stone
In silence on the pile.   It stands there yet.
And Indians from the distant West, who come
To visit where their fathers' bones are laid,
Yet tell the sorrowful tale, and to this day
The mountain where the hapless maiden died
Is called the Mountain of the Monument.

AFTER A TEMPEST.

The day had been a day of wind and storm,
The wind was laid, the storm was overpast,
And stooping from the zenith, bright and warm,
Shone the great sun on the wide earth at last.
I stood upon the upland slope, and cast
Mine eye upon a broad and beauteous scene,
Where the vast plain lay girt by mountains vast,
And hills o'er hills lifted their heads of green,
With pleasant vales scooped out and villages between.

The rain-drops glistened on the trees around,
Whose shadows on the tall grass were not stirred,
Save when a shower of diamonds, to the ground,
Was shaken by the flight of startled bird ;
For birds were warbling round, and bees were heard
About the flowers ; the cheerful rivulet sung
And gossiped, as he hastened oceanward ;
To the gray oak the squirrel, chiding, clung,
And chirping from the ground the grasshopper upsprung.

And from beneath the leaves that kept them dry
Flew many a glittering insect here and there,
And darted up and down the butterfly,
That seemed a living blossom of the air,
The flocks came scattering from the thicket, where
The violent rain had pent them ; in the way
Strolled groups of damsels frolicsome and fair ;
The farmer swung the scythe or turned the hay,
And 'twixt the heavy swaths his children were at play.

It was a scene of peace—and, like a spell,
Did that serene and golden sunlight fall
Upon the motionless wood that clothed the fell,
And precipice upspringing like a wall,
And glassy river and white waterfall,
And happy living things that trod the bright
And beauteous scene ; while far beyond them all,
On many a lovely valley, out of sight,
Was poured from the blue heavens the same soft golden light.

I looked, and thought the quiet of the scene
An emblem of the peace that yet shall be,
When o'er earth's continents, and isles between,
The noise of war shall cease from sea to sea,
And married nations dwell in harmony ;
When millions, crouching in the dust to one,
No more shall beg their lives on bended knee,
Nor the black stake be dressed, nor in the sun
The o'erlabored captive toil, and wish his life were done.

Too long, at clash of arms amid her bower:
And pools of blood, the earth has stood aghast,
The fair earth, that should only blush with flowers
And ruddy fruits ; but not for aye can last
The storm, and sweet the sunshine when 'tis past.
Lo, the clouds roll away—they break—they fly,
And, like the glorious light of summer, cast
O'er the wide landscape from the embracing sky,
On all the peaceful world the smile of heaven shall lie.

AUTUMN WOODS.

ERE, in the northern gale,
The summer tresses of the trees are gone,
The woods of Autumn, all around our vale,
Have put their glory on.

The mountains that infold,
In their wide sweep, the colored landscape round,
Seem groups of giant kings, in purple and gold,
That guard the enchanted ground.

I roam the woods that crown
The uplands, where the mingled splendors glow,
Where the gay company of trees look down
On the green fields below.

. My steps are not alone
In these bright walks ; the sweet southwest, at play,
Flies, rustling, where the painted leaves are strown
Along the winding way.

And far in heaven, the while,
The sun, that sends that gale to wander here,
Pours out on the fair earth his quiet smile—
The sweetest of the year.

Where now the solemn shade,
Verdure and gloom where many branches meet
So grateful, when the noon of summer made
    The valleys sick with heat?

Let in through all the trees
Come the strange rays ; the forest depths are bright ;
Their sunny colored foliage, in the breeze,
    Twinkles, like beams of light.

The rivulet, late unseen,
Where bickering through the shrubs its waters run,
Shines with the image of its golden screen,
    And glimmerings of the sun.

But 'neath you crimson tree,
Lover to listening maid might breathe his flame,
Nor mark, within its roseate canopy,
    Her blush of maiden shame.

Oh, Autumn ! why so soon
Depart the hues that make thy forests glad,
Thy gentle wind and thy fair sunny noon,
    And leave thee wild and sad !

Ah ! 'twere a lot too blest
Forever in thy colored shades to stray ;
Amid the kisses of the soft southwest
    To roam and dream for aye ;

And leave the vain low strife
That makes men mad—the tug for wealth and power—
The passions and the cares that wither life,
    And waste its little hour.

MUTATION.

THEY talk of short-lived pleasure—be it so—
    Pain dies as quickly : stern, hard-featured pain
Expires, and lets her weary prisoner go.
    The fiercest agonies have shortest reign ;
    And after dreams of horror, comes again
The welcome morning with its rays of peace.
    Oblivion, softly wiping out the stain,
Makes the strong secret pangs of shame to cease .
Remorse is virtue's root ; its fair increase
    Are fruits of innocence and blessedness :
Thus joy, o'erborne and bound, doth still release
    His young limbs from the chains that round him press,
Weep not that the world changes—did it keep
A stable, changeless state, 'twere cause indeed to weep.

NOVEMBER.

YET one smile more, departing, distant sun !
    One mellow smile through the soft vapory air,
Ere, o'er the frozen earth, the loud winds run,
    Or snows are sifted o'er the meadows bare.
One smile on the brown hills and naked trees,
    And the dark rocks whose summer wreaths are cast,
And the blue gentian-flower, that, in the breeze,
    Nods lonely, of her beauteous race the last.
Yet a few sunny days, in which the bee
    Shall murmur by the hedge that skirts the way,
The cricket chirp upon the russet lea,
    And man delight to linger in thy ray.
Yet one rich smile, and we will try to bear
The piercing winter frost, and winds, and darkened air.

SONG OF THE GREEK AMAZON.

I BUCKLE to my slender side
  The pistol and the scimitar,
And in my maiden flower and pride
  Am come to share the task of war.
And yonder stands the fiery steed,
  That paws the ground and neighs to go,
My charger of the Arab breed—
  I took him from the routed foe.

My mirror is the mountain-spring,
  At which I dress my ruffled hair ;
My dimmed and dusty arms I bring,
  And wash away the blood-stain there.
Why should I guard from wind and sun
  This cheek, whose virgin rose is fled?
It was for one—oh, only one—
  I kept its bloom, and he is dead.

But they who slew him—unaware
  Of coward murderers lurking nigh—
And left him to the fowls of air,
  Are yet alive—and they must die !
They slew him—and my virgin years
  Are vowed to Greece and vengeance now
And many an Othman dame, in tears,
  Shall rue the Grecian maiden's vow.

I touched the lute in better days,
  I led in dance the joyous band ;
Ah ! they may move to mirthful lays
  Whose hands can touch a lover's hand.
The march of hosts that haste to meet
  Seems gayer than the dance to me ;
The lute's sweet tones are not so sweet
  As the fierce shout of victory.

TO A CLOUD.

BEAUTIFUL cloud ! with folds so soft and fair,
  Swimming in the pure quiet air !
Thy fleeces bathed in sunlight, while below
  Thy shadow o'er the vale moves slow ;
Where, midst their labor, pause the reaper train,
  As cool it comes along the grain.
Beautiful cloud ! I would I were with thee
  In thy calm way o'er land and sea ;
To rest on thy unrolling skirts, and look
  On Earth as on an open book ;
On streams that tie her realms with silver bands,
  And the long ways that seam her lands ;
And hear her humming cities, and the sound
  Of the great ocean breaking round.
Ay—I would sail, upon thy air-borne car,
  To blooming regions distant far,
To where the sun of Andalusia shines
  On his own olive-groves and vines,
Or the soft lights of Italy's clear sky
  In smiles upon her ruins lie.
But I would woo the winds to let us rest
  O'er Greece, long fettered and oppressed,
Whose sons at length have heard the call that comes
  From the old battle-fields and tombs,
And risen, and drawn the sword, and on the foe
  Have dealt the swift and desperate blow,
And the Othman power is cloven, and the stroke
  Has touched its chains, and they are broke.
Ay, we would linger, till the sunset there
  Should come, to purple all the air,
And thou reflect upon the sacred ground
  The ruddy radiance streaming round.
Bright meteor ! for the summer noontide made !
  Thy peerless beauty yet shall fade.
The sun, that fills with light each glistening fold,
  Shall set, and leave thee dark and cold :

The blast shall rend thy skirts, or thou mayst frown
  In the dark heaven when storms come down ;
And weep in rain, till man's inquiring eye
  Miss thee, forever, from the sky.

THE MURDERED TRAVELLER.

WHEN Spring, to woods and wastes around,
  Brought bloom and joy again,
The murdered traveller's bones were found,
  Far down a narrow glen.

The fragrant birch, above him, hung
  Her tassels in the sky ;
And many a vernal blossom sprung,
  And nodded careless by.

The red-bird warbled, as he wrought
  His hanging nest o'erhead,
And fearless, near the fatal spot,
  Her young the partridge led.

But there was weeping far away,
  And gentle eyes, for him,
With watching many an anxious day,
  Were sorrowful and dim.

They little knew, who loved him so,
  The fearful death he met,
When shouting o'er the desert snow,
  Unarmed, and hard beset ;—

Nor how, when round the frosty pole
  The northern dawn was red,
The mountain-wolf and wild-cat stole
  To banquet on the dead —

Nor how, when strangers found his bones,
  They dressed the hasty bier,
And marked his grave with nameless stones,
  Unmoistened by a tear.

But long they looked, and feared, and wept,
  Within his distant home ;
And dreamed, and started as they slept,
  For joy that he was come.

Long, long they looked—but never spied
  His welcome step again,
Nor knew the fearful death he died
  Far down that narrow glen.

HYMN TO THE NORTH STAR.

THE sad and solemn night
Hath yet her multitude of cheerful fires ;
  The glorious host of light
Walk the dark hemisphere till she retires ;
All through her silent watches, gliding slow,
Her constellations come, and climb the heavens, and go.

  Day, too, hath many a star
To grace his gorgeous reign, as bright as they :
  Through the blue fields afar,
Unseen, they follow in his flaming way :
Many a bright lingerer, as the eve grows dim,
Tells what a radiant troop arose and set with him.

  And thou dost see them rise,
Star of the Pole ! and thou dost see them set.
  Alone, in thy cold skies,
Thou keep'st thy old unmoving station yet,
Nor join'st the dances of that glittering train,
Nor dipp'st thy virgin orb in the blue western main.

There, at morn's rosy birth,
Thou lookest meekly through the kindling air,
And eve, that round the earth
Chases the day, beholds thee watching there ;
There noontide finds thee, and the hour that calls
The shapes of polar flame to scale heaven's azure walls.

Alike, beneath thine eye,
The deeds of darkness and of light are done ;
High toward the starlit sky
Towns blaze, the smoke of battle blots the sun,
The night storm on a thousand hills is loud,
And the strong wind of day doth mingle sea and cloud.

On thy unaltering blaze
The half-wrecked mariner, his compass lost,
Fixes his steady gaze,
And steers, undoubting, to the friendly coast ;
And they who stray in perilous wastes, by night,
Are glad when thou dost shine to guide their footsteps right.

And, therefore, bards of old,
Sages and hermits of the solemn wood,
Did in thy beams behold
A beauteous type of that unchanging good,
That bright eternal beacon, by whose ray
The voyager of time should shape his heedful way.

———

THE LAPSE OF TIME.

LAMENT who will, in fruitless tears,
The speed with which our moments fly ;
I sigh not over vanished years,
But watch the years that hasten by.
14

Look, how they come—a mingled crowd
  Of bright and dark, but rapid days ;
Beneath them, like a summer cloud,
  The wide world changes as I gaze.

What ! grieve that time has brought so soon
  The sober age of manhood on !
As idly might I weep, at noon,
  To see the blush of morning gone.

Could I give up the hopes that glow
  In prospect like Elysian isles ;
And let the cheerful future go,
  With all her promises and smiles ?

The future !—cruel were the power
  Whose doom would tear thee from my heart,
Thou sweetener of the present hour !
  We cannot—no—we will not part.

Oh, leave me, still, the rapid flight
  That makes the changing seasons gay,
The grateful speed that brings the night,
  The swift and glad return of day ;

The months that touch, with added grace,
  This little prattler at my knee,
In whose arch eye and speaking face
  New meaning every hour I see ;

The years, that o'er each sister land
  Shall lift the country of my birth,
And nurse her strength, till she shall stand
  The pride and pattern of the earth :

Till younger commonwealths, for aid,
  Shall cling about her ample robe,
And from her frown shall shrink afraid
  The crowned oppressors of the globe.

True—time will seam and blanch my brow—
    Well—I shall sit with aged men,
And my good glass will tell me how
    A grizzly beard becomes me then.

And then, should no dishonor lie
    Upon my head, when I am gray,
Love yet shall watch my fading eye,
    And smooth the path of my decay.

Then haste thee, Time—'tis kindness all
    That speeds thy wingèd feet so fast :
Thy pleasures stay not till they pall,
    And all thy pains are quickly past.

Thou fliest and bear'st away our woes,
    And as thy shadowy train depart,
The memory of sorrow grows
    A lighter burden on the heart.

THE SONG OF THE STARS.

WHEN the radiant morn of creation broke,
And the world in the smile of God awoke,
And the empty realms of darkness and death
Were moved through their depths by his mighty breath,
And orbs of beauty and spheres of flame
From the void abyss by myriads came—
In the joy of youth as they darted away,
Through the widening wastes of space to play,
Their silver voices in chorus rang,
And this was the song the bright ones sang :

" Away, away, through the wide, wide sky,
The fair blue fields that before us lie—
Each sun with the worlds that round him roll,
Each planet, poised on her turning pole ;
With her isles of green, and her clouds of white,
And her waters that lie like fluid light.

"For the source of glory uncovers his face,
And the brightness o'erflows unbounded space,
And we drink as we go to the luminous tides
In our ruddy air and our blooming sides :
Lo, yonder tho living splendors play ;
Away, on our joyous path, away !

"Look, look, through our glittering ranks afar,
In the infinite azure, star after star,
How they brighten and bloom as they swiftly pass !
How the verdure runs o'er each rolling mass !
And the path of the gentle winds is seen,
Where the small waves dance, and the young woods lean.

"And see, where the brighter day-beams pour,
How the rainbows hang in the sunny shower ;
And the morn and eve, with their pomp of hues,
Shift o'er the bright planets and shed their dews ;
And 'twixt them both, o'er the teeming ground,
With her shadowy cone the night goes round !

"Away, away ! in our blossoming bowers,
In the soft airs wrapping these spheres of ours,
In the seas and fountains that shine with morn,
See, Love is brooding, and Life is born,
And breathing myriads are breaking from night,
To rejoice, like us, in motion and light.

"Glide on in your beauty, ye youthful spheres,
To weave the dance that measures the years ;
Glide on, in the glory and gladness sent
To the furthest wall of the firmament—
The boundless visible smile of Him
To the veil of whose brow your lamps are dim."

A FOREST HYMN.

THE groves were God's first temples. Ere man learned
To hew the shaft, and lay the architrave,
And spread the roof above them—ere he framed
The lofty vault, to gather and roll back
The sound of anthems ; in the darkling wood,
Amid the cool and silence, he knelt down,
And offered to the Mightiest solemn thanks
And supplication. For his simple heart
Might not resist the sacred influences
Which, from the stilly twilight of the place,
And from the gray old trunks that high in heaven
Mingled their mossy boughs, and from the sound
Of the invisible breath that swayed at once
All their green tops, stole over him, and bowed
His spirit with the thought of boundless power
And inaccessible majesty. Ah, why
Should we, in the world's riper years, neglect
God's ancient sanctuaries, and adore
Only among the crowd, and under roofs
That our frail hands have raised ? Let me, at least,
Here, in the shadow of this aged wood,
Offer one hymn—thrice happy, if it find
Acceptance in His ear.

     Father, thy hand
Hath reared these venerable columns, thou
Didst weave this verdant roof. Thou didst look down
Upon the naked earth, and, forthwith, rose
All these fair ranks of trees. They, in thy sun,
Budded, and shook their green leaves in thy breeze,
And shot toward heaven. The century-living crow
Whose birth was in their tops, grew old and died
Among their branches, till, at last, they stood,
As now they stand, massy, and tall, and dark,
Fit shrine for humble worshipper to hold
Communion with his Maker. These dim vaults,

These winding aisles, of human pomp or pride
Report not.   No fantastic carvings show
The boast of our vain race to change the form
Of thy fair works.   But thou art here—thou fill'st
The solitude.   Thou art in the soft winds
That run along the summit of these trees
In music ; thou art in the cooler breath
That from the inmost darkness of the place
Comes, scarcely felt ; the barky trunks, the ground,
The fresh moist ground, are all instinct w:th thee.
Here is continual worship ;—Nature, here,
In the tranquillity that thou dost love,
Enjoys thy presence.   Noiselessly, around,
From perch to perch, the solitary bird
Passes ; and yon clear spring, that, midst its herbs,
Wells softly forth and wandering steeps the roots
Of half the mighty forest, tells no tale
Of all the good it does.   Thou hast not left
Thyself without a witness, in the shades,
Of thy perfections.   Grandeur, strength, and grace
Are here to speak of thee.   This mighty oak—
By whose immovable stem I stand and seem
Almost annihilated—not a prince,
In all that proud old world beyond the deep,
E'er wore his crown as loftily as he
Wears the green coronal of leaves with which
Thy hand has graced him.   Nestled at his root
Is beauty, such as blooms not in the glare
Of the broad sun.   That delicate forest flower,
With scented breath and look so like a smile,
Seems, as it issues from the shapeless mould,
An emanation of the indwelling Life,
A visible token of the upholding Love,
That are the soul of this great universe.

   My heart is awed within me when I think
Of the great miracle that still goes on,
In silence, round me—the perpetual work
Of thy creation, finished, yet renewed

" . . . yon clear spring, that, midst its herbs,
Wells softly forth and wandering steeps the roots
Of half the mighty forest."

Forever.   Written on thy works I read
The lesson of thy own eternity.
Lo ! all grow old and die—but see again,
How on the faltering footsteps of decay
Youth presses—ever gay and beautiful youth
In all its beautiful forms.   These lofty trees
Wave not less proudly that their ancestors
Moulder beneath them.   Oh, there is not lost
One of earth's charms : upon her bosom yet,
After the flight of untold centuries,
The freshness of her far beginning lies
And yet shall lie.   Life mocks the idle hate
Of his arch-enemy Death—yea, seats himself
Upon the tyrant's throne—the sepulchre,
And of the triumphs of his ghastly foe
Makes his own nourishment.   For he came forth
From thine own bosom, and shall have no end.

There have been holy men who hid themselves
Deep in the woody wilderness, and gave
Their lives to thought and prayer, till they outlived
The generation born with them, nor seemed
Less aged than the hoary trees and rocks
Around them ;—and there have been holy men
Who deemed it were not well to pass life thus.
But let me often to these solitudes
Retire, and in thy presence reassure
My feeble virtue.   Here its enemies,
The passions, at thy plainer footsteps shrink
And tremble and are still.   O God ! when thou
Dost scare the world with tempests, set on fire
The heavens with falling thunderbolts, or fill,
With all the waters of the firmament,
The swift dark whirlwind that uproots the woods
And drowns the villages ; when, at thy call,
Uprises the great deep and throws himself
Upon the continent, and overwhelms
Its cities—who forgets not, at the sight
Of these tremendous tokens of thy power,

His pride, and lays his strifes and follies by?
Oh, from these sterner aspects of thy face
Spare me and mine, nor let us need the wrath
Of the mad unchained elements to teach
Who rules them.   Be it ours to meditate,
In these calm shades, thy milder majesty,
And to the beautiful order of thy works
Learn to conform the order of our lives.

"OH FAIREST OF THE RURAL MAIDS."

Oh fairest of the rural maids !
Thy birth was in the forest shades ;
Green boughs, and glimpses of the sky,
Were all that met thine infant eye.

Thy sports, thy wanderings, when a child,
Were ever in the sylvan wild ;
And all the beauty of the place
Is in thy heart and on thy face.

The twilight of the trees and rocks
Is in the light shade of thy locks ;
Thy step is as the wind, that weaves
Its playful way among the leaves.

Thine eyes are springs, in whose serene
And silent waters heaven is seen ;
Their lashes are the herbs that look
On their young figures in the brook.

The forest depths, by foot unpressed,
Are not more sinless than thy breast ;
The holy peace, that fills the air
Of those calm solitudes, is there.

"I BROKE THE SPELL THAT HELD ME LONG."

I BROKE the spell that held me long,
The dear, dear witchery of song.
I said, the poet's idle lore
Shall waste my prime of years no more,
For Poetry, though heavenly born,
Consorts with poverty and scorn.

I broke the spell—nor deemed its power
Could fetter me another hour.
Ah, thoughtless! how could I forget
Its causes were around me yet?
For wheresoe'er I looked, the while,
Was Nature's everlasting smile.

Still came and lingered on my sight
Of flowers and streams the bloom and light,
And glory of the stars and sun ;—
And these and poetry are one.
They, ere the world had held me long,
Recalled me to the love of song.

JUNE.

I GAZED upon the glorious sky
    And the green mountains round,
And thought that when I came to lie
    At rest within the ground,
'Twere pleasant, that in flowery June,
When brooks send up a cheerful tune,
    And groves a joyous sound,
The sexton's hand, my grave to make,
The rich, green mountain-turf should break.

A cell within the frozen mould,
    A coffin borne through sleet,
And icy clods above it rolled,
    While fierce the tempests beat—
Away !—I will not think of these—
Blue be the sky and soft the breeze,
    Earth green beneath the feet,
And be the damp mould gently pressed
Into my narrow place of rest.

There through the long, long summer hours,
    The golden light should lie,
And thick young herbs and groups of flowers
    Stand in their beauty by.
The oriole should build and tell
His love-tale close beside my cell ;
    The idle butterfly
Should rest him there, and there be heard
The housewife bee and humming-bird.

And what if cheerful shouts at noon
    Come, from the village sent,
Or songs of maids, beneath the moon
    With fairy laughter blent ?
And what if, in the evening light,
Betrothèd lovers walk in sight
    Of my low monument ?
I would the lovely scene around
Might know no sadder sight nor sound.

I know that I no more should see
    The season's glorious show,
Nor would its brightness shine for me,
    Nor its wild music flow ;
But if, around my place of sleep,
The friends I love should come to weep
    They might not haste to go.
Soft airs, and song, and light, and bloom
Should keep them lingering by my tomb.

These to their softened hearts should bear
    The thought of what has been,
And speak of one who cannot share
    The gladness of the scene ;
Whose part, in all the pomp that fills
The circuit of the summer hills,
    Is that his grave is green ;
And deeply would their hearts rejoice
To hear again his living voice.

A SONG OF PITCAIRN'S ISLAND.

COME, take our boy, and we will go
    Before our cabin-door ;
The winds shall bring us, as they blow,
    The murmurs of the shore ;
And we will kiss his young blue eyes
And I will sing him, as he lies,
    Songs that were made of yore :
I'll sing, in his delighted ear,
The island lays thou lov'st to hear.

And thou, while stammering I repeat,
    Thy country's tongue shalt teach ;
'Tis not so soft, but far more sweet
    Than my own native speech :
For thou no other tongue didst know,
When, scarcely twenty moons ago,
    Upon Tahete's beach,
Thou cam'st to woo me to be thine,
With many a speaking look and sign.

I knew thy meaning—thou didst praise
    My eyes, my locks of jet ;
Ah ! well for me they won thy gaze,
    But thine were fairer yet !

I'm glad to see my infant wear
Thy soft blue eyes and sunny hair,
   And when my sight is met
By his white brow and blooming cheek,
I feel a joy I cannot speak.

Come, talk of Europe's maids with me,
   Whose necks and cheeks, they tell,
Outshine the beauty of the sea,
   White foam and crimson shell.
I'll shape like theirs my simple dress,
And bind like them each jetty tress,
   A sight to please thee well ;
And for my dusky brow will braid
A bonnet like an English maid.

Come, for the soft low sunlight calls,
   We lose the pleasant hours ;
'Tis lovelier than these cottage walls,—
   That seat among the flowers.
And I will learn of thee a prayer,
To Him who gave a home so fair,
   A lot so blest as ours—
The God who made, for thee and me,
This sweet lone isle amid the sea.

THE FIRMAMENT.

Ay ! gloriously thou standest there,
   Beautiful, boundless firmament !
That, swelling wide o'er earth and air,
   And round the horizon bent,
With thy bright vault, and sapphire wall,
Dost overhang and circle all.

Far, far below thee, tall gray trees
   Arise, and piles built up of old,
And hills, whose ancient summits freeze
   In the fierce light and cold.
The eagle soars his utmost height,
Yet far thou stretchest o'er his flight.

Thou hast thy frowns—with thee on high
   The storm has made his airy seat,
Beyond that soft blue curtain lie
   His stores of hail and sleet.
Thence the consuming lightnings break,
There the strong hurricanes awake.

Yet art thou prodigal of smiles—
   Smiles, sweeter than thy frowns are stern.
Earth sends, from all her thousand isles,
   A shout at their return.
The glory that comes down from thee,
Bathes, in deep joy, the land and sea.

The sun, the gorgeous sun is thine,
   The pomp that brings and shuts the day,
The clouds that round him change and shine,
   The airs that fan his way.
Thence look the thoughtful stars, and there
The meek moon walks the silent air.

The sunny Italy may boast
   The beauteous tints that flush her skies,
And lovely, round the Grecian coast,
   May thy blue pillars rise.
I only know how fair they stand
Around my own beloved land.

And they are fair—a charm is theirs,
   That earth, the proud green earth, has not,
With all the forms, and hues, and airs,
   That haunt her sweetest spot.

We gaze upon thy calm pure sphere,
And read of Heaven's eternal year.

Oh, when, amid the throng of men,
    The heart grows sick of hollow mirth,
How willingly we turn us then
    Away from this cold earth,
And look into thy azure breast,
For seats of innocence and rest!

"I CANNOT FORGET WITH WHAT FERVID DEVOTION."

I CANNOT forget with what fervid devotion
    I worshipped the visions of verse and of fame;
Each gaze at the glories of earth, sky, and ocean,
    To my kindled emotions, was wind over flame.

And deep were my musings in life's early blossom,
    Mid the twilight of mountain-groves wandering long;
How thrilled my young veins, and how throbbed my full bosom,
    When o'er me descended the spirit of song!

'Mong the deep-cloven fells that for ages had listened
    To the rush of the pebble-paved river between,
Where the kingfisher screamed and gray precipice glistened,
    All breathless with awe have I gazed on the scene;

Till I felt the dark power o'er my reveries stealing,
    From the gloom of the thicket that over me hung,
And the thoughts that awoke, in that rapture of feeling,
    Were formed into verse as they rose to my tongue.

Bright visions! I mixed with the world, and ye faded,
    No longer your pure rural worshipper now;
In the haunts your continual presence pervaded,
    Ye shrink from the signet of care on my brow.

In the old mossy groves on the breast of the mountains,
  In deep lonely glens where the waters complain,
By the shade of the rock, by the gush of the fountain,
  I seek your loved footsteps, but seek them in vain.

Oh, leave not forlorn and forever forsaken,
  Your pupil and victim to life and its tears!
But sometimes return, and in mercy awaken
  The glories ye showed to his earlier years.

TO A MOSQUITO.

Fair insect! that, with threadlike legs spread out,
  And blood-extracting bill and filmy wing,
Dost murmur, as thou slowly sail'st about,
  In pitiless ears full many a plaintive thing,
And tell how little our large veins would bleed,
Would we but yield them to thy bitter need.

Unwillingly, I own, and, what is worse,
  Full angrily men hearken to thy plaint;
Thou gettest many a brush, and many a curse,
  For saying thou art gaunt, and starved, and faint;
Even the old beggar, while he asks for food,
Would kill thee, hapless stranger, if he could.

I call thee stranger, for the town, I ween,
  Has not the honor of so proud a birth,—
Thou com'st from Jersey meadows, fresh and green,
  The offspring of the gods, though born on earth
For Titan was thy sire, and fair was she,
The ocean-nymph that nursed thy infancy.

Beneath the rushes was thy cradle swung,
  And when at length thy gauzy wings grew strong,
Abroad to gentle airs their folds were flung,
  Rose in the sky and bore thee soft along;
The south wind breathed to waft thee on the way,
And danced and shone beneath the billowy bay.

Calm rose afar the city spires, and thence
   Came the deep murmur of its throng of men,
And as its grateful odors met thy sense,
   They seemed the perfumes of thy native fen.
Fair lay its crowded streets, and at the sight
Thy tiny song grew shriller with delight.

At length thy pinions fluttered in Broadway—
   Ah, there were fairy steps, and white necks kissed
By wanton airs, and eyes whose killing ray
   Shone through the snowy veils like stars through mist ;
And fresh as morn, on many a cheek and chin,
Bloomed the bright blood through the transparent skin.

Sure these were sights to touch an anchorite !
   What ! do I hear thy slender voice complain ?
Thou wailest when I talk of beauty's light,
   As if it brought the memory of pain :
Thou art a wayward being—well—come near,
And pour thy tale of sorrow in my ear.

What sayest thou—slanderer !—rouge makes thee sick ?
   And China bloom at best is sorry food ?
And Rowland's Kalydor, if laid on thick,
   Poisons the thirsty wretch that bores for blood ?
Go ! 'twas a just reward that met thy crime—
But shun the sacrilege another time.

That bloom was made to look at, not to touch ;
   To worship, not approach, that radiant white ;
And well might sudden vengeance light on such
   As dared, like thee, most impiously to bite.
Thou shouldst have gazed at distance and admired,
Murmured thy adoration, and retired.

Thou'rt welcome to the town ; but why come here
   To bleed a brother poet, gaunt like thee ?
Alas ! the little blood I have is dear,
   And thin will be the banquet drawn from me.
Look round—the pale-eyed sisters in my cell,
Thy old acquaintance, Song and Famine, dwell.

Try some plump alderman, and suck the blood
    Enriched by generous wine and costly meat ;
On well-filled skins, sleek as thy native mud,
    Fix thy light pump and press thy freckled feet.
Go to the men for whom, in ocean's halls,
The oyster breeds, and the green turtle sprawls.

There corks are drawn, and the red vintage flows
    To fill the swelling veins for thee, and now
The ruddy cheek and now the ruddier nose
    Shall tempt thee, as thou flittest round the brow ;
And when the hour of sleep its quiet brings,
No angry hands shall rise to brush thy wings.

LINES ON REVISITING THE COUNTRY.

I STAND upon my native hills again,
    Broad, round, and green, that in the summer sky
With garniture of waving grass and grain,
    Orchards, and beechen forests, basking lie,
While deep the sunless glens are scooped between,
Where brawl o'er shallow beds the streams unseen.

A lisping voice and glancing eyes are near,
    And ever-restless feet of one, who, now,
Gathers the blossoms of her fourth bright year ;
    There plays a gladness o'er her fair young brow
As breaks the varied scene upon her sight,
Upheaved and spread in verdure and in light.

For I have taught her, with delighted eye,
    To gaze upon the mountains,—to behold,
With deep affection, the pure ample sky
    And clouds along its blue abysses rolled,
To love the song of waters, and to hear
The melody of winds with charmèd ear.
    15

Here, have I 'scaped the city's stifling heat,
  Its horrid sounds, and its polluted air,
And, where the season's milder fervors beat,
  And gales, that sweep the forest borders, bear
The song of bird and sound of running stream,
Am come awhile to wander and to dream.

Ay, flame thy fiercest, sun ! thou canst not wake,
  In this pure air, the plague that walks unseen.
The maize-leaf and the maple-bough but take,
  From thy strong heats, a deeper, glossier green.
The mountain wind, that faints not in thy ray,
Sweeps the blue steams of pestilence away.

The mountain wind ! most spiritual thing of all
  The wide earth knows ; when, in the sultry time,
He stoops him from his vast cerulean hall,
  He seems the breath of a celestial clime !
As if from heaven's wide-open gates did flow
Health and refreshment on the world below.

THE DEATH OF THE FLOWERS.

THE melancholy days are come, the saddest of the year,
Of wailing winds, and naked woods, and meadows brown and
      sere.
Heaped in the hollows of the grove, the autumn leaves lie dead ;
They rustle to the eddying gust, and to the rabbit's tread ;
The robin and the wren are flown, and from the shrubs the jay,
And from the wood-top calls the crow through all the gloomy
      day.

Where are the flowers, the fair young flowers, that lately sprang
      and stood
In brighter light and softer airs, a beauteous sisterhood ?
Alas ! they all are in their graves, the gentle race of flowers
Are lying in their lowly beds, with the fair and good of ours.
The rain is falling where they lie, but the cold November rain
Calls not from out the gloomy earth the lovely ones again.

The wind-flower and the violet, they perished long ago,
And the brier-rose and the orchis died amid the summer glow ;
But on the hills the golden-rod, and the aster in the wood,
And the yellow sun-flower by the brook in autumn beauty stood,
Till fell the frost from the clear cold heaven, as falls the plague
    on men,
And the brightness of their smile was gone, from upland, glade,
    and glen.

And now, when comes the calm mild day, as still such days will
    come,
To call the squirrel and the bee from out their winter home ;
When the sound of dropping nuts is heard, though all the trees
    are still,
And twinkle in the smoky light the waters of the rill,
The south wind searches for the flowers whose fragrance late he
    bore,
And sighs to find them in the wood and by the stream no more.

And then I think of one who in her youthful beauty died,
The fair meek blossom that grew up and faded by my side.
In the cold moist earth we laid her, when the forests cast the
    leaf,
And we wept that one so lovely should have a life so brief :
Yet not unmeet it was that one, like that young friend of ours,
So gentle and so beautiful, should perish with the flowers.

ROMERO.

WHEN freedom, from the land of Spain,
    By Spain's degenerate sons was driven.
Who gave their willing limbs again
    To wear the chain so lately riven ;
Romero broke the sword he wore—
    " Go, faithful brand," the warrior said,
" Go, undishonored, never more

The blood of man shall make thee red.
I grieve for that already shed ;
And I am sick at heart to know,
That faithful friend and noble foe
Have only bled to make more strong
The yoke that Spain has worn so long.
Wear it who will, in abject fear—
I wear it not who have been free ;
The perjured Ferdinand shall hear
No oath of loyalty from me."
Then, hunted by the hounds of power,
Romero chose a safe retreat,
Where bleak Nevada's summits tower
Above the beauty at their feet.
There once, when on his cabin lay
The crimson light of setting day,
When, even on the mountain's breast,
The chainless winds were all at rest,
And he could hear the river's flow
From the calm paradise below ;
Warmed with his former fires again
He framed this rude but solemn strain :

I.

" Here will I make my home—for here at least I see,
Upon this wild Sierra's side, the steps of Liberty ;
Where the locust chirps unscared beneath the unpruned lime,
And the merry bee doth hide from man the spoil of the moun-
tain-thyme ;
Where the pure winds come and go, and the wild-vine strays at
will,
An outcast from the haunts of men, she dwells with Nature still.

II.

" I see the valleys, Spain ! where thy mighty rivers run,
And the hills that lift thy harvests and vineyards to the sun,

And the flocks that drink thy brooks and sprinkle all the green,
Where lie thy plains, with sheep-walks seamed, and olive-shades
    between :
I see thy fig-trees bask, with the fair pomegranate near,
And the fragrance of thy lemon-groves can almost reach me here.

III.

"Fair—fair—but fallen Spain ! 'tis with a swelling heart,
That I think on all thou mightst have been, and look at what
    thou art ;
But the strife is over now, and all the good and brave,
That would have raised thee up, are gone, to exile or the grave.
Thy fleeces are for monks, thy grapes for the convent feast,
And the wealth of all thy harvest-fields for the pampered lord
    and priest.

IV.

"But I shall see the day—it will come before I die—
I shall see it in my silver hairs, and with an age-dimmed eye ;
When the spirit of the land to liberty shall bound,
As yonder fountain leaps away from the darkness of the ground :
And to my mountain-cell, the voices of the free
Shall rise as from the beaten shore the thunders of the sea."

A MEDITATION ON RHODE ISLAND COAL.

> " Decolor, obscurus, vilis, non ille repexam
>   Cesariem regum, non candida virginis ornat
> Colla, nec insigni splendet per cingula morsu
> Sed nova si nigri videas miracula saxi,
>   Tune superat pulchros cultus et quicquid Eois
> Indus litoribus rubra scrutatur in alga."
>   CLAUDIAN.

I SAT beside the glowing grate, fresh heaped
  With Newport coal, and as the flame grew bright
—The many-colored flame—and played and leaped,
  I thought of rainbows, and the northern light,

Moore's Lalla Rookh, the Treasury Report,
And other brilliant matters of the sort.

And last I thought of that fair isle which sent
 The mineral fuel ; on a summer day
I saw it once, with heat and travel spent,
 And scratched by dwarf-oaks in the hollow way.
Now dragged through sand, now jolted over stone—
A rugged road through rugged Tiverton.

And hotter grew the air, and hollower grew
 The deep-worn path, and horror-struck, I thought,
Where will this dreary passage lead me to ?
 This long dull road, so narrow, deep, and hot ?
I looked to see it dive in earth outright ;
I looked—but saw a far more welcome sight.

Like a soft mist upon the evening shore,
 At once a lovely isle before me lay,
Smooth, and with tender verdure covered o'er,
 As if just risen from its calm inland bay ;
Sloped each way gently to the grassy edge,
And the small waves that dallied with the sedge.

The barley was just reaped ; the heavy sheaves
 Lay on the stubble-field ; the tall maize stood
Dark in its summer growth, and shook its leaves,
 And bright the sunlight played on the young wood—
For fifty years ago, the old men say,
The Briton hewed their ancient groves away.

I saw where fountains freshened the green land,
 And where the pleasant road, from door to door,
With rows of cherry-trees on either hand,
 Went wandering all that fertile region o'er—
Rogue's Island once—but when the rogues were dead,
Rhode Island was the name it took instead.

Beautiful island ! then it only seemed
  A lovely stranger ; it has grown a friend.
I gazed on its smooth slopes, but never dreamed
  How soon that green and quiet isle would send
The treasures of its womb across the sea,
To warm a poet's room and boil his tea.

Dark anthracite ! that reddenest on my hearth,
  Thou in those island mines didst slumber long ;
But now thou art come forth to move the earth,
  And put to shame the men that mean thee wrong
Thou shalt be coals of fire to those that hate thee,
And warm the shins of all that underrate thee.

Yea, they did wrong thee foully—they who mocked
  Thy honest face, and said thou wouldst not burn ;
Of hewing thee to chimney-pieces talked,
  And grew profane, and swore, in bitter scorn,
That men might to thy inner caves retire,
And there, unsinged, abide the day of fire.

Yet is thy greatness nigh.   I pause to state,
  That I too have seen greatness—even I—
Shook hands with Adams, stared at La Fayette,
  When, barehead, in the hot noon of July,
He would not let the umbrella be held o'er him,
For which three cheers burst from the mob before him.

And I have seen—not many months ago—
  An eastern Governor in chapeau bras
And military coat, a glorious show !
  Ride forth to visit the reviews, and ah !
How oft he smiled and bowed to Jonathan !
How many hands were shook and votes were won !

'Twas a great Governor ; thou too shalt be
  Great in thy turn, and wide shall spread thy fame
And swiftly ; furthest Maine shall hear of thee,
  And cold New Brunswick gladden at thy name ;

And, faintly through its sleets, the weeping isle
That sends the Boston folks their cod shall smile.

For thou shalt forge vast railways, and shalt heat
    The hissing rivers into steam, and drive
Huge masses from thy mines, on iron feet,
    Walking their steady way, as if alive,
Northward, till everlasting ice besets thee,
And South as far as the grim Spaniard lets thee.

Thou shalt make mighty engines swim the sea,
    Like its own monsters—boats that for a guinea
Will take a man to Havre—and shalt be
    The moving soul of many a spinning-jenny,
And ply thy shuttles, till a bard can wear
As good a suit of broadcloth as the mayor.

Then we will laugh at winter when we hear
    The grim old churl about our dwellings rave :
Thou, from that "ruler of the inverted year,"
    Shalt pluck the knotty sceptre Cowper gave,
And pull him from his sledge, and drag him in,
And melt the icicles from off his chin.

THE NEW MOON.

When, as the garish day is done,
Heaven burns with the descended sun,
        'Tis passing sweet to mark,
Amid that flush of crimson light,
The new moon's modest bow grow bright,
        As earth and sky grow dark.

Few are the hearts too cold to feel
A thrill of gladness o'er them steal,
        When first the wandering eye
Sees faintly, in the evening blaze,

That glimmering curve of tender rays
   Just planted in the sky.

The sight of that young crescent brings
Thoughts of all fair and youthful things—
   The hopes of early years ;
And childhood's purity and grace,
And joys that like a rainbow chase
   The passing shower of tears.

The captive yields him to the dream
Of freedom, when that virgin beam
   Comes out upon the air ;
And painfully the sick man tries
To fix his dim and burning eyes
   On the sweet promise there.

Most welcome to the lover's sight
Glitters that pure, emerging light ;
   For prattling poets say,
That sweetest is the lovers' walk,
And tenderest is their murmured talk,
   Beneath its gentle ray.

And there do graver men behold
A type of errors, loved of old,
   Forsaken and forgiven ;
And thoughts and wishes not of earth
Just opening in their early birth,
   Like that new light in heaven.

OCTOBER.

Ay. thou art welcome, heaven's delicious breath !
  When woods begin to wear the crimson leaf,
  And suns grow meek, and the meek suns grow brief,
And the year smiles as it draws near its death.

Wind of the sunny south ! oh, still delay
   In the gay woods and in the golden air,
    Like to a good old age released from care,
Journeying, in long serenity, away.
In such a bright, late quiet, would that I
   Might wear out life like thee, mid bowers and brooks.
   And, dearer yet, the sunshine of kind looks,
And music of kind voices ever nigh ;
And when my last sand twinkled in the glass,
Pass silently from men, as thou dost pass.

THE DAMSEL OF PERU.

WHERE olive-leaves were twinkling in every wind that blew,
There sat beneath the pleasant shade a damsel of Peru.
Betwixt the slender boughs, as they opened to the air,
Came glimpses of her ivory neck and of her glossy hair ;
And sweetly rang her silver voice, within that shady nook,
As from the shrubby glen is heard the sound of hidden brook.

'Tis a song of love and valor, in the noble Spanish tongue,
That once upon the sunny plains of old Castile was sung ;
When, from their mountain-holds, on the Moorish rout below,
Had rushed the Christians like a flood, and swept away the foe.
Awhile that melody is still, and then breaks forth anew
A wilder rhyme, a livelier note, of freedom and Peru.

For she has bound the sword to a youthful lover's side,
And sent him to the war the day she should have been his bride,
And bade him bear a faithful heart to battle for the right,
And held the fountains of her eyes till he was out of sight.
Since the parting kiss was given, six weary months are fled,
And yet the foe is in the land, and blood must yet be shed.

A white hand parts the branches, a lovely face looks forth,
And bright dark eyes gaze steadfastly and sadly toward the north.

Thou look'st in vain, sweet maiden, the sharpest sight would fail
To spy a sign of human life abroad in all the vale ;
For the noon is coming on, and the sunbeams fiercely beat,
And the silent hills and forest-tops seem reeling in the heat.

That white hand is withdrawn, that fair sad face is gone,
But the music of that silver voice is flowing sweetly on,
Not as of late, in cheerful tones, but mournfully and low,—
A ballad of a tender maid heart-broken long ago,
Of him who died in battle, the youthful and the brave,
And her who died of sorrow, upon his early grave.

And see, along that mountain-slope, a fiery horseman ride ;
Mark his torn plume, his tarnished belt, the sabre at his side.
His spurs are buried rowel-deep, he rides with loosened rain,
There's blood upon his charger's flank and foam upon the mane.
He speeds him toward the olive-grove, along that shaded hill !
God shield the helpless maiden there, if he should mean her ill !

And suddenly that song has ceased, and suddenly I hear
A shriek sent up amid the shade, a shriek—but not of fear.
For tender accents follow, and tender pauses speak
The overflow of gladness, when words are all too weak ;
" I lay my good sword at thy feet, for now Peru is free,
And I am come to dwell beside the olive-grove with thee.'

THE AFRICAN CHIEF.

CHAINED in the market-place he stood,
   A man of giant frame,
Amid the gathering multitude
   That shrunk to hear his name—
All stern of look and strong of limb,
   His dark eye on the ground :—
And silently they gazed on him,
   As on a lion bound.

Vainly, but well that chief had fought,
  He was a captive now,
Yet pride, that fortune humbles not,
  Was written on his brow.
The scars his dark broad bosom wore
  Showed warrior true and brave ;
A prince among his tribe before,
  He could not be a slave.

Then to his conqueror he spake :
  " My brother is a king ;
Undo this necklace from my neck,
  And take this bracelet ring,
And send me where my brother reigns,
  And I will fill thy hands
With store of ivory from the plains,
  And gold-dust from the sands."

" Not for thy ivory nor thy gold
  Will I unbind thy chain ;
That bloody hand shall never hold
  The battle-spear again.
A price that nation never gave
  Shall yet be paid for thee ;
For thou shalt be the Christian's slave,
  In lands beyond the sea."

Then wept the warrior chief, and bade
  To shred his locks away ;
And one by one, each heavy braid
  Before the victor lay.
Thick were the platted locks, and long,
  And closely hidden there
Shone many a wedge of gold among
  The dark and crispèd hair.

" Look, feast thy greedy eye with gold
  Long kept for sorest need ;
Take it—thou askest sums untold—
  And say that I am freed.

Take it—my wife, the long, long day,
  Weeps by the cocoa-tree,
And my young children leave their play,
  And ask in vain for me."

" I take thy gold, but I have made
  Thy fetters fast and strong,
And ween that by the cocoa-shade
  Thy wife will wait thee long."
Strong was the agony that shook
  The captive's frame to hear,
And the proud meaning of his look
  Was changed to mortal fear.

His heart was broken—crazed his brain :
  At once his eye grew wild ;
He struggled fiercely with his chain,
  Whispered, and wept, and smiled ;
Yet wore not long those fatal bands,
  And once, at shut of day,
They drew him forth upon the sands,
  The foul hyena's prey.

SPRING IN TOWN.

THE country ever has a lagging Spring,
  Waiting for May to call its violets forth,
And June its roses ; showers and sunshine bring,
  Slowly, the deepening verdure o'er the earth ;
To put their foliage out, the woods are slack,
And one by one the singing-birds come back.

Within the city's bounds the time of flowers
  Comes earlier.   Let a mild and sunny day,
Such as full often, for a few bright hours,
  Breathes through the sky of March the airs of May

Shine on our roofs and chase the wintry gloom—
And lo ! our borders glow with sudden bloom.

For the wide sidewalks of Broadway are then
 Gorgeous as are a rivulet's banks in June,
That overhung with blossoms, through its glen,
 Slides soft away beneath the sunny noon,
And they who search the untrodden wood for flowers
Meet in its depths no lovelier ones than ours.

For here are eyes that shame the violet,
 Or the dark drop that on the pansy lies,
And foreheads, white, as when in clusters set,
 The anemones by forest-mountains rise ;
And the spring-beauty boasts no tenderer streak
Than the soft red on many a youthful cheek.

And thick about those lovely temples lie
 Locks that the lucky Vignardonne has curled,
Thrice happy man ! whose trade it is to buy,
 And bake, and braid those love-knots of the world ;
Who curls of every glossy color keepest,
And sellest, it is said, the blackest cheapest.

And well thou mayst—for Italy's brown maids
 Send the dark locks with which their brows are dressed,
And Gascon lasses, from their jetty braids,
 Crop half, to buy a ribbon for the rest ;
But the fresh Norman girls their tresses spare,
And the Dutch damsel keeps her flaxen hair.

Then, henceforth, let no maid nor matron grieve,
 To see her locks of an unlovely hue,
Frouzy or thin, for liberal art shall give
 Such piles of curls as Nature never knew.
Eve, with her veil of tresses, at the sight
Had blushed, outdone, and owned herself a fright.

Soft voices and light laughter wake the street,
 Like notes of woodbirds, and where'er the eye

Threads the long way, plumes wave, and twinkling **feet**
    Fall light, as hastes that crowd of beauty by.
The ostrich, hurrying o'er the desert space,
Scarce bore those tossing plumes with fleeter **pace.**

No swimming Juno gait, of languor born,
    Is theirs, but a light step of freest grace,—
Light as Camilla's o'er the unbent corn,—
    A step that speaks the spirit of the place,
Since Quiet, meek old dame, was driven away
To Sing Sing and the shores of Tappan Bay.

Ye that dash by in chariots ! who will care
    For steeds or footmen now ? ye cannot show
Fair face, and dazzling dress, and graceful air,
    And last edition of the shape ! Ah, no,
These sights are for the earth and open sky,
And your loud wheels unheeded rattle by.

THE GLADNESS OF NATURE.

Is this a time to be cloudy and sad,
    When our mother Nature laughs around ;
When even the deep blue heavens look glad,
    And gladness breathes from the blossoming ground ?

There are notes of joy from the hang-bird and wren,
    And the gossip of swallows through all the sky ;
The ground-squirrel gayly chirps by his den,
    And the wilding bee hums merrily by.

The clouds are at play in the azure space
    And their shadows at play on the bright-green **vale,**
And here they stretch to the frolic chase,
    And there they roll on the easy gale.

There's a dance of leaves in that aspen bower,
  There's a titter of winds in that beechen tree,
There's a smile on the fruit, and a smile on the flower,
  And a laugh from the brook that runs to the sea.

And look at the broad-faced sun, how he smiles
  On the dewy earth that smiles in his ray,
On the leaping waters and gay young isles ;
  Ay, look, and he'll smile thy gloom away.

THE DISINTERRED WARRIOR.

GATHER him to his grave again,
  And solemnly and softly lay,
Beneath the verdure of the plain,
  The warrior's scattered bones away.
Pay the deep reverence, taught of old,
  The homage of man's heart to death ;
Nor dare to trifle with the mould
  Once hallowed by the Almighty's breath.

The soul hath quickened every part—
  That remnant of a martial brow,
Those ribs that held the mighty heart,
  That strong arm—strong no longer now.
Spare them, each mouldering relic spare,
  Of God's own image ; let them rest,
Till not a trace shall speak of where
  The awful likeness was impressed.

For he was fresher from the hand
  That formed of earth the human face,
And to the elements did stand
  In nearer kindred than our race.
In many a flood to madness tossed,
  In many a storm has been his path ;
He hid him not from heat or frost,
  But met them, and defied their wrath.

Then they were kind—the forests here,
  Rivers, and stiller waters, paid
A tribute to the net and spear
  Of the red ruler of the shade.
Fruits on the woodland branches lay,
  Roots in the shaded soil below ;
The stars looked forth to teach his way ;
  The still earth warned him of the foe.

A noble race ! but they are gone,
  With their old forests wide and deep,
And we have built our homes upon
  Fields where their generations sleep.
Their fountains slake our thirst at noon,
  Upon their fields our harvest waves,
Our lovers woo beneath their moon—
  Then let us spare, at least, their graves.

MIDSUMMER.

A POWER is on the earth and in the air
  From which the vital spirit shrinks afraid,
  And shelters him, in nooks of deepest shade,
From the hot steam and from the fiery glare.
Look forth upon the earth—her thousand plants
  Are smitten ; even the dark sun-loving maize
  Faints in the field beneath the torrid blaze ;
The herd beside the shaded fountain pants ;
For life is driven from all the landscape brown ;
  The bird has sought his tree, the snake his den,
  The trout floats dead in the hot stream, and men
Drop by the sun-stroke in the populous town ;
  As if the Day of Fire had dawned, and sent
  Its deadly breath into the firmament.

16

THE GREEK PARTISAN.

OUR free flag is dancing
  In the free mountain air,
And burnished arms are glancing,
  And warriors gathering there ;
And fearless is the little train
  Whose gallant bosoms shield it ;
The blood that warms their hearts shall stain
  That banner, ere they yield it.
—Each dark eye is fixed on earth,
  And brief each solemn greeting ;
There is no look nor sound of mirth,
  Where those stern men are meeting.

They go to the slaughter
  To strike the sudden blow,
And pour on earth, like water,
  The best blood of the foe ;
To rush on them from rock and height,
  And clear the narrow valley,
Or fire their camp at dead of night,
  And fly before they rally.
—Chains are round our country pressed,
  And cowards have betrayed her,
And we must make her bleeding breast
  The grave of the invader.

Not till from her fetters
  We raise up Greece again,
And write, in bloody letters,
  That tyranny is slain,—
Oh, not till then the smile shall steal
  Across those darkened faces,
Nor one of all those warriors feel
  His children's dear embraces.
—Reap we not the ripened wheat,
  Till yonder hosts are flying,
And all their bravest, at our feet,
  Like autumn sheaves are lying.

THE TWO GRAVES.

'Tis a bleak wild hill, but green and bright
In the summer warmth and the mid-day light ;
There's the hum of the bee and the chirp of the wren
And the dash of the brook from the alder-glen.
There's the sound of a bell from the scattered flock,
And the shade of the beech lies cool on the rock,
And fresh from the west is the free wind's breath ;—
There is nothing here that speaks of death.

Far yonder, where orchards and gardens lie,
And dwellings cluster, 'tis there men die,
They are born, they die, and are buried near,
Where the populous graveyard lightens the bier.
For strict and close are the ties that bind
In death the children of human-kind ;
Yea, stricter and closer than those of life,—
'Tis a neighborhood that knows no strife.
They are noiselessly gathered—friend and foe—
To the still and dark assemblies below.
Without a frown or a smile they meet,
Each pale and calm in his winding-sheet ;
In that sullen home of peace and gloom,
Crowded, like guests in a banquet-room.

Yet there are graves in this lonely spot,
Two humble graves,—but I meet them not.
I have seen them,—eighteen years are past
Since I found their place in the brambles last,—
The place where, fifty winters ago
An aged man in his locks of snow,
And an aged matron, withered with years,
Were solemnly laid !—but not with tears.
For none, who sat by the light of their hearth,
Beheld their coffins covered with earth ;
Their kindred were far, and their children dead,
When the funeral-prayer was coldly said.

Two low green hillocks, two small gray stones,
Rose over the place that held their bones ;
But the grassy hillocks are levelled again,
And the keenest eye might search in vain,
'Mong briers, and ferns, and paths of sheep,
For the spot where the aged couple sleep.

Yet well might they lay, beneath the soil
Of this lonely spot, that man of toil,
And trench the strong hard mould with the spade,
Where never before a grave was made ;
For he hewed the dark old woods away,
And gave the virgin fields to the day ;
And the gourd and the bean, beside his door,
Bloomed where their flowers ne'er opened before ;
And the maize stood up, and the bearded rye
Bent low in the breath of an unknown sky.

'Tis said that when life is ended here,
The spirit is borne to a distant sphere ;
That it visits its earthly home no more,
Nor looks on the haunts it loved before.
But why should the bodiless soul be sent
Far off, to a long, long banishment ?
Talk not of the light and the living green !
It will pine for the dear familiar scene ;
It will yearn, in that strange bright world, to behold
The rock and the stream it knew of old.

'Tis a cruel creed, believe it not !
Death to the good is a milder lot.
They are here,—they are here,—that harmless pair,
In the yellow sunshine and flowing air,
In the light cloud-shadows that slowly pass,
In the sounds that rise from the murmuring grass.
They sit where their humble cottage stood,
They walk by the waving edge of the wood,
And list to the long-accustomed flow
Of the brook that wets the rocks below,

Patient, and peaceful, and passionless,
As seasons on seasons swiftly press,
They watch, and wait, and linger around,
Till the day when their bodies shall leave the ground.

THE CONJUNCTION OF JUPITER AND VENUS.

I would not always reason.   The straight path
Wearies us with the never-varying lines,
And we grow melancholy.   I would make
Reason my guide, but she should sometimes sit
Patiently by the way-side, while I traced
The mazes of the pleasant wilderness
Around me.   She should be my counsellor,
But not my tyrant.   For the spirit needs
Impulses from a deeper source than hers,
And there are motions, in the mind of man,
That she must look upon with awe.   I bow
Reverently to her dictates, but not less
Hold to the fair illusions of old time—
Illusions that shed brightness over life,
And glory over Nature.   Look, even now,
Where two bright planets in the twilight meet,
Upon the saffron heaven,—the imperial star
Of Jove, and she that from her radiant urn
Pours forth the light of love.   Let me believe,
Awhile, that they are met for ends of good,
Amid the evening glory, to confer
Of men and their affairs, and to shed down
Kind influence.   Lo ! they brighten as we gaze,
And shake out softer fires ! The great earth feels
The gladness and the quiet of the time.
Meekly the mighty river, that infolds
This mighty city, smooths his front, and far
Glitters and burns even the rocky base
Of the dark heights that bound him to the west ;

And a deep murmur, from the many streets,
Rises like a thanksgiving. Put we hence
Dark and sad thoughts awhile—there's time for them
Hereafter—on the morrow we will meet,
With melancholy looks, to tell our griefs,
And make each other wretched ; this calm hour,
This balmy, blessed evening, we will give
To cheerful hopes and dreams of happy days,
Born of the meeting of those glorious stars.

   Enough of drought has parched the year, and scared
The land with dread of famine. Autumn, yet,
Shall make men glad with unexpected fruits.
The dog-star shall shine harmless : genial days
Shall softly glide away into the keen
And wholesome cold of winter ; he that fears
The pestilence, shall gaze on those pure beams,
And breathe, with confidence, the quiet air.

   Emblems of power and beauty ! well may they
Shine brightest on our borders, and withdraw
Toward the great Pacific, marking out
The path of empire. Thus in our own land,
Ere long, the better Genius of our race,
Having encompassed earth, and tamed its tribes,
Shall sit him down beneath the farthest west,
By the shore of that calm ocean, and look back
On realms made happy.

              Light the nuptial torch,
And say the glad, yet solemn rite, that knits
The youth and maiden. Happy days to them
That wed this evening !—a long life of love,
And blooming sons and daughters ! Happy they
Born at this hour, for they shall see an age
Whiter and holier than the past, and go
Late to their graves. Men shall wear softer hearts,
And shudder at the butcheries of war,
As now at other murders.

Hapless Greece !
Enough of blood has wet thy rocks, and stained
Thy rivers ; deep enough thy chains have worn
Their links into thy flesh ; the sacrifice
Of thy pure maidens, and thy innocent babes,
And reverend priests, has expiated all
Thy crimes of old.   In yonder mingling lights
There is an omen of good days for thee.
Thou shalt arise from midst the dust and sit
Again among the nations.   Thine own arm
Shall yet redeem thee.   Not in wars like thine
The world takes part.   Be it a strife of kings,—
Despot with despot battling for a throne,—
And Europe shall be stirred throughout her realms,
Nations shall put on harness, and shall fall
Upon each other, and in all their bounds
The wailing of the childless shall not cease.
Thine is a war for liberty, and thou
Must fight it single-handed.   The old world
Looks coldly on the murderers of thy race,
And leaves thee to the struggle ; and the new,—
I fear me thou couldst tell a shameful tale
Of fraud and lust of gain ;—thy treasury drained,
And Missolonghi fallen.   Yet thy wrongs
Shall put new strength into thy heart and hand,
And God and thy good sword shall yet work out,
For thee, a terrible deliverance.

A SUMMER RAMBLE.

THE quiet August noon has come ;
    A slumberous silence fills the sky,
The fields are still, the woods are dumb
    In glassy sleep the waters lie.

And mark yon soft white clouds that rest
    Above our vale, a moveless throng ;
The cattle on the mountain's breast
    Enjoy the grateful shadow long.

Oh, how unlike those merry hours,
  In early June, when Earth laughs out,
When the fresh winds make love to flowers,
  And woodlands sing and waters shout.

When in the grass sweet voices talk,
  And strains of tiny music swell
From every moss-cup of the rock,
  From every nameless blossom's bell.

But now a joy too deep for sound,
  A peace no other season knows,
Hushes the heavens and wraps the ground,
  The blessing of supreme repose.

Away ! I will not be, to-day,
  The only slave of toil and care,
Away from desk and dust ! away !
  I'll be as idle as the air.

Beneath the open sky abroad,
  Among the plants and breathing things,
The sinless, peaceful works of God,
  I'll share the calm the season brings.

Come, thou, in whose soft eyes I see
  The gentle meanings of thy heart,
One day amid the woods with me,
  From men and all their cares apart.

And where, upon the meadow's breast,
  The shadow of the thicket lies,
The blue wild-flowers thou gatherest
  Shall glow yet deeper near thine eyes.

Come, and when mid the calm profound,
  I turn, those gentle eyes to seek,
They, like the lovely landscape round,
  Of innocence and peace shall speak.

Rest here, beneath the unmoving shade,
  And on the silent valleys gaze,
Winding and widening, till they fade
  In yon soft ring of summer haze.

The village trees their summits rear
  Still as its spire, and yonder flock
At rest in those calm fields appear
  As chiselled from the lifeless rock.

One tranquil mount the scene o'erlooks—
  There the hushed winds their sabbath keep,
While a near hum from bees and brooks
  Comes faintly like the breath of sleep.

Well may the gazer deem that when,
  Worn with the struggle and the strife,
And heart-sick at the wrongs of men,
  The good forsakes the scene of life ;

Like this deep quiet that, awhile,
  Lingers the lovely landscape o'er,
Shall be the peace whose holy smile
  Welcomes him to a happier shore.

A SCENE ON THE BANKS OF THE HUDSON.

Cool shades and dews are round my way,
And silence of the early day ;
Mid the dark rocks that watch his bed,
Glitters the mighty Hudson spread,
Unrippled, save by drops that fall
From shrubs that fringe his mountain wall ;
And o'er the clear still water swells
The music of the Sabbath bells.

All, save this little nook of land,
Circled with trees, on which I stand ;
All, save that line of hills which lie
Suspended in the mimic sky—
Seems a blue void, above, below,
Through which the white clouds come and go ;
And from the green world's farthest steep
I gaze into the airy deep.

Loveliest of lovely things are they,
On earth, that soonest pass away.
The rose that lives its little hour
Is prized beyond the sculptured flower.
Even love, long tried and cherished long,
Becomes more tender and more strong
At thought of that insatiate grave
From which its yearnings cannot save.

River ! in this still hour thou hast
Too much of heaven on earth to last ;
Nor long may thy still waters lie,
An image of the glorious sky.
Thy fate and mine are not repose,
And ere another evening close,
Thou to thy tides shalt turn again,
And I to seek the crowd of men.

THE HURRICANE.

Lord of the winds ! I feel thee nigh,
I know thy breath in the burning sky !
And I wait, with a thrill in every vein,
For the coming of the hurricane !

And lo ! on the wing of the heavy gales,
Through the boundless arch of heaven he sails ;
Silent and slow, and terribly strong,
The mighty shadow is borne along,

"Heavily poured on the shuddering ground.

Like the dark eternity to come ;
While the world below, dismayed and dumb,
Through the calm of the thick hot atmosphere,
Looks up at its gloomy folds with fear.

They darken fast ; and the golden blaze
Of the sun is quenched in the lurid haze,
And he sends through the shade a funeral ray—
A glare that is neither night nor day,
A beam that touches, with hues of death,
The clouds above and the earth beneath.
To its covert glides the silent bird,
While the hurricane's distant voice is heard
Uplifted among the mountains round,
And the forests hear and answer the sound.

He is come ! he is come ! do ye not behold
His ample robes on the wind unrolled ?
Giant of air ! we bid thee hail !—
How his gray skirts toss in the whirling gale ;
How his huge and writhing arms are bent
To clasp the zone of the firmament,
And fold at length, in their dark embrace,
From mountain to mountain the visible space.

Darker—still darker ! the whirlwinds bear
The dust of the plains to the middle air :
And hark to the crashing, long and loud,
Of the chariot of God in the thunder-cloud !
You may trace its path by the flashes that start
From the rapid wheels where'er they dart,
As the fire-bolts leap to the world below,
And flood the skies with a lurid glow.

What roar is that?—'tis the rain that breaks
In torrents away from the airy lakes,
Heavily poured on the shuddering ground,
And shedding a nameless horror round.
Ah ! well-known woods, and mountains, and skies
With the very clouds !—ye are lost to my eyes.

I seek ye vainly, and see in your place
The shadowy tempest that sweeps through space,
A whirling ocean that fills the wall
Of the crystal heaven, and buries all.
And I, cut off from the world, remain
Alone with the terrible hurricane.

WILLIAM TELL.

CHAINS may subdue the feeble spirit, but thee,
   TELL, of the iron heart ! they could not tame !
   For thou wert of the mountains ; they proclaim
The everlasting creed of liberty.
That creed is written on the untrampled snow,
   Thundered by torrents which no power can hold,
   Save that of God, when He sends forth His cold,
And breathed by winds that through the free heaven blow
Thou, while thy prison-walls were dark around,
   Didst meditate the lesson Nature taught,
   And to thy brief captivity was brought
A vision of thy Switzerland unbound.
   The bitter cup they mingled, strengthened thee
   For the great work to set thy country free.

THE HUNTER'S SERENADE.

THY bower is finished, fairest !
   Fit bower for hunter's bride,
Where old woods overshadow
   The green savanna's side.
I've wandered long, and wandered far,
   And never have I met,

In all this lovely Western land,
  A spot so lovely yet.
But I shall think it fairer
  When thou art come to bless,
With thy sweet smile and silver voice,
  Its silent loveliness.

For thee the wild-grape glistens
  On sunny knoll and tree,
The slim papaya ripens
  Its yellow fruit for thee.
For thee the duck, on glassy stream,
  The prairie-fowl shall die ;
My rifle for thy feast shall bring
  The wild-swan from the sky.
The forest's leaping panther,
  Fierce, beautiful, and fleet,
Shall yield his spotted hide to be
  A carpet for thy feet.

I know, for thou hast told me,
  Thy maiden love of flowers ;
Ah, those that deck thy gardens
  Are pale compared with ours.
When our wide woods and mighty lawns
  Bloom to the April skies,
The earth has no more gorgeous sight
  To show to human eyes.
In meadows red with blossoms,
  All summer long, the bee
Murmurs, and loads his yellow thighs,
  For thee, my love, and me.

Or wouldst thou gaze at tokens
  Of ages long ago—
Our old oaks stream with mosses,
  And sprout with mistletoe ;
And mighty vines, like serpents, climb
  The giant sycamore ;

And trunks, o'erthrown for centuries,
　　Cumber the forest floor ;
And in the great savanna,
　　The solitary mound,
Built by the elder world, o'erlooks
　　The loneliness around.

Come, thou hast not forgotten
　　Thy pledge and promise quite,
With many blushes murmured,
　　Beneath the evening light.
Come, the young violets crowd my door,
　　Thy earliest look to win,
And at my silent window-sill
　　The jessamine peeps in.
All day the red-bird warbles
　　Upon the mulberry near,
And the night-sparrow trills her song
　　All night, with none to hear.

THE GREEK BOY.

Gone are the glorious Greeks of old,
　　Glorious in mien and mind ;
Their bones are mingled with the mould,
　　Their dust is on the wind ;
The forms they hewed from living stone
Survive the waste of years, alone,
And, scattered with their ashes, show
What greatness perished long ago.

Yet fresh the myrtles there ; the springs
　　Gush brightly as of yore ;
Flowers blossom from the dust of kings,
　　As many an age before.
There Nature moulds as nobly now,
As e'er of old, the human brow ;

And copies still the martial form
That braved Plataea's battle-storm.

Boy ! thy first looks were taught to seek
    Their heaven in Hellas' skies ;
Her airs have tinged thy dusky cheek,
    Her sunshine lit thine eyes ;
Thine ears have drunk the woodland strains
Heard by old poets, and thy veins
Swell with the blood of demigods,
That slumber in thy country's sods.

Now is thy nation free, though late ;
    Thy elder brethren broke—
Broke, ere thy spirit felt its weight—
    The intolerable yoke.
And Greece, decayed, dethroned, doth see
Her youth renewed in such as thee :
A shoot of that old vine that made
The nations silent in its shade.

THE PAST.

    Thou unrelenting Past !
Strong are the barriers round thy dark domain,
    And fetters, sure and fast,
Hold all that enter thy unbreathing reign.

    Far in thy realm withdrawn,
Old empires sit in sullenness and gloom,
    And glorious ages gone
Lie deep within the shadow of thy womb.

    Childhood, with all its mirth,
Youth, Manhood, Age that draws us to the ground,
    And last, Man's Life on earth,
Glide to thy dim dominions, and are bound.

Thou hast my better years ;
Thou hast my earlier friends, the good, the kind,
Yielded to thee with tears—
The venerable form, the exalted mind.

My spirit yearns to bring
The lost ones back—yearns with desire intense,
And struggles hard to wring
Thy bolts apart, and pluck thy captives thence.

In vain ; thy gates deny
All passage save to those who hence depart ;
Nor to the streaming eye
Thou giv'st them back—nor to the broken heart.

In thy abysses hide
Beauty and excellence unknown ; to thee
Earth's wonder and her pride
Are gathered, as the waters to the sea ;

Labors of good to man,
Unpublished charity, unbroken faith,
Love, that midst grief began,
And grew with years, and faltered not in death.

Full many a mighty name
Lurks in thy depths, unuttered, unrevered ;
With thee are silent fame,
Forgotten arts, and wisdom disappeared.

Thine for a space are they—
Yet shalt thou yield thy treasures up at last
Thy gates shall yet give way,
Thy bolts shall fall, inexorable Past !

All that of good and fair
Has gone into thy womb from earliest time,
Shall then come forth to wear
The glory and the beauty of its prime.

They have not perished—no !
Kind words, remembered voices once so sweet,
  Smiles, radiant long ago,
And features, the great soul's apparent seat.

All shall come back ; each tie
Of pure affection shall be knit again ;
  Alone shall Evil die,
And Sorrow dwell a prisoner in thy reign.

And then shall I behold
Him, by whose kind paternal side I sprung,
  And her, who, still and cold,
Fills the next grave—the beautiful and young.

"UPON THE MOUNTAIN'S DISTANT HEAD."

Upon the mountain's distant head,
  With trackless snows forever white,
Where all is still, and cold, and dead,
  Late shines the day's departing light.

But far below those icy rocks,
  The vales, in summer bloom arrayed,
Woods full of birds, and fields of flocks,
  Are dim with mist and dark with shade.

'Tis thus, from warm and kindly hearts,
  And eyes where generous meanings burn,
Earliest the light of life departs,
  But lingers with the cold and stern.

THE EVENING WIND.

Spirit that breathest through my lattice, thou
    That cool'st the twilight of the sultry day,
Gratefully flows thy freshness round my brow ;
    Thou hast been out upon the deep at play,
Riding all day the wild blue waves till now,
    Roughening their crests, and scattering high their spray,
And swelling the white sail.   I welcome thee
To the scorched land, thou wanderer of the sea !

Nor I alone ; a thousand bosoms round
    Inhale thee in the fulness of delight ;
And languid forms rise up, and pulses bound
    Livelier, at coming of the wind of night ;
And, languishing to hear thy grateful sound,
    Lies the vast inland stretched beyond the sight.
Go forth into the gathering shade ; go forth,
God's blessing breathed upon the fainting earth !

Go, rock the little wood-bird in his nest,
    Curl the still waters, bright with stars, and rouse
The wide old wood from his majestic rest,
    Summoning from the innumerable boughs
The strange, deep harmonies that haunt his breast :
    Pleasant shall be thy way where meekly bows
The shutting flower, and darkling waters pass,
And where the o'ershadowing branches sweep the grass.

The faint old man shall lean his silver head
    To feel thee ; thou shalt kiss the child asleep,
And dry the moistened curls that overspread
    His temples, while his breathing grows more deep ;
And they who stand about the sick man's bed,
    Shall joy to listen to thy distant sweep,
And softly part his curtains to allow
Thy visit, grateful to his burning brow.

Go—but the circle of eternal change,
   Which is the life of Nature, shall restore,
With sounds and scents from all thy mighty range,
   Thee to thy birthplace of the deep once more ;
Sweet odors in the sea-air sweet and strange,
   Shall tell the home-sick mariner of the shore ;
And, listening to thy murmur, he shall deem
He hears the rustling leaf and running stream.

"WHEN THE FIRMAMENT QUIVERS WITH DAYLIGHT'S YOUNG BEAM."

When the firmament quivers with daylight's young beam,
   And the woodlands awaking burst into a hymn,
And the glow of the sky blazes back from the stream,
   How the bright ones of heaven in the brightness grow dim !

Oh ! 'tis sad, in that moment of glory and song,
   To see, while the hill-tops are waiting the sun,
The glittering band that kept watch all night long
   O'er Love and o'er Slumber, go out one by one :

Till the circle of ether, deep, ruddy, and vast,
   Scarce glimmers with one of the train that were there ;
And their leader, the day-star, the brightest and last,
   Twinkles faintly and fades in that desert of air.

Thus, Oblivion, from midst of whose shadow we came,
   Steals o'er us again when life's twilight is gone ;
And the crowd of bright names, in the heaven of fame,
   Grow pale and are quenched as the years hasten on.

Let them fade—but we'll pray that the age, in whose flight,
   Of ourselves and our friends the remembrance shall die,
May rise o'er the world, with the gladness and light
   Of the morning that withers the stars from the sky.

"INNOCENT CHILD AND SNOW–WHITE FLOWER."

INNOCENT child and snow-white flower !
Well are ye paired in your opening hour.
Thus should the pure and the lovely meet,
Stainless with stainless, and sweet with sweet.

White as those leaves, just blown apart,
Are the folds of thy own young heart;
Guilty passion and cankering care
Never have left their traces there.

Artless one ! though thou gazest now
O'er the white blossom with earnest brow,
Soon will it tire thy childish eye ;
Fair as it is, thou wilt throw it by.

Throw it aside in thy weary hour,
Throw to the ground the fair white flower ;
Yet, as thy tender years depart,
Keep that white and innocent heart.

TO THE RIVER ARVE.

SUPPOSED TO BE WRITTEN AT A HAMLET NEAR THE FOOT OF MONT BLANC.

NOT from the sands or cloven rocks,
 Thou rapid Arve ! thy waters flow ;
Nor earth, within her bosom, locks
 Thy dark unfathomed wells below.
Thy springs are in the cloud, thy stream
 Begins to move and murmur first
Where ice-peaks feel the noonday beam,
 Or rain-storms on the glacier burst.

Born where the thunder and the blast
 And morning's earliest light are born,
Thou rushest swoln, and loud, and fast,
 By these low homes, as if in scorn :
Yet humbler springs yield purer waves ;
 And brighter, glassier streams than thine,
Sent up from earth's unlighted caves,
 With heaven's own beam and image shine.

Yet stay ; for here are flowers and trees ;
 Warm rays on cottage-roofs are here ;
And laugh of girls, and hum of bees,
 Here linger till thy waves are clear.
Thou heedest not—thou hastest on ;
 From steep to steep thy torrent falls ;
Till, mingling with the mighty Rhone,
 It rests beneath Geneva's walls.

Rush on—but were there one with me
 That loved me, I would light my hearth
Here, where with God's own majesty
 Are touched the features of the earth.
By these old peaks, white, high, and vast,
 Still rising as the tempests beat,
Here would I dwell, and sleep, at last,
 Among the blossoms at their feet.

———

TO COLE, THE PAINTER, DEPARTING FOR EUROPE.

THINE eyes shall see the light of distant skies ;
 Yet, COLE ! thy heart shall bear to Europe's strand
 A living image of our own bright land,
Such as upon thy glorious canvas lies ;
Lone lakes—savannas where the bison roves—
 Rocks rich with summer garlands—solemn streams—
 Skies, where the desert eagle wheels and screams—

Spring bloom and autumn blaze of boundless groves.
Fair scenes shall greet thee where thou goest—fair,
 But different—everywhere the trace of men,
 Paths, homes, graves, ruins, from the lowest glen
To where life shrinks from the fierce Alpine air.
 Gaze on them, till the tears shall dim thy sight,
 But keep that earlier, wilder image bright.

TO THE FRINGED GENTIAN.

Thou blossom bright with autumn dew,
And colored with the heaven's own blue,
That openest when the quiet light
Succeeds the keen and frosty night.

Thou comest not when violets lean
O'er wandering brooks and springs unseen,
Or columbines, in purple dressed,
Nod o'er the ground-bird's hidden nest.

Thou waitest late and com'st alone,
When woods are bare and birds are flown,
And frosts and shortening days portend
The aged year is near his end.

Then doth thy sweet and quiet eye
Look through its fringes to the sky,
Blue—blue—as if that sky let fall
A flower from its cerulean wall.

I would that thus, when I shall see
The hour of death draw near to me,
Hope, blossoming within my heart,
May look to heaven as I depart.

THE TWENTY-SECOND OF DECEMBER.

Wild was the day ; the wintry sea
　Moaned sadly on New-England's strand,
When first the thoughtful and the free,
　Our fathers, trod the desert land.

They little thought how pure a light,
　With years, should gather round that day ;
How love should keep their memories bright,
　How wide a realm their sons should sway.

Green are their bays ; but greener still
　Shall round their spreading fame be wreathed,
And regions, now untrod, shall thrill
　With reverence when their names are breathed.

Till where the sun, with softer fires,
　Looks on the vast Pacific's sleep,
The children of the pilgrim sires
　This hallowed day like us shall keep.

HYMN OF THE CITY.

　Not in the solitude
Alone may man commune with Heaven, or see,
　Only in savage wood
And sunny vale, the present Deity ;
　Or only hear his voice
Where the winds whisper and the waves rejoice.

　Even here do I behold
Thy steps, Almighty !—here, amidst the crowd
　Through the great city rolled,
With everlasting murmur deep and loud—
　Choking the ways that wind
'Mongst the proud piles, the work of human kind.

Thy golden sunshine comes
From the round heaven, and on their dwellings lies
   And lights their inner homes ;
For them thou fill'st with air the unbounded skies,
   And givest them the stores
Of ocean, and the harvests of its shores.

   Thy Spirit is around,
Quickening the restless mass that sweeps along ;
   And this eternal sound—
Voices and footfalls of the numberless throng—
   Like the resounding sea,
Or like the rainy tempest, speaks of Thee.

   And when the hour of rest
Comes, like a calm upon the mid-sea brine,
   Hushing its billowy breast—
The quiet of that moment too is thine ;
   It breathes of Him who keeps
The vast and helpless city while it sleeps.

THE PRAIRIES.

THESE are the gardens of the Desert, these
The unshorn fields, boundless and beautiful,
For which the speech of England has no name—
The Prairies. I behold them for the first,
And my heart swells, while the dilated sight
Takes in the encircling vastness. Lo ! they stretch,
In airy undulations, far away,
As if the ocean, in his gentlest swell,
Stood still, with all his rounded billows fixed,
And motionless forever.—Motionless ?—
No—they are all unchained again. The clouds
Sweep over with their shadows, and, beneath,
The surface rolls and fluctuates to the eye ;

Dark hollows seem to glide along and chase
The sunny ridges.   Breezes of the South !
Who toss the golden and the flame-like flowers,
And pass the prairie-hawk that, poised on high,
Flaps his broad wings, yet moves not—ye have played
Among the palms of Mexico and vines
Of Texas, and have crisped the limpid brooks
That from the fountains of Sonora glide
Into the calm Pacific—have ye fanned
A nobler or a lovelier scene than this ?
Man hath no power in all this glorious work :
The hand that built the firmament hath heaved
And smoothed these verdant swells, and sown their slopes
With herbage, planted them with island groves,
And hedged them round with forests.   Fitting floor
For this magnificent temple of the sky—
Witn flowers whose glory and whose multitude
Rival the constellations !   The great heavens
Seem to stoop down upon the scene in love,—
A nearer vault, and of a tenderer blue,
Than that which bends above our eastern hills.

   As o'er the verdant waste I guide my steed,
Among the high rank grass that sweeps his sides
The hollow beating of his footstep seems
A sacrilegious sound.   I think of those
Upon whose rest he tramples.   Are they here—
The dead of other days ?—and did the dust
Of these fair solitudes once stir with life
And burn with passion ?   Let the mighty mounds
That overlook the rivers, or that rise
In the dim forest crowded with old oaks,
Answer.   A race, that long has passed away,
Built them ;—a disciplined and populous race
Heaped, with long toil, the earth, while yet the Greek
Was hewing the Pentelicus to forms
Of symmetry, and rearing on its rock
The glittering Parthenon.   These ample fields
Nourished their harvests, here their herds were fed,

When haply by their stalls the bison lowed,
And bowed his manèd shoulder to the yoke.
All day this desert murmured with their toils,
Till twilight blushed, and lovers walked, and wooed
In a forgotten language, and old tunes,
From instruments of unremembered form,
Gave the soft winds a voice.   The red man came—
The roaming hunter tribes, warlike and fierce,
And the mound-builders vanished from the earth.
The solitude of centuries untold
Has settled where they dwelt.   The prairie-wolf
Hunts in their meadows, and his fresh-dug den
Yawns by my path.   The gopher mines the ground
Where stood their swarming cities.   All is gone ;
All--save the piles of earth that hold their bones,
The platforms where they worshipped unknown gods,
The barriers which they builded from the soil
To keep the foe at bay—till o'er the walls
The wild beleaguerers broke, and, one by one,
The strongholds of the plain were forced, and heaped
With corpses.   The brown vultures of the wood
Flocked to those vast uncovered sepulchres,
And sat unscared and silent at their feast.
Haply some solitary fugitive,
Lurking in marsh and forest, till the sense
Of desolation and of fear became
Bitterer than death, yielded himself to die.
Man's better nature triumphed then.   Kind words
Welcomed and soothed him ; the rude conquerors
Seated the captive with their chiefs ; he chose
A bride among their maidens, and at length
Seemed to forget—yet ne'er forgot—the wife
Of his first love, and her sweet little ones,
Butchered, amid their shrieks, with all his race.

    Thus change the forms of being.   Thus arise
Races of living things, glorious in strength,
And perish, as the quickening breath of God
Fills them, or is withdrawn.   The red man, too,

Has left the blooming wilds he ranged so long,
And, nearer to the Rocky Mountains, sought
A wilder hunting-ground. The beaver builds
No longer by these streams, but far away,
On waters whose blue surface ne'er gave back
The white man's face—among Missouri's springs,
And pools whose issues swell the Oregon—
He rears his little Venice. In these plains
The bison feeds no more. Twice twenty leagues
Beyond remotest smoke of hunter's camp,
Roams the majestic brute, in herds that shake
The earth with thundering steps—yet here I meet
His ancient footprints stamped beside the pool.

   Still this great solitude is quick with life.
Myriads of insects, gaudy as the flowers
They flutter over, gentle quadrupeds,
And birds, that scarce have learned the fear of man,
Are here, and sliding reptiles of the ground,
Startlingly beautiful. The graceful deer
Bounds to the wood at my approach. The bee,
A more adventurous colonist than man,
With whom he came across the eastern deep,
Fills the savannas with his murmurings,
And hides his sweets, as in the golden age,
Within the hollow oak. I listen long
To his domestic hum, and think I hear
The sound of that advancing multitude
Which soon shall fill these deserts. From the ground
Comes up the laugh of children, the soft voice
Of maidens, and the sweet and solemn hymn
Of Sabbath worshippers. The low of herds
Blends with the rustling of the heavy grain
Over the dark brown furrows. All at once
A fresher wind sweeps by, and breaks my dream,
And I am in the wilderness alone.

SONG OF MARION'S MEN.

Our band is few but true and tried,
  Our leader frank and bold ;
The British soldier trembles
  When Marion's name is told.
Our fortress is the good greenwood,
  Our tent the cypress-tree ;
We know the forest round us,
  As seamen know the sea.
We know its walls of thorny vines,
  Its glades of reedy grass,
Its safe and silent islands
  Within the dark morass.

Woe to the English soldiery
  That little dread us near !
On them shall light at midnight
  A strange and sudden fear :
When, waking to their tents on fire,
  They grasp their arms in vain,
And they who stand to face us
  Are beat to earth again ;
And they who fly in terror deem
  A mighty host behind,
And hear the tramp of thousands
  Upon the hollow wind.

Then sweet the hour that brings release
  From danger and from toil :
We talk the battle over,
  And share the battle's spoil.
The woodland rings with laugh and shout,
  As if a hunt were up,
And woodland flowers are gathered
  To crown the soldier's cup.
With merry songs we mock the wind
  That in the pine-top grieves,
And slumber long and sweetly
  On beds of oaken leaves.

Well knows the fair and friendly moon
  The band that Marion leads—
The glitter of their rifles,
  The scampering of their steeds.
'Tis life to guide the fiery barb
  Across the moonlight plain ;
'Tis life to feel the night-wind
  That lifts the tossing mane.
A moment in the British camp—
  A moment—and away
Back to the pathless forest,
  Before the peep of day.

Grave men there are by broad Santee,
  Grave men with hoary hairs ;
Their hearts are all with Marion,
  For Marion are their prayers.
And lovely ladies greet our band
  With kindliest welcoming,
With smiles like those of summer,
  And tears like those of spring.
For them we wear these trusty arms,
  And lay them down no more
Till we have driven the Briton,
  Forever, from our shore.

———

THE ARCTIC LOVER.

Gone is the long, long winter night ;
  Look, my belovèd one !
How glorious, through his depths of light,
  Rolls the majestic sun !
The willows, waked from winter's death,
Give out a fragrance like thy breath—
  The summer is begun !

Ay, 'tis the long bright summer day :
  Hark to that mighty crash !
The loosened ice-ridge breaks away—
  The smitten waters flash ;
Seaward the glittering mountain rides,
While, down its green translucent sides,
  The foamy torrents dash.

See, love, my boat is moored for thee
  By ocean's weedy floor—
The petrel does not skim the sea
  More swiftly than my oar.
We'll go where, on the rocky isles,
Her eggs the screaming sea-fowl piles
  Beside the pebbly shore.

Or, bide thou where the poppy blows,
  With wind-flowers frail and fair,
While I, upon his isle of snow,
  Seek and defy the bear.
Fierce though he be, and huge of frame,
This arm his savage strength shall tame,
  And drag him from his lair.

When crimson sky and flamy cloud
  Bespeak the summer o'er,
And the dead valleys wear a shroud
  Of snows that melt no more,
I'll build of ice thy winter home,
With glistening walls and glassy dome,
  And spread with skins the floor.

The white fox by thy couch shall play ;
  And, from the frozen skies,
The meteors of a mimic day
  Shall flash upon thine eyes.
And I—for such thy vow—meanwhile
Shall hear thy voice and see thy smile,
  Till that long midnight flies.

THE JOURNEY OF LIFE.

BENEATH the waning moon I walk at night,
    And muse on human life—for all around
Are dim uncertain shapes that cheat the sight,
    And pitfalls lurk in shade along the ground,
And broken gleams of brightness, here and there,
Glance through, and leave unwarmed the death-like air.

The trampled earth returns a sound of fear—
    A hollow sound, as if I walked on tombs ;
And lights, that tell of cheerful homes, appear
    Far off, and die like hope amid the glooms.
A mournful wind across the landscape flies,
And the wide atmosphere is full of sighs.

And I, with faltering footsteps, journey on,
    Watching the stars that roll the hours away,
Till the faint light that guides me now is gone,
    And, like another life, the glorious day
Shall open o'er me from the empyreal height,
With warmth, and certainty, and boundless light.

TRANSLATIONS.

___

VERSION OF A FRAGMENT OF SIMONIDES.

The night winds howled, the billows dashed
 Against the tossing chest,
As Danaë to her broken heart
 Her slumbering infant pressed.

"My little child"—in tears she said—
 "To wake and weep is mine,
But thou canst sleep—thou dost not know
 Thy mother's lot, and thine.

"The moon is up, the moonbeams smile—
 They tremble on the main ;
But dark, within my floating cell,
 To me they smile in vain.

"Thy folded mantle wraps thee warm.
 Thy clustering locks are dry ;
Thou dost not hear the shrieking gust,
 Nor breakers booming high.

"As o'er thy sweet unconscious face
 A mournful watch I keep,
I think, didst thou but know thy fate,
 How thou wouldst also weep.

" Yet, dear one, sleep, and sleep, ye winds,
   That vex the restless brine—
When shall these eyes, my babe, be sealed
   As peacefully as thine ! "

FROM THE SPANISH OF VILLEGAS.

'TIS sweet, in the green Spring,
To gaze upon the wakening fields around ;
   Birds in the thicket sing,
Winds whisper, waters prattle from the ground.
   A thousand odors rise,
Breathed up from blossoms of a thousand dyes.

   Shadowy, and close, and cool,
The pine and poplar keep their quiet nook ;
   Forever fresh and full,
Shines, at their feet, the thirst-inviting brook ;
   And the soft herbage seems
Spread for a place of banquets and of dreams.

   Thou, who alone art fair,
And whom alone I love, art far away.
   Unless thy smile be there,
It makes me sad to see the earth so gay ;
   I care not if the train
Of leaves, and flowers, and zephyrs go again.

MARY MAGDALEN.

FROM THE SPANISH OF BARTOLOME LEONARDO DE ARGENSOLA.

BLESSED, yet sinful one, and broken-hearted !
   The crowd are pointing at the thing forlorn,
      In wonder and in scorn !
18

Thou weepest days of innocence departed ;
    Thou weepest, and thy tears have power to move
        The Lord to pity and love.

The greatest of thy follies is forgiven,
    Even for the least of all the tears that shine
        On that pale cheek of thine.
Thou didst kneel down, to Him who came from heaven,
    Evil and ignorant, and thou shalt rise
        Holy, and pure, and wise.

It is not much that to the fragrant blossom
    The ragged brier should change, the bitter fir
        Distil Arabian myrrh ;
Nor that, upon the wintry desert's bosom,
    The harvest should rise plenteous, and the swain
        Bear home the abundant grain.

But come and see the bleak and barren mountains
    Thick to their tops with roses ; come and see
        Leaves on the dry dead tree.
The perished plant, set out by living fountains,
    Grows fruitful, and its beauteous branches rise,
        Forever, toward the skies.

THE LIFE OF THE BLESSED.

FROM THE SPANISH OF LUIS PONCE DE LEON.

Region of life and light !
Land of the good whose earthly toils are o'er !
    Nor frost nor heat may blight
    Thy vernal beauty, fertile shore,
Yielding thy blessed fruits for evermore.

There, without crook or sling,
Walks the good shepherd ; blossoms white and red
Round his meek temples cling ;
And to sweet pastures led,
The flock he loves beneath his eye is fed.

He guides, and near him they
Follow delighted, for he makes them go
Where dwells eternal May,
And heavenly roses blow,
Deathless, and gathered but again to grow.

He leads them to the height
Named of the infinite and long-sought Good,
And fountains of delight ;
And where his feet have stood
Springs up, along the way, their tender food.

And when, in the mid skies,
The climbing sun has reached his highest bound,
Reposing as he lies,
With all his flock around,
He witches the still air with numerous sound.

From his sweet lute flow forth
Immortal harmonies, of power to still
All passions born of earth,
And draw the ardent will
Its destiny of goodness to fulfil.

Might but a little part,
A wandering breath of that high melody,
Descend into my heart,
And change it till it be
Transformed and swallowed up, oh love, in thee !

Ah ! then my soul should know,
Beloved ! where thou liest at noon of day,
And from this place of woe
Released, should take its way
To mingle with thy flock and never stray.

FATIMA AND RADUAN.

FROM THE SPANISH.

Diamante falso y fingido,
Engastado en pedernal, etc.

"FALSE diamond set in flint ! hard heart in haughty breast !
By a softer, warmer bosom the tiger's couch is prest.
Thou art fickle as the sea, thou art wandering as the wind,
And the restless ever-mounting flame is not more hard to bind.
If the tears I shed were tongues, yet all too few would be
To tell of all the treachery that thou hast shown to me.
Oh ! I could chide thee sharply—but every maiden knows
That she who chides her lover, forgives him ere he goes.

"Thou hast called me oft the flower of all Granada's maids,
Thou hast said that by the side of me the first and fairest fades ;
And they thought thy heart was mine, and it seemed to every one
That what thou didst to win my love, for love of me was done.
Alas ! if they but knew thee, as mine it is to know,
They well might see another mark to which thine arrows go ;
But thou giv'st me little heed—for I speak to one who knows
That she who chides her lover, forgives him ere he goes.

" It wearies me, mine enemy, that I must weep and bear
What fills thy heart with triumph, and fills my own with care.
Thou art leagued with those that hate me, and ah ! thou know'st
        I feel
That cruel words as surely kill as sharpest blades of steel.
'Twas the doubt that thou wert false that wrung my heart with
        pain ;
But, now I know thy perfidy, I shall be well again.
I would proclaim thee as thou art—but every maiden knows
That she who chides her lover, forgives him ere he goes."

Thus Fatima complained to the valiant Raduan,
Where underneath the myrtles Alhambra's fountains ran.
The Moor was inly moved, and blameless as he was,
He took her white hand in his own, and pleaded thus his cause :

" Oh, lady, dry those star-like eyes—their dimness does me wrong
If my heart be made of flint, at least 'twill keep thy image long.
Thou hast uttered cruel words—but I grieve the less for those,
Since she who chides her lover, forgives him ere he goes."

LOVE AND FOLLY.

FROM LA FONTAINE.

Love's worshippers alone can know
   The thousand mysteries that are his ;
His blazing torch, his twanging bow,
   His blooming age are mysteries.
A charming science—but the day
   Were all too short to con it o'er ;
So take of me this little lay,
   A sample of its boundless lore.

As once, beneath the fragrant shade
   Of myrtles fresh in heaven's pure air,
The children, Love and Folly, played,
   A quarrel rose betwixt the pair.
Love said the gods should do him right—
   But Folly vowed to do it then,
And struck him, o'er the orbs of sight,
   So hard he never saw again.

His lovely mother's grief was deep,
   She called for vengeance on the deed ;
A beauty does not vainly weep,
   Nor coldly does a mother plead.
A shade came o'er the eternal bliss
   That fills the dwellers of the skies ;
Even stony-hearted Nemesis,
   And Rhadamanthus, wiped their eyes.

" Behold," she said, " this lovely boy,"
     While streamed afresh her graceful tears—
" Immortal, yet shut out from joy
     And sunshine, all his future years.
The child can never take, you see,
     A single step without a staff—
The hardest punishment would be
     Too lenient for the crime by half."

All said that Love had suffered wrong,
     And well that wrong should be repaid ;
Then weighed the public interest long,
     And long the party's interest weighed.
And thus decreed the court above :
     " Since Love is blind from Folly's blow,
Let Folly be the guide of Love,
     Where'er the boy may choose to go."

THE SIESTA.

FROM THE SPANISH.

> Vientecico murmurador,
> Que lo gozas y andas todo, etc.

AIRS, that wander and murmur round,
     Bearing delight where'er ye blow !
Make in the elms a lulling sound,
     While my lady sleeps in the shade below.

Lighten and lengthen her noonday rest,
     Till the heat of the noonday sun is o'er.
Sweet be her slumbers ! though in my breast
     The pain she has waked may slumber no more.

Breathing soft from the blue profound,
     Bearing delight where'er ye blow,
Make in the elms a lulling sound,
     While my lady sleeps in the shade below.

Airs ! that over the bending boughs,
  And under the shade of pendent leaves,
Murmur soft, like my timid vows
  Or the secret sighs my bosom heaves—

Gently sweeping the grassy ground,
  Bearing delight where'er ye blow,
Make in the elms a lulling sound,
  While my lady sleeps in the shade below.

THE ALCAYDE OF MOLINA.

FROM THE SPANISH.

To the town of Atienza, Molina's brave Alcayde,
The courteous and the valorous, led forth his bold brigade.
The Moor came back in triumph, he came without a wound,
With many a Christian standard, and Christian captive bound.
He passed the city portals, with swelling heart and vain,
And toward his lady's dwelling he rode with slackened rein ;
Two circuits on his charger he took, and at the third,
From the door of her balcony Zelinda's voice was heard.
" Now if thou wert not shameless," said the lady to the Moor,
" Thou wouldst neither pass my dwelling, nor stop before my door
Alas for poor Zelinda, and for her wayward mood,
That one in love with peace should have loved a man of blood
Since not that thou wert noble I chose thee for my knight,
But that thy sword was dreaded in tournay and in fight.
Ah, thoughtless and unhappy ! that I should fail to see
How ill the stubborn flint and the yielding wax agree.
Boast not thy love for me, while the shrieking of the fife
Can change thy mood of mildness to fury and to strife.
Say not my voice is magic—thy pleasure is to hear
The bursting of the carbine, and shivering of the spear.
Well, follow thou thy choice—to the battle-field away,
To thy triumphs and thy trophies, since I am less than they.

Thrust thy arm into thy buckler, gird on thy crooked brand,
And call upon thy trusty squire to bring thy spears in hand.
Lead forth thy band to skirmish, by mountain and by mead,
On thy dappled Moorish barb, or thy fleeter border steed.
Go, waste the Christian hamlets, and sweep away their flocks,
From Almazan's broad meadows to Siguënza's rocks.
Leave Zelinda altogether, whom thou leavest oft and long
And in the life thou lovest, forget whom thou dost wrong.
These eyes shall not recall thee, though they meet no more thine
　　own,
Though they weep that thou art absent, and that I am all alone.
She ceased, and turning from him her flushed and angry cheek,
Shut the door of her balcony before the Moor could speak.

THE DEATH OF ALIATAR.

FROM THE SPANISH.

'Tis not with gilded sabres
　　That gleam in baldricks blue,
Nor nodding plumes in caps of Fez,
　　Of gay and gaudy hue—
But, habited in mourning weeds,
　　Come marching from afar,
By four and four, the valiant men
　　Who fought with Aliatar.
All mournfully and slowly
　　The afflicted warriors come,
To the deep wail of the trumpet,
　　And beat of muffled drum.

The banner of the Phœnix,
　　The flag that loved the sky,
That scarce the wind dared wanton with,
　　It flew so proud and high—
Now leaves its place in battle-field,
　　And sweeps the ground in grief,

The bearer drags its glorious folds
   Behind the fallen chief,
As mournfully and slowly
   The afflicted warriors come,
To the deep wail of the trumpet,
   And beat of muffled drum.

Brave Aliatar led forward
   A hundred Moors to go
To where his brother held Motril
   Against the leaguering foe.
On horseback went the gallant Moor.
   That gallant band to lead ;
And now his bier is at the gate,
   From which he pricked his steed.
While mournfully and slowly
   The afflicted warriors come,
To the deep wail of the trumpet,
   And beat of muffled drum.

The knights of the Grand Master
   In crowded ambush lay ;
They rushed upon him where the reeds
   Were thick beside the way ;
They smote the valiant Aliatar,
   They smote the warrior dead,
And broken, but not beaten, were
   The gallant ranks he led.
Now mournfully and slowly
   The afflicted warriors come,
To the deep wail of the trumpet,
   And beat of muffled drum.

Oh ! what was Zayda's sorrow,
   How passionate her cries !
Her lover's wounds streamed not more free
   Than that poor maiden's eyes.
Say, Love—for didst thou see her tears—
   Oh, no ! he drew more tight

The blinding fillet o'er his lids
    To spare his eyes the sight.
While mournfully and slowly
    The afflicted warriors come,
To the deep wail of the trumpet,
    And beat of muffled drum.

Nor Zayda weeps him only,
    But all that dwell between
The great Alhambra's palace walls
    And springs of Albaicin.
The ladies weep the flower of knights,
    The brave the bravest here;
The people weep a champion,
    The Alcaydes a noble peer.
While mournfully and slowly
    The afflicted warriors come,
To the deep wail of the trumpet,
    And beat of muffled drum.

LOVE IN THE AGE OF CHIVALRY.

FROM PEYRE VIDAL, THE TROUBADOUR.

THE earth was sown with early flowers,
    The heavens were blue and bright—
I met a youthful cavalier
    As lovely as the light.
I knew him not—but in my heart
    His graceful image lies,
And well I marked his open brow,
    His sweet and tender eyes,
His ruddy lips that ever smiled,
    His glittering teeth betwixt,
And flowing robe embroidered o'er,
    With leaves and blossoms mixed.

He wore a chaplet of the rose ;
  His palfrey, white and sleek,
Was marked with many an ebon spot,
  And many a purple streak ;
Of jasper was his saddle-bow,
  His housings sapphire stone,
And brightly in his stirrup glanced
  The purple calcedon.
Fast rode the gallant cavalier,
  As youthful horsemen ride ;
" Peyre Vidal ! know that I am Love,"
  The blooming stranger cried ;
" And this is Mercy by my side,
  A dame of high degree ;
This maid is Chastity," he said,
  " This squire is Loyalty."

THE LOVE OF GOD.

FROM THE PROVENÇAL OF BERNARD RASCAS.

ALL things that are on earth shall wholly pass away,
Except the love of God, which shall live and last for aye.
The forms of men shall be as they had never been ;
The blasted groves shall lose their fresh and tender green ;
The birds of the thicket shall end their pleasant song,
And the nightingale shall cease to chant the evening long ;
The kine of the pasture shall feel the dart that kills,
And all the fair white flocks shall perish from the hills.
The goat and antlered stag, the wolf and the fox,
The wild-boar of the wood, and the chamois of the rocks,
And the strong and fearless bear, in the trodden dust shall lie ;
And the dolphin of the sea, and the mighty whale, shall die.
And realms shall be dissolved, and empires be no more,
And they shall bow to death, who ruled from shore to shore ;

And the great globe itself, so the holy writings tell,
With the rolling firmament, where the starry armies dwell,
Shall melt with fervent heat—they shall all pass away,
Except the love of God, which shall live and last for aye.

FROM THE SPANISH OF PEDRO DE CASTRO Y AÑAYA.

STAY, rivulet, nor haste to leave
  The lovely vale that lies around thee.
Why wouldst thou be a sea at eve,
  When but a fount the morning found thee?

Born when the skies began to glow,
  Humblest of all the rock's cold daughters,
No blossom bowed its stalk to show
  Where stole thy still and scanty waters.

Now on the stream the noonbeams look,
  Usurping, as thou downward driftest,
Its crystal from the clearest brook,
  Its rushing current from the swiftest.

Ah! what wild haste!—and all to be
  A river and expire in ocean.
Each fountain's tribute hurries thee
  To that vast grave with quicker motion.

Far better 'twere to linger still
  In this green vale, these flowers to cherish,
And die in peace, an aged rill,
  Than thus, a youthful Danube, perish.

SONNET.

FROM THE PORTUGUESE OF SEMEDO.

It is a fearful night ; a feeble glare
  Streams from the sick moon in the o'erclouded sky ;
  The ridgy billows, with a mighty cry,
Rush on the foamy beaches wild and bare ;
No bark the madness of the waves will dare ;
  The sailors sleep ; the winds are loud and high.
  Ah, peerless Laura ! for whose love I die,
Who gazes on thy smiles while I despair ?
  As thus, in bitterness of heart, I cried,
I turned, and saw my Laura, kind and bright,
  A messenger of gladness, at my side ;
To my poor bark she sprang with footstep light,
  And as we furrowed Tago's heaving tide,
I never saw so beautiful a night.

SONG.

FROM THE SPANISH OF IGLESIAS.

Alexis calls me cruel :
  The rifted crags that hold
The gathered ice of winter,
  He says, are not more cold.

When even the very blossoms
  Around the fountain's brim,
And forest-walks, can witness
  The love I bear to him.

I would that I could utter
  My feelings without shame,
And tell him how I love him,
  Nor wrong my virgin fame.

Alas ! to seize the moment
  When heart inclines to heart,
And press a suit with passion,
  Is not a woman's part.

If man come not to gather
  The roses where they stand,
They fade among their foliage ;
  They cannot seek his hand.

THE COUNT OF GREIERS.

FROM THE GERMAN OF UHLAND.

At morn the Count of Greiers before his castle stands ;
He sees afar the glory that lights the mountain-lands ;
The horned crags are shining, and in the shade between
A pleasant Alpine valley lies beautifully green.

"Oh, greenest of the valleys, how shall I come to thee !
Thy herdsmen and thy maidens, how happy must they be !
I have gazed upon thee coldly, all lovely as thou art,
But the wish to walk thy pastures now stirs my inmost heart."

He hears a sound of timbrels, and suddenly appear
A troop of ruddy damsels and herdsmen drawing near :
They reach the castle greensward, and gayly dance across ;
The white sleeves flit and glimmer, the wreaths and ribbons toss.

The youngest of the maidens, slim as a spray of spring,
She takes the young count's fingers, and draws him to the ring ,
They fling upon his forehead a crown of mountain flowers,
"And ho, young Count of Greiers ! this morning thou art ours !"

Then hand in hand departing, with dance and roundelay,
Through hamlet after hamlet, they lead the Count away.
They dance through wood and meadow, they dance across the
    linn,
Till the mighty Alpine summits have shut the music in.

The second morn is risen, and now the third is come ;
Where stays the Count of Greiers ? has he forgot his home?
Again the evening closes, in thick and sultry air ;
There's thunder on the mountains, the storm is gathering there.

The cloud has shed its waters, the Brook comes swollen down ;
You see it by the lightning—a river wide and brown.
Around a struggling swimmer the eddies dash and roar,
Till, seizing on a willow, he leaps upon the shore.

" Here am I cast by tempests far from your mountain-dell.
Amid our evening dances the bursting deluge fell.
Ye all, in cots and caverns, have 'scaped the water-spout,
While me alone the tempest o'erwhelmed and hurried out.

" Farewell, with thy glad dwellers, green vale among the rocks !
Farewell the swift sweet moments, in which I watched thy flocks !
Why rocked they not my cradle in that delicious spot,
That garden of the happy, where Heaven endures me not?

" Rose of the Alpine valley ! I feel, in every vein,
Thy soft touch on my fingers ; oh, press them not again !
Bewitch me not, ye garlands, to tread that upward track,
And thou, my cheerless mansion, receive thy master back."

THE SERENADE.

FROM THE SPANISH.

If slumber, sweet Lisena !
   Have stolen o'er thine eyes,
As night steals o'er the glory
   Of spring's transparent skies ;

Wake, in thy scorn and beauty,
   And listen to the strain
That murmurs my devotion,
   That mourns for thy disdain.

Here, by thy door at midnight,
  I pass the dreary hour,
With plaintive sounds profaning
  The silence of thy bower ;

A tale of sorrow cherished
  Too fondly to depart,
Of wrong from love the flatterer
  And my own wayward heart.

Twice, o'er this vale, the seasons
  Have brought and borne away
The January tempest,
  The genial wind of May ;

Yet still my plaint is uttered,
  My tears and sighs are given
To earth's unconscious waters,
  And wandering winds of heaven.

I saw, from this fair region,
  The smile of summer pass,
And myriard frost-stars glitter
  Among the russet grass.

While winter seized the streamlet
  That fled along the ground,
And fast in chains of crystal
  The truant murmurers bound.

I saw that to the forest
  The nightingales had flown,
And every sweet-voiced fountain
  Had hushed its silver tone.

The maniac winds, divorcing
  The turtle from his mate,
Raved through the leafy beeches,
  And left them desolate.

Now May, with life and music,
  The blooming valley fills,
And rears her flowery arches
  For all the little rills.

The minstrel bird of evening
  Comes back on joyous wings,
And, like the harp's soft murmur,
  Is heard the gush of springs.

And deep within the forest
  Are wedded turtles seen,
Their nuptial chambers seeking,
  Their chambers close and green.

The rugged trees are mingling
  Their flowery sprays in love ;
The ivy climbs the laurel,
  To clasp the boughs above.

They change—but thou, Lisena,
  Art cold while I complain :
Why to thy lover only
  Should spring return in vain ?

A NORTHERN LEGEND

FROM THE GERMAN OF UHLAND.

THERE sits a lovely maiden,
  The ocean murmuring nigh ;
She throws the hook, and watches ;
  The fishes pass it by.

A ring, with a red jewel,
  Is sparkling on her hand ;
Upon the hook she binds it,
  And flings it from the land.

Uprises from the water
  A hand like ivory fair.
What gleams upon its finger?
  The golden ring is there.

Uprises from the bottom
  A young and handsome knight;
In golden scales he rises,
  That glitter in the light.

The maid is pale with terror—
  "Nay, Knight of Ocean, nay,
It was not thou I wanted;
  Let go the ring, I pray."

"Ah, maiden, not to fishes
  The bait of gold is thrown;
Thy ring shall never leave me,
  And thou must be my own."

THE PARADISE OF TEARS.

FROM THE GERMAN OF N. MÜELLER.

BESIDE the River of Tears, with branches low,
And bitter leaves, the weeping-willows grow;
The branches stream like the dishevelled hair
Of women in the sadness of despair.

On rolls the stream with a perpetual sigh;
The rocks moan wildly as it passes by;
Hyssop and wormwood border all the strand,
And not a flower adorns the dreary land.

Then comes a child, whose face is like the sun,
And dips the gloomy waters as they run,
And waters all the region, and behold
The ground is bright with blossoms manifold.

Where fall the tears of love the rose appears,
And where the ground is bright with friendship's tears,
Forget-me-not, and violets, heavenly blue,
Spring, glittering with the cheerful drops like dew.

The souls of mourners, all whose tears are dried,
Like swans, come gently floating down the tide,
Walk up the golden sands by which it flows,
And in that Paradise of Tears repose.

There every heart rejoins its kindred heart;
There, in a long embrace that none may part,
Fulfilment meets desire, and that fair shore
Beholds its dwellers happy evermore.

THE LADY OF CASTLE WINDECK.

FROM THE GERMAN OF CHAMISSO.

REIN in thy snorting charger!
  That stag but cheats thy sight;
He is luring thee on to Windeck,
  With his seeming fear and flight.

Now, where the mouldering turrets
  Of the outer gate arise,
The knight gazed over the ruins
  Where the stag was lost to his eyes.

The sun shone hot above him;
  The castle was still as death;
He wiped the sweat from his forehead,
  With a deep and weary breath.

"Who now will bring me a beaker
  Of the rich old wine that here,
In the choked-up vaults of Windeck,
  Has lain for many a year?"

The careless words had scarcely
    Time from his lips to fall,
When the lady of Castle Windeck,
    Came round the ivy-wall.

He saw the glorious maiden
    In her snow-white drapery stand,
The bunch of keys at her girdle,
    The beaker high in her hand.

He quaffed that rich old vintage ;
    With an eager lip he quaffed ;
But he took into his bosom
    A fire with the grateful draught.

Her eyes' unfathomed brightness !
    The flowing gold of her hair !
He folded his hands in homage,
    And murmured a lover's prayer.

She gave him a look of pity,
    A gentle look of pain ;
And, quickly as he had seen her,
    She passed from his sight again.

And ever, from that moment,
    He haunted the ruins there,
A sleepless, restless wanderer,
    A watcher with despair.

Ghost-like and pale he wandered,
    With a dreamy, haggard eye ;
He seemed not one of the living,
    And yet he could not die.

'Tis said that the lady met him,
    When many years had past,
And kissing his lips, released him
    From the burden of life at last.

LATER POEMS.

TO THE APENNINES.

Your peaks are beautiful, ye Apennines !
  In the soft light of these serenest skies ;
From the broad highland region, black with pines,
  Fair as the hills of Paradise they rise,
Bathed in the tint Peruvian slaves behold
In rosy flushes on the virgin gold.

There, rooted to the aërial shelves that wear
  The glory of a brighter world, might spring
Sweet flowers of heaven to scent the unbreathed air,
  And heaven's fleet messengers might rest the wing
To view the fair earth in its summer sleep,
Silent, and cradled by the glimmering deep.

Below you lie men's sepulchres, the old
  Etrurian tombs, the graves of yesterday ;
The herd's white bones lie mixed with human moula,
  Yet up the radiant steeps that I survey
Death never climbed, nor life's soft breath, with pain,
Was yielded to the elements again.

Ages of war have filled these plains with fear ;
  How oft the hind has started at the clash
Of spears, and yell of meeting armies here,
  Or seen the lightning of the battle flash
From clouds, that rising with the thunder's sound,
Hung like an earth-born tempest o'er the ground !

Ah me ! what armèd nations—Asian horde,
    And Libyan host, the Scythian and the Gaul—
Have swept your base and through your passes poured,
    Like ocean-tides uprising at the call
Of tyrant winds—against your rocky side
The bloody billows dashed, and howled, and died !

How crashed the towers before beleaguering foes,
    Sacked cities smoked and realms were rent in twain
And commonwealths against their rivals rose,
    Trode out their lives and earned the curse of Cain !
While, in the noiseless air and light that flowed
Round your fair brows, eternal Peace abode.

Here pealed the impious hymn, and altar-flames
    Rose to false gods, a dream-begotten throng,
Jove, Bacchus, Pan, and earlier, fouler names ;
    While, as the unheeding ages passed along,
Ye, from your station in the middle skies,
Proclaimed the essential Goodness, strong and wise.

In you the heart that sighs for freedom seeks
    Her image ; there the winds no barrier know,
Clouds come and rest and leave your fairy peaks ;
    While even the immaterial Mind, below,
And Thought, her wingèd offspring, chained by power,
Pine silently for the redeeming hour.

EARTH.

    A midnight black with clouds is in the sky ;
I seem to feel, upon my limbs, the weight
Of its vast brooding shadow. All in vain
Turns the tired eye in search of form ; no star
Pierces the pitchy veil ; no ruddy blaze,
From dwellings lighted by the cheerful hearth,
Tinges the flowering summits of the grass.

"*Ah me! what armèd nations—Asian horde,*
And Libyan host, the Scythian and the Gaul—
Have swept your base and through your passes poured."

No sound of life is heard, no village hum,
Nor measured tramp of footstep in the path,
Nor rush of wind, while, on the breast of Earth,
I lie and listen to her mighty voice :
A voice of many tones—sent up from streams
That wander through the gloom, from woods unseen
Swayed by the sweeping of the tides of air,
From rocky chasms where darkness dwells all day,
And hollows of the great invisible hills,
And sands that edge the ocean, stretching far
Into the night—a melancholy sound !

   O Earth ! dost thou too sorrow for the past
Like man thy offspring ?   Do I hear thee mourn
Thy childhood's unreturning hours, thy springs
Gone with their genial airs and melodies,
The gentle generations of thy flowers,
And thy majestic groves of olden time,
Perished with all their dwellers ?   Dost thou wail
For that fair age of which the poets tell,
Ere yet the winds grew keen with frost, or fire
Fell with the rains or spouted from the hills,
To blast thy greenness, while the virgin night
Was guiltless and salubrious as the day ?
Or haply dost thou grieve for those that die—
For living things that trod thy paths awhile,
The love of thee and heaven—and now they sleep
Mixed with the shapeless dust on which thy herds
Trample and graze ?   I too must grieve with thee,
O'er loved ones lost.   Their graves are far away
Upon thy mountains ; yet, while I recline
Alone, in darkness, on thy naked soil,
The mighty nourisher and burial-place
Of man, I feel that I embrace their dust.

   Ha ! how the murmur deepens !   I perceive
And tremble at its dreadful import.   Earth
Uplifts a general cry for guilt and wrong,
And heaven is listening.   The forgotten graves

Of the heart-broken utter forth their plaint.
The dust of her who loved and was betrayed,
And him who died neglected in his age ;
The sepulchres of those who for mankind
Labored, and earned the recompense of scorn ;
Ashes of martyrs for the truth, and bones
Of those who, in the strife for liberty,
Were beaten down, their corses given to dogs,
Their names to infamy, all find a voice.
The nook in which the captive, overtoiled,
Lay down to rest at last, and that which holds
Childhood's sweet blossoms, crushed by cruel hands,
Send up a plaintive sound.   From battle-fields,
Where heroes madly drave and dashed their hosts
Against each other, rises up a noise,
As if the armèd multitudes of dead
Stirred in their heavy slumber.   Mournful tones
Come from the green abysses of the sea—
A story of the crimes the guilty sought
To hide beneath its waves.   The glens, the groves,
Paths in the thicket, pools of running brook,
And banks and depths of lake, and streets and lanes
Of cities, now that living sounds are hushed,
Murmur of guilty force and treachery.

Here, where I rest, the vales of Italy
Are round me, populous from early time,
And field of the tremendous warfare waged
'Twixt good and evil.   Who, alas ! shall dare
Interpret to man's ear the mingled voice
That comes from her old dungeons yawning now
To the black air, her amphitheatres,
Where the dew gathers on the mouldering stones,
And fanes of banished gods, and open tombs,
And roofless palaces, and streets and hearths
Of cities dug from their volcanic graves ?
I hear a sound of many languages,
The utterance of nations now no more,
Driven out by mightier, as the days of heaven

Chase one another from the sky.   The blood
Of freemen shed by freemen, till strange lords
Came in their hour of weakness, and made fast
The yoke that yet is worn, cries out to heaven.

What then shall cleanse thy bosom, gentle Earth,
From all its painful memories of guilt?
The whelming flood, or the renewing fire,
Or the slow change of time?—that so, at last,
The horrid tale of perjury and strife,
Murder and spoil, which men call history,
May seem a fable, like the inventions told
By poets of the gods of Greece.   O thou,
Who sittest far beyond the Atlantic deep,
Among the sources of thy glorious streams,
My native Land of Groves! a newer page
In the great record of the world is thine;
Shall it be fairer?   Fear, and friendly Hope,
And Envy, watch the issue, while the lines,
By which thou shalt be judged, are written down.

THE KNIGHT'S EPITAPH.

This is the church which Pisa, great and free,
Reared to St. Catharine.   How the time-stained walls,
That earthquakes shook not from their poise, appear
To shiver in the deep and voluble tones
Rolled from the organ!   Underneath my feet
There lies the lid of a sepulchral vault.
The image of an armèd knight is graven
Upon it, clad in perfect panoply—
Cuishes, and greaves, and cuirass, with barred helm,
Gauntleted hand, and sword, and blazoned shield.
Around, in Gothic characters, worn dim
By feet of worshippers, are traced his name,
And birth, and death, and words of eulogy.
Why should I pore upon them?   This old tomb,

This effigy, the strange disusèd form
Of this inscription, eloquently show
His history.   Let me clothe in fitting words
The thoughts they breathe, and frame his epitaph :

  " He whose forgotten dust for centuries
Has lain beneath this stone, was one in whom
Adventure, and endurance, and emprise,
Exalted the mind's faculties and strung
The body's sinews.   Brave he was in figh:,
Courteous in banquet, scornful of repose,
And bountiful, and cruel, and devout,
And quick to draw the sword in private feud,
He pushed his quarrels to the death, yet prayed
The saints as fervently on bended knees
As ever shaven cenobite.   He loved
As fiercely as he fought.   He would have borne
The maid that pleased him from her bower by nighl
To his hill castle, as the eagle bears
His victim from the fold, and rolled the rocks
On his pursuers.   He aspired to see
His native Pisa queen and arbitress
Of cities ; earnestly for her he raised
His voice in council, and affronted death
In battle-field, and climbed the galley's deck,
And brought the captured flag of Genoa back,
Or piled upon the Arno's crowded quay
The glittering spoils of the tamed Saracen.
He was not born to brook the stranger's yoke,
But would have joined the exiles that withdrew
Forever, when the Florentine broke in
The gates of Pisa, and bore off the bolts
For trophies—but he died before that day.

  " He lived, the impersonation of an age
That never shall return.   His soul of fire
Was kindled by the breath of the rude time
He lived in.   Now a gentler race succeeds,
Shuddering at blood ; the effeminate cavalier,

Turning his eyes from the reproachful past,
And from the hopeless future, gives to ease,
And love, and music, his inglorious life."

———

THE HUNTER OF THE PRAIRIES.

Ay, this is freedom!—these pure skies
  Were never stained with village smoke :
The fragrant wind, that through them flies,
  Is breathed from wastes by plough unbroke.
Here, with my rifle and my steed,
  And her who left the world for me,
I plant me, where the red deer feed
  In the green desert—and am free.

For here the fair savannas know
  No barriers in the bloomy grass ;
Wherever breeze of heaven may blow,
  Or beam of heaven may glance, I pass.
In pastures, measureless as air,
  The bison is my noble game ;
The bounding elk, whose antlers tear
  The branches, falls before my aim.

Mine are the river-fowl that scream
  From the long stripe of waving sedge ;
The bear that marks my weapon's gleam,
  Hides vainly in the forest's edge ;
In vain the she-wolf stands at bay ;
  The brinded catamount, that lies
High in the boughs to watch his prey,
  Even in the act of springing, dies.

With what free growth the elm and plane
  Fling their huge arms across my way,
Gray, old, and cumbered with a train
  Of vines, as huge, and old, and gray !

Free stray the lucid streams, and find
    No taint in these fresh lawns and shades ;
Free spring the flowers that scent the wind
    Where never scythe has swept the glades.

Alone the Fire, when frost-winds sere
    The heavy herbage of the ground,
Gathers his annual harvest here,
    With roaring like the battle's sound,
And hurrying flames that sweep the plain,
    And smoke-streams gushing up the sky :
I meet the flames with flames again,
    And at my door they cower and die.

Here, from dim woods, the aged past
    Speaks solemnly ; and I behold
The boundless future in the vast
    And lonely river, seaward rolled.
Who feeds its founts with rain and dew ?
    Who moves, I ask, its gliding mass,
And trains the bordering vines, whose blue
    Bright clusters tempt me as I pass ?

Broad are these streams—my steed obeys,
    Plunges, and bears me through the tide.
Wide are these woods—I thread the maze
    Of giant stems, nor ask a guide.
I hunt till day's last glimmer dies
    O'er woody vale and grassy height ;
And kind the voice and glad the eyes
    That welcome my return at night.

SEVENTY–SIX.

WHAT heroes from the woodland sprung,
    When, through the fresh-awakened land,
The thrilling cry of freedom rung,
And to the work of warfare strung
    The yeoman's iron hand !

Hills flung the cry to hills around,
　And ocean-mart replied to mart,
And streams, whose springs were yet unfound,
Pealed far away the startling sound
　Into the forest's heart.

Then marched the brave from rocky steep,
　From mountain-river swift and cold ;
The borders of the stormy deep,
The vales where gathered waters sleep,
　Sent up the strong and bold,—

As if the very earth again
　Grew quick with God's creating breath,
And, from the sods of grove and glen,
Rose ranks of lion-hearted men
　To battle to the death.

The wife, whose babe first smiled that day,
　The fair fond bride of yestereve,
And aged sire and matron gray,
Saw the loved warriors haste away,
　And deemed it sin to grieve.

Already had the strife begun ;
　Already blood, on Concord's plain,
Along the springing grass had run,
And blood had flowed at Lexington,
　Like brooks of April rain.

That death-stain on the vernal sward
　Hallowed to freedom all the shore ;
In fragments fell the yoke abhorred—
The footstep of a foreign lord
　Profaned the soil no more.

THE LIVING LOST.

Matron! the children of whose love,
  Each to his grave, in youth have passed ;
And now the mould is heaped above
  The dearest and the last !
Bride ! who dost wear the widow's veil
Before the wedding flowers are pale !
Ye deem the human heart endures
No deeper, bitterer grief than yours.

Yet there are pangs of keener woe,
  Of which the sufferers never speak,
Nor to the world's cold pity show
  The tears that scald the cheek,
Wrung from their eyelids by the shame
And guilt of those they shrink to name,
Whom once they loved with cheerful will,
And love, though fallen and branded, still.

Weep, ye who sorrow for the dead,
  Thus breaking hearts their pain relieve,
And reverenced are the tears they shed,
  And honored ye who grieve.
The praise of those who sleep in earth,
The pleasant memory of their worth,
The hope to meet when life is past,
Shall heal the tortured mind at last.

But ye, who for the living lost
  That agony in secret bear,
Who shall with soothing words accost
  The strength of your despair ?
Grief for your sake is scorn for them
Whom ye lament and all condemn ;
And o'er the world of spirits lies
A gloom from which ye turn your eyes.

"*Midst greens and shades the Catterskill leaps.*"

CATTERSKILL FALLS.

MIDST greens and shades the Catterskill leaps,
From cliffs where the wood-flower clings ;
All summer he moistens his verdant steeps,
With the sweet light spray of the mountain-springs,
And he shakes the woods on the mountain-side,
When they drip with the rains of autumn-tide.

But when, in the forest bare and old,
The blast of December calls,
He builds, in the starlight clear and cold,
A palace of ice where his torrent falls,
With turret, and arch, and fretwork fair,
And pillars blue as the summer air.

For whom are those glorious chambers wrought,
In the cold and cloudless night ?
Is there neither spirit nor motion of thought
In forms so lovely, and hues so bright ?
Hear what the gray-haired woodmen tell
Of this wild stream and its rocky dell.

'Twas hither a youth of dreamy mood,
A hundred winters ago,
Had wandered over the mighty wood,
When the panther's track was fresh on the snow.
And keen were the winds that came to stir
The long dark boughs of the hemlock-fir.

Too gentle of mien he seemed and fair,
For a child of those rugged steeps ;
His home lay low in the valley where
The kingly Hudson rolls to the deeps ;
But he wore the hunter's frock that day,
And a slender gun on his shoulder lay.

And here he paused, and against the trunk
Of a tall gray linden leant,
When the broad clear orb of the sun had sunk,
From his path in the frosty firmament,

And over the round dark edge of the hill
A cold green light was quivering still.

And the crescent moon, high over the green,
　From a sky of crimson shone,
On that icy palace, whose towers were seen
　To sparkle as if with stars of their own,
While the water fell with a hollow sound,
'Twixt the glistening pillars ranged around.

Is that a being of life, that moves
　Where the crystal battlements rise ?
A maiden watching the moon she loves,
　At the twilight hour, with pensive eyes ?
Was that a garment which seemed to gleam
Betwixt the eye and the falling stream ?

'Tis only the torrent tumbling o'er,
　In the midst of those glassy walls,
Gushing, and plunging, and beating the floor
　Of the rocky basin in which it falls.
'Tis only the torrent—but why that start ?
Why gazes the youth with a throbbing heart ?

He thinks no more of his home afar,
　Where his sire and sister wait.
He heeds no longer how star after star
　Looks forth on the night as the hour grows late.
He heeds not the snow-wreaths, lifted and cast
From a thousand boughs, by the rising blast.

His thoughts are alone of those who dwell
　In the halls of frost and snow,
Who pass where the crystal domes upswell
　From the alabaster floors below,
Where the frost-trees shoot with leaf and spray,
And frost-gems scatter a silvery day.

"And oh that those glorious haunts were mine!"
  He speaks, and throughout the glen
Thin shadows swim in the faint moonshine,
  And take a ghastly likeness of men,
As if the slain by the wintry storms
Came forth to the air in their earthly forms.

There pass the chasers of seal and whale,
  With their weapons quaint and grim,
And bands of warriors in glittering mail,
  And herdsmen and hunters huge of limb;
There are naked arms, with bow and spear,
And furry gauntlets the carbine rear.

There are mothers—and oh how sadly their eyes
  On their children's white brows rest!
There are youthful lovers—the maiden lies,
  In a seeming sleep, on the chosen breast;
There are fair wan women with moonstruck air,
The snow-stars flecking their long loose hair.

They eye him not as they pass along,
  But his hair stands up with dread,
When he feels that he moves with that phantom throng,
  Till those icy turrets are over his head,
And the torrent's roar as they enter seems
Like a drowsy murmur heard in dreams.

The glittering threshold is scarcely passed,
  When there gathers and wraps him round
A thick white twilight, sullen and vast,
  In which there is neither form nor sound;
The phantoms, the glory, vanish all,
With the dying voice of the waterfall.

Slow passes the darkness of that trance,
  And the youth now faintly sees
Huge shadows and gushes of light that dance
  On a rugged ceiling of unhewn trees,
  20

And walls where the skins of beasts are hung,
And rifles glitter on antlers strung.

On a couch of shaggy skins he lies ;
   As he strives to raise his head,
Hard-featured woodmen, with kindly eyes,
   Come round him and smooth his furry bed,
And bid him rest, for the evening star
Is scarcely set and the day is far.

They had found at eve the dreaming one
   By the base of that icy steep,
When over his stiffening limbs begun
   The deadly slumber of frost to creep,
And they cherished the pale and breathless form,
Till the stagnant blood ran free and warm.

THE STRANGE LADY.

THE summer morn is bright and fresh, the birds are darting by.
As if they loved to breast the breeze that sweeps the cool clear
   sky ;
Young Albert, in the forest's edge, has heard a rustling sound,
An arrow slightly strikes his hand and falls upon the ground.

A dark-haired woman from the wood comes suddenly in sight ;
Her merry eye is full and black, her cheek is brown and bright ;
Her gown is of the mid-sea blue, her belt with beads is strung,
And yet she speaks in gentle tones, and in the English tongue.

" It was an idle bolt I sent, against the villain crow ;
Fair sir, I fear it harmed thy hand ; beshrew my erring bow ! "
" Ah ! would that bolt had not been spent ! then, lady, might
   wear
A lasting token on my hand of one so passing fair ! "

"Thou art a flatterer like the rest, but wouldst thou take with me
A day of hunting in the wild beneath the greenwood tree,
I know where most the pheasants feed, and where the red-deer
    herd,
And thou shouldst chase the nobler game, and I bring down the
    bird."

Now Albert in her quiver lays the arrow in its place,
And wonders as he gazes on the beauty of her face :
"Those hunting-grounds are far away, and, lady, 'twere not meet
That night, amid the wilderness, should overtake thy feet."

"Heed not the night ; a summer lodge amid the wild is mine—
'Tis shadowed by the tulip-tree, 'tis mantled by the vine ;
The wild-plum sheds its yellow fruit from fragrant thickets nigh,
And flowery prairies from the door stretch till they meet the sky.

"There in the boughs that hide the roof the mock-bird sits and
    sings,
And there the hang-bird's brood within its little hammock swings ;
A pebbly brook, where rustling winds among the hopples sweep,
Shall lull thee till the morning sun looks in upon thy sleep."

Away, into the forest depths by pleasant paths they go,
He with his rifle on his arm, the lady with her bow,
Where cornels arch their cool dark boughs o'er beds of winter-
    green,
And never at his father's door again was Albert seen.

That night upon the woods came down a furious hurricane,
With howl of winds and roar of streams, and beating of the rain ;
The mighty thunder broke and drowned the noises in its crash ;
The old trees seemed to fight like fiends beneath the lightning
    flash.

Next day, within a mossy glen, 'mid mouldering trunks were found
The fragments of a human form upon the bloody ground ;
White bones from which the flesh was torn, and locks of glossy
    hair ;
They laid them in the place of graves, yet wist not whose they
    were.

And whether famished evening wolves had mangled Albert so,
Or that strange dame so gay and fair were some mysterious foe,
Or whether to that forest-lodge, beyond the mountains blue,
He went to dwell with her, the friends who mourned him never
    knew.

LIFE.

OH Life ! I breathe thee in the breeze,
  I feel thee bounding in my veins,
I see thee in these stretching trees,
    These flowers, this still rock's mossy stains.

This stream of odors flowing by
  From clover-field and clumps of pine,
This music, thrilling all the sky,
    From all the morning birds, are thine.

Thou fill'st with joy this little one,
  That leaps and shouts beside me here,
Where Isar's clay-white rivulets run
    Through the dark woods like frighted deer.

Ah ! must thy mighty breath, that wakes
  Insect and bird, and flower and tree,
From the low-trodden dust, and makes
    Their daily gladness, pass from me—

Pass, pulse by pulse, till o'er the ground
  These limbs, now strong, shall creep with pain,
And this fair world of sight and sound
    Seem fading into night again?

The things, oh LIFE ! thou quickenest, all
  Strive upward toward the broad bright sky,
Upward and outward, and they fall
    Back to earth's bosom when they die.

All that have borne the touch of death,
   All that shall live, lie mingled there,
Beneath that veil of bloom and breath,
   That living zone 'twixt earth and air.

There lies my chamber dark and still,
   The atoms trampled by my feet
There wait, to take the place I fill
   In the sweet air and sunshine sweet.

Well, I have had my turn, have been
   Raised from the darkness of the clod,
And for a glorious moment seen
   The brightness of the skirts of God ;

And knew the light within my breast,
   Though wavering oftentimes and dim,
The power, the will, that never rest,
   And cannot die, were all from him.

Dear child ! I know that thou wilt grieve
   To see me taken from thy love,
Wilt seek my grave at Sabbath eve
   And weep, and scatter flowers above.

Thy little heart will soon be healed,
   And being shall be bliss, till thou
To younger forms of life must yield
   The place thou fill'st with beauty now.

When we descend to dust again,
   Where will the final dwelling be
Of thought and all its memories then,
   My love for thee, and thine for me ?

"EARTH'S CHILDREN CLEAVE TO EARTH."

EARTH's children cleave to Earth—her frail
   Decaying children dread decay.
Yon wreath of mist that leaves the vale
   And lessens in the morning ray—
Look, how, by mountain rivulet,
   It lingers as it upward creeps,
And clings to fern and copsewood set
   Along the green and dewy steeps :
Clings to the flowery kalmia, clings
   To precipices fringed with grass,
Dark maples where the wood-thrush sings,
   And bowers of fragrant sassafras.
Yet all in vain—it passes still
   From hold to hold, it cannot stay,
And in the very beams that fill
   The world with glory, wastes away,
Till, parting from the mountain's brow,
   It vanishes from human eye,
And that which sprung of earth is now
   A portion of the glorious sky.

THE HUNTER'S VISION.

UPON a rock that, high and sheer,
   Rose from the mountain's breast,
A weary hunter of the deer
   Had sat him down to rest,
And bared to the soft summer air
His hot red brow and sweaty hair.

All dim in haze the mountains lay,
   With dimmer vales between ;
And rivers glimmered on their way
   By forests faintly seen ;

While ever rose a murmuring sound
From brooks below and bees around.

He listened, till he seemed to hear
  A strain, so soft and low,
That whether in the mind or ear
  The listener scarce might know.
With such a tone, so sweet, so mild,
The watching mother lulls her child.

" Thou weary huntsman," thus it said,
  " Thou faint with toil and heat,
The pleasant land of rest is spread
  Before thy very feet,
And those whom thou wouldst gladly see
Are waiting there to welcome thee."

He looked, and 'twixt the earth and sky,
  Amid the noontide haze,
A shadowy region met his eye,
  And grew beneath his gaze,
As if the vapors of the air
Had gathered into shapes so fair.

Groves freshened as he looked, and flowers
  Showed bright on rocky bank,
And fountains welled beneath the bowers,
  Where deer and pheasant drank.
He saw the glittering streams, he heard
The rustling bough and twittering bird.

And friends, the dead, in boyhood dear
  There lived and walked again,
And there was one who many a year
  Within her grave had lain,
A fair young girl, the hamlet's pride—
His heart was breaking when she died ·

Bounding, as was her wont, she came
　　Right toward his resting-place,
And stretched her hand and called his name
　　With that sweet smiling face.
Forward with fixed and eager eyes,
The hunter leaned in act to rise :

Forward he leaned, and headlong down
　　Plunged from that craggy wall ;
He saw the rocks, steep, stern, and brown,
　　An instant, in his fall ;
A frightful instant—and no more,
The dream and life at once were o'er.

THE GREEN MOUNTAIN BOYS.

I.

HERE halt we our march, and pitch our tent
　　On the rugged forest-ground,
And light our fire with the branches rent
　　By winds from the beeches round.
Wild storms have torn this ancient wood,
　　But a wilder is at hand,
With hail of iron and rain of blood,
　　To sweep and waste the land.

II.

How the dark wood rings with our voices shrill,
　　That startle the sleeping bird !
To-morrow eve must the voice be still,
　　And the step must fall unheard.
The Briton lies by the blue Champlain,
　　In Ticonderoga's towers,
And ere the sun rise twice again,
　　Must they and the lake be ours.

III.

Fill up the bowl from the brook that glides
    Where the fire-flies light the brake ;
A ruddier juice the Briton hides
    In his fortress by the lake.
Build high the fire, till the panther leap
    From his lofty perch in flight,
And we'll strengthen our weary arms with sleep
    For the deeds of to-morrow night.

A PRESENTIMENT.

"Oh father, let us hence—for hark,
    A fearful murmur shakes the air ;
The clouds are coming swift and dark ;—
    What horrid shapes they wear !
A wingèd giant sails the sky ;
Oh father, father, let us fly ! "

"Hush, child ; it is a grateful sound,
    That beating of the summer shower ;
Here, where the boughs hang close around,
    We'll pass a pleasant hour,
Till the fresh wind, that brings the rain,
Has swept the broad heaven clear again."

"Nay, father, let us haste—for see,
    That horrid thing with hornèd brow—
His wings o'erhang this very tree,
    He scowls upon us now ;
His huge black arm is lifted high ;
Oh father, father, let us fly ! "

"Hush, child ; " but, as the father spoke,
    Downward the livid firebolt came,
Close to his ear the thunder broke,
    And, blasted by the flame,
The child lay dead ; while dark and still
Swept the grim cloud along the hill.

THE CHILD'S FUNERAL.

Fair is thy sight, Sorrento, green thy shore,
    Black crags behind thee pierce the clear blue skies;
The sea, whose borderers ruled the world of yore,
    As clear and bluer still before thee lies.

Vesuvius smokes in sight, whose fount of fire,
    Outgushing, drowned the cities on his steeps;
And murmuring Naples, spire o'ertopping spire,
    Sits on the slope beyond where Virgil sleeps.

Here doth the earth, with flowers of every hue,
    Prank her green breast when April suns are bright;
Flowers of the morning-red, or ocean-blue,
    Or like the mountain-frost of silvery white.

Currents of fragrance, from the orange-tree,
    And sward of violets, breathing to and fro,
Mingle, and, wandering out upon the sea,
    Refresh the idle boatsman where they blow.

Yet even here, as under harsher climes,
    Tears for the loved and early lost are shed;
That soft air saddens with the funeral-chimes,
    Those shining flowers are gathered for the dead.

Here once a child, a smiling playful one,
    All the day long caressing and caressed,
Died when its little tongue had just begun
    To lisp the names of those it loved the best.

The father strove his struggling grief to quell,
    The mother wept as mothers use to weep,
Two little sisters wearied them to tell
    When their dear Carlo would awake from sleep.

Within an inner room his couch they spread,
    His funeral-couch; with mingled grief and love,
They laid a crown of roses on his head,
    And murmured, "Brighter is his crown above."

They scattered round him, on the snowy sheet,
  Laburnum's strings of sunny-colored gems,
Sad hyacinths, and violets dim and sweet,
  And orange-blossoms on their dark-green stems.

And now the hour is come, the priest is there ;
  Torches are lit and bells are tolled ; they go,
With solemn rites of blessing and of prayer,
  To lay the little one in earth below.

The door is opened ; hark ! tnat quick glad cry ;
  Carlo has waked, has waked, and is at play ;
The little sisters laugh and leap, and try
  To climb the bed on which the infant lay.

And there he sits alive, and gayly shakes
  In his full hands the blossoms red and white,
And smiles with winking eyes, like one who wakes
  From long deep slumbers at the morning light.

THE BATTLE-FIELD.

Once this soft turf, this rivulet's sands,
  Were trampled by a hurrying crowd,
And fiery hearts and armèd hands
  Encountered in the battle-cloud.

Ah ! never shall the land forget
  How gushed the life-blood of her brave—
Gushed, warm with hope and courage yet,
  Upon the soil they fought to save.

Now all is calm, and fresh, and still ;
  Alone the chirp of flitting bird,
And talk of children on the hill,
  And bell of wandering kine, are heard.

No solemn host goes trailing by
　　The black-mouthed gun and staggering wain ;
Men start not at the battle-cry,
　　Oh, be it never heard again !

Soon rested those who fought ; but thou
　　Who minglest in the harder strife
For truths which men receive not now,
　　Thy warfare only ends with life.

A friendless warfare ! lingering long
　　Through weary day and weary year,
A wild and many-weaponed throng
　　Hang on thy front, and flank, and rear.

Yet nerve thy spirit to the proof,
　　And blench not at thy chosen lot.
The timid good may stand aloof,
　　The sage may frown—yet faint thou not.

Nor heed the shaft too surely cast,
　　The foul and hissing bolt of scorn ;
For with thy side shall dwell, at last,
　　The victory of endurance born.

Truth, crushed to earth, shall rise again ;
　　Th' eternal years of God are hers ;
But Error, wounded, writhes in pain,
　　And dies among his worshippers.

Yea, though thou lie upon the dust,
　　When they who helped thee flee in fear,
Die full of hope and manly trust,
　　Like those who fell in battle here.

Another hand thy sword shall wield,
　　Another hand the standard wave,
Till from the trumpet's mouth is pealed
　　The blast of triumph o'er thy grave.

THE FUTURE LIFE.

How shall I know thee in the sphere which keeps
　The disembodied spirits of the dead,
When all of thee that time could wither sleeps
　And perishes among the dust we tread?

For I shall feel the sting of ceaseless pain
　If there I meet thy gentle presence not;
Nor hear the voice I love, nor read again
　In thy serenest eyes the tender thought.

Will not thy own meek heart demand me there?
　That heart whose fondest throbs to me were given—
My name on earth was ever in thy prayer,
　And wilt thou never utter it in heaven?

In meadows fanned by heaven's life-breathing wind,
　In the resplendence of that glorious sphere,
And larger movements of the unfettered mind,
　Wilt thou forget the love that joined us here?

The love that lived through all the stormy past,
　And meekly with my harsher nature bore,
And deeper grew, and tenderer to the last,
　Shall it expire with life, and be no more?

A happier lot than mine, and larger light,
　Await thee there, for thou hast bowed thy will
In cheerful homage to the rule of right,
　And lovest all, and renderest good for ill.

For me, the sordid cares in which I dwell
　Shrink and consume my heart, as heat the scroll;
And wrath has left its scar—that fire of hell
　Has left its frightful scar upon my soul.

Yet, though thou wear'st the glory of the sky,
    Wilt thou not keep the same beloved name,
The same fair thoughtful brow, and gentle eye,
    Lovelier in heaven's sweet climate, yet the same?

Shalt thou not teach me, in that calmer home,
    The wisdom that I learned so ill in this—
The wisdom which is love—till I become
    Thy fit companion in that land of bliss?

THE DEATH OF SCHILLER.

'TIS said, when Schiller's death drew nigh,
    The wish possessed his mighty mind,
To wander forth wherever lie
    The homes and haunts of humankind.

Then strayed the poet, in his dreams,
    By Rome and Egypt's ancient graves ;
Went up the New World's forest-streams,
    Stood in the Hindoo's temple-caves ;

Walked with the Pawnee, fierce and stark,
    The sallow Tartar, midst his herds,
The peering Chinese, and the dark
    False Malay, uttering gentle words.

How could he rest? even then he trod
    The threshold of the world unknown ;
Already, from the seat of God,
    A ray upon his garments shone ;—

Shone and awoke the strong desire
    For love and knowledge reached not here,
Till, freed by death, his soul of fire
    Sprang to a fairer, ampler sphere.

THE FOUNTAIN.

FOUNTAIN, that springest on this grassy slope,
Thy quick cool murmur mingles pleasantly,
With the cool sound of breezes in the beech,
Above me in the noontide. Thou dost wear
No stain of thy dark birthplace ; gushing up
From the red mould and slimy roots of earth
Thou flashest in the sun. The mountain-air,
In winter, is not clearer, nor the dew
That shines on mountain-blossom. Thus doth God
Bring, from the dark and foul, the pure and bright.

This tangled thicket on the bank above
Thy basin, how thy waters keep it green !
For thou dost feed the roots of the wild-vine
That trails all over it, and to the twigs
Ties fast her clusters. There the spice-bush lifts
Her leafy lances ; the viburnum there,
Paler of foliage, to the sun holds up
Her circlet of green berries. In and out
The chipping-sparrow, in her coat of brown,
Steals silently lest I should mark her nest.

Not such thou wert of yore, ere yet the axe
Had smitten the old woods. Then hoary trunks
Of oak, and plane, and hickory, o'er thee held
A mighty canopy. When April winds
Grew soft, the maple burst into a flush
Of scarlet flowers. The tulip-tree, high up,
Opened, in airs of June, her multitude
Of golden chalices to humming-birds
And silken-wingèd insects of the sky.

Frail wood-plants clustered round thy edge in spring ;
The liver-leaf put forth her sister blooms
Of faintest blue. Here the quick-footed wolf,
Passing to lap thy waters, crushed the flower
Of sanguinaria, from whose brittle stem

The red drops fell like blood. The deer, too, left
Her delicate footprint in the soft moist mould,
And on the fallen leaves. The slow-paced bear,
In such a sultry summer noon as this,
Stopped at thy stream, and drank, and leaped across.

But thou hast histories that stir the heart
With deeper feeling ; while I look on thee
They rise before me. I behold the scene
Hoary again with forests ; I behold
The Indian warrior, whom a hand unseen
Has smitten with his death-wound in the woods,
Creep slowly to thy well-known rivulet,
And slake his death-thirst. Hark, that quick fierce cry
That rends the utter silence ! 'tis the whoop
Of battle, and a throng of savage men
With naked arms and faces stained like blood,
Fill the green wilderness ; the long bare arms
Are heaved aloft, bows twang and arrows stream ;
Each makes a tree his shield, and every tree
Sends forth its arrow. Fierce the fight and short,
As is the whirlwind. Soon the conquerors
And conquered vanish, and the dead remain
Mangled by tomahawks. The mighty woods
Are still again, the frighted bird comes back
And plumes her wings ; but thy sweet waters run
Crimson with blood. Then, as the sun goes down,
Amid the deepening twilight I descry
Figures of men that crouch and creep unheard,
And bear away the dead. The next day's shower
Shall wash the tokens of the fight away.

I look again—a hunter's lodge is built,
With poles and boughs, beside thy crystal well,
While the meek autumn stains the woods with gold,
And sheds his golden sunshine. To the door
The red-man slowly drags the enormous bear
Slain in the chestnut-thicket, or flings down
The deer from his strong shoulders. Shaggy fells

Of wolf and cougar hang upon the walls,
And loud the black-eyed Indian maidens laugh,
That gather, from the rustling heaps of leaves,
The hickory's white nuts, and the dark fruit
That falls from the gray butternut's long boughs.

So centuries passed by, and still the woods
Blossomed in spring, and reddened when the year
Grew chill, and glistened in the frozen rains
Of winter, till the white man swung the axe
Beside thee—signal of a mighty change.
Then all around was heard the crash of trees,
Trembling awhile and rushing to the ground,
The low of ox, and shouts of men who fired
The brushwood, or who tore the earth with ploughs;
The grain sprang thick and tall, and hid in green
The blackened hill-side ; ranks of spiky maize
Rose like a host embattled ; the buckwheat
Whitened broad acres, sweetening with its flowers
The August wind.   White cottages were seen
With rose-trees at the windows ; barns from which
Came loud and shrill the crowing of the cock ;
Pastures where rolled and neighed the lordly horse,
And white flocks browsed and bleated.   A rich turf
Of grasses brought from far o'ercrept thy bank,
Spotted with the white clover.   Blue-eyed girls
Brought pails, and dipped them in thy crystal pool ;
And children, ruddy-cheeked and flaxen-haired,
Gathered the glistening cowslip from thy edge.

Since then, what steps have trod thy border !   Here
On thy green bank, the woodman of the swamp
Has laid his axe, the reaper of the hill
His sickle, as they stooped to taste thy stream.
The sportsman, tired with wandering in the still
September noon, has bathed his heated brow
In thy cool current.   Shouting boys, let loose
For a wild holiday, have quaintly shaped
Into a cup the folded linden-leaf,
21

And dipped thy sliding crystal.　From the wars
Returning, the plumed soldier by thy side
Has sat, and mused how pleasant 'twere to dwell
In such a spot, and be as free as thou,
And move for no man's bidding more.　At eve,
When thou wert crimson with the crimson sky,
Lovers have gazed upon thee, and have thought
Their mingled lives should flow as peacefully
And brightly as thy waters.　Here the sage,
Gazing into thy self-replenished depth,
Has seen eternal order circumscribe
And bound the motions of eternal change,
And from the gushing of thy simple fount
Has reasoned to the mighty universe.

Is there no other change for thee, that lurks
Among the future ages?　Will not man
Seek out strange arts to wither and deform
The pleasant landscape which thou makest green?
Or shall the veins that feed thy constant stream
Be choked in middle earth, and flow no more
For ever, that the water-plants along
Thy channel perish, and the bird in vain
Alight to drink?　Haply shall these green hills
Sink, with the lapse of years, into the gulf
Of ocean waters, and thy source be lost
Amidst the bitter brine?　Or shall they rise,
Upheaved in broken cliffs and airy peaks,
Haunts of the eagle and the snake, and thou
Gush midway from the bare and barren steep?

THE WINDS.

I.

YE winds, ye unseen currents of the air,
　　Softly ye played a few brief hours ago;
Ye bore the murmuring bee; ye tossed the hair
　　O'er maiden cheeks, that took a fresher glow;

Ye rolled the round white cloud through depths of blue ;
Ye shook from shaded flowers the lingering dew ;
Before you the catalpa's blossoms flew,
   Light blossoms, dropping on the grass like snow.

II.

What change is this ! Ye take the cataract's sound ;
   Ye take the whirlpool's fury and its might ;
The mountain shudders as ye sweep the ground ;
   The valley woods lie prone beneath your flight.
The clouds before you shoot like eagles past ;
The homes of men are rocking in your blast ;
Ye lift the roofs like autumn leaves, and cast,
   Skyward, the whirling fragments out of sight.

III.

The weary fowls of heaven make wing in vain,
   To escape your wrath ; ye seize and dash them dead ;
Against the earth ye drive the roaring rain ;
   The harvest-field becomes a river's bed ;
And torrents tumble from the hills around,
Plains turn to lakes, and villages are drowned,
And wailing voices, midst the tempest's sound,
   Rise, as the rushing waters swell and spread.

IV.

Ye dart upon the deep, and straight is heard
   A wilder roar, and men grow pale, and pray ;
Ye fling its floods around you, as a bird
   Flings o'er his shivering plumes the fountain's spray.
See ! to the breaking mast the sailor clings ;
Ye scoop the ocean to its briny springs,
And take the mountain-billow on your wings,
   And pile the wreck of navies round the bay.

V.

Why rage ye thus ?—no strife for liberty
   Has made you mad ; no tyrant, strong through fear,
Has chained your pinions till ye wrenched them free,
   And rushed into the unmeasured atmosphere ;

For ye were born in freedom where ye blow ;
Free o'er the mighty deep to come and go ;
Earth's solemn woods were yours, her wastes of snow,
    Her isles where summer blossoms all the year.

VI.

O ye wild winds ! a mightier Power than yours
    In chains upon the shore of Europe lies ;
The sceptred throng whose fetters he endures
    Watch his mute throes with terror in their eyes ;
And armèd warriors all around him stand,
And, as he struggles, tighten every band,
And lift the heavy spear, with threatening hand,
    To pierce the victim, should he strive to rise.

VII.

Yet oh, when that wronged Spirit of our race
    Shall break, as soon he must, his long-worn chains,
And leap in freedom from his prison-place,
    Lord of his ancient hills and fruitful plains,
Let him not rise, like these mad winds of air,
To waste the loveliness that time could spare,
To fill the earth with woe, and blot her fair
    Unconscious breast with blood from human veins.

VIII.

But may he like the spring-time come abroad,
    Who crumbles winter's gyves with gentle might,
When in the genial breeze, the breath of God,
    The unsealed springs come spouting up to light ;
Flowers start from their dark prisons at his feet,
The woods, long dumb, awake to hymnings sweet,
And morn and eve, whose glimmerings almost meet,
    Crowd back to narrow bounds the ancient night

THE OLD MAN'S COUNSEL.

AMONG our hills and valleys, I have known
Wise and grave men, who, while their diligent hands
Tended or gathered in the fruits of earth,
Were reverent learners in the solemn school
Of Nature. Not in vain to them were sent
Seed-time and harvest, or the vernal shower
That darkened the brown tilth, or snow that beat
On the white winter hills. Each brought, in turn,
Some truth, some lesson on the life of man,
Or recognition of the Eternal mind
Who veils his glory with the elements.

One such I knew long since, a white-haired man,
Pithy of speech, and merry when he would ;
A genial optimist, who daily drew
From what he saw his quaint moralities.
Kindly he held communion, though so old,
With me a dreaming boy, and taught me much
That books tell not, and I shall ne'er forget.

The sun of May was bright in middle heaven,
And steeped the sprouting forests, the green hills,
And emerald wheat-fields, in his yellow light.
Upon the apple-tree, where rosy buds
Stood clustered, ready to burst forth in bloom,
The robin warbled forth his full clear note
For hours, and wearied not. Within the woods,
Whose young and half transparent leaves scarce cast
A shade, gay circles of anemones
Danced on their stalks ; the shad-bush, white with flower
Brightened the glens ; the new-leaved butternut
And quivering poplar to the roving breeze
Gave a balsamic fragrance. In the fields
I saw the pulses of the gentle wind
On the young grass. My heart was touched with joy
At so much beauty, flushing every hour

Into a fuller beauty ; but my friend,
The thoughtful ancient, standing at my side,
Gazed on it mildly sad.   I asked him why.

  " Well mayst thou join in gladness," he replied,
" With the glad earth, her springing plants and flowers,
And this soft wind, the herald of the green
Luxuriant summer.   Thou art young like them,
And well mayst thou rejoice.   But while the flight
Of seasons fills and knits thy spreading frame,
It withers mine, and thins my hair, and dims
These eyes, whose fading light shall soon be quenched
In utter darkness.   Hearest thou that bird ? "

  I listened, and from midst the depth of woods
Heard the love-signal of the grouse, that wears
A sable ruff around his mottled neck ;
Partridge they call him by our northern streams,
And pheasant by the Delaware.   He beat
His barred sides with his speckled wings, and made
A sound like distant thunder ; slow the strokes
At first, then fast and faster, till at length
They passed into a murmur and were still.

  " There hast thou," said my friend, " a fitting type
Of human life.   'Tis an old truth, I know,
But images like these revive the power
Of long familiar truths.   Slow pass our days
In childhood, and the hours of light are long
Betwixt the morn and eve ; with swifter lapse
They glide in manhood, and in age they fly ;
Till days and seasons flit before the mind
As flit the snow-flakes in a winter storm,
Seen rather than distinguished.   Ah ! I seem
As if I sat within a helpless bark,
By swiftly-running waters hurried on
To shoot some mighty cliff.   Along the banks
Grove after grove, rock after frowning rock,
Bare sands and pleasant homes, and flowery nooks,

And isles and whirlpools in the stream, appear
Each after each, but the devoted skiff
Darts by so swiftly that their images
Dwell not upon the mind, or only dwell
In dim confusion ; faster yet I sweep
By other banks, and the great gulf is near.

" Wisely, my son, while yet thy days are long,
And this fair change of seasons passes slow,
Gather and treasure up the good they yield—
All that they teach of virtue, of pure thoughts
And kind affections, reverence for thy God
And for thy brethren ; so when thou shalt come
Into these barren years, thou mayst not bring
A mind unfurnished and a withered heart."

Long since that white-haired ancient slept—but still,
When the red flower-buds crowd the orchard-bough,
And the ruffed grouse is drumming far within
The woods, his venerable form again
Is at my side, his voice is in my ear.

IN MEMORY OF WILLIAM LEGGETT.

THE earth may ring, from shore to shore,
  With echoes of a glorious name,
But he, whose loss our tears deplore,
  Has left behind him more than fame.

For when the death-frost came to lie
  On Leggett's warm and mighty heart,
And quench his bold and friendly eye,
  His spirit did not all depart.

The words of fire that from his pen
  Were flung upon the fervid page,
Still move, still shake the hearts of men,
  Amid a cold and coward age.

His love of truth, too warm, too strong
　For Hope or Fear to chain or chill,
His hate of tyranny and wrong,
　Burn in the breasts he kindled still.

AN EVENING REVERY.

THE summer day is closed—the sun is set :
Well they have done their office, those bright hours,
The latest of whose train goes softly out
In the red west.　The green blade of the ground
Has risen, and herds have cropped it ; the young twig
Has spread its plaited tissues to the sun ;
Flowers of the garden and the waste have blown
And withered ; seeds have fallen upon the soil,
From bursting cells, and in their graves await
Their resurrection.　Insects from the pools
Have filled the air awhile with humming wings,
That now are still for ever ; painted moths
Have wandered the blue sky, and died again ;
The mother-bird hath broken for her brood
Their prison shell, or shoved them from the nest,
Plumed for their earliest flight.　In bright alcoves,
In woodland cottages with barky walls,
In noisome cells of the tumultuous town,
Mothers have clasped with joy the new-born babe.
Graves by the lonely forest, by the shore
Of rivers and of ocean, by the ways
Of the thronged city, have been hollowed out
And filled, and closed.　This day hath parted friends
That ne'er before were parted ; it hath knit
New friendships ; it hath seen the maiden plight
Her faith, and trust her peace to him who long
Had wooed ; and it hath heard, from lips which late
Were eloquent of love, the first harsh word,
That told the wedded one her peace was flown.

Farewell to the sweet sunshine !   One glad day
Is added now to Childhood's merry days,
And one calm day to those of quiet Age.
Still the fleet hours run on ; and as I lean,
Amid the thickening darkness, lamps are lit,
By those who watch the dead, and those who twine
Flowers for the bride.   The mother from the eyes
Of her sick infant shades the painful light,
And sadly listens to his quick-drawn breath.

   O thou great Movement of the Universe,
Or Change, or Flight of Time—for ye are one !
That bearest, silently, this visible scene
Into night's shadow and the streaming rays
Of starlight, whither art thou bearing me ?
I feel the mighty current sweep me on,
Yet know not whither.   Man foretells afar
The courses of the stars ; the very hour
He knows when they shall darken or grow bright ;
Yet doth the eclipse of Sorrow and of Death
Come unforewarned.   Who next, of those I love,
Shall pass from life, or, sadder yet, shall fall
From virtue ?   Strife with foes, or bitterer strife
With friends, or shame and general scorn of men—
Which who can bear ?—or the fierce rack of pain—
Lie they within my path ?   Or shall the years
Push me, with soft and inoffensive pace,
Into the stilly twilight of my age ?
Or do the portals of another life
Even now, while I am glorying in my strength,
Impend around me ?   Oh ! beyond that bourne,
In the vast cycle of being which begins
At that dread threshold, with what fairer forms
Shall the great law of change and progress clothe
Its workings ?   Gently—so have good men taught—
Gently, and without grief, the old shall glide
Into the new ; the eternal flow of things,
Like a bright river of the fields of heaven,
Shall journey onward in perpetual peace.

THE PAINTED CUP.

THE fresh savannas of the Sangamon
Here rise in gentle swells, and the long grass
Is mixed with rustling hazels.   Scarlet tufts
Are glowing in the green, like flakes of fire ;
The wanderers of the prairie know them well,
And call that brilliant flower the Painted Cup.

Now, if thou art a poet, tell me not
That these bright chalices were tinted thus
To hold the dew for fairies, when they meet
On moonlight evenings in the hazel-bowers,
And dance till they are thirsty.   Call not up,
Amid this fresh and virgin solitude,
The faded fancies of an elder world ;
But leave these scarlet cups to spotted moths
Of June, and glistening flies, and humming-birds,
To drink from, when on all these boundless lawns
The morning sun looks hot.   Or let the wind
O'erturn in sport their ruddy brims, and pour
A sudden shower upon the strawberry-plant,
To swell the reddening fruit that even now
Breathes a slight fragrance from the sunny slope.

But thou art of a gayer fancy.   Well—
Let then the gentle Manitou of flowers,
Lingering amid the bloomy waste he loves,
Though all his swarthy worshippers are gone—
Slender and small, his rounded cheek all brown
And ruddy with the sunshine ; let him come
On summer mornings, when the blossoms wake,
And part with little hands the spiky grass,
And touching, with his cherry lips, the edge
Of these bright beakers, drain the gathered dew.

A DREAM.

I HAD a dream—a strange, wild dream—
    Said a dear voice at early light;
And even yet its shadows seem
    To linger in my waking sight.

Earth, green with spring, and fresh with dew,
    And bright with morn, before me stood;
And airs just wakened softly blew
    On the young blossoms of the wood.

Birds sang within the sprouting shade,
    Bees hummed amid the whispering grass,
And children prattled as they played
    Beside the rivulet's dimpling glass.

Fast climbed the sun : the flowers were flown,
    There played no children in the glen ;
For some were gone, and some were grown
    To blooming dames and bearded men.

'Twas noon, 'twas summer : I beheld
    Woods darkening in the flush of day,
And that bright rivulet spread and swelled,
    A mighty stream, with creek and bay.

And here was love, and there was strife,
    And mirthful shouts, and wrathful cries,
And strong men, struggling as for life,
    With knotted limbs and angry eyes.

Now stooped the sun—the shades grew thin ;
    The rustling paths were piled with leaves,
And sunburnt groups were gathering in,
    From the shorn field, its fruits and sheaves.

The river heaved with sullen sounds ;
　The chilly wind was sad with moans ;
Black hearses passed, and burial-grounds
　Grew thick with monumental stones.

Still waned the day ; the wind that chased
　The jagged clouds blew chiller yet ;
The woods were stripped, the fields were waste
　The wintry sun was near his set.

And of the young, and strong, and fair,
　A lonely remnant, gray and weak,
Lingered, and shivered to the air
　Of that bleak shore and water bleak.

Ah ! age is drear, and death is cold !
　I turned to thee, for thou wert near,
And saw thee withered, bowed, and old,
　And woke all faint with sudden fear.

'Twas thus I heard the dreamer say,
　And bade her clear her clouded brow ;
" For thou and I, since childhood's day,
　Have walked in such a dream till now.

" Watch we in calmness, as they rise,
　The changes of that rapid dream,
And note its lessons, till our eyes
　Shall open in the morning beam."

THE ANTIQUITY OF FREEDOM.

Here are old trees, tall oaks, and gnarléd pines,
That stream with gray-green mosses ; here the ground
Was never trenched by spade, and flowers spring up
Unsown, and die ungathered.　It is sweet

"Here are old trees, tall oaks, and gnarlèd pines."

To linger here, among the flitting birds
And leaping squirrels, wandering brooks, and winds
That shake the leaves, and scatter, as they pass,
A fragrance from the cedars, thickly set
With pale-blue berries.   In these peaceful shades—
Peaceful, unpruned, immeasurably old—
My thoughts go up the long dim path of years,
Back to the earliest days of liberty.

   O FREEDOM ! thou art not, as poets dream,
A fair young girl, with light and delicate limbs,
And wavy tresses gushing from the cap
With which the Roman master crowned his slave
When he took off the gyves.   A bearded man,
Armed to the teeth, art thou ; one mailéd hand
Grasps the broad shield, and one the sword ; thy brow,
Glorious in beauty though it be, is scarred
With tokens of old wars ; thy massive limbs
Are strong with struggling.   Power at thee has launched
His bolts, and with his lightnings smitten thee ;
They could not quench the life thou hast from heaven ;
Merciless Power has dug thy dungeon deep,
And his swart armorers, by a thousand fires,
Have forged thy chain ; yet, while he deems thee bound,
The links are shivered, and the prison-walls
Fall outward ; terribly thou springest forth,
As springs the flame above a burning pile,
And shoutest to the nations, who return
Thy shoutings, while the pale oppressor flies.

   Thy birthright was not given by human hands :
Thou wert twin-born with man.   In pleasant fields,
While yet our race was few, thou sat'st with him,
To tend the quiet flock and watch the stars,
And teach the reed to utter simple airs.
Thou by his side, amid the tangled wood,
Didst war upon the panther and the wolf,
His only foes ; and thou with him didst draw
The earliest furrow on the mountain-side,

Soft with the deluge.   Tyranny himself,
Thy enemy, although of reverend look,
Hoary with many years, and far obeyed,
Is later born than thou ; and as he meets
The grave defiance of thine elder eye,
The usurper trembles in his fastnesses.

Thou shalt wax stronger with the lapse of years,
But he shall fade into a feebler age—
Feebler, yet subtler.   He shall weave his snares,
And spring them on thy careless steps, and clap
His withered hands, and from their ambush call
His hordes to fall upon thee.   He shall send
Quaint maskers, wearing fair and gallant forms
To catch thy gaze, and uttering graceful words
To charm thy ear ; while his sly imps, by stealth,
Twine round thee threads of steel, light thread on thread,
That grow to fetters ; or bind down thy arms
With chains concealed in chaplets.   Oh ! not yet
Mayst thou unbrace thy corslet, nor lay by
Thy sword ; nor yet, O Freedom ! close thy lids
In slumber ; for thine enemy never sleeps,
And thou must watch and combat till the day
Of the new earth and heaven.   But wouldst thou rest
Awhile from tumult and the frauds of men,
These old and friendly solitudes invite
Thy visit.   They, while yet the forest-trees
Were young upon the unviolated earth,
And yet the moss-stains on the rock were new,
Beheld thy glorious childhood, and rejoiced.

THE MAIDEN'S SORROW.

SEVEN long years has the desert rain
    Dropped on the clods that hide thy face ;
Seven long years of sorrow and pain
    I have thought of thy burial-place ;

"*There, when the winter woods are bare,*
Walks the wolf on the crackling snow."

Thought of thy fate in the distant West,
  Dying with none that loved thee near,
They who flung the earth on thy breast
  Turned from the spot without a tear.

There, I think, on that lonely grave,
  Violets spring in the soft May shower ;
There, in the summer breezes, wave
  Crimson phlox and moccasin-flower.

There the turtles alight, and there
  Feeds with her fawn the timid doe ;
There, when the winter woods are bare,
  Walks the wolf on the crackling snow.

Soon wilt thou wipe my tears away ;
  All my task upon earth is done ;
My poor father, old and gray,
  Slumbers beneath the churchyard stone.

In the dreams of my lonely bed,
  Ever thy form before me seems,
All night long I talk with the dead,
  All day long I think of my dreams.

This deep wound that bleeds and aches,
  This long pain, a sleepless pain—
When the Father my spirit takes,
  I shall feel it no more again.

THE RETURN OF YOUTH.

My friend, thou sorrowest for thy golden prime,
  For thy fair youthful years too swift of flight ;
Thou musest, with wet eyes, upon the time
  Of cheerful hopes that filled the world with light—

Years when thy heart was bold, thy hand was strong,
    And quick the thought that moved thy tongue to speak,
And willing faith was thine, and scorn of wrong
    Summoned the sudden crimson to thy cheek.

Thou lookest forward on the coming days,
    Shuddering to feel their shadow o'er thee creep ;
A path, thick-set with changes and decays,
    Slopes downward to the place of common sleep ;
And they who walked with thee in life's first stage,
    Leave one by one thy side, and, waiting near,
Thou seest the sad companions of thy age—
    Dull love of rest, and weariness and fear.

Yet grieve thou not, nor think thy youth is gone,
    Nor deem that glorious season e'er could die.
Thy pleasant youth, a little while withdrawn,
    Waits on the horizon of a brighter sky ;
Waits, like the morn, that folds her wings and hides
    Till the slow stars bring back her dawning hour ;
Waits, like the vanished spring, that slumbering bides
    Her own sweet time to waken bud and flower.

There shall he welcome thee, when thou shalt stand
    On his bright morning hills, with smiles more sweet
Than when at first he took thee by the hand,
    Through the fair earth to lead thy tender feet.
He shall bring back, but brighter, broader still,
    Life's early glory to thine eyes again,
Shall clothe thy spirit with new strength, and fill
    Thy leaping heart with warmer love than then.

Hast thou not glimpses, in the twilight here,
    Of mountains where immortal morn prevails ?
Comes there not, through the silence, to thine ear
    A gentle rustling of the morning gales ;
A murmur, wafted from that glorious shore,
    Of streams that water banks forever fair,
And voices of the loved ones gone before,
    More musical in that celestial air ?

A HYMN OF THE SEA.

THE sea is mighty, but a mightier sways
His restless billows. Thou, whose hands have scooped
His boundless gulfs and built his shore, thy breath,
That moved in the beginning o'er his face,
Moves o'er it evermore. The obedient waves
To its strong motion roll, and rise and fall.
Still from that realm of rain thy cloud goes up,
As at the first, to water the great earth,
And keep her valleys green. A hundred realms
Watch its broad shadow warping on the wind,
And in the dropping shower, with gladness hear
Thy promise of the harvest. I look forth
Over the boundless blue, where joyously
The bright crests of innumerable waves
Glance to the sun at once, as when the hands
Of a great multitude are upward flung
In acclamation. I behold the ships
Gliding from cape to cape, from isle to isle,
Or stemming toward far lands, or hastening home
From the Old World. It is thy friendly breeze
That bears them, with the riches of the land,
And treasure of dear lives, till, in the port,
The shouting seaman climbs and furls the sail.

But who shall bide thy tempest, who shall face
The blast that wakes the fury of the sea ?
O God ! thy justice makes the world turn pale,
When on the armèd fleet, that royally
Bears down the surges, carrying war, to smite
Some city, or invade some thoughtless realm,
Descends the fierce tornado. The vast hulks
Are whirled like chaff upon the waves ; the sails
Fly, rent like webs of gossamer ; the masts
Are snapped asunder ; downward from the decks,
Downward are slung, into the fathomless gulf,
Their cruel engines ; and their hosts, arrayed
22

In trappings of the battle-field, are whelmed
By whirlpools, or dashed dead upon the rocks.
Then stand the nations still with awe, and pause,
A moment, from the bloody work of war.

These restless surges eat away the shores
Of earth's old continents ; the fertile plain
Welters in shallows, headlands crumble down,
And the tide drifts the sea-sand in the streets
Of the drowned city.   Thou, meanwhile, afar
In the green chambers of the middle sea,
Where broadest spread the waters and the line
Sinks deepest, while no eye beholds thy work,
Creator ! thou dost teach the coral-worm
To lay his mighty reefs.   From age to age,
He builds beneath the waters, till, at last,
His bulwarks overtop the brine, and check
The long wave rolling from the southern pole
To break upon Japan.   Thou bidd'st the fires,
That smoulder under ocean, heave on high
The new-made mountains, and uplift their peaks,
A place of refuge for the storm-driven bird.
The birds and wafting billows plant the rifts
With herb and tree ; sweet fountains gush ; sweet airs
Ripple the living lakes that, fringed with flowers,
Are gathered in the hollows.   Thou dost look
On thy creation and pronounce it good.
Its valleys, glorious in their summer green,
Praise thee in silent beauty, and its woods,
Swept by the murmuring winds of ocean, join
The murmuring shores in a perpetual hymn.

NOON.

FROM AN UNFINISHED POEM.

'Tis noon. At noon the Hebrew bowed the knee
And worshipped, while the husbandmen withdrew
From the scorched field, and the wayfaring man
Grew faint, and turned aside by bubbling fount,
Or rested in the shadow of the palm.

I, too, amid the overflow of day,
Behold the power which wields and cherishes
The frame of Nature. From this brow of rock
That overlooks the Hudson's western marge,
I gaze upon the long array of groves,
The piles and gulfs of verdure drinking in
The grateful heats. They love the fiery sun ;
Their broadening leaves grow glossier, and their sprays
Climb as he looks upon them. In the midst,
The swelling river, into his green gulfs,
Unshadowed save by passing sails above,
Takes the redundant glory, and enjoys
The summer in his chilly bed. Coy flowers,
That would not open in the early light,
Push back their plaited sheaths. The rivulet's pool,
That darkly quivered all the morning long
In the cool shade, now glimmers in the sun ;
And o'er its surface shoots, and shoots again,
The glittering dragon-fly, and deep within
Run the brown water-beetles to and fro.

A silence, the brief sabbath of an hour,
Reigns o'er the fields ; the laborer sits within
His dwelling ; he has left his steers awhile,
Unyoked, to bite the herbage, and his dog
Sleeps stretched beside the door-stone in the shade.
Now the gray marmot, with uplifted paws,
No more sits listening by his den, but steals

Abroad, in safety, to the clover-field,
And crops its juicy blossoms.   All the while
A ceaseless murmur from the populous town
Swells o'er these solitudes : a mingled sound
Of jarring wheels, and iron hoofs that clash
Upon the stony ways, and hammer-clang,
And creak of engines lifting ponderous bulks,
And calls and cries, and tread of eager feet,
Innumerable, hurrying to and fro.
Noon, in that mighty mart of nations, brings
No pause to toil and care.   With early day
Began the tumult, and shall only cease
When midnight, hushing one by one the sounds
Of bustle, gathers the tired brood to rest.

   Thus, in this feverish time, when love of gain
And luxury possess the hearts of men,
Thus is it with the noon of human life.
We, in our fervid manhood, in our strength
Of reason, we, with hurry, noise, and care,
Plan, toil, and strive, and pause not to refresh
Our spirits with the calm and beautiful
Of God's harmonious universe, that won
Our youthful wonder ; pause not to inquire
Why we are here ; and what the reverence
Man owes to man, and what the mystery
That links us to the greater world, beside
Whose borders we but hover for a space.

THE CROWDED STREET.

Let me move slowly through the street,
  Filled with an ever-shifting train,
Amid the sound of steps that beat
  The murmuring walks like autumn rain.

How fast the flitting figures come !
 The mild, the fierce, the stony face ;
Some bright with thoughtless smiles, and some
 Where secret tears have left their trace.

They pass—to toil, to strife, to rest ;
 To halls in which the feast is spread ;
To chambers where the funeral guest
 In silence sits beside the dead.

And some to happy homes repair,
 Where children, pressing cheek to cheek,
With mute caresses shall declare
 The tenderness they cannot speak.

And some, who walk in calmness here,
 Shall shudder as they reach the door
Where one who made their dwelling dear,
 Its flower, its light, is seen no more.

Youth, with pale cheek and slender frame,
 And dreams of greatness in thine eye !
Go'st thou to build an early name,
 Or early in the task to die ?

Keen son of trade, with eager brow !
 Who is now fluttering in thy snare ?
Thy golden fortunes, tower they now,
 Or melt the glittering spires in air ?

Who of this crowd to-night shall tread
 The dance till daylight gleam again ?
Who sorrow o'er the untimely dead ?
 Who writhe in throes of mortal pain?

Some, famine-struck, shall think how long
 The cold dark hours, how slow the light ;
And some, who flaunt amid the throng,
 Shall hide in dens of shame to-night.

Each, where his tasks or pleasures call,
  They pass, and heed each other not.
There is who heeds, who holds them all,
  In His large love and boundless thought.

These struggling tides of life that seem
  In wayward, aimless course to tend,
Are eddies of the mighty stream
  That rolls to its appointed end.

THE WHITE-FOOTED DEER.

It was a hundred years ago,
  When, by the woodland ways,
The traveller saw the wild-deer drink,
  Or crop the birchen sprays.

Beneath a hill, whose rocky side
  O'erbrowed a grassy mead,
And fenced a cottage from the wind,
  A deer was wont to feed.

She only came when on the cliffs
  The evening moonlight lay,
And no man knew the secret haunts
  In which she walked by day.

White were her feet, her forehead showed
  A spot of silvery white,
That seemed to glimmer like a star
  In autumn's hazy night.

And here, when sang the whippoorwill,
  She cropped the sprouting leaves,
And here her rustling steps were heard
  On still October eves.

But when the broad midsummer moon
　　Rose o'er that grassy lawn,
Beside the silver-footed deer
　　There grazed a spotted fawn.

The cottage dame forbade her son
　　To aim the rifle here ;
" It were a sin," she said, " to harm
　　Or fright that friendly deer.

" This spot has been my pleasant home
　　Ten peaceful years and more ;
And ever, when the moonlight shines,
　　She feeds before our door.

" The red-men say that here she walked
　　A thousand moons ago ;
They never raise the war-whoop here,
　　And never twang the bow.

" I love to watch her as she feeds,
　　And think that all is well
While such a gentle creature haunts
　　The place in which we dwell."

The youth obeyed, and sought for game
　　In forests far away,
Where, deep in silence and in moss,
　　The ancient woodland lay.

But once, in autumn's golden time
　　He ranged the wild in vain,
Nor roused the pheasant nor the deer
　　And wandered home again.

The crescent moon and crimson eve
　　Shone with a mingling light ;
The deer, upon the grassy mead,
　　Was feeding full in sight.

He raised the rifle to his eye,
  And from the cliffs around
A sudden echo, shrill and sharp,
  Gave back its deadly sound.

Away, into the neighboring wood,
  The startled creature flew,
And crimson drops at morning lay
  Amid the glimmering dew.

Next evening shone the waxing moon
  As brightly as before ;
The deer upon the grassy mead
  Was seen again no more.

But ere that crescent moon was old,
  By night the red-men came,
And burnt the cottage to the ground,
  And slew the youth and dame.

Now woods have overgrown the mead,
  And hid the cliffs from sight ;
There shrieks the hovering hawk at noon,
  And prowls the fox at night.

THE WANING MOON.

I'VE watched too late ; the morn is near ;
  One look at God's broad silent sky !
Oh, hopes and wishes vainly dear,
  How in your very strength ye die !

Even while your glow is on the cheek,
  And scarce the high pursuit begun,
The heart grows faint, the hand grows weak,
  The task of life is left undone.

See where, upon the horizon's brim,
　Lies the still cloud in gloomy bars ;
The waning moon, all pale and dim,
　Goes up amid the eternal stars.

Late, in a flood of tender light,
　She floated through the ethereal blue,
A softer sun, that shone all night
　Upon the gathering beads of dew.

And still thou wanest, pallid moon !
　The encroaching shadow grows apace ;
Heaven's everlasting watchers soon
　Shall see thee blotted from thy place.

Oh, Night's dethroned and crownless queen !
　Well may thy sad, expiring ray
Be shed on those whose eyes have seen
　Hope's glorious visions fade away.

Shine thou for forms that once were bright,
　For sages in the mind's eclipse,
For those whose words were spells of might,
　But falter now on stammering lips !

In thy decaying beam there lies
　Full many a grave on hill and plain,
Of those who closed their dying eyes
　In grief that they had lived in vain.

Another night, and thou among
　The spheres of heaven shalt cease to shine,
All rayless in the glittering throng
　Whose lustre late was quenched in thine.

Yet soon a new and tender light
　From out thy darkened orb shall beam,
And broaden till it shines all night
　On glistening dew and glimmering stream.

THE STREAM OF LIFE.

OH silvery streamlet of the fields,
　That flowest full and free,
For thee the rains of spring return,
　The summer dews for thee ;
And when thy latest blossoms die
　In autumn's chilly showers,
The winter fountains gush for thee,
　Till May brings back the flowers.

Oh Stream of Life ! the violet springs
　But once beside thy bed ;
But one brief summer, on thy path,
　The dews of heaven are shed.
Thy parent fountains shrink away,
　And close their crystal veins,
And where thy glittering current flowed
　The dust alone remains.

THE UNKNOWN WAY.

A BURNING sky is o'er me,
　The sands beneath me glow,
As onward, onward, wearily,
　In the sultry morn I go.

From the dusty path there opens,
　Eastward, an unknown way ;
Above its windings, pleasantly,
　The woodland branches play.

A silvery brook comes stealing
　From the shadow of its trees,
Where slender herbs of the forest stoop
　Before the entering breeze.

Along those pleasant windings
  I would my journey lay,
Where the shade is cool and the dew of night
  Is not yet dried away.

Path of the flowery woodland !
  Oh whither dost thou lead,
Wandering by grassy orchard-grounds,
  Or by the open mead ?

Goest thou by nestling cottage ?
  Goest thou by stately hall,
Where the broad elm droops, a leafy dome,
  And woodbines flaunt on the wall ?

By steeps where children gather
  Flowers of the yet fresh year ?
By lonely walks where lovers stray
  Till the tender stars appear ?

Or haply dost thou linger
  On barren plains and bare,
Or clamber the bald mountain-side
  Into the thinner air ?—

Where they who journey upward
  Walk in a weary track,
And oft upon the shady vale
  With longing eyes look back ?

I hear a solemn murmur,
  And, listening to the sound,
I know the voice of the mighty Sea,
  Beating his pebbly bound.

Dost thou, oh path of the woodland !
  End where those waters roar,
Like human life, on a trackless beach,
  With a boundless Sea before ?

"OH MOTHER OF A MIGHTY RACE."

OH mother of a mighty race,
Yet lovely in thy youthful grace !
The elder dames, thy haughty peers,
Admire and hate thy blooming years.
    With words of shame
And taunts of scorn they join thy name.

For on thy cheeks the glow is spread
That tints thy morning hills with red ;
Thy step—the wild-deer's rustling feet
Within thy woods are not more fleet ;
    Thy hopeful eye
Is bright as thine own sunny sky.

Ay, let them rail—those haughty ones,
While safe thou dwellest with thy sons.
They do not know how loved thou art,
How many a fond and fearless heart
    Would rise to throw
Its life between thee and the foe.

They know not, in their hate and pride,
What virtues with thy children bide ;
How true, how good, thy graceful maids
Make bright, like flowers, the valley-shades ;
    What generous men
Spring, like thine oaks, by hill and glen ;—

What cordial welcomes greet the guest
By thy lone rivers of the West ;
How faith is kept, and truth revered,
And man is loved, and God is feared,
    In woodland homes,
And where the ocean border foams.

There's freedom at thy gates and rest
For Earth's down-trodden and opprest,
A shelter for the hunted head,
For the starved laborer toil and bread.
        Power, at thy bounds,
Stops and calls back his baffled hounds.

Oh, fair young mother! on thy brow
Shall sit a nobler grace than now.
Deep in the brightness of the skies
The thronging years in glory rise,
        And, as they fleet,
Drop strength and riches at thy feet.

Thine eye, with every coming hour,
Shall brighten, and thy form shall tower;
And when thy sisters, elder born,
Would brand thy name with words of scorn,
        Before thine eye,
Upon their lips the taunt shall die.

THE LAND OF DREAMS.

A MIGHTY realm is the Land of Dreams,
  With steeps that hang in the twilight sky,
And weltering oceans and trailing streams,
  That gleam where the dusky valleys lie.

But over its shadowy border flow
  Sweet rays from the world of endless morn,
And the nearer mountains catch the glow,
  And flowers in the nearer fields are born.

The souls of the happy dead repair,
  From their bowers of light, to that bordering land,
And walk in the fainter glory there,
  With the souls of the living hand in hand.

One calm sweet smile, in that shadowy sphere,
  From eyes that open on earth no more—
One warning word from a voice once dear—
  How they rise in the memory o'er and o'er!

Far off from those hills that shine with day,
  And fields that bloom in the heavenly gales,
The Land of Dreams goes stretching away
  To dimmer mountains and darker vales.

There lie the chambers of guilty delight,
  There walk the spectres of guilty fear,
And soft low voices, that float through the night,
  Are whispering sin in the helpless ear.

Dear maid, in thy girlhood's opening flower,
  Scarce weaned from the love of childish play!
The tears on whose cheeks are but the shower
  That freshens the blooms of early May!

Thine eyes are closed, and over thy brow
  Pass thoughtful shadows and joyous gleams,
And I know, by thy moving lips, that now
  Thy spirit strays in the Land of Dreams.

Light-hearted maiden, oh, heed thy feet!
  O keep where that beam of Paradise falls:
And only wander where thou mayst meet
  The blessed ones from its shining walls!

So shalt thou come from the Land of Dreams,
  With love and peace to this world of strife:
And the light which over that border streams
  Shall lie on the path of thy daily life.

THE BURIAL OF LOVE.

Two dark-eyed maids, at shut of day,
Sat where a river rolled away,
With calm sad brows and raven hair,
And one was pale and both were fair.

Bring flowers, they sang, bring flowers unblown,
Bring forest-blooms of name unknown ;
Bring budding sprays from wood and wild,
To strew the bier of Love, the child.

Close softly, fondly, while ye weep,
His eyes, that death may seem like sleep,
And fold his hands in sign of rest,
His waxen hands, across his breast.

And make his grave where violets hide,
Where star-flowers strew the rivulet's side,
And bluebirds in the misty spring
Of cloudless skies and summer sing.

Place near him, as ye lay him low,
His idle shafts, his loosened bow,
The silken fillet that around
His waggish eyes in sport he wound.

But we shall mourn him long, and miss
His ready smile, his ready kiss,
The patter of his little feet,
Sweet frowns and stammered phrases sweet :

And graver looks, serene and high,
A light of heaven in that young eye,
All these shall haunt us till the heart
Shall ache and ache—and tears will start.

The bow, the band shall fail to dust,
The shining arrows waste with rust,
And all of Love that earth can claim,
Be but a memory and a name.

Not thus his nobler part shall dwell
A prisoner in this narrow cell ;
But he whom now we hide from men,
In the dark ground, shall live again :

Shall break these clods, a form of light,
With nobler mien and purer sight,
And in the eternal glory stand,
Highest and nearest God's right hand.

"THE MAY SUN SHEDS AN AMBER LIGHT."

THE May sun sheds an amber light
　　On new-leaved woods and lawns between ;
But she who, with a smile more bright,
　　Welcomed and watched the springing green,
　　　　　Is in her grave,
　　　　　Low in her grave.

The fair white blossoms of the wood
　　In groups beside the pathway stand ;
But one, the gentle and the good,
　　Who cropped them with a fairer hand,
　　　　　Is in her grave,
　　　　　Low in her grave.

Upon the woodland's morning airs
　　The small birds' mingled notes are flung ;
But she, whose voice, more sweet than theirs,
　　Once bade me listen while they sung,
　　　　　Is in her grave,
　　　　　Low in her grave.

That music of the early year
  Brings tears of anguish to my eyes ;
My heart aches when the flowers appear ;
  For then I think of her who lies
            Within her grave,
            Low in her grave.

THE VOICE OF AUTUMN.

THERE comes, from yonder height,
  A soft repining sound,
Where forest-leaves are bright,
And fall, like flakes of light,
      To the ground.

It is the autumn breeze,
  That, lightly floating on,
Just skims the weedy leas,
Just stirs the glowing trees,
      And is gone.

He moans by sedgy brook,
  And visits, with a sigh,
The last pale flowers that look,
From out their sunny nook,
      At the sky.

O'er shouting children flies
  That light October wind,
And, kissing cheeks and eyes,
He leaves their merry cries
      Far behind,

And wanders on to make
  That soft uneasy sound
By distant wood and lake,
Where distant fountains break
      From the ground

23

No bower where maidens dwell
　　Can win a moment's stay ;
Nor fair untrodden dell ;
He sweeps the upland swell,
　　　　And away !

Mourn'st thou thy homeless state ?
　　O soft, repining wind !
That early seek'st and late
The rest it is thy fate
　　　　Not to find.

Not on the mountain's breast,
　　Not on the ocean's shore,
In all the East and West :
The wind that stops to rest
　　　　Is no more.

By valleys, woods, and springs,
　　No wonder thou shouldst grieve
For all the glorious things
Thou touchest with thy wings
　　　　And must leave.

THE CONQUEROR'S GRAVE.

WITHIN this lowly grave a Conqueror lies,
　　And yet the monument proclaims it not,
Nor round the sleeper's name hath chisel wrought
　　The emblems of a fame that never dies,—
Ivy and amaranth, in a graceful sheaf,
Twined with the laurel's fair, imperial leaf.
　　　　A simple name alone,
　　　　To the great world unknown,
Is graven here, and wild-flowers, rising round,
Meek meadow-sweet and violets of the ground,
　　Lean lovingly against the humble stone.

Here, in the quiet earth, they laid apart
  No man of iron mould and bloody hands,
Who sought to wreak upon the cowering lands
  The passions that consumed his restless heart ;
But one of tender spirit and delicate frame,
        Gentlest, in mien and mind,
        Of gentle womankind,
Timidly shrinking from the breath of blame :
One in whose eyes the smile of kindness made
  Its haunt, like flowers by sunny brooks in May,
Yet, at the thought of others' pain, a shade
Of sweeter sadness chased the smile away.

Nor deem that when the hand that moulders here
Was raised in menace, realms were chilled with fear,
  And armies mustered at the sign, as when
Clouds rise on clouds before the rainy East—
    Gray captains leading bands of veteran men
And fiery youths to be the vulture's feast.
Not thus were waged the mighty wars that gave
The victory to her who fills this grave :
        Alone her task was wrought,
        Alone the battle fought ;
Through that long strife her constant hope was staid
On God alone, nor looked for other aid.

She met the hosts of Sorrow with a look
  That altered not beneath the frown they wore,
And soon the lowering brood were tamed, and took,
  Meekly, her gentle rule, and frowned no more.
Her soft hand put aside the assaults of wrath,
        And calmly broke in twain
        The fiery shafts of pain,
And rent the nets of passion from her path.
  By that victorious hand despair was slain.
With love she vanquished hate and overcame
Evil with good, in her Great Master's name.

Her glory is not of this shadowy state,
  Glory that with the fleeting season dies ;
But when she entered at the sapphire gate
  What joy was radiant in celestial eyes !
How heaven's bright depths with sounding welcomes rung,
And flowers of heaven by shining hands were flung !
    And He who, long before,
    Pain, scorn, and sorrow bore,
The Mighty Sufferer, with aspect sweet,
Smiled on the timid stranger from his seat ;
He who returning, glorious, from the grave,
Dragged Death, disarmed, in chains, a crouching slave.

See, as I linger here, the sun grows low ;
  Cool airs are murmuring that the night is near.
Oh, gentle sleeper, from thy grave I go
  Consoled though sad, in hope and yet in fear.
    Brief is the time, I know,
    The warfare scarce begun ;
Yet all may win the triumphs thou hast won.
Still flows the fount whose waters strengthened thee,
  The victors' names are yet too few to fill
Heaven's mighty roll ; the glorious armory,
  That ministered to thee, is open still.

THE PLANTING OF THE APPLE-TREE.

  Come, let us plant the apple-tree.
Cleave the tough greensward with the spade ;
Wide let its hollow bed be made ;
There gently lay the roots, and there
Sift the dark mould with kindly care,
  And press it o'er them tenderly,
As, round the sleeping infant's feet,
We softly fold the cradle-sheet ;
  So plant we the apple-tree.

What plant we in this apple-tree?
Buds, which the breath of summer days
Shall lengthen into leafy sprays;
Boughs where the thrush, with crimson breast,
Shall haunt and sing and hide her nest;
   We plant, upon the sunny lea,
A shadow for the noontide hour,
A shelter from the summer shower,
   When we plant the apple-tree.

What plant we in this apple-tree?
Sweets for a hundred flowery springs
To load the May-wind's restless wings,
When, from the orchard-row, he pours
Its fragrance through our open doors;
   A world of blossoms for the bee,
Flowers for the sick girl's silent room,
For the glad infant sprigs of bloom,
   We plant with the apple-tree.

What plant we in this apple-tree?
Fruits that shall swell in sunny June,
And redden in the August noon,
And drop, when gentle airs come by,
That fan the blue September sky,
   While children come, with cries of glee,
And seek them where the fragrant grass
Betrays their bed to those who pass,
   At the foot of the apple-tree.

And when, above this apple-tree,
The winter stars are quivering bright,
And winds go howling through the night,
Girls, whose young eyes o'erflow with mirth,
Shall peel its fruit by cottage-hearth,
   And guests in prouder homes shall see,
Heaped with the grape of Cintra's vine
And golden orange of the line,
   The fruit of the apple-tree.

The fruitage of this apple-tree
Winds and our flag of stripe and star
Shall bear to coasts that lie afar,
Where men shall wonder at the view,
And ask in what fair groves they grew ;
    And sojourners beyond the sea
Shall think of childhood's careless day,
And long, long hours of summer play,
    In the shade of the apple-tree.

Each year shall give this apple-tree
A broader flush of roseate bloom,
A deeper maze of verdurous gloom,
And loosen, when the frost-clouds lower,
The crisp brown leaves in thicker shower.
    The years shall come and pass, but we
Shall hear no longer, where we lie,
The summer's songs, the autumn's sigh,
    In the boughs of the apple-tree.

And time shall waste this apple-tree.
Oh, when its aged branches throw
Thin shadows on the ground below,
Shall fraud and force and iron will
Oppress the weak and helpless still?
    What shall the tasks of mercy be,
Amid the toils, the strifes, the tears
Of those who live when length of years
    Is wasting this little apple-tree?

"Who planted this old apple-tree?"
The children of that distant day
Thus to some aged man shall say ;
And, gazing on its mossy stem,
The gray-haired man shall answer them :
    "A poet of the land was he,
Born in the rude but good old times ;
'Tis said he made some quaint old rhymes,
    On planting the apple-tree."

*"Flake after flake
They sink in the dark and silent lake."*

THE SNOW-SHOWER.

STAND here by my side and turn, I pray,
  On the lake below thy gentle eyes ;
The clouds hang over it, heavy and gray,
  And dark and silent the water lies ;
And out of that frozen mist the snow
In wavering flakes begins to flow ;
          Flake after flake
They sink in the dark and silent lake.

See how in a living swarm they come
  From the chambers beyond that misty veil ;
Some hover awhile in air, and some
  Rush prone from the sky like summer hail.
All, dropping swiftly or settling slow,
Meet, and are still in the depths below ;
          Flake after flake
Dissolved in the dark and silent lake.

Here delicate snow-stars, out of the cloud,
  Come floating downward in airy play,
Like spangles dropped from the glistening crowd
  That whiten by night the milky way ;
There broader and burlier masses fall ;
The sullen water buries them all—
          Flake after flake—
All drowned in the dark and silent lake.

And some, as on tender wings they glide
  From their chilly birth-cloud, dim and gray,
Are joined in their fall, and, side by side,
  Come clinging along their unsteady way ;
As friend with friend, or husband with wife,
Makes hand in hand the passage of life ;
          Each mated flake
Soon sinks in the dark and silent lake.

Lo ! while we are gazing, in swifter haste
  Stream down the snows, till the air is white,
As, myriads by myriads madly chased,
    They fling themselves from their shadowy height.
The fair, frail creatures of middle sky,
What speed they make, with their grave so nigh ;
        Flake after flake,
To lie in the dark and silent lake !

I see in thy gentle eyes a tear ;
  They turn to me in sorrowful thought ;
Thou thinkest of friends, the good and dear,
    Who were for a time, and now are not ;
Like these fair children of cloud and frost,
That glisten a moment and then are lost,
        Flake after flake—
All lost in the dark and silent lake.

Yet look again, for the clouds divide ;
  A gleam of blue on the water lies ;
And far away, on the mountain-side,
    A sunbeam falls from the opening skies,
But the hurrying host that flew between
The cloud and the water, no more is seen ;
        Flake after flake,
At rest in the dark and silent lake.

A RAIN-DREAM.

THESE strifes, these tumults of the noisy world,
Where Fraud, the coward, tracks his prey by stealth,
And Strength, the ruffian, glories in his guilt,
Oppress the heart with sadness.   Oh, my friend,
In what serener mood we look upon
The gloomiest aspects of the elements
Among the woods and fields !   Let us awhile,
As the slow wind is rolling up the storm,
In fancy leave this maze of dusty streets,

Forever shaken by the importunate jar
Of commerce, and upon the darkening air
Look from the shelter of our rural home.
 Who is not awed that listens to the Rain,
Sending his voice before him ?   Mighty Rain !
The upland steeps are shrouded by thy mists ;
Thy shadow fills the hollow vale ; the pools
No longer glimmer, and the silvery streams
Darken to veins of lead at thy approach.
O mighty Rain ! already thou art here ;
And every roof is beaten by thy streams,
And, as thou passest, every glassy spring
Grows rough, and every leaf in all the woods
Is struck, and quivers.   All the hill-tops slake
Their thirst from thee ; a thousand languishing fields,
A thousand fainting gardens, are refreshed ;
A thousand idle rivulets start to speed,
And with the graver murmur of the storm
Blend their light voices as they hurry on.
 Thou fill'st the circle of the atmosphere
Alone ; there is no living thing abroad,
No bird to wing the air nor beast to walk
The field ; the squirrel in the forest seeks
His hollow tree ; the marmot of the field
Has scampered to his den ; the butterfly
Hides under her broad leaf ; the insect crowds,
That made the sunshine populous, lie close
In their mysterious shelters, whence the sun
Will summon them again.   The mighty Rain
Holds the vast empire of the sky alone.
 I shut my eyes, and see, as in a dream,
The friendly clouds drop down spring violets
And summer columbines, and all the flowers
That tuft the woodland floor, or overarch
The streamlet :—spiky grass for genial June,
Brown harvests for the waiting husbandman,
And for the woods a deluge of fresh leaves.
 I see these myriad drops that slake the dust,
Gathered in glorious streams, or rolling blue

In billows on the lake or on the deep,
And bearing navies. I behold them change
To threads of crystal as they sink in earth
And leave its stains behind, to rise again
In pleasant nooks of verdure, where the child,
Thirsty with play, in both his little hands
Shall take the cool, clear water, raising it
To wet his pretty lips. To-morrow noon
How proudly will the water-lily ride
The brimming pool, o'erlooking, like a queen,
Her circle of broad leaves ! In lonely wastes,
When next the sunshine makes them beautiful,
Gay troops of butterflies shall light to drink
At the replenished hollows of the rock.

 Now slowly falls the dull blank night, and still,
All through the starless hours, the mighty Rain
Smites with perpetual sound the forest-leaves,
And beats the matted grass, and still the earth
Drinks the unstinted bounty of the clouds—
Drinks for her cottage wells, her woodland brooks—
Drinks for the springing trout, the toiling bee,
And brooding bird—drinks for her tender flowers,
Tall oaks, and all the herbage of her hills.

 A melancholy sound is in the air,
A deep sigh in the distance, a shrill wail
Around my dwelling. 'Tis the Wind of night ;
A lonely wanderer between earth and cloud,
In the black shadow and the chilly mist,
Along the streaming mountain-side, and through
The dripping woods, and o'er the plashy fields,
Roaming and sorrowing still, like one who makes
The journey of life alone, and nowhere meets
A welcome or a friend, and still goes on
In darkness. Yet a while, a little while,
And he shall toss the glittering leaves in play,
And dally with the flowers, and gayly lift
The slender herbs, pressed low by weight of rain,
And drive, in joyous triumph, through the sky,
White clouds, the laggard remnants of the storm.

ROBERT OF LINCOLN.

MERRILY swinging on brier and weed,
　Near to the nest of his little dame,
Over the mountain-side or mead,
　　Robert of Lincoln is telling his name :
　　　Bob-o'-link, bob-o'-link,
　　　Spink, spank, spink ;
Snug and safe is that nest of ours,
Hidden among the summer flowers.
　　　　　Chee, chee, chee.

Robert of Lincoln is gayly drest,
　Wearing a bright black wedding-coat ;
White are his shoulders and white his crest.
　　Hear him call in his merry note :
　　　Bob-o'-link, bob-o'-link,
　　　Spink, spank, spink ;
Look, what a nice new coat is mine,
Sure there was never a bird so fine.
　　　　　Chee, chee, chee.

Robert of Lincoln's Quaker wife,
　Pretty and quiet, with plain brown wings,
Passing at home a patient life,
　　Broods in the grass while her husband sings :
　　　Bob-o'-link, bob-o'-link,
　　　Spink, spank, spink ;
Brood, kind creature ; you need not fear
Thieves and robbers while I am here.
　　　　　Chee, chee, chee.

Modest and shy as a nun is she ;
　One weak chirp is her only note.
Braggart and prince of braggarts is he,
　　Pouring boasts from his little throat :
　　　Bob-o'-link, bob-o'-link,
　　　Spink, spank, spink ;

Never was I afraid of man ;
Catch me, cowardly knaves, if you can !
      Chee, chee, chee.

Six white eggs on a bed of hay,
   Flecked with purple, a pretty sight !
There as the mother sits all day,
   Robert is singing with all his might :
     Bob-o'-link, bob-o'-link,
     Spink, spank, spink ;
Nice good wife, that never goes out,
Keeping house while I frolic about.
      Chee, chee, chee.

Soon as the little ones chip the shell,
   Six wide mouths are open for food ;
Robert of Lincoln bestirs him well,
   Gathering seeds for the hungry brood.
     Bob-o'-link, bob-o'-link,
     Spink, spank, spink ;
This new life is likely to be
Hard for a gay young fellow like me.
      Chee, chee, chee.

Robert of Lincoln at length is made
   Sober with work, and silent with care ;
Off is his holiday garment laid,
   Half forgotten that merry air :
     Bob-o'-link, bob-o'-link,
     Spink, spank, spink ;
Nobody knows but my mate and I
Where our nest and our nestlings lie.
      Chee, chee, chee.

Summer wanes ; the children are grown ;
   Fun and frolic no more he knows ;
Robert of Lincoln's a humdrum crone ;
   Off he flies, and we sing as he goes :
     Bob-o'-link, bob-o'-link,
     Spink, spank, spink ;

When you can pipe that merry old strain,
Robert of Lincoln, come back again.
Chee, chee, chee.

THE TWENTY-SEVENTH OF MARCH.

OH, gentle one, thy birthday sun should rise
Amid a chorus of the merriest birds
That ever sang the stars out of the sky
In a June morning. Rivulets should send
A voice of gladness from their winding paths,
Deep in o'erarching grass, where playful winds,
Stirring the loaded stems, should shower the dew
Upon the grassy water. Newly-blown
Roses, by thousands, to the garden-walks
Should tempt the loitering moth and diligent bee.
The longest, brightest day in all the year
Should be the day on which thy cheerful eyes
First opened on the earth, to make thy haunts
Fairer and gladder for thy kindly looks.
    Thus might a poet say ; but I must bring
A birthday offering of an humbler strain,
And yet it may not please thee less. I hold
That 'twas the fitting season for thy birth
When March, just ready to depart, begins
To soften into April. Then we have
The delicatest and most welcome flowers,
And yet they take least heed of bitter wind
And lowering sky. The periwinkle then,
In an hour's sunshine, lifts her azure blooms
Beside the cottage-door ; within the woods
Tufts of ground-laurel, creeping underneath
The leaves of the last summer, send their sweets
Up to the chilly air, and, by the oak,
The squirrel-cups, a graceful company,
Hide in their bells, a soft aërial blue—

Sweet flowers, that nestle in the humblest nook,
And yet within whose smallest bud is wrapped
A world of promise ! Still the north wind breathes
His frost, and still the sky sheds snow and sleet ;
Yet ever, when the sun looks forth again,
The flowers smile up to him from their low seats.
   Well hast thou borne the bleak March day of life.
Its storms and its keen winds to thee have been
Most kindly tempered, and through all its gloom
There has been warmth and sunshine in thy heart ;
The griefs of life to thee have been like snows,
That light upon the fields in early spring,
Making them greener. In its milder hours,
The smile of this pale season, thou hast seen
The glorious bloom of June, and in the note
Of early bird, that comes a messenger
From climes of endless verdure, thou hast heard
The choir that fills the summer woods with song.
   Now be the hours that yet remain to thee
Stormy or sunny, sympathy and love,
That inextinguishably dwell within
Thy heart, shall give a beauty and a light
To the most desolate moments, like the glow
Of a bright fireside in the wildest day ;
And kindly words and offices of good
Shall wait upon thy steps, as thou goest on,
Where God shall lead thee, till thou reach the gates
Of a more genial season, and thy path
Be lost to human eye among the bowers
And living fountains of a brighter land.
    March, 1855.

AN INVITATION TO THE COUNTRY.

ALREADY, close by our summer dwelling,
  The Easter sparrow repeats her song ;
A merry warbler, she chides the blossoms—
  The idle blossoms that sleep so long

The bluebird chants, from the elm's long branches,
  A hymn to welcome the budding year.
The south wind wanders from field to forest,
  And softly whispers, "The Spring is here."

Come, daughter mine, from the gloomy city,
  Before those lays from the elm have ceased ;
The violet breathes, by our door, as sweetly
  As in the air of her native East.

Though many a flower in the wood is waking,
  The daffodil is our doorside queen ;
She pushes upward the sward already,
  To spot with sunshine the early green.

No lays so joyous as these are warbled
  From wiry prison in maiden's bower ;
No pampered bloom of the green-house chamber
  Has half the charm of the lawn's first flower.

Yet these sweet sounds of the early season,
  And these fair sights of its sunny days,
Are only sweet when we fondly listen,
  And only fair when we fondly gaze.

There is no glory in star or blossom
  Till looked upon by a loving eye ;
There is no fragrance in April breezes
  Till breathed with joy as they wander by.

Come, Julia dear, for the sprouting willows,
  The opening flowers, and the gleaming brooks,
And hollows, green in the sun, are waiting
  Their dower of beauty from thy glad looks.

A SONG FOR NEW-YEAR'S EVE.

STAY yet, my friends, a moment stay—
  Stay till the good old year,
So long companion of our way,
  Shakes hands, and leaves us here.
    Oh stay, oh stay,
One little hour, and then away.

The year, whose hopes were high and strong,
  Has now no hopes to wake ;
Yet one hour more of jest and song
  For his familiar sake.
    Oh stay, oh stay,
One mirthful hour, and then away.

The kindly year, his liberal hands
  Have lavished all his store.
And shall we turn from where he stands,
  Because he gives no more?
    Oh stay, oh stay,
One grateful hour, and then away.

Days brightly came and calmly went,
  While yet he was our guest ;
How cheerfully the week was spent !
  How sweet the seventh day's rest !
    Oh stay, oh stay,
One golden hour, and then away.

Dear friends were with us, some who sleep
  Beneath the coffin-lid :
What pleasant memories we keep
  Of all they said and did !
    Oh stay, oh stay,
One tender hour, and then away.

Even while we sing, he smiles his last,
  And leaves our sphere behind.
The good old year is with the past ;

Oh be the new as kind !
Oh stay, oh stay,
One parting strain, and then away.

THE WIND AND STREAM.

A BROOK came stealing from the ground ,
  You scarcely saw its silvery gleam
Among the herbs that hung around
  The borders of the winding stream,
The pretty stream, the placid stream,
The softly-gliding, bashful stream.

A breeze came wandering from the sky,
  Light as the whispers of a dream ;
He put the o'erhanging grasses by,
  And softly stooped to kiss the stream,
The pretty stream, the flattered stream,
The shy, yet unreluctant stream.

The water, as the wind passed o'er,
  Shot upward many a glancing beam,
Dimpled and quivered more and more,
  And tripped along, a livelier stream,
The flattered stream, the simpering stream
The fond, delighted, silly stream.

Away the airy wanderer flew
  To where the fields with blossoms teem.
To sparkling springs and rivers blue,
  And left alone that little stream,
The flattered stream, the cheated stream,
The sad, forsaken, lonely stream.

That careless wind came never back ;
  He wanders yet the fields, I deem,

24

But, on its melancholy track,
  Complaining went that little stream,
The cheated stream, the hopeless stream,
The ever-murmuring, mourning stream.

THE LOST BIRD.

FROM THE SPANISH OF CAROLINA CORONADO DE PERRY.

My bird has flown away,
Far out of sight has flown, I know not where.
  Look in your lawn, I pray,
  Ye maidens, kind and fair,
And see if my beloved bird be there.

  His eyes are full of light;
The eagle of the rock has such an eye;
  And plumes, exceeding bright,
  Round his smooth temples lie,
And sweet his voice and tender as a sigh.

  Look where the grass is gay
With summer blossoms, haply there he cowers;
  And search, from spray to spray,
  The leafy laurel-bowers,
For well he loves the laurels and the flowers.

  Find him, but do not dwell,
With eyes too fond, on the fair form you see,
  Nor love his song too well;
  Send him, at once, to me,
Or leave him to the air and liberty.

  For only from my hand
He takes the seed into his golden beak,
  And all unwiped shall stand
  The tears that wet my cheek,
Till I have found the wanderer I seek.

My sight is darkened o'er,
Whene'er I miss his eyes, which are my day,
And when I hear no more
The music of his lay,
My heart in utter ʟadness faints away.

THE NIGHT JOURNEY OF A RIVER.

Oh River, gentle River ! gliding on
In silence underneath the starless sky !
Thine is a ministry that never rests
Even while the living slumber. For a time
The meddler, man, hath left the elements
In peace ; the ploughman breaks the clods no more ;
The miner labors not, with steel and fire,
To rend the rock, and he that hews the stone,
And he that fells the forest, he that guides
The loaded wain, and the poor animal
That drags it, have forgotten, for a time,
Their toils, and share the quiet of the earth.
    Thou pausest not in thine allotted task,
Oh darkling River ! Through the night I hear
Thy wavelets rippling on the pebbly beach ;
I hear thy current stir the rustling sedge,
That skirts thy bed ; thou intermittest not
Thine everlasting journey, drawing on
A silvery train from many a woodland spring
And mountain-brook.   The dweller by thy side,
Who moored his little boat upon thy beach,
Though all the waters that upbore it then
Have slid away o'er night, shall find, at morn,
Thy channel filled with waters freshly drawn
From distant cliffs, and hollows where the rill
Comes up amid the water-flags.   All night
Thou givest moisture to the thirsty roots
Of the lithe willow and o'erhanging plane,

And cherishest the herbage of thy bank,
Spotted with little flowers, and sendest up
Perpetually the vapors from thy face,
To steep the hills with dew, or darken heaven
With drifting clouds, that trail the shadowy shower.
    Oh River! darkling River! what a voice
Is that thou utterest while all else is still—
The ancient voice that, centuries ago,
Sounded between thy hills, while Rome was yet
A weedy solitude by Tiber's stream!
How many, at this hour, along thy course,
Slumber to thine eternal murmurings,
That mingle with the utterance of their dreams!
At dead of night the child awakes and hears
Thy soft, familiar dashings, and is soothed,
And sleeps again.   An airy multitude
Of little echoes, all unheard by day,
Faintly repeat, till morning, after thee,
The story of thine endless goings forth.
    Yet there are those who lie beside thy bed
For whom thou once didst rear the bowers that screen
Thy margin, and didst water the green fields;
And now there is no night so still that they
Can hear thy lapse; their slumbers, were thy voice
Louder than Ocean's, it could never break.
For them the early violet no more
Opens upon thy bank, nor, for their eyes,
Glitter the crimson pictures of the clouds,
Upon thy bosom, when the sun goes down.
Their memories are abroad, the memories
Of those who last were gathered to the earth,
Lingering within the homes in which they sat,
Hovering above the paths in which they walked,
Haunting them like a presence.   Even now
They visit many a dreamer in the forms
They walked in, ere at last they wore the shroud.
And eyes there are which will not close to dream,
For weeping and for thinking of the grave,
The new-made grave, and the pale one within.

" . . . *Haste thee to the deep,*
There to be tossed by shifting winds."

These memories and these sorrows all shall fade
And pass away, and fresher memories
And newer sorrows come and dwell awhile
Beside thy borders, and, in turn, depart.
    On glide thy waters, till at last they flow
Beneath the windows of the populous town,
And all night long give back the gleam of lamps,
And glimmer with the trains of light that stream
From halls where dancers whirl.   A dimmer ray
Touches thy surface from the silent room
In which they tend the sick, or gather round
The dying ; and a slender, steady beam
Comes from the little chamber, in the roof
Where, with a feverous crimson on her cheek,
The solitary damsel, dying, too,
Plies the quick needle till the stars grow pale.
There, close beside the haunts of revel, stand
The blank, unlighted windows, where the poor,
In hunger and in darkness, wake till morn.
There, drowsily, on the half-conscious ear
Of the dull watchman, pacing on the wharf,
Falls the soft ripple of the waves that strike
On the moored bark ; but guiltier listeners
Are nigh, the prowlers of the night, who steal
From shadowy nook to shadowy nook, and start
If other sounds than thine are in the air.
    Oh, glide away from those abodes, that bring
Pollution to thy channel and make foul
Thy once clear current ; summon thy quick waves
And dimpling eddies ; linger not, but haste,
With all thy waters, haste thee to the deep,
There to be tossed by shifting winds and rocked
By that mysterious force which lives within
The sea's immensity, and wields the weight
Of its abysses, swaying to and fro
The billowy mass, until the stain, at length,
Shall wholly pass away, and thou regain
The crystal brightness of thy mountain-springs.

THE LIFE THAT IS.

THOU, who so long hast pressed the couch of pain,
　　Oh welcome, welcome back to life's free breath—
To life's free breath and day's sweet light again,
　　From the chill shadows of the gate of death !

For thou hadst reached the twilight bound between
　　The world of spirits and this grosser sphere ;
Dimly by thee the things of earth were seen,
　　And faintly fell earth's voices on thine ear.

And now, how gladly we behold, at last,
　　The wonted smile returning to thy brow !
The very wind's low whisper, breathing past,
　　In the light leaves, is music to thee now.

Thou wert not weary of thy lot ; the earth
　　Was ever good and pleasant in thy sight ;
Still clung thy loves about the household hearth,
　　And sweet was every day's returning light.

Then welcome back to all thou wouldst not leave,
　　To this grand march of seasons, days, and hours ;
The glory of the morn, the glow of eve,
　　The beauty of the streams, and stars, and flowers ;

To eyes on which thine own delight to rest ;
　　To voices which it is thy joy to hear ;
To the kind toils that ever pleased thee best,
　　The willing tasks of love, that made life dear.

Welcome to grasp of friendly hands ; to prayers
　　Offered where crowds in reverent worship come,
Or softly breathed amid the tender cares
　　And loving inmates of thy quiet home.

Thou bring'st no tidings of the better land,
　　Even from its verge ; the mysteries opened there
Are what the faithful heart may understand
　　In its still depths, yet words may not declare.

And well I deem, that, from the brighter side
  Of life's dim border, some o'erflowing rays
Streamed from the inner glory, shall abide
  Upon thy spirit through the coming days.

Twice wert thou given me ; once in thy fair prime,
  Fresh from the fields of youth, when first we met,
And all the blossoms of that hopeful time
  Clustered and glowed where'er thy steps were set.

And now, in thy ripe autumn, once again
  Given back to fervent prayers and yearnings strong,
From the drear realm of sickness and of pain
  When we had watched, and feared, and trembled long.

Now may we keep thee from the balmy air
  And radiant walks of heaven a little space,
Where He, who went before thee to prepare
  For His meek followers, shall assign thy place.

CASTELLAMARE, *May*, 1858.

SONG.

"THESE PRAIRIES GLOW WITH FLOWERS."

THESE prairies glow with flowers,
  These groves are tall and fair,
The sweet lay of the mocking-bird
  Rings in the morning air ;
And yet I pine to see
  My native hill once more,
And hear the sparrow's friendly chirp
  Beside its cottage-door.

And he, for whom I left
  My native hill and brook,
Alas, I sometimes think I trace
  A coldness in his look !

If I have lost his love,
  I know my heart will break ;
And haply, they I left for him
  Will sorrow for my sake.

———

A SICK-BED.

LONG hast thou watched my bed,
  And smoothed the pillow oft
For this poor, aching head,
  With touches kind and soft.

Oh ! smooth it yet again,
  As softly as before ;
Once—only once—and then
  I need thy hand no more.

Yet here I may not stay,
  Where I so long have lain,
Through many a restless day
  And many a night of pain.

But bear me gently forth
  Beneath the open sky,
Where, on the pleasant earth,
  Till night the sunbeams lie.

There, through the coming days,
  I shall not look to thee
My weary side to raise,
  And shift it tenderly.

There sweetly shall I sleep ;
  Nor wilt thou need to bring
And put to my hot lip
  Cool water from the spring ;

Nor wet the kerchief laid
　Upon my burning brow ;
Nor from my eyeballs shade
　The light that wounds them now ;

Nor watch that none shall tread,
　With noisy footstep, nigh ;
Nor listen by my bed,
　To hear my faintest sigh,

And feign a look of cheer,
　And words of comfort speak,
Yet turn to hide the tear
　That gathers on thy cheek.

Beside me, where I rest,
　Thy loving hands will set
The flowers that please me best—
　Moss-rose and violet.

Then to the sleep I crave
　Resign me, till I see
The face of Him who gave
　His life for thee and me.

Yet, with the setting sun,
　Come, now and then, at eve,
And think of me as one
　For whom thou shouldst not grieve ;

Who, when the kind release
　From sin and suffering came,
Passed to the appointed peace
　In murmuring thy name.

Leave at my side a space,
　Where thou shalt come, at last,
To find a resting-place,
　When many years are past.

THE SONG OF THE SOWER.

I.

The maples redden in the sun ;
  In autumn gold the beeches stand ;
Rest, faithful plough, thy work is done
  Upon the teeming land.
Bordered with trees whose gay leaves fly
On every breath that sweeps the sky,
The fresh dark acres furrowed lie,
  And ask the sower's hand.
Loose the tired steer and let him go
To pasture where the gentians blow,
And we, who till the grateful ground,
Fling we the golden shower around.

II.

Fling wide the generous grain ; we fling
O'er the dark mould the green of spring.
For thick the emerald blades shall grow,
When first the March winds melt the snow,
And to the sleeping flowers, below,
  The early bluebirds sing.
Fling wide the grain ; we give the fields
  The ears that nod in summer's gale,
The shining stems that summer gilds,
  The harvest that o'erflows the vale,
And swells, an amber sea, between
The full-leaved woods, its shores of green.
Hark ! from the murmuring clods I hear
Glad voices of the coming year ;
The song of him who binds the grain,
The shout of those that load the wain,
And from the distant grange there comes
  The clatter of the thresher's flail,
And steadily the millstone hums
  Down in the willowy vale.

III.

Fling wide the golden shower ; we trust
The strength of armies to the dust.
This peaceful lea may haply yield
Its harvest for the tented field.
Ha ! feel ye not your fingers thrill,
    As o'er them, in the yellow grains,
Glide the warm drops of blood that fill,
    For mortal strife, the warrior's veins ;
Such as, on Solferino's day,
Slaked the brown sand and flowed away—
Flowed till the herds, on Mincio's brink,
Snuffed the red stream and feared to drink ;—
Blood that in deeper pools shall lie,
    On the sad earth, as time grows gray,
When men by deadlier arts shall die,
And deeper darkness blot the sky
    Above the thundering fray ;
And realms, that hear the battle-cry,
    Shall sicken with dismay ;
And chieftains to the war shall lead
Whole nations, with the tempest's speed,
    To perish in a day ;—
Till man, by love and mercy taught,
Shall rue the wreck his fury wrought,
    And lay the sword away !
Oh strew, with pausing, shuddering hand,
The seed upon the helpless land,
As if, at every step, ye cast
The pelting hail and riving blast.

IV.

Nay, strew, with free and joyous sweep,
    The seed upon the expecting soil ;
For hence the plenteous year shall heap
    The garners of the men who toil.
Strew the bright seed for those who tear
The matted sward with spade and share,

And those whose sounding axes gleam
Beside the lonely forest-stream,
   Till its broad banks lie bare ;
And him who breaks the quarry-ledge,
  With hammer-blows, plied quick and strong,
And him who, with the steady sledge,
  Smites the shrill anvil all day long.
Sprinkle the furrow's even trace
  For those whose toiling hands uprear
The roof-trees of our swarming race,
  By grove and plain, by stream and mere ;
Who forth, from crowded city, lead
  The lengthening street, and overlay
Green orchard-plot and grassy mead
  With pavement of the murmuring way.
Cast, with full hands the harvest cast,
For the brave men that climb the mast,
When to the billow and the blast
  It swings and stoops, with fearful strain,
And bind the fluttering mainsail fast,
  Till the tossed bark shall sit, again,
  Safe as a sea-bird on the main.

v.

Fling wide the grain for those who throw
The clanking shuttle to and fro,
In the long row of humming rooms,
  And into ponderous masses wind
The web that, from a thousand looms,
  Comes forth to clothe mankind.
Strew, with free sweep, the grain for them,
  By whom the busy thread
Along the garment's even hem
  And winding seam is led ;
A pallid sisterhood, that keep
  The lonely lamp alight,
In strife with weariness and sleep,
  Beyond the middle night.

Large part be theirs in what the year
Shall ripen for the reaper here.

VI.

Still, strew, with joyous hand, the wheat
On the soft mould beneath our feet,
　　For even now I seem
To hear a sound that lightly rings
From murmuring harp and viol's strings,
　　As in a summer dream.
The welcome of the wedding-guest,
　　The bridegroom's look of bashful pride,
　　The faint smile of the pallid bride,
And bridemaid's blush at matron's jest,
And dance and song and generous dower,
Are in the shining grains we shower.

VII.

Scatter the wheat for shipwrecked men,
Who, hunger-worn, rejoice again
　　In the sweet safety of the shore,
And wanderers, lost in woodlands drear,
Whose pulses bound with joy to hear
　　The herd's light bell once more.
　　Freely the golden spray be shed
For him whose heart, when night comes down
On the close alleys of the town,
　　Is faint for lack of bread.
In chill roof-chambers, bleak and bare,
Or the damp cellar's stifling air,
She who now sees, in mute despair,
　　Her children pine for food,
Shall feel the dews of gladness start
To lids long tearless, and shall part
The sweet loaf with a grateful heart,
　　Among her thin pale brood.
Dear, kindly Earth, whose breast we till!
Oh, for thy famished children, fill,
　　Where'er the sower walks,

Fill the rich ears that shade the mould
With grain for grain, a hundredfold,
    To bend the sturdy stalks.

VIII.

Strew silently the fruitful seed,
    As softly o'er the tilth ye tread,
For hands that delicately knead
    The consecrated bread—
The mystic loaf that crowns the board,
When, round the table of their Lord,
    Within a thousand temples set,
In memory of the bitter death
Of Him who taught at Nazareth,
    His followers are met,
And thoughtful eyes with tears are wet,
    As of the Holy One they think,
The glory of whose rising yet
    Makes bright the grave's mysterious brink.

IX.

Brethren, the sower's task is done.
The seed is in its winter bed.
Now let the dark-brown mould be spread,
    To hide it from the sun,
And leave it to the kindly care
Of the still earth and brooding air,
As when the mother, from her breast,
Lays the hushed babe apart to rest,
And shades its eyes, and waits to see
How sweet its waking smile will be.
The tempest now may smite, the sleet
All night on the drowned furrow beat,
And winds that, from the cloudy hold,
Of winter breathe the bitter cold,
Stiffen to stone the mellow mould,
    Yet safe shall lie the wheat ;
Till, out of heaven's unmeasured blue,
    Shall walk again the genial year,

" The ancient East shall welcome thee
To mighty marts beyond the sea."

To wake with warmth and nurse with dew
  The germs we lay to slumber here.

x.

Oh blessed harvest yet to be!
  Abide thou with the Love that keeps,
In its warm bosom, tenderly,
  The Life which wakes and that which sleeps.
The Love that leads the willing spheres
Along the unending track of years,
And watches o'er the sparrow's nest,
Shall brood above thy winter rest,
And raise thee from the dust, to hold
  Light whisperings with the winds of **May,**
And fill thy spikes with living gold,
  From summer's yellow ray;
Then, as thy garners give thee forth,
  On what glad errands shalt thou go,
Wherever, o'er the waiting earth,
  Roads wind and rivers flow!
The ancient East shall welcome thee
To mighty marts beyond the sea,
And they who dwell where palm-groves sound
To summer winds the whole year round,
Shall watch, in gladness, from the shore,
The sails that bring thy glistening store.

THE NEW AND THE OLD.

NEW are the leaves on the oaken spray,
  New the blades of the silky grass;
Flowers, that were buds but yesterday,
  Peep from the ground where'er I pass.

These gay idlers, the butterflies,
  Broke, to-day, from their winter shroud;
These light airs, that winnow the skies,
  Blow, just born, from the soft, white cloud.

Gushing fresh in the little streams,
  What a prattle the waters make !
Even the sun, with his tender beams,
  Seems as young as the flowers they wake.

Children are wading, with cheerful cries,
  In the shoals of the sparkling brook ;
Laughing maidens, with soft, young eyes,
  Walk or sit in the shady nook.

What am I doing, thus alone,
  In the glory of Nature here,
Silver-haired, like a snow-flake thrown
  On the greens of the springing year ?

Only for brows unploughed by care,
  Eyes that glisten with hope and mirth,
Cheeks unwrinkled, and unblanched hair,
  Shines this holiday of the earth.

Under the grass, with the clammy clay,
  Lie in darkness the last year's flowers,
Born of a light that has passed away,
  Dews long dried and forgotten showers.

"Under the grass is the fitting home,"
  So they whisper, " for such as thou,
When the winter of life is come,
  Chilling the blood, and frosting the brow."

THE CLOUD ON THE WAY.

See, before us, in our journey, broods a mist upon the ground ;
Thither leads the path we walk in, blending with that gloomy
    bound.
Never eye hath pierced its shadows to the mystery they screen ;
Those who once have passed within it never more on earth are
    seen.

"*The sheltered glens are lovely and the rivulet's song is sweet.*"

Now it seems to stoop beside us, now at seeming distance lowers,
Leaving banks that tempt us onward bright with summer-green
and flowers.
Yet it blots the way forever ; there our journey ends at last ;
Into that dark cloud we enter, and are gathered to the past.
Thou who, in this flinty pathway, leading through a stranger-land,
Passest down the rocky valley, walking with me hand in hand,
Which of us shall be the soonest folded to that dim Unknown ?
Which shall leave the other walking in this flinty path alone ?
Even now I see thee shudder, and thy cheek is white with fear,
And thou clingest to my side as comes that darkness sweeping
near.
'Here," thou sayst, "the path is rugged, sown with thorns that
wound the feet ;
But the sheltered glens are lovely, and the rivulet's song is sweet ;
Roses breathe from tangled thickets ; lilies bend from ledges
brown ;
Pleasantly between the pelting showers the sunshine gushes
down ;
Dear are those who walk beside us, they whose looks and voices
make
All this rugged region cheerful, till I love it for their sake.
Far be yet the hour that takes me where that chilly shadow lies,
From the things I know and love, and from the sight of loving
eyes ! "
So thou murmurest, fearful one ; but see, we tread a rougher way ;
Fainter glow the gleams of sunshine that upon the dark rocks
play ;
Rude winds strew the faded flowers upon the crags o'er which we
pass ;
Banks of verdure, when we reach them, hiss with tufts of withered
grass.
One by one we miss the voices which we loved so well to hear ;
One by one the kindly faces in that shadow disappear.
Yet upon the mist before us fix thine eyes with closer view ;
See, beneath its sullen skirts, the rosy morning glimmers through.
One whose feet the thorns have wounded passed that barrier and
came back,
With a glory on His footsteps lighting yet the dreary track.
25

Boldly enter where He entered ; all that seems but darkness here,
When thou once hast passed beyond it, haply shall be crystal
    clear.
Viewed from that serener realm, the walks of human life may lie,
Like the page of some familiar volume, open to thine eye ;
Haply, from the o'erhanging shadow, thou mayst stretch an un-
    seen hand,
To support the wavering steps that print with blood the rugged
    land.
Haply, leaning o'er the pilgrim, all unweeting thou art near,
Thou mayst whisper words of warning or of comfort in his ear
Till, beyond the border where that brooding mystery bars the
    sight,
Those whom thou hast fondly cherished stand with thee in peace
    and light.

THE TIDES.

THE moon is at her full, and, riding high,
    Floods the calm fields with light ;
The airs that hover in the summer-sky
    Are all asleep to-night.

There comes no voice from the great woodlands round
    That murmured all the day ;
Beneath the shadow of their boughs the ground
    Is not more still than they.

But ever heaves and moans the restless Deep ;
    His rising tides I hear,
Afar I see the glimmering billows leap ;
    I see them breaking near.

Each wave springs upward, climbing toward the fair
    Pure light that sits on high—
Springs eagerly, and faintly sinks, to where
    The mother-waters lie.

Upward again it swells ; the moonbeams show
    Again its glimmering crest ;
Again it feels the fatal weight below,
    And sinks, but not to rest.

Again and yet again ; until the Deep
    Recalls his brood of waves ;
And, with a sullen moan, abashed, they creep
    Back to his inner caves.

Brief respite ! they shall rush from that recess
    With noise and tumult soon,
And fling themselves, with unavailing stress,
    Up toward the placid moon.

O restless Sea, that, in thy prison here,
    Dost struggle and complain ;
Through the slow centuries yearning to be near
    To that fair orb in vain ;

The glorious source of light and heat must warm
    Thy billows from on high,
And change them to the cloudy trains that form
    The curtain of the sky.

Then only may they leave the waste of brine
    In which they welter here,
And rise above the hills of earth, and shine
    In a serener sphere.

ITALY.

Voices from the mountains speak,
    Apennines to Alps reply ;
Vale to vale and peak to peak
    Toss an old-remembered cry :

" Italy
Shall be free ! "
Such the mighty shout that fills
All the passes of her hills.

All the old Italian lakes
    Quiver at that quickening word ;
Como with a thrill awakes ;
    Garda to her depths is stirred ;
        Mid the steeps
        Where he sleeps,
Dreaming of the elder years,
Startled Thrasymenus hears.

Sweeping Arno, swelling Po,
    Murmur freedom to their meads.
Tiber swift and Liris slow
    Send strange whispers from their reeds.
        " Italy
        Shall be free ! "
Sing the glittering brooks that slide,
Toward the sea, from Etna's side.

Long ago was Gracchus slain ;
    Brutus perished long ago ;
Yet the living roots remain
    Whence the shoots of greatness grow ;
        Yet again,
        Godlike men,
Sprung from that heroic stem,
Call the land to rise with them.

They who haunt the swarming street,
    They who chase the mountain-boar,
Or, where cliff and billow meet,
    Prune the vine or pull the oar,
        With a stroke
        Break their yoke ;
Slaves but yestereve were they-
Freemen with the dawning day.

Looking in his children's eyes,
　While his own with gladness flash,
"These," the Umbrian father cries,
　"Ne'er shall crouch beneath the lash !
　　　These shall ne'er
　　　Brook to wear
Chains whose cruel links are twined
Round the crushed and withering mind."

Monarchs ! ye whose armies stand
　Harnessed for the battle-field !
Pause, and from the lifted hand
　Drop the bolts of war ye wield.
　　　Stand aloof
　　　While the proof
Of the people's might is given ;
Leave their kings to them and Heaven !

Stand aloof, and see the oppressed
　Chase the oppressor, pale with fear,
As the fresh winds of the west
　Blow the misty valleys clear.
　　　Stand and see
　　　Italy
Cast the gyves she wears no more
To the gulfs that steep her shore.

————

A DAY-DREAM.

A DAY-DREAM by the dark-blue deep ;
　Was it a dream, or something more ?
I sat where Posilippo's steep,
　With its gray shelves, o'erhung the shore

On ruined Roman walls around
　The poppy flaunted, for 'twas May ;
And at my feet, with gentle sound,
　Broke the light billows of the bay

I sat and watched the eternal flow
   Of those smooth billows toward the shore,
While quivering lines of light below
   Ran with them on the ocean-floor :

Till, from the deep, there seemed to rise
   White arms upon the waves outspread,
Young faces, lit with soft blue eyes,
   And smooth, round cheeks, just touched with red.

Their long, fair tresses, tinged with gold,
   Lay floating on the ocean-streams,
And such their brows as bards behold—
   Love-stricken bards—in morning dreams.

Then moved their coral lips ; a strain
   Low, sweet and sorrowful, I heard,
As if the murmurs of the main
   Were shaped to syllable and word.

"The sight thou dimly dost behold,
   Oh, stranger from a distant sky !
Was often, in the days of old,
   Seen by the clear, believing eye.

"Then danced we on the wrinkled sand,
   Sat in cool caverns by the sea,
Or wandered up the bloomy land,
   To talk with shepherds on the lea.

" To us, in storms, the seaman prayed,
   And where our rustic altars stood,
His little children came and laid
   The fairest flowers of field and wood.

"Oh woe, a long, unending woe !
   For who shall knit the ties again
That linked the sea-nymphs, long ago,
   In kindly fellowship with men ?

"Earth rears her flowers for us no more ;
   A half-remembered dream are we ;
Unseen we haunt the sunny shore,
   And swim, unmarked, the glassy sea.

"And we have none to love or aid,
   But wander, heedless of mankind,
With shadows by the cloud-rack made,
   With moaning wave and sighing wind.

"Yet sometimes, as in elder days,
   We come before the painter's eye,
Or fix the sculptor's eager gaze,
   With no profaner witness nigh.

"And then the words of men grow warm
   With praise and wonder, asking where
The artist saw the perfect form
   He copied forth in lines so fair."

As thus they spoke, with wavering sweep
   Floated the graceful forms away ;
Dimmer and dimmer, through the deep,
   I saw the white arms gleam and play.

Fainter and fainter, on mine ear,
   Fell the soft accents of their speech,
Till I, at last, could only hear
   The waves run murmuring up the beach.

THE RUINS OF ITALICA.

FROM THE SPANISH OF RIOJA.

I.

FABIUS, this region, desolate and drear,
   These solitary fields, this shapeless mound,
   Were once Italica, the far-renowned ;

For Scipio, the mighty, planted here
His conquering colony, and now, o'erthrown,
Lie its once-dreaded walls of massive stone,
    Sad relics, sad and vain,
    Of those invincible men
    Who held the region then.
Funereal memories alone remain
    Where forms of high example walked of yore.
Here lay the forum, there arose the fane—
    The eye beholds their places, and no more.
Their proud gymnasium and their sumptuous baths,
Resolved to dust and cinders, strew the paths ;
Their towers, that looked defiance at the sky,
Fallen by their own vast weight, in fragments lie.

II.

This broken circus, where the rock-weeds climb,
    Flaunting with yellow blossoms, and defy
    The gods to whom its walls were piled so high,
Is now a tragic theatre, where Time
Acts his great fable, spreads a stage that shows
Past grandeur's story and its dreary close.
    Why, round this desert pit,
    Shout not the applauding rows
    Where the great people sit ?
Wild beasts are here, but where the combatant ;
    With his bare arms, the strong athleta where ?
All have departed from this once gay haunt
    Of noisy crowds, and silence holds the air.
Yet, on this spot, Time gives us to behold
A spectacle as stern as those of old.
As dreamily I gaze, there seem to rise,
From all the mighty ruin, wailing cries.

III.

The terrible in war, the pride of Spain,
    Trajan, his country's father, here was born ;
Good, fortunate, triumphant, to whose reign
    Submitted the far regions, where the morn

Rose from her cradle, and the shore whose steeps
O'erlooked the conquered Gaditanian deeps.
  Of mighty Adrian here,
  Of Theodosius, saint,
  Of Silius, Virgil's peer,
Were rocked the cradles, rich with gold, and quaint
With ivory carvings ; here were laurel-boughs
And sprays of jasmine gathered for their brows,
  From gardens now a marshy, thorny waste.
Where rose the palace, reared for Cæsar, yawn
  Foul rifts to which the scudding lizards haste.
Palaces, gardens, Cæsars, all are gone,
And even the stones their names were graven on.

                    IV.

Fabius, if tears prevent thee not, survey
  The long-dismantled streets, so thronged of old,
The broken marbles, arches in decaӯ,
  Proud statues, toppled from their place and rolled
In dust, when Nemesis, the avenger, came,
    And buried, in forgetfulness profound,
      The owners and their fame.
      Thus Troy, I deem, must be,
      With many a mouldering mound ;
And thou, whose name alone remains to thee,
Rome, of old gods and kings the native ground ;
And thou, sage Athens, built by Pallas, whom
Just laws redeemed not from the appointed doom.
The envy of earth's cities once wert thou—
A weary solitude and ashes now !
For Fate and Death respect ye not ; they strike
The mighty city and the wise alike.

                    V.

But why goes forth the wandering thought to frame
  New themes of sorrow, sought in distant lands ?
  Enough the example that before me stands ;
For here are smoke-wreaths seen, and glimmering flame,

And hoarse lamentings on the breezes die ;
So doth the mighty ruin cast its spell
    On those who near it dwell.
    And under night's still sky,
    As awe-struck peasants tell,
A melancholy voice is heard to cry,
    "Italica is fallen !" the echoes then
    Mournfully shout "Italica" again.
The leafy alleys of the forest nigh
    Murmur "Italica," and all around,
    A troop of mighty shadows, at the sound
Of that illustrious name, repeat the call,
"Italica !" from ruined tower and wall.

WAITING BY THE GATE.

BESIDE a massive gateway built up in years gone by,
Upon whose top the clouds in eternal shadow lie,
While streams the evening sunshine on quiet wood and lea,
I stand and calmly wait till the hinges turn for me.

The tree-tops faintly rustle beneath the breeze's flight,
A soft and soothing sound, yet it whispers of the night ;
I hear the wood-thrush piping one mellow descant more,
And scent the flowers that blow when the heat of day is o'er.

Behold, the portals open, and o'er the threshold, now,
There steps a weary one with a pale and furrowed brow ;
His count of years is full, his allotted task is wrought ;
He passes to his rest from a place that needs him not.

In sadness then I ponder how quickly fleets the hour
Of human strength and action, man's courage and his power.
I muse while still the wood-thrush sings down the golden day,
And as I look and listen the sadness wears away.

Again the hinges turn, and a youth, departing, throws
A look of longing backward, and sorrowfully goes ;
A blooming maid, unbinding the roses from her hair,
Moves mournfully away from amid the young and fair.

O glory of our race that so suddenly decays !
O crimson flush of morning that darkens as we gaze !
O breath of summer blossoms that on the restless air
Scatters a moment's sweetness, and flies we know not where !

I grieve for life's bright promise, just shown and then withdrawn ;
But still the sun shines round me : the evening bird sings on,
And I again am soothed, and, beside the ancient gate,
In this soft evening sunlight, I calmly stand and wait.

Once more the gates are opened ; an infant group go out,
The sweet smile quenched forever, and stilled the sprightly shout.
O frail, frail tree of Life, that upon the greensward strows
Its fair young buds unopened, with every wind that blows !

So come from every region, so enter, side by side,
The strong and faint of spirit, the meek and men of pride.
Steps of earth's great and mighty, between those pillars gray
And prints of little feet, mark the dust along the way.

And some approach the threshold whose looks are blank with fear,
And some whose temples brighten with joy in drawing near,
As if they saw dear faces, and caught the gracious eye
Of Him, the Sinless Teacher, who came for us to die.

I mark the joy, the terror ; yet these, within my heart,
Can neither wake the dread nor the longing to depart ;
And, in the sunshine streaming on quiet wood and lea,
I stand and calmly wait till the hinges turn for me.

NOT YET.

OH COUNTRY, marvel of the earth !
  Oh realm to sudden greatness grown !
The age that gloried in thy birth,
  Shall it behold thee overthrown ?
Shall traitors lay that greatness low ?
No, land of Hope and Blessing, No !

And we, who wear thy glorious name,
  Shall we, like cravens, stand apart,
When those whom thou hast trusted aim
  The death-blow at thy generous heart ?
Forth goes the battle-cry, and lo !
Hosts rise in harness, shouting, No !

And they who founded, in our land,
  The power that rules from sea to sea,
Bled they in vain, or vainly planned
  To leave their country great and free ?
Their sleeping ashes, from below,
Send up the thrilling murmur, No !

Knit they the gentle ties which long
  These sister States were proud to wear,
And forged the kindly links so strong
  For idle hands in sport to tear ?
For scornful hands aside to throw ?
No, by our fathers' memory, No !

Our humming marts, our iron ways,
  Our wind-tossed woods on mountain-crest,
The hoarse Atlantic, with its bays,
  The calm, broad Ocean of the West,
And Mississippi's torrent-flow,
And loud Niagara, answer, No !

Not yet the hour is nigh when they
  Who deep in Eld's dim twilight sit,
Earth's ancient kings, shall rise and say,
  " Proud country, welcome to the pit !
So soon art thou, like us, brought low ! "
No, sullen group of shadows, No !

For now, behold, the arm that gave
  The victory in our fathers' day,
Strong, as of old, to guard and save—
  That mighty arm which none can stay—
On clouds above and fields below,
Writes, in men's sight, the answer, No !

July, 1861.

OUR COUNTRY'S CALL.

LAY down the axe ; fling by the spade ;
  Leave in its track the toiling plough ;
The rifle and the bayonet-blade
  For arms like yours were fitter now ;
And let the hands that ply the pen
  Quit the light task, and learn to wield
The horseman's crooked brand, and rein
  The charger on the battle-field.

Our country calls ; away ! away !
  To where the blood-stream blots the green.
Strike to defend the gentlest sway
  That Time in all his course has seen.
See, from a thousand coverts—see,
  Spring the armed foes that haunt her track ;
They rush to smite her down, and we
  Must beat the banded traitors back.

Ho ! sturdy as the oaks ye cleave,
  And moved as soon to fear and flight,
Men of the glade and forest ! leave
  Your woodcraft for the field of fight.

The arms that wield the axe must pour
    An iron tempest on the foe ;
His serried ranks shall reel before
    The arm that lays the panther low.

And ye, who breast the mountain-storm
    By grassy steep or highland lake,
Come, for the land ye love, to form
    A bulwark that no foe can break.
Stand, like your own gray cliffs that mock
    The whirlwind, stand in her defence ;
The blast as soon shall move the rock
    As rushing squadrons bear ye thence.

And ye, whose homes are by her grand
    Swift rivers, rising far away,
Come from the depth of her green land,
    As mighty in your march as they ;
As terrible as when the rains
    Have swelled them over bank and bourne,
With sudden floods to drown the plains
    And sweep along the woods uptorn.

And ye, who throng, beside the deep,
    Her ports and hamlets of the strand,
In number like the waves that leap
    On his long-murmuring marge of sand—
Come like that deep, when, o'er his brim,
    He rises, all his floods to pour,
And flings the proudest barks that swim,
    A helpless wreck, against the shore !

Few, few were they whose swords of old
    Won the fair land in which we dwell ;
But we are many, we who hold
    The grim resolve to guard it well.
Strike, for that broad and goodly land,
    Blow after blow, till men shall see
That Might and Right move hand in hand,
    And glorious must their triumph be !
September, 1861.

THE CONSTELLATIONS.

O CONSTELLATIONS of the early night,
That sparkled brighter as the twilight died,
And made the darkness glorious! I have seen
Your rays grow dim upon the horizon's edge,
And sink behind the mountains. I have seen
The great Orion, with his jewelled belt,
That large-limbed warrior of the skies, go down
Into the gloom. Beside him sank a crowd
Of shining ones. I look in vain to find
The group of sister-stars, which mothers love
To show their wondering babes, the gentle Seven.
Along the desert space mine eyes in vain
Seek the resplendent cressets which the Twins
Uplifted in their ever-youthful hands.
The streaming tresses of the Egyptian Queen
Spangle the heavens no more. The Virgin trails
No more her glittering garments through the blue.
Gone! all are gone! and the forsaken Night,
With all her winds, in all her dreary wastes,
Sighs that they shine upon her face no more
    Now only here and there a little star
Looks forth alone. Ah me! I know them not,
Those dim successors of the numberless host
That filled the heavenly fields, and flung to earth
Their quivering fires. And now the middle watch
Betwixt the eve and morn is past, and still
The darkness gains upon the sky, and still
It closes round my way. Shall, then, the Night
Grow starless in her later hours? Have these
No train of flaming watchers, that shall mark
Their coming and farewell? O Sons of Light!
Have ye then left me ere the dawn of day
To grope along my journey sad and faint?
    Thus I complained, and from the darkness round
A voice replied—was it indeed a voice,
Or seeming accents of a waking dream

Heard by the inner ear ?   But thus it said :
O Traveller of the Night ! thine eyes are dim
With watching ; and the mists, that chill the vale
Down which thy feet are passing, hide from view
The ever-burning stars.   It is thy sight
That is so dark, and not the heavens.   Thine eyes,
Were they but clear, would see a fiery host
Above thee ; Hercules, with flashing mace,
The Lyre with silver chords, the Swan uppoised
On gleaming wings, the Dolphin gliding on
With glistening scales, and that poetic steed,
With beamy mane, whose hoof struck out from earth
The fount of Hippocrene, and many more,
Fair clustered splendors, with whose rays the Night
Shall close her march in glory, ere she yield,
To the young Day, the great earth steeped in dew.
    So spake the monitor, and I perceived
How vain were my repinings, and my thought
Went backward to the vanished years and all
The good and great who came and passed with them,
And knew that ever would the years to come
Bring with them, in their course, the good and great,
Lights of the world, though, to my clouded sight,
Their rays might seem but dim, or reach me not.

THE THIRD OF NOVEMBER, 1861.

SOFTLY breathes the west-wind beside the ruddy forest,
    Taking leaf by leaf from the branches where he flies.
Sweetly streams the sunshine, this third day of November,
    Through the golden haze of the quiet autumn skies.

Tenderly the season has spared the grassy meadows,
    Spared the petted flowers that the old world gave the new
Spared the autumn-rose and the garden's group of pansies,
    Late-blown dandelions and periwinkles blue.

On my cornice linger the ripe black grapes ungathered;
   Children fill the groves with the echoes of their glee,
Gathering tawny chestnuts, and shouting when beside them
   Drops the heavy fruit of the tall black-walnut tree.

Glorious are the woods in their latest gold and crimson,
   Yet our full-leaved willows are in their freshest green.
Such a kindly autumn, so mercifully dealing
   With the growths of summer, I never yet have seen.

Like this kindly season may life's decline come o'er me;
   Past is manhood's summer, the frosty months are here;
Yet be genial airs and a pleasant sunshine left me,
   Leaf, and fruit, and blossom, to mark the closing year!

Dreary is the time when the flowers of earth are withered;
   Dreary is the time when the woodland leaves are cast—
When, upon the hillside, all hardened into iron,
   Howling, like a wolf, flies the famished northern blast.

Dreary are the years when the eye can look no longer
   With delight on Nature, or hope on human kind;
Oh, may those that whiten my temples, as they pass me,
   Leave the heart unfrozen, and spare the cheerful mind!

THE MOTHER'S HYMN.

LORD, who ordainest for mankind
   Benignant toils and tender cares!
We thank Thee for the ties that bind
   The mother to the child she bears.

We thank Thee for the hopes that rise,
   Within her heart, as, day by day,
The dawning soul, from those young eyes,
   Looks, with a clearer, steadier ray.

And grateful for the blessing given
  With that dear infant on her knee,
She trains the eye to look to heaven,
  The voice to lisp a prayer to Thee.

Such thanks the blessed Mary gave,
  When, from her lap, the Holy Child,
Sent from on high to seek and save
  The lost of earth, looked up and smiled.

All-Gracious ! grant, to those that bear
  A mother's charge, the strength and light
To lead the steps that own their care
  In ways of Love, and Truth, and Right.

SELLA.

HEAR now a legend of the days of old—
The days when there were goodly marvels yet,
When man to man gave willing faith, and loved
A tale the better that 'twas wild and strange.
  Beside a pleasant dwelling ran a brook
Scudding along a narrow channel, paved
With green and yellow pebbles ; yet full clear
Its waters were, and colorless and cool,
As fresh from granite rocks.   A maiden oft
Stood at the open window, leaning out,
And listening to the sound the water made,
A sweet, eternal murmur, still the same,
And not the same ; and oft, as spring came on,
She gathered violets from its fresh moist bank,
To place within her bower, and when the herbs
Of summer drooped beneath the mid-day sun,
She sat within the shade of a great rock,
Dreamily listening to the streamlet's song.

Ripe were the maiden's years ; her stature showed
Womanly beauty, and her clear, calm eye
Was bright with venturous spirit, yet her face
Was passionless, like those by sculptor graved
For niches in a temple. Lovers oft
Had wooed her, but she only laughed at love,
And wondered at the silly things they said.
'Twas her delight to wander where wild-vines
O'erhang the river's brim, to climb the path
Of woodland streamlet to its mountain-springs,
To sit by gleaming wells and mark below
The image of the rushes on its edge,
And, deep beyond, the trailing clouds that slid
Across the fair blue space. No little fount
Stole forth from hanging rock, or in the side
Of hollow dell, or under roots of oak ;
No rill came trickling, with a stripe of green,
Down the bare hill, that to this maiden's eye
Was not familiar. Often did the banks
Of river or of sylvan lakelet hear
The dip of oars with which the maiden rowed
Her shallop, pushing ever from the prow
A crowd of long, light ripples toward the shore.
    Two brothers had the maiden, and she thought,
Within herself : " I would I were like them ;
For then I might go forth alone, to trace
The mighty rivers downward to the sea,
And upward to the brooks that, through the year,
Prattle to the cool valleys. I would know
What races drink their waters ; how their chiefs
Bear rule, and how men worship there, and how
They build, and to what quaint device they frame,
Where sea and river meet, their stately ships ;
What flowers are in their gardens, and what trees
Bear fruit within their orchards ; in what garb
Their bowmen meet on holidays, and how
Their maidens bind the waist and braid the hair.
Here, on these hills, my father's house o'erlooks
Broad pastures grazed by flocks and herds, but there

I hear they sprinkle the great plains with corn
And watch its springing up, and when the green
Is changed to gold, they cut the stems and bring
The harvest in, and give the nations bread.
And there they hew the quarry into shafts,
And pile up glorious temples from the rock,
And chisel the rude stones to shapes of men.
All this I pine to see, and would have seen,
But that I am a woman, long ago."
    Thus in her wanderings did the maiden dream,
Until, at length, one morn in early spring,
When all the glistening fields lay white with frost,
She came half breathless where her mother sat :
"See, mother dear," she said, " what I have found,
Upon our rivulet's bank ; two slippers, white
As the midwinter snow, and spangled o'er
With twinkling points, like stars, and on the edge
My name is wrought in silver ; read, I pray,
Sella, the name thy mother, now in heaven,
Gave at my birth ; and sure, they fit my feet ! "
" A dainty pair," the prudent matron said,
" But thine they are not.   We must lay them by
For those whose careless hands have left them here ;
Or haply they were placed beside the brook
To be a snare.   I cannot see thy name
Upon the border—only characters
Of mystic look and dim are there, like signs
Of some strange art ; nay, daughter, wear them not."
    Then Sella hung the slippers in the porch
Of that broad rustic lodge, and all who passed
Admired their fair contexture, but none knew
Who left them by the brook.   And now, at length,
May, with her flowers and singing birds, had gone,
And on bright streams and into deep wells shone
The high, midsummer sun.   One day, at noon,
Sella was missed from the accustomed meal.
They sought her in her favorite haunts, they looked
By the great rock and far along the stream,
And shouted in the sounding woods her name.

Night came, and forth the sorrowing household went
With torches over the wide pasture-grounds,
To pool and thicket, marsh and briery dell,
And solitary valley far away.
The morning came, and Sella was not found.
The sun climbed high ; they sought her still ; the noon,
The hot and silent noon, heard Sella's name,
Uttered with a despairing cry, to wastes
O'er which the eagle hovered.   As the sun
Stooped toward the amber west to bring the close
Of that sad second day, and, with red eyes,
The mother sat within her home alone,
Sella was at her side.   A shriek of joy
Broke the sad silence ; glad, warm tears were shed,
And words of gladness uttered.   " Oh, forgive,"
The maiden said, " that I could e'er forget
Thy wishes for a moment.   I just tried
The slippers on, amazed to see them shaped
So fairly to my feet, when, all at once,
I felt my steps upborne and hurried on
Almost as if with wings.   A strange delight,
Blent with a thrill of fear, o'ermastered me,
And, ere I knew, my splashing steps were set
Within the rivulet's pebbly bed, and I
Was rushing down the current.   By my side
Tripped one as beautiful as ever looked
From white clouds in a dream ; and, as we ran,
She talked with musical voice and sweetly laughed.
Gayly we leaped the crag and swam the pool,
And swept with dimpling eddies round the rock,
And glided between shady meadow-banks.
The streamlet, broadening as we went, became
A swelling river, and we shot along
By stately towns, and under leaning masts
Of gallant barks, nor lingered by the shore
Of blooming gardens ; onward, onward still,
The same strong impulse bore me, till, at last,
We entered the great deep, and passed below
His billows, into boundless spaces, lit

With a green sunshine. Here were mighty groves
Far down the ocean-valleys, and between
Lay what might seem fair meadows, softly tinged
With orange and with crimson. Here arose
Tall stems, that, rooted in the depths below,
Swung idly with the motions of the sea ;
And here were shrubberies in whose mazy screen
The creatures of the deep made haunt. My friend
Named the strange growths, the pretty coralline,
The dulse with crimson leaves, and, streaming far,
Sea-thong and sea-lace. Here the tangle spread
Its broad, thick fronds, with pleasant bowers beneath ;
And oft we trod a waste of pearly sands,
Spotted with rosy shells, and thence looked in
At caverns of the sea whose rock-roofed halls
Lay in blue twilight. As we moved along,
The dwellers of the deep, in mighty herds,
Passed by us, reverently they passed us by,
Long trains of dolphins rolling through the brine,
Huge whales, that drew the waters after them,
A torrent-stream, and hideous hammer-sharks,
Chasing their prey. I shuddered as they came ;
Gently they turned aside and gave us room."
    Hereat broke in the mother : " Sella dear,
This is a dream, the idlest, vainest dream."
    " Nay, mother, nay ; behold this sea-green scarf,
Woven of such threads as never human hand
Twined from the distaff. She who led my way
Through the great waters, bade me wear it home,
A token that my tale is true. ' And keep,'
She said, ' the slippers thou hast found, for thou,
When shod with them, shalt be like one of us,
With power to walk at will the ocean-floor,
Among its monstrous creatures, unafraid,
And feel no longing for the air of heaven
To fill thy lungs, and send the warm, red blood
Along thy veins. But thou shalt pass the hours
In dances with the sea-nymphs, or go forth,
To look into the mysteries of the abyss

"... Oft we trod a waste of pearly sands,
Spotted with rosy shells, and thence looked in
At caverns of the sea whose rock-roofed halls
Lay in blue twilight."

Where never plummet reached.   And thou shalt sleep
Thy weariness away on downy banks
Of sea-moss, where the pulses of the tide
Shall gently lift thy hair, or thou shalt float
On the soft currents that go forth and wind
From isle to isle, and wander through the sea.'
   "So spake my fellow-voyager, her words
Sounding like wavelets on a summer shore,
And then we stopped beside a hanging rock,
With a smooth beach of white sands at its foot,
Where three fair creatures like herself were set
At their sea-banquet, crisp and juicy stalks,
Culled from the ocean's meadows, and the sweet
Midrib of pleasant leaves, and golden fruits
Dropped from the trees that edge the southern isles,
And gathered on the waves.   Kindly they prayed
That I would share their meal, and I partook
With eager appetite, for long had been
My journey, and I left the spot refreshed.
   "And then we wandered off amid the groves
Of coral loftier than the growths of earth ;
The mightiest cedar lifts no trunk like theirs,
So huge, so high toward heaven, nor overhangs
Alleys and bowers so dim.   We moved between
Pinnacles of black rock, which, from beneath,
Molten by inner fires, so said my guide,
Gushed long ago into the hissing brine,
That quenched and hardened them, and now they stand
Motionless in the currents of the sea
That part and flow around them.   As we went,
We looked into the hollows of the abyss,
To which the never-resting waters sweep
The skeletons of sharks, the long white spines
Of narwhal and of dolphin, bones of men
Shipwrecked, and mighty ribs of foundered barks.
Down the blue pits we looked, and hastened on.
   "But beautiful the fountains of the sea
Sprang upward from its bed : the silvery jets
Shot branching far into the azure brine,

And where they mingled with it, the great deep
Quivered and shook, as shakes the glimmering air
Above a furnace. So we wandered through
The mighty world of waters, till at length
I wearied of its wonders, and my heart
Began to yearn for my dear mountain-home.
I prayed my gentle guide to lead me back
To the upper air. 'A glorious realm,' I said,
'Is this thou openest to me ; but I stray
Bewildered in its vastness ; these strange sights
And this strange light oppress me. I must see
The faces that I love, or I shall die.'
   "She took my hand, and, darting through the waves,
Brought me to where the stream, by which we came,
Rushed into the main ocean. Then began
A slower journey upward. Wearily
We breasted the strong current, climbing through
The rapids, tossing high their foam. The night
Came down, and in the clear depth of a pool,
Edged with o'erhanging rock, we took our rest
Till morning ; and I slept, and dreamed of home
And thee. A pleasant sight the morning showed ;
The green fields of this upper world, the herds
That grazed the bank, the light on the red clouds,
The trees, with all their host of trembling leaves,
Lifting and lowering to the restless wind
Their branches. As I woke, I saw them all
From the clear stream ; yet strangely was my heart
Parted between the watery world and this,
And as we journeyed upward, oft I thought
Of marvels I had seen, and stopped and turned,
And lingered, till I thought of thee again ;
And then again I turned and clambered up
The rivulet's murmuring path, until we came
Beside the cottage-door. There tenderly
My fair conductor kissed me, and I saw
Her face no more. I took the slippers off.
Oh ! with what deep delight my lungs drew in
The air of heaven again, and with what joy

I felt my blood bound with its former glow ;
And now I never leave thy side again ! ''
  So spoke the maiden Sella, with large tears
Standing in her mild eyes, and in the porch
Replaced the slippers. Autumn came and went ;
The winter passed ; another summer warmed
The quiet pools ; another autumn tinged
The grape with red, yet while it hung unplucked,
The mother ere her time was carried forth
To sleep among the solitary hills.
  A long, still sadness settled on that home
Among the mountains. The stern father there
Wept with his children, and grew soft of heart,
And Sella, and the brothers twain, and one
Younger than they, a sister fair and shy,
Strewed the new grave with flowers, and round it set
Shrubs that all winter held their lively green.
Time passed ; the grief with which their hearts were wrung
Waned to a gentle sorrow. Sella, now,
Was often absent from the patriarch's board ;
The slippers hung no longer in the porch ;
And sometimes after summer nights her couch
Was found unpressed at dawn, and well they knew
That she was wandering with the race who make
Their dwelling in the waters. Oft her looks
Fixed on blank space, and oft the ill-suited word
Told that her thoughts were far away. In vain
Her brothers reasoned with her tenderly :
"Oh leave not thus thy kindred ! '' so they prayed ;
" Dear Sella, now that she who gave us birth
Is in her grave, oh go not hence, to seek
Companions in that strange cold realm below,
For which God made not us nor thee, but stay
To be the grace and glory of our home.''
She looked at them with those mild eyes and wept,
But said no word in answer, nor refrained
From those mysterious wanderings that filled
Their loving hearts with a perpetual pain.
  And now the younger sister, fair and shy,

Had grown to early womanhood, and one
Who loved her well had wooed her for his bride,
And she had named the wedding-day. The herd
Had given its fatlings for the marriage-feast ;
The roadside garden and the secret glen
Were rifled of their sweetest flowers to twine
The door-posts, and to lie among the locks
Of maids, the wedding-guests, and from the boughs
Of mountain-orchards had the fairest fruit
Been plucked to glisten in the,canisters.
    Then, trooping over hill and valley, came
Matron and maid, grave men and smiling youths,
Like swallows gathering for their autumn flight,
In costumes of that simpler age they came,
That gave the limbs large play, and wrapped the form
In easy folds, yet bright with glowing hues
As suited holidays. All hastened on
To that glad bridal. There already stood
The priest prepared to say the spousal rite,
And there the harpers in due order sat,
And there the singers. Sella, midst them all,
Moved strangely and serenely beautiful,
With clear blue eyes, fair locks, and brow and cheek
Colorless as the lily of the lakes,
Yet moulded to such shape as artists give
To beings of immortal youth. Her hands
Had decked her sister for the bridal hour
With chosen flowers, and lawn whose delicate threads
Vied with the spider's spinning. There she stood
With such a gentle pleasure in her looks
As.might beseem a river-nymph's soft eyes
Gracing a bridal of the race whose flocks
Were pastured on the borders of her stream.
    She smiled, but from that calm sweet face the smile
Was soon to pass away. That very morn
The elder of the brothers, as he stood
Upon the hillside, had beheld the maid,
Emerging from the channel of the brook,
With three fresh water-lilies in her hand,

" *The elder of the brothers, as he stood*
Upon the hillside, had beheld the maid,
Emerging from the channel of the brook,
With three fresh water-lilies in her hand."

Wring dry her dripping locks, and in a cleft
Of hanging rock, beside a screen of boughs,
Bestow the spangled slippers. None before
Had known where Sella hid them. Then she laid
The light-brown tresses smooth, and in them twined
The lily-buds, and hastily drew forth
And threw across her shoulders a light robe
Wrought for the bridal, and with bounding steps
Ran toward the lodge. The youth beheld and marked
The spot and slowly followed from afar.
  Now had the marriage-rite been said ; the bride
Stood in the blush that from her burning cheek
Glowed down the alabaster neck, as morn
Crimsons the pearly heaven half-way to the west.
At once the harpers struck their chords ; a gush
Of music broke upon the air ; the youths
All started to the dance. Among them moved
The queenly Sella with a grace that seemed
Caught from the swaying of the summer sea.
The young drew forth the elders to the dance,
Who joined it half abashed, but when they felt
The joyous music tingling in their veins,
They called for quaint old measures, which they trod
As gayly as in youth, and far abroad
Came through the open windows cheerful shouts
And bursts of laughter. They who heard the sound
Upon the mountain footpaths paused and said,
" A merry wedding." Lovers stole away
That sunny afternoon to bowers that edged
The garden-walks, and what was whispered there
The lovers of these later times can guess.
  Meanwhile the brothers, when the merry din
Was loudest, stole to where the slippers lay,
And took them thence, and followed down the brook
To where a little rapid rushed between
Its borders of smooth rock, and dropped them in.
The rivulet, as they touched its face, flung up
Its small bright waves like hands, and seemed to take
The prize with eagerness and draw it down.

They, gleaming through the waters as they went,
And striking with light sound the shining stones,
Slid down the stream.　The brothers looked and watched,
And listened with full beating hearts, till now
The sight and sound had passed, and silently
And half repentant hastened to the lodge.
　　The sun was near his set ; the music rang
Within the dwelling still, but the mirth waned ;
For groups of guests were sauntering toward their homes
Across the fields, and far, on hillside paths,
Gleamed the white robes of maidens.　Sella grew
Weary of the long merriment ; she thought
Of her still haunts beneath the soundless sea,
And all unseen withdrew and sought the cleft
Where she had laid the slippers.　They were gone !
She searched the brookside near, yet found them not.
Then her heart sank within her, and she ran
Wildly from place to place, and once again
She searched the secret cleft, and next she stooped
And with spread palms felt carefully beneath
The tufted herbs and bushes, and again,
And yet again, she searched the rocky cleft.
" Who could have taken them ? "　That question cleared
The mystery.　She remembered suddenly
That when the dance was in its gayest whirl,
Her brothers were not seen, and when, at length,
They reappeared, the elder joined the sports
With shouts of boisterous mirth, and from her eye
The younger shrank in silence.　" Now, I know
The guilty ones," she said, and left the spot,
And stood before the youths with such a look
Of anguish and reproach that well they knew
Her thought, and almost wished the deed undone.
　　Frankly they owned the charge : " And pardon us ;
We did it all in love ; we could not bear
That the cold world of waters and the strange
Beings that dwell within it should beguile
Our sister from us."　Then they told her all ;
How they had seen her stealthily bestow

The slippers in the cleft, and how by stealth
They took them thence and bore them down the brook,
And dropped them in, and how the eager waves
Gathered and drew them down ; but at that word
The maiden shrieked—a broken-hearted shriek—
And all who heard it shuddered and turned pale
At the despairing cry, and "They are gone,"
She said, " gone—gone forever ! Cruel ones !
'Tis you who shut me out eternally
From that serener world which I had learned
To love so well. Why took ye not my life ?
Ye cannot know what ye have done !" She spake
And hurried to her chamber, and the guests
Who yet had lingered silently withdrew.
    The brothers followed to the maiden's bower,
But with a calm demeanor, as they came,
She met them at the door. " The wrong is great,"
She said, " that ye have done me, but no power
Have ye to make it less, nor yet to soothe
My sorrow ; I shall bear it as I may,
The better for the hours that I have passed
In the calm region of the middle sea.
Go, then. I need you not." They, overawed,
Withdrew from that grave presence. Then her tears
Broke forth a flood, as when the August cloud,
Darkening beside the mountain, suddenly
Melts into streams of rain. That weary night
She paced her chamber, murmuring as she walked,
" O peaceful region of the middle sea !
O azure bowers and grots, in which I loved
To roam and rest ! Am I to long for you,
And think how strangely beautiful ye are,
Yet never see you more ? And dearer yet,
Ye gentle ones in whose sweet company
I trod the shelly pavements of the deep,
And swam its currents, creatures with calm eyes
Looking the tenderest love, and voices soft
As ripple of light waves along the shore,
Uttering the tenderest words ! Oh ! ne'er again

Shall I, in your mild aspects, read the peace
That dwells within, and vainly shall I pine
To hear your sweet low voices. Haply now
Ye miss me in your deep-sea home, and think
Of me with pity, as of one condemned
To haunt this upper world, with its harsh sounds
And glaring lights, its withering heats, its frosts,
Cruel and killing, its delirious strifes,
And all its feverish passions, till I die."
    So mourned she the long night, and when the morn
Brightened the mountains, from her lattice looked
The maiden on a world that was to her
A desolate and dreary waste. That day
She passed in wandering by the brook that oft
Had been her pathway to the sea, and still
Seemed, with its cheerful murmur, to invite
Her footsteps thither. "Well mayst thou rejoice,
Fortunate stream!" she said, "and dance along
Thy bed, and make thy course one ceaseless strain
Of music, for thou journeyest toward the deep,
To which I shall return no more." The night
Brought her to her lone chamber, and she knelt
And prayed, with many tears, to Him whose hand
Touches the wounded heart and it is healed.
With prayer there came new thoughts and new desires
She asked for patience and a deeper love
For those with whom her lot was henceforth cast,
And that in acts of mercy she might lose
The sense of her own sorrow. When she rose
A weight was lifted from her heart. She sought
Her couch, and slept a long and peaceful sleep.
At morn she woke to a new life. Her days
Henceforth were given to quiet tasks of good
In the great world. Men hearkened to her words,
And wondered at their wisdom and obeyed,
And saw how beautiful the law of love
Can make the cares and toils of daily life.
    Still did she love to haunt the springs and brooks
As in her cheerful childhood, and she taught

The skill to pierce the soil and meet the veins
Of clear cold water winding underneath,
And call them forth to daylight.   From afar
She bade men bring the rivers on long rows
Of pillared arches to the sultry town,
And on the hot air of the summer fling
The spray of dashing fountains.   To relieve
Their weary hands, she showed them how to tame
The rushing stream, and make him drive the wheel
That whirls the humming millstone and that wields
The ponderous sledge.   The waters of the cloud,
That drench the hillside in the time of rains,
Were gathered, at her bidding, into pools,
And in the months of drought led forth again,
In glimmering rivulets, to refresh the vales,
Till the sky darkened with returning showers.
   So passed her life, a long and blameless life,
And far and near her name was named with love
And reverence.   Still she kept, as age came on,
Her stately presence ; still her eyes looked forth
From under their calm brows as brightly clear
As the transparent wells by which she sat
So oft in childhood.   Still she kept her fair
Unwrinkled features, though her locks were white
A hundred times had summer, since her birth,
Opened the water-lily on the lakes,
So old traditions tell, before she died.
A hundred cities mourned her, and her death
Saddened the pastoral valleys.   By the brook,
That bickering ran beside the cottage-door
Where she was born, they reared her monument.
Ere long the current parted and flowed round
The marble base, forming a little isle,
And there the flowers that love the running stream,
Iris and orchis, and the cardinal-flower,
Crowded and hung caressingly around
The stone engraved with Sella's honored name.

THE FIFTH BOOK OF HOMER'S ODYSSEY.

TRANSLATED.

Aurora, rising from her couch beside
The famed Tithonus, brought the light of day
To men and to immortals. Then the gods
Came to their seats in council. With them came
High-thundering Jupiter, among them all
The mightiest. Pallas, mindful of the past,
Spoke of Ulysses and his many woes,
Grieved that he still was with the island-nymph.
  " Oh, father Jove, and all ye blessed ones
Who live forever ! let not sceptred king,
Henceforth, be gracious, mild, and merciful,
And righteous ; rather be he deaf to prayer,
And prone to deeds of wrong, since no one now
Remembers the divine Ulysses more
Among the people over whom he ruled,
Benignly, like a father. Still he lies,
Weighed down by many sorrows, in the isle
And dwelling of Calypso, who so long
Constrains his stay. To his dear native land
Depart he cannot ; ship, arrayed with oars,
And seamen has he none, to bear him o'er
The breast of the broad ocean. Nay, even now,
Against his well-beloved son a plot
Is laid, to slay him as he journeys home
From Pylos the divine, and from the walls
Of famous Sparta, whither he had gone
To gather tidings of his father's fate."
  Then answered her the ruler of the storms :
" My child, what words are these that pass thy lips ?
Was not thy long-determined counsel this,
That, in good time, Ulysses should return,
To be avenged ? Guide, then, Telemachus,
Wisely, for thou canst, that, all unharmed,

He reach his native land, and, in their barks,
Homeward the suitor-train retrace their way."
   He spake, and turned to Hermes, his dear son :
" Hermes, for thou, in this, my messenger
Art, as in all things, to the bright-haired nymph
Make known my steadfast purpose, the return
Of suffering Ulysses.   Neither gods
Nor men shall guide his voyage.   On a raft,
Made firm with bands, he shall depart and reach,
After long hardships, on the twentieth day,
The fertile shore of Scheria, on whose isle
Dwell the Pheacians, kinsmen of the gods.
They like a god shall honor him, and thence
Send him to his loved country in a ship,
With ample gifts of brass and gold, and store
Of raiment—wealth like which he ne'er had brought
From conquered Ilion, had he reached his home
Safely, with all his portion of the spoil.
So is it preordained, that he behold
His friends again, and stand once more within
His high-roofed palace, on his native soil."
   He spake ; the herald Argicide obeyed,
And hastily beneath his feet he bound
The fair, ambrosial, golden sandals, worn
To bear him over ocean like the wind,
And o'er the boundless land.   His wand he took,
Wherewith he softly seals the eyes of men,
And opens them at will from sleep.   With this
In hand, the mighty Argos-queller flew,
And lighting on Pieria, from the sky
Plunged downward to the deep, and skimmed its fair
Like hovering sea-mew, that on the broad gulfs
Of the unfruitful ocean seeks her prey,
And often dips her pinions in the brine.
So Hermes flew along the waste of waves.
   But when he reached that island, far away,
Forth from the dark-blue ocean-swell he stepped
Upon the sea-beach, walking till he came
To the vast cave in which the bright-haired nymph
27

Made her abode.   He found the nymph within.
A fire blazed brightly on the hearth, and far
Was wafted o'er the isle the fragrant smoke
Of cloven cedar, burning in the flame,
And cypress-wood.   Meanwhile, in her recess,
She sweetly sang, as busily she threw
The golden shuttle through the web she wove.
And all about the grotto alders grew,
And poplars, and sweet-smelling cypresses,
In a green forest, high among whose boughs
Birds of broad wing, wood-owls and falcons, built
Their nests, and crows, with voices sounding far,
All haunting for their food the ocean-side.
A vine, with downy leaves and clustering grapes,
Crept over all the cavern-rock.   Four springs
Poured forth their glittering waters in a row,
And here and there went wandering side by side.
Around were meadows of soft green, o'ergrown
With violets and parsley.   'Twas a spot
Where even an Immortal might, awhile,
Linger, and gaze with wonder and delight.
The herald Argos-queller stood, and saw,
And marvelled : but as soon as he had viewed
The wonders of the place, he turned his steps,
Entering the broad-roofed cave.   Calypso there,
The glorious goddess, saw him as he came,
And knew him, for the ever-living gods
Are to each other known, though one may dwell
Far from the rest.   Ulysses, large of heart,
Was not within.   Apart, upon the shore,
He sat and sorrowed, where he oft, in tears
And sighs and vain repinings, passed the hours,
Gazing with wet eyes on the barren deep.
Now, placing Hermes on a shining seat
Of state, Calypso, glorious goddess, said :
    "Thou of the golden wand, revered and loved,
What, Hermes, brings thee hither ?   Passing few
Have been thy visits.   Make thy pleasure known,
My heart enjoins me to obey, if aught

That thou commandest be within my power.
But first accept the offerings due a guest."
   The goddess, speaking thus, before him placed
A table where the heaped ambrosia lay,
And mingled the red nectar. Ate and drank
The herald Argos-queller, and, refreshed,
Answered the nymph, and made his message known :
   "Art thou a goddess, and dost ask of me,
A god, why came I hither? Yet, since thou
Requirest, I will truly tell the cause.
I came unwillingly at Jove's command,
For who, of choice, would traverse the wide waste
Of the salt ocean, with no city near,
Where men adore the gods with solemn rites
And chosen hecatombs? No god has power
To elude or to resist the purposes
Of ægis-bearing Jove. With thee abides,
He bids me say, the most unhappy man
Of all who round the city of Priam waged
The battle through nine years, and, in the tenth,
Laying it waste, departed for their homes.
But in their voyage, they provoked the wrath
Of Pallas, who called up the furious winds
And angry waves against them. By his side
Sank all his gallant comrades in the deep.
Him did the winds and waves drive hither. Him
Jove bids thee send away with speed, for here
He must not perish, far from all he loves.
So is it preordained that he behold
His friends again, and stand once more within
His high-roofed palace, on his native soil."
   He spoke ; Calypso, glorious goddess, heard,
And shuddered, and with wingèd words replied :
   "Ye are unjust, ye gods, and, envious far
Beyond all other beings, cannot bear
That ever goddess openly should make
A mortal man her consort. Thus it was
When once Aurora, rosy-fingered, took
Orion for her husband ; ye were stung,

Amid your blissful lives, with envious hate,
Till chaste Diana, of the golden throne,
Smote him with silent arrows from her bow,
And slew him in Ortygia.   Thus, again,
When bright-haired Ceres, swayed by her own heart,
In fields which bore three yearly harvests, met
Iasion as a lover, this was known
Ere long to Jupiter, who flung from high
A flaming thunderbolt, and laid him dead.
And now ye envy me, that with me dwells
A mortal man.   I saved him, as he clung,
Alone, upon his floating keel, for Jove
Had cloven, with a bolt of fire from heaven,
His galley in the midst of the black sea,
And all his gallant comrades perished there.
Him kindly I received ; I cherished him,
And promised him a life that ne'er should know
Decay or death.   But, since no god has power
To elude or to withstand the purposes
Of ægis-bearing Jove, let him depart,
If so the sovereign moves him and commands,
Over the barren deep.   I send him not ;
For neither ship arrayed with oars have I,
Nor seamen, o'er the boundless waste of waves
To bear him hence.   My counsel I will give,
And nothing will I hide that he should know,
To place him safely on his native shore."
   The herald Argos-queller answered her :
" Dismiss him thus, and bear in mind the wrath
Of Jove, lest it be kindled against thee."
   Thus having said, the mighty Argicide
Departed, and the nymph, who now had heard
The doom of Jove, sought the great-hearted man
Ulysses.   Him she found beside the deep,
Seated alone, with eyes from which the tears
Were never dried, for now no more the nymph
Delighted him ; he wasted his sweet life
In yearning for his home.   Night after night
He slept constrained within the hollow cave,

The unwilling by the fond, and, day by day,
He sat upon the rocks that edged the shore,
And in continual weeping and in sighs
And vain repinings, wore the hours away,
Gazing through tears upon the barren deep.
The glorious goddess stood by him and spoke :
"Unhappy ! sit no longer sorrowing here,
Nor waste life thus. Lo ! I most willingly
Dismiss thee hence. Rise, hew down trees, and bind
Their trunks, with brazen clamps, into a raft,
And fasten planks above, a lofty floor,
That it may bear thee o'er the dark-blue deep.
Bread will I put on board, water, and wine,
Red wine, that cheers the heart, and wrap thee well
In garments, and send after thee the wind,
That safely thou attain thy native shore ;
If so the gods permit thee, who abide
In the broad heaven above, and better know
By far than I, and far more wisely judge."
Ulysses, the great sufferer, as she spoke,
Shuddered, and thus with wingèd words replied :
" Some other purpose than to send me home
Is in thy heart, oh goddess, bidding me
To cross this frightful sea upon a raft,
This perilous sea, where never even ships
Pass with their rapid keels, though Jove bestow
The wind that glads the seamen. Nay, I climb
No raft, against thy wish, unless thou swear
The great oath of the gods, that thou, in this,
Dost meditate no other harm to me."
He spake ; Calypso, glorious goddess, smiled,
And smoothed his forehead with her hand, and said :
"Perverse ! and slow to see where guile is not !
How could thy heart permit thee thus to speak ?
Now bear me witness, Earth, and ye broad Heavens
Above us, and ye waters of the Styx
That flow beneath us, mightiest oath of all,
And most revered by all the blessed gods,
That I design no other harm to thee ;

But that I plan for thee and counsel thee
What I would do were I in need like thine.
I bear a juster mind ; my bosom holds
A pitying heart, and not a heart of steel."
   Thus having said, the glorious goddess moved
Away with hasty steps, and where she trod
He followed, till they reached the vaulted cave,
The goddess and the hero.   There he took
The seat whence Hermes had just risen.   The nymph
Brought forth whatever mortals eat and drink
To set before him.   She, right opposite
To that of Ulysses, took her seat,
Ambrosia there her maidens laid, and there
Poured nectar.   Both put forth their hands, and took
The ready viands, till at length the calls
Of hunger and of thirst were satisfied ;
Calypso, glorious goddess, then began :
   "Son of Laertes, man of many wiles,
High-born Ulysses !   Thus wilt thou depart
Home to thy native country ?   Then farewell ;
But, couldst thou know the sufferings Fate ordains
For thee ere yet thou landest on its shore,
Thou wouldst remain to keep this home with me,
And be immortal, strong as is thy wish
To see thy wife—a wish that, day by day,
Possesses thee.   I cannot deem myself
In form or face less beautiful than she ;
For never with immortals can the race
Of mortal dames in form or face compare."
   Ulysses, the sagacious, answered her :
"Bear with me, gracious goddess ; well I know
All thou couldst say.   The sage Penelope
In feature and in stature comes not nigh
To thee ; for she is mortal, deathless thou
And ever young ; yet, day by day, I long
To be at home once more, and pine to see
The hour of my return.   Even though some god
Smite me on the black ocean, I shall bear
The stroke, for in my bosom dwells a mind

Patient of suffering ; much have I endured,
And much survived, in tempests on the deep,
And in the battle ; let this happen too."
　　He spoke ; the sun went down ; the night came on,
And now the twain withdrew to a recess
Deep in the vaulted cave, where, side by side,
They took their rest.　But when the child of dawn,
Aurora, rosy-fingered, looked abroad,
Ulysses put his vest and mantle on ;
The nymph too, in a robe of silver white,
Ample, and delicate, and beautiful,
Arrayed herself, and round about her loins
Wound a fair golden girdle, drew a veil
Over her head, and planned to send away
Magnanimous Ulysses.　She bestowed
A heavy axe, of steel, and double-edged,
Well fitted to the hand, the handle wrought
Of olive-wood, firm set and beautiful.
A polished adze she gave him next, and led
The way to a far corner of the isle,
Where lofty trees, alders and poplars, stood,
And firs that reach the clouds, sapless and dry
Long since, and fitter thus to ride the waves.
Then, having shown where grew the tallest trees,
Calypso, glorious goddess, sought her home.
　　Trees then he felled, and soon the task was done.
Twenty in all he brought to earth, and squared
Their trunks with the sharp steel, and carefully
He smoothed their sides, and wrought them by a line.
Calypso, gracious goddess, having brought
Wimbles, he bored the beams, and, fitting them
Together, made them fast with nails and clamps.
As when some builder, skillful in his art,
Frames, for a ship of burden, the broad keel,
Such ample breadth Ulysses gave the raft.
Upon the massy beams he reared a deck,
And floored it with long planks from end to end.
On this a mast he raised, and to the mast
Fitted a yard ; he shaped a rudder next,

To guide the raft along her course, and round
With woven work of willow-boughs he fenced
Her sides against the dashings of the sea.
Calypso, gracious goddess, brought him store
Of canvas, which he fitly shaped to sails,
And, rigging her with cords, and ropes, and stays,
Heaved her with levers into the great deep.
　'Twas the fourth day ; his labors now were done,
And, on the fifth, the goddess from her isle
Dismissed him, newly from the bath, arrayed
In garments given by her, that shed perfumes.
A skin of dark-red wine she put on board,
A larger one of water, and for food
A basket, stored with viands such as please
The appetite.　A friendly wind and soft
She sent before.　The great Ulysses spread
His canvas joyfully, to catch the breeze,
And sat and guided with nice care the helm,
Gazing with fixed eye on the Pleiades,
Boötes setting late, and the Great Bear,
By others called the Wain, which, wheeling round,
Looks ever toward Orion, and alone
Dips not into the waters of the deep.
For so Calypso, glorious goddess, bade
That, on his ocean journey, he should keep
That constellation ever on his left.
Now seventeen days were in the voyage past,
And on the eighteenth shadowy heights appeared,
The nearest point of the Pheacian land,
Lying on the dark ocean like a shield.
　But mighty Neptune, coming from among
The Ethiopians, saw him.　Far away
He saw, from mountain-heights of Solyma,
The voyager, and burned with fiercer wrath,
And shook his head, and said within himself :
　"Strange ! now I see the gods have new designs
For this Ulysses, formed while I was yet
In Ethiopia.　He draws near the land
Of the Pheacians, where it is decreed

He shall o'erpass the boundary of his woes ;
But first, I think, he will have much to bear."
   He spoke, and round about him called the clouds
And roused the ocean, wielding in his hand
The trident, summoned all the hurricanes
Of all the winds, and covered earth and sky
At once with mists, while from above, the night
Fell suddenly. The east wind and the south
Rushed forth at once, with the strong-blowing west,
And the clear north rolled up his mighty waves.
Ulysses trembled in his knees and heart,
And thus to his great soul, lamenting, said :
   "What will become of me ? unhappy man !
I fear that all the goddess said was true,
Foretelling what disasters should o'ertake
My voyage, ere I reach my native land.
Now are her words fulfilled. Now Jupiter
Wraps the great heaven in clouds and stirs the deep
To tumult ! Wilder grow the hurricanes
Of all the winds, and now my fate is sure.
Thrice happy, four times happy they, who fell
On Troy's wide field, warring for Atreus' sons :
O, had I met my fate and perished there,
That very day on which the Trojan host,
Around the dead Achilles, hurled at me
Their brazen javelins ! I had then received
Due burial and great glory with the Greeks ;
Now must I die a miserable death."
   As thus he spoke, upon him, from on high,
A huge and frightful billow broke ; it whirled
The raft around, and far from it he fell.
His hands let go the rudder ; a fierce rush
Of all the winds together snapped in twain
The mast ; far off the yard and canvas flew
Into the deep ; the billow held him long
Beneath the waters, and he strove in vain
Quickly to rise to air from that huge swell
Of ocean, for the garments weighed him down
Which fair Calypso gave him. But, at length,

Emerging, he rejected from his throat
The bitter brine that down his forehead streamed.
Even then, though hopeless with dismay, his thought
Was on the raft, and, struggling through the waves,
He seized it, sprang on board, and seated there
Escaped the threatened death.   Still to and fro
The rolling billows drove it.   As the wind
In autumn sweeps the thistles o'er the field,
Clinging together, so the blasts of heaven
Hither and thither drove it o'er the sea.
And now the south wind flung it to the north
To buffet ; now the east wind to the west.
   Ino Leucothea saw him clinging there,
The delicate-footed child of Cadmus, once
A mortal, speaking with a mortal voice ;
Though now within the ocean-gulfs, she shares
The honors of the gods.   With pity she
Beheld Ulysses struggling thus distressed,
And, rising from the abyss below, in form
A cormorant, the sea-nymph took her perch
On the well-banded raft, and thus she said :
   " Ah, luckless man, how hast thou angered thus
Earth-shaking Neptune, that he visits thee
With these disasters ?   Yet he cannot take,
Although he seek it earnestly, thy life.
Now do my bidding, for thou seemest wise.
Laying aside thy garments, let the raft
Drift with the winds, while thou, by strength of arm.
Makest thy way in swimming to the land
Of the Pheacians, where thy safety lies.
Receive this veil and bind its heavenly woof
Beneath thy breast, and have no further fear
Of hardship or of danger.   But, as soon
As thou shalt touch the island, take it off,
And turn away thy face, and fling it far
From where thou standest, into the black deep."
   The goddess gave the veil as thus she spoke,
And to the tossing deep went down, in form
A cormorant ; the black wave covered her.

But still Ulysses, mighty sufferer,
Pondered, and thus to his great soul he said :
    "Ah me ! perhaps some god is planning here
Some other fraud against me, bidding me
Forsake my raft.   I will not yet obey,
For still far off I see the land in which
'Tis said my refuge lies.   This will I do,
For this seems wisest.   While the fastenings last
That hold these timbers, I will keep my place
And bide the tempest here.   But when the waves
Shall dash my raft in pieces, I will swim,
For nothing better will remain to do."
    As he revolved this purpose in his mind,
Earth-shaking Neptune sent a mighty wave,
Horrid, and huge, and high, and where he sat
It smote him.   As a violent wind uplifts
The dry chaff heaped upon a threshing-floor,
And sends it scattered through the air abroad,
So did that wave fling loose the ponderous beams.
To one of these, Ulysses, clinging fast,
Bestrode it, like a horseman on his steed ;
And now he took the garments off, bestowed
By fair Calypso, binding round his breast
The veil, and forward plunged into the deep,
With palms outspread, prepared to swim.   Meanwhile,
Neptune beheld him, Neptune, mighty king,
And shook his head, and said within himself :
    " Go thus, and, laden with mischances, roam
The waters, till thou come among the race
Cherished by Jupiter ; but well I deem
Thou wilt not find thy share of suffering light."
    Thus having spoke, he urged his coursers on,
With their fair-flowing manes, until he came
To Ægæ, where his glorious palace stands.
    But Pallas, child of Jove, had other thoughts.
She stayed the course of every wind beside,
And bade them rest, and lulled them into sleep,
But summoned the swift north to break the waves,
That so Ulysses, the high-born, escaped

From death and from the fates, might be the guest
Of the Pheacians, men who love the sea.
    Two days and nights, among the mighty waves
He floated, oft his heart foreboding death,
But when the bright-haired Eos had fulfilled
The third day's course, and all the winds were laid,
And calm was on the watery waste, he saw
The land was near, as, lifted on the crest
Of a huge swell, he looked with sharpened sight ;
And as a father's life preserved makes glad
His children's hearts, when long time he has lain
Sick, wrung with pain, and wasting by the power
Of some malignant genius, till, at length,
The gracious gods bestow a welcome cure ;
So welcome to Ulysses was the sight
Of woods and fields.   By swimming on he thought
To climb and tread the shore, but when he drew
So near that one who shouted could be heard
From land, the sound of ocean on the rocks
Came to his ear, for there huge breakers roared
And spouted fearfully, and all around
Was covered with the sea-foam.   Haven here
Was none for ships, nor sheltering creek, but shores
Beetling from high, and crags and walls of rock.
Ulysses trembled both in knees and heart,
And thus, to his great soul, lamenting, said :
    "Now woe is me ! as soon as Jove has shown
What I had little hoped to see, the land,
And I through all these waves have ploughed my way,
I find no issue from the hoary deep.
For sharp rocks border it, and all around
Roar the wild surges ; slippery cliffs arise
Close to deep gulfs, and footing there is none,
Where I might plant my steps and thus escape.
All effort now were fruitless to resist
The mighty billow hurrying me away
To dash me on the pointed rocks.   If yet
I strive, by swimming further, to descry
Some sloping shore or harbor of the isle,

I fear the tempest, lest it hurl me back,
Heavily groaning, to the fishy deep,
Or huge sea-monster, from the multitude
Which sovereign Amphitrite feeds, be sent
Against me by some god, for well I know
The power who shakes the shores is wroth with me."
    While he revolved these doubts within his mind,
A huge wave hurled him toward the rugged coast.
Then had his limbs been flayed, and all his bones
Broken at once, had not the blue-eyed maid,
Minerva, prompted him. Borne toward the rock,
He clutched it instantly, with both his hands,
And panting clung till that huge wave rolled by,
And so escaped its fury. But it came,
And smote him once again, and flung him far
Seaward. As to the claws of polypus,
Plucked from its bed, the pebbles thickly cling,
So flakes of skin, from off his powerful hands,
Were left upon the rock. The mighty surge
O'erwhelmed him ; he had perished ere his time,
Hapless Ulysses, but the blue-eyed maid,
Pallas, informed his mind with forecast. Straight
Emerging from the wave that shoreward rolled,
He swam along the coast and eyed it well,
In hope of sloping beach or sheltered creek.
But when, in swimming, he had reached the mouth
Of a soft-flowing river, here appeared
The spot he wished for, smooth, without a rock,
And here was shelter from the wind. He felt
The current's flow, and thus devoutly prayed :
    "Hear me, oh sovereign power, whoe'er thou art ;
To thee, the long-desired, I come. I seek
Escape from Neptune's threatenings on the sea.
The deathless gods respect the prayer of him
Who looks to them for help, a fugitive,
As I am now, when to thy stream I come,
And to thy knees, from many a hardship past,
Oh thou that here art ruler, I declare
Myself thy suppliant ; be thou merciful."

He spoke ; the river stayed his current, checked
The billows, smoothed them to a calm, and gave
The swimmer a safe landing at his mouth.
Then dropped his knees and sinewy arms, at once
Unstrung, for faint with struggling was his heart.
His body was all swoln ; the brine gushed forth
From mouth and nostrils ; all unnerved he lay,
Breathless and speechless ; utter weariness
O'ermastered him.   But when he breathed again,
And his flown senses had returned, he loosed
The veil that Ino gave him from his breast,
And to the salt flood cast it.   A great wave
Bore it far down the stream ; the goddess there
In her own hands received it.   He, meanwhile,
Withdrawing from the brink, lay down among
The reeds, and kissed the harvest-bearing earth,
And thus to his great soul, lamenting, said :
    " Ah me ! what must I suffer more ! what yet
Will happen to me ?   If, by the river's side,
I pass the unfriendly watches of the night,
The cruel cold and dews that steep the bank
May, in this weakness, end me utterly,
For chilly blows the river-air at dawn.
But should I climb this hill, to sleep within
The shadowy wood, among their shrubs, if cold
And weariness allow me, then I fear,
That, while the pleasant slumbers o'er me steal,
I may become the prey of savage beasts."
    Yet, as he longer pondered, this seemed best.
He rose and sought the wood, and found it near
The water, on a height, o'erlooking far
The region round.   Between two shrubs, that sprung
Both from one spot, he entered—olive-trees,
One wild, one fruitful.   The damp-blowing wind
Ne'er pierced their covert ; never blazing sun
Darted his beams within, nor pelting shower
Beat through, so closely intertwined they grew.
Here entering, Ulysses heaped a bed
Of leaves with his own hands ; he made it broad

And high, for thick the leaves had fallen around.
Two men and three, in that abundant store,
Might bide the winter-storm, though keen the cold.
Ulysses, the great sufferer, on his couch
Looked and rejoiced, and placed himself within,
And heaped the leaves high o'er him and around.
As one who, dwelling in the distant fields,
Without a neighbor near him, hides a brand
In the dark ashes, keeping carefully
The seeds of fire alive, lest he, perforce,
To light his hearth must bring them from afar ;
So did Ulysses, in that pile of leaves,
Bury himself, while Pallas o'er his eyes
Poured sleep and closed his lids, that he might take,
After his painful toils, the fitting rest.

THE LITTLE PEOPLE OF THE SNOW.

Alice.—One of your old-world stories, Uncle John,
Such as you tell us by the winter fire,
Till we all wonder it is grown so late.
    Uncle John.—The story of the witch that ground to death
Two children in her mill, or will you have
The tale of Goody Cutpurse ?
    Alice.—   Nay now, nay ;
Those stories are too childish, Uncle John,
Too childish even for little Willy here,
And I am older, two good years, than he ;
No, let us have a tale of elves that ride,
By night, with jingling reins, or gnomes of the mine,
Or water-fairies, such as you know how
To spin, till Willy's eyes forget to wink,
And good Aunt Mary, busy as she is,
Lays down her knitting.
    Uncle John.—   Listen to me, then.
'Twas in the olden time, long, long ago,
And long before the great oak at our door

Was yet an acorn, on a mountain's side
Lived, with his wife, a cottager. They dwelt
Beside a glen and near a dashing brook,
A pleasant spot in spring, where first the wren
Was heard to chatter, and, among the grass,
Flowers opened earliest ; but when winter came,
That little brook was fringed with other flowers,—
White flowers, with crystal leaf and stem, that grew
In clear November nights. And, later still,
That mountain-glen was filled with drifted snows
From side to side, that one might walk across ;
While, many a fathom deep, below, the brook
Sang to itself, and leaped and trotted on
Unfrozen, o'er its pebbles, toward the vale.

    Alice.—A mountain-side, you said ; the Alps, perhaps,
Or our own Alleghanies.
     Uncle John.—   Not so fast,
My young geographer, for then the Alps,
With their broad pastures, haply were untrod
Of herdsman's foot, and never human voice
Had sounded in the woods that overhang
Our Alleghany's streams. I think it was
Upon the slopes of the great Caucasus,
Or where the rivulets of Ararat
Seek the Armenian vales. That mountain rose
So high, that, on its top, the winter-snow
Was never melted, and the cottagers
Among the summer-blossoms, far below,
Saw its white peaks in August from their door.

   One little maiden, in that cottage-home,
Dwelt with her parents, light of heart and limb,
Bright, restless, thoughtless, flitting here and there,
Like sunshine on the uneasy ocean-waves,
And sometimes she forgot what she was bid,
As Alice does.
    Alice.—   Or Willy, quite as oft.
    Uncle John.—But you are older, Alice, two good years,
And should be wiser. Eva was the name
Of this young maiden, now twelve summers old.

Now you must know that, in those early times,
When autumn days grew pale, there came a troop
Of childlike forms from that cold mountain-top ;
With trailing garments through the air they came,
Or walked the ground with girded loins, and threw
Spangles of silvery frost upon the grass,
And edged the brooks with glistening parapets,
And built it crystal bridges, touched the pool,
And turned its face to glass, or, rising thence,
They shook from their full laps the soft, light snow,
And buried the great earth, as autumn winds
Bury the forest-floor in heaps of leaves.
   A beautiful race were they, with baby brows,
And fair, bright locks, and voices like the sound
Of steps on the crisp snow, in which they talked
With man, as friend with friend. A merry sight
It was, when, crowding round the traveller,
They smote him with their heaviest snow-flakes, flung
Needles of frost in handfuls at his cheeks,
And, of the light wreaths of his smoking breath,
Wove a white fringe for his brown beard, and laughed
Their slender laugh to see him wink and grin
And make grim faces as he floundered on.
   But, when the spring came on, what terror reigned
Among these Little People of the Snow !
To them the sun's warm beams were shafts of fire,
And the soft south-wind was the wind of death.
Away they flew, all with a pretty scowl
Upon their childish faces, to the north,
Or scampered upward to the mountain's top,
And there defied their enemy, the Spring ;
Skipping and dancing on the frozen peaks,
And moulding little snow-balls in their palms,
And rolling them, to crush her flowers below,
Down the steep snow-fields.
   Alice.—   That, too, must have been
A merry sight to look at.
   Uncle John.—   You are right,
But I must speak of graver matters now.
   28

Midwinter was the time, and Eva stood,
Within the cottage, all prepared to dare
The outer cold, with ample furry robe
Close-belted round her waist, and boots of fur,
And a broad kerchief, which her mother's hand
Had closely drawn about her ruddy cheek.
" Now, stay not long abroad," said the good dame,
" For sharp is the outer air, and, mark me well,
Go not upon the snow beyond the spot
Where the great linden bounds the neighboring field."
   The little maiden promised, and went forth,
And climbed the rounded snow-swells firm with frost
Beneath her feet, and slid, with balancing arms,
Into the hollows. Once, as up a drift
She slowly rose, before her, in the way,
She saw a little creature, lily-cheeked,
With flowing flaxen locks, and faint blue eyes,
That gleamed like ice, and robe that only seemed
Of a more shadowy whiteness than her cheek.
On a smooth bank she sat.
   Alice.—   She must have been
One of your Little People of the Snow.
   Uncle John.—She was so, and, as Eva now drew near,
The tiny creature bounded from her seat ;
" And come," she said, " my pretty friend ; to-day
We will be playmates.   I have watched thee long,
And seen how well thou lov'st to walk these drifts,
And scoop their fair sides into little cells,
And carve them with quaint figures, huge-limbed men,
Lions, and griffins.   We will have, to-day,
A merry ramble over these bright fields,
And thou shalt see what thou hast never seen."
On went the pair, until they reached the bound
Where the great linden stood, set deep in snow,
Up to the lower branches.   " Here we stop,"
Said Eva, " for my mother has my word
That I will go no farther than this tree."
Then the snow-maiden laughed : " And what is this ?
This fear of the pure snow, the innocent snow,

That never harmed aught living ? Thou mayst roam
For leagues beyond this garden, and return
In safety ; here the grim wolf never prowls,
And here the eagle of our mountain-crags
Preys not in winter. I will show the way,
And bring thee safely home. Thy mother, sure,
Counselled thee thus because thou hadst no guide."
   By such smooth words was Eva won to break
Her promise, and went on with her new friend,
Over the glistening snow and down a bank
Where a white shelf, wrought by the eddying wind,
Like to a billow's crest in the great sea,
Curtained an opening. "Look, we enter here."
And straight, beneath the fair o'erhanging fold,
Entered the little pair that hill of snow,
Walking along a passage with white walls,
And a white vault above where snow-stars shed
A wintry twilight. Eva moved in awe,
And held her peace, but the snow-maiden smiled,
And talked and tripped along, as down the way,
Deeper they went into that mountainous drift.
   And now the white walls widened, and the vault
Swelled upward, like some vast cathedral-dome,
Such as the Florentine, who bore the name
Of heaven's most potent angel, reared, long since,
Or the unknown builder of that wondrous fane,
The glory of Burgos. Here a garden lay,
In which the Little People of the Snow
Were wont to take their pastime when their tasks
Upon the mountain's side and in the clouds
Were ended. Here they taught the silent frost
To mock, in stem and spray, and leaf and flower,
The growths of summer. Here the palm upreared
Its white columnar trunk and spotless sheaf
Of plume-like leaves ; here cedars, huge as those
Of Lebanon, stretched far their level boughs,
Yet pale and shadowless ; the sturdy oak
Stood, with its huge gnarled roots of seeming strength,
Fast anchored in the glistening bank ; light sprays

Of myrtle, roses in their bud and bloom,
Drooped by the winding walks ; yet all seemed wrought
Of stainless alabaster ; up the trees
Ran the lithe jessamine, with stalk and leaf
Colorless as her flowers.   " Go softly on,"
Said the snow-maiden ; " touch not, with thy hand,
The frail creation round thee, and beware
To sweep it with thy skirts.   Now look above.
How sumptuously these bowers are lighted up
With shifting gleams that softly come and go !
These are the northern lights, such as thou seest
In the midwinter nights, cold, wandering flames,
That float with our processions, through the air ;
And here, within our winter palaces,
Mimic the glorious daybreak."   Then she told
How, when the wind, in the long winter nights,
Swept the light snows into the hollow dell,
She and her comrades guided to its place
Each wandering flake, and piled them quaintly up,
In shapely colonnade and glistening arch,
With shadowy aisles between, or bade them grow,
Beneath their little hands, to bowery walks
In gardens such as these, and, o'er them all,
Built the broad roof.   " But thou hast yet to see
A fairer sight," she said, and led the way
To where a window of pellucid ice
Stood in the wall of snow, beside their path.
" Look, but thou mayst not enter."   Eva looked,
And lo ! a glorious hall, from whose high vault
Stripes of soft light, ruddy and delicate green,
And tender blue, flowed downward to the floor
And far around, as if the aërial hosts,
That march on high by night, with beamy spears,
And streaming banners, to that place had brought
Their radiant flags to grace a festival.
   And in that hall a joyous multitude
Of these by whom its glistening walls were reared,
Whirled in a merry dance to silvery sounds,
That rang from cymbals of transparent ice,

" And in that hall a joyous multitude
Of these by whom its glistening walls were reared."

And ice-cups, quivering to the skilful touch
Of little fingers. Round and round they flew,
As when, in spring, about a chimney-top,
A cloud of twittering swallows, just returned,
Wheel round and round, and turn and wheel again,
Unwinding their swift track. So rapidly
Flowed the meandering stream of that fair dance,
Beneath that dome of light. Bright eyes that looked
From under lily-brows, and gauzy scarfs
Sparkling like snow-wreaths in the early sun,
Shot by the window in their mazy whirl.
And there stood Eva, wondering at the sight
Of those bright revellers and that graceful sweep
Of motion as they passed her ;—long she gazed,
And listened long to the sweet sounds that thrilled
The frosty air, till now the encroaching cold
Recalled her to herself. " Too long, too long
I linger here," she said, and then she sprang
Into the path, and with a hurried step
Followed it upward. Ever by her side
Her little guide kept pace. As on they went,
Eva bemoaned her fault : " What must they think—
The dear ones in the cottage, while so long,
Hour after hour, I stay without ? I know
That they will seek me far and near, and weep
To find me not. How could I, wickedly,
Neglect the charge they gave me ? " As she spoke,
The hot tears started to her eyes ; she knelt
In the mid-path. " Father ! forgive this sin ;
Forgive myself I cannot "—thus she prayed,
And rose and hastened onward. When, at last,
They reached the outer air, the clear north breathed
A bitter cold, from which she shrank with dread,
But the snow-maiden bounded as she felt
The cutting blast, and uttered shouts of joy,
And skipped, with boundless glee, from drift to drift,
And danced round Eva, as she labored up
The mounds of snow. " Ah me ! I feel my eyes
Grow heavy," Eva said ; " they swim with sleep ;

I cannot walk for utter weariness,
And I must rest a moment on this bank,
But let it not be long." As thus she spoke,
In half formed words, she sank on the smooth snow,
With closing lids. Her guide composed the robe
About her limbs, and said : " A pleasant spot
Is this to slumber in ; on such a couch
Oft have I slept away the winter night,
And had the sweetest dreams." So Eva slept,
But slept in death ; for when the power of frost
Locks up the motions of the living frame,
The victim passes to the realm of Death
Through the dim porch of Sleep. The little guide,
Watching beside her, saw the hues of life
Fade from the fair smooth brow and rounded cheek,
As fades the crimson from a morning cloud,
Till they were white as marble, and the breath
Had ceased to come and go, yet knew she not
At first that this was death. But when she marked
How deep the paleness was, how motionless
That once lithe form, a fear came over her.
She strove to wake the sleeper, plucked her robe,
And shouted in her ear, but all in vain ;
The life had passed away from those young limbs.
Then the snow-maiden raised a wailing cry,
Such as the dweller in some lonely wild,
Sleepless through all the long December night,
Hears when the mournful East begins to blow.

But suddenly was heard the sound of steps,
Grating on the crisp snow ; the cottagers
Were seeking Eva ; from afar they saw
The twain, and hurried toward them. As they came
With gentle chidings ready on their lips,
And marked that deathlike sleep, and heard the tale
Of the snow-maiden, mortal anguish fell
Upon their hearts, and bitter words of grief
And blame were uttered : " Cruel, cruel one,
To tempt our daughter thus, and cruel we,
Who suffered her to wander forth alone

"*Around that little grave, in the long night,
Frost-wreaths were laid and tufts of silvery rime
In shape like blades and blossoms of the field.*"

In this fierce cold ! " They lifted the dear child,
And bore her home and chafed her tender limbs,
And strove, by all the simple arts they knew,
To make the chilled blood move, and win the breath
Back to her bosom ; fruitlessly they strove ;
The little maid was dead. In blank despair
They stood, and gazed at her who never more
Should look on them. " Why die we not with her ? "
They said ; " without her, life is bitterness."
    Now came the funeral-day ; the simple folk
Of all that pastoral region gathered round
To share the sorrow of the cottagers.
They carved a way into the mound of snow
To the glen's side, and dug a little grave
In the smooth slope, and, following the bier,
In long procession from the silent door,
Chanted a sad and solemn melody :
    " Lay her away to rest within the ground.
Yea, lay her down whose pure and innocent life
Was spotless as these snows ; for she was reared
In love, and passed in love life's pleasant spring,
And all that now our tenderest love can do
Is to give burial to her lifeless limbs."
    They paused. A thousand slender voices round,
Like echoes softly flung from rock and hill,
Took up the strain, and all the hollow air
Seemed mourning for the dead ; for, on that day,
The Little People of the Snow had come,
From mountain-peak, and cloud, and icy hall,
To Eva's burial. As the murmur died,
The funeral-train renewed the solemn chant :
    " Thou, Lord, hast taken her to be with Eve,
Whose gentle name was given her. Even so,
For so Thy wisdom saw that it was best
For her and us. We bring our bleeding hearts,
And ask the touch of healing from Thy hand,
As, with submissive tears, we render back
The lovely and beloved to Him who gave."
    They ceased. Again the plaintive murmur rose.

From shadowy skirts of low-hung cloud it came,
And wide white fields, and fir-trees capped with snow,
Shivering to the sad sounds.   They sank away
To silence in the dim-seen distant woods.
  The little grave was closed ; the funeral-train
Departed ; winter wore away ; the Spring
Steeped, with her quickening rains, the violet-tufts,
By fond hands planted where the maiden slept.
But, after Eva's burial, never more
The Little People of the Snow were seen
By human eye, nor ever human ear
Heard from their lips articulate speech again ;
For a decree went forth to cut them off,
Forever, from communion with mankind.
The winter-clouds, along the mountain-side,
Rolled downward toward the vale, but no fair form
Leaned from their folds, and, in the icy glens,
And aged woods, under snow-loaded pines,
Where once they made their haunt, was emptiness.
  But ever, when the wintry days drew near,
Around that little grave, in the long night,
Frost-wreaths were laid and tufts of silvery rime
In shape like blades and blossoms of the field
As one would scatter flowers upon a bier.

THE POET.

Thou, who wouldst wear the name
    Of poet mid thy brethren of mankind,
And clothe in words of flame
    Thoughts that shall live within the general mind !
Deem not the framing of a deathless lay
The pastime of a drowsy summer day.

But gather all thy powers,
    And wreak them on the verse that thou dost weave,
And in thy lonely hours,
    At silent morning or at wakeful eve,

"*Deem not the framing of a deathless lay
The pastime of a drowsy summer day.*"

While the warm current tingles through thy veins,
Set forth the burning words in fluent strains.

No smooth array of phrase,
    Artfully sought and ordered though it be,
Which the cold rhymer lays
    Upon his page with languid industry,
Can wake the listless pulse to livelier speed,
Or fill with sudden tears the eyes that read.

The secret wouldst thou know
    To touch the heart or fire the blood at will?
Let thine own eyes o'erflow ;
    Let thy lips quiver with the passionate thrill ;
Seize the great thought, ere yet its power be past,
And bind, in words, the fleet emotion fast.

Then, should thy verse appear
    Halting and harsh, and all unaptly wrought,
Touch the crude line with fear,
    Save in the moment of impassioned thought ;
Then summon back the original glow, and mend
The strain with rapture that with fire was penned.

Yet let no empty gust
    Of passion find an utterance in thy lay,
A blast that whirls the dust
    Along the howling street and dies away ;
But feelings of calm power and mighty sweep,
Like currents journeying through the windless deep.

Seek'st thou, in living lays,
    To limn the beauty of the earth and sky?
Before thine inner gaze
    Let all that beauty in clear vision lie ;
Look on it with exceeding love, and write
The words inspired by wonder and delight.

Of tempests wouldst thou sing,
    Or tell of battles—make thyself a part

Of the great tumult ; cling
  To the tossed wreck with terror in thy heart ;
Scale, with the assaulting host, the rampart's height,
And strike and struggle in the thickest fight.

So shalt thou frame a lay
  That haply may endure from age to age,
And they who read shall say :
  " What witchery hangs upon this poet's page !
What art is his the written spells to find
That sway from mood to mood the willing mind ! "

THE PATH.

THE path we planned beneath October's sky,
  Along the hillside, through the woodland shade,
Is finished ; thanks to thee, whose kindly eye
  Has watched me, as I plied the busy spade ;
Else had I wearied, ere this path of ours
Had pierced the woodland to its inner bowers.

Yet, 'twas a pleasant toil to trace and beat,
  Among the glowing trees, this winding way,
While the sweet autumn sunshine, doubly sweet,
  Flushed with the ruddy foliage, round us lay,
As if some gorgeous cloud of morning stood,
In glory, mid the arches of the wood.

A path ! what beauty does a path bestow
  Even on the dréariest wild ! its savage nooks
Seem homelike where accustomed footsteps go,
  And the grim rock puts on familiar looks.
The tangled swamp, through which a pathway strays,
Becomes a garden with strange flowers and sprays.

See from the weedy earth a rivulet break
  And purl along the untrodden wilderness ;

There the shy cuckoo comes his thirst to slake,
　There the shrill jay alights his plumes to dress;
And there the stealthy fox, when morn is gray,
Laps the clear stream and lightly moves away.

But let a path approach that fountain': brink,
　And nobler forms of life, behold ! are there :
Boys kneeling with protruded lips to drink,
　And slender maids that homeward slowly bear
The brimming pail, and busy dames that lay
Their webs to whiten in the summer ray.

Then know we that for herd and flock are poured
　Those pleasant streams that o'er the pebbles slip ;
Those pure sweet waters sparkle on the board ;
　Those fresh cool waters wet the sick man's lip ;
Those clear bright waters from the font are shed,
In dews of baptism, on the infant's head.

What different steps the rural footway trace !
　The laborer afield at early day ;
The schoolboy sauntering with uneven pace ;
　The Sunday worshipper in fresh array ;
And mourner in the weeds of sorrow drest ;
And, smiling to himself, the wedding guest.

There he who cons a speech and he who hums
　His yet unfinished verses, musing walk.
There, with her little brood, the matron comes,
　To break the spring flower from its juicy stalk ;
And lovers, loitering, wonder that the moon
Has risen upon their pleasant stroll so soon.

Bewildered in vast woods, the traveller feels
　His heavy heart grow lighter, if he meet
The traces of a path, and straight he kneels,
　And kisses the dear print of human feet,
And thanks his God, and journeys without fear,
For now he knows the abodes of men are near

Pursue the slenderest path across a lawn :
   Lo ! on the broad highway it issues forth,
And, blended with the greater track, goes on,
   Over the surface of the mighty earth,
Climbs hills and crosses vales, and stretches far,
Through silent forests, toward the evening star—

And enters cities murmuring with the feet
   Of multitudes, and wanders forth again,
And joins the climes of frost to climes of heat,
   Binds East to West, and marries main to main,
Nor stays till at the long-resounding shore
Of the great deep, where paths are known no more.

Oh, mighty instinct, that dost thus unite
   Earth's neighborhoods and tribes with friendly bands,
What guilt is theirs who, in their greed or spite,
   Undo thy holy work with violent hands,
And post their squadrons, nursed in war's grim trade,
To bar the ways for mutual succor made !

THE RETURN OF THE BIRDS.

I HEAR, from many a little throat,
   A warble interrupted long ;
I hear the robin's flute-like note,
   The bluebird's slenderer song.

Brown meadows and the russet hill,
   Not yet the haunt of grazing herds,
And thickets by the glimmering rill,
   Are all alive with birds.

Oh choir of spring, why come so soon ?
   On leafless grove and herbless lawn
Warm lie the yellow beams of moon ;
   Yet winter is not gone.

For frost shall sheet the pools again ;
　Again the blustering East shall blow—
Whirl a white tempest through the glen,
　And load the pines with snow.

Yet, haply, from the region where,
　Waked by an earlier spring than here,
The blossomed wild-plum scents the air,
　Ye come in haste and fear.

For there is heard the bugle-blast,
　The booming gun, the jarring drum,
And on their chargers, spurring fast,
　Armed warriors go and come.

There mighty hosts have pitched the camp
　In valleys that were yours till then,
And Earth has shuddered to the tramp
　Of half a million men !

In groves where once ye used to sing,
　In orchards where ye had your birth,
A thousand glittering axes swing
　To smite the trees to earth.

Ye love the fields by ploughmen trod ;
　But there, when sprouts the beechen spray,
The soldier only breaks the sod
　To hide the slain away.

Stay, then, beneath our ruder sky ;
　Heed not the storm-clouds rising black,
Nor yelling winds that with them fly ;
　Nor let them fright you back,—

Back to the stifling battle-cloud,
　To burning towns that blot the day,
And trains of mounting dust that shroud
　The armies on their way.

Stay, for a tint of green shall creep
  Soon o'er the orchard's grassy floor,
And from its bed the crocus peep
  Beside the housewife's door.

Here build, and dread no harsher sound,
  To scare you from the sheltering tree,
Than winds that stir the branches round,
  And murmur of the bee.

And we will pray that, ere again
  The flowers of autumn bloom and die,
Our generals and their strong-armed men
  May lay their weapons by.

Then may ye warble, unafraid,
  Where hands, that wear the fetter now,
Free as your wings shall ply the spade,
  And guide the peaceful plough.

Then, as our conquering hosts return,
  What shouts of jubilee shall break
From placid vale and mountain stern,
  And shore of mighty lake !

And midland plain and ocean-strand
  Shall thunder : " Glory to the brave,
Peace to the torn and bleeding land,
  And freedom to the slave ! "

March, 1864.

HE HATH PUT ALL THINGS UNDER HIS
FEET."

O NORTH, with all thy vales of green !
  O South, with all thy palms !
From peopled towns and fields between
  Uplift the voice of psalms ;

Raise, ancient East, the anthem high,
And let the youthful West reply.

Lo ! in the clouds of heaven appears
    God's well-belovèd Son ;
He brings a train of brighter years :
    His kingdom is begun.
He comes, a guilty world to bless
With mercy, truth, and righteousness.

Oh, Father ! haste the promised hour
    When, at His feet, shall lie
All rule, authority, and power,
    Beneath the ample sky ;
When He shall reign from pole to pole,
The lord of every human soul ;

When all shall heed the words He said
    Amid their daily cares,
And, by the loving life He led,
    Shall seek to pattern theirs ;
And He, who conquered Death, shall win
The nobler conquest over Sin.

MY AUTUMN WALK.

On woodlands ruddy with autumn
    The amber sunshine lies ;
I look on the beauty round me,
    And tears come into my eyes.

For the wind that sweeps the meadows
    Blows out of the far Southwest,
Where our gallant men are fighting,
    And the gallant dead are at rest.

The golden-rod is leaning,
  And the purple aster waves
In a breeze from the land of battles,
  A breath from the land of graves.

Full fast the leaves are dropping
  Before that wandering breath;
As fast, on the field of battle,
  Our brethren fall in death.

Beautiful over my pathway
  The forest spoils are shed;
They are spotting the grassy hillocks
  With purple and gold and red.

Beautiful is the death-sleep
  Of those who bravely fight
In their country's holy quarrel,
  And perish for the Right.

But who shall comfort the living,
  The light of whose homes is gone:
The bride that, early widowed,
  Lives broken-hearted on;

The matron whose sons are lying
  In graves on a distant shore;
The maiden, whose promised husband
  Comes back from the war no more?

I look on the peaceful dwellings
  Whose windows glimmer in sight,
With croft and garden and orchard,
  That bask in the mellow light;

And I know that, when our couriers
  With news of victory come,
They will bring a bitter message
  Of hopeless grief to some.

Again I turn to the woodlands,
  And shudder as I see
The mock-grape's blood-red banner
  Hung out on the cedar-tree ;

And I think of days of slaughter,
  And the night-sky red with flames,
On the Chattahoochee's meadows,
  And the wasted banks of the James.

Oh, for the fresh spring-season,
  When the groves are in their prime ;
And far away in the future
  Is the frosty autumn-time !

Oh, for that better season,
  When the pride of the foe shall yield,
And the hosts of God and Freedom
  March back from the well-won field ;

And the matron shall clasp her first-born
  With tears of joy and pride ;
And the scarred and war-worn lover
  Shall claim his promised bride !

The leaves are swept from the branches ;
  But the living buds are there,
With folded flower and foliage,
  To sprout in a kinder air.

October, 1864.

DANTE.

W<small>HO</small>, mid the grasses of the field
  That spring beneath our careless feet,
First found the shining stems that yield
  The grains of life-sustaining wheat :

29

Who first, upon the furrowed land,
   Strewed the bright grains to sprout, and grow,
And ripen for the reaper's hand—
   We know not, and we cannot know.

But well we know the hand that brought
   And scattered, far as sight can reach,
The seeds of free and living thought
   On the broad field of modern speech.

Mid the white hills that round us lie,
   We cherish that Great Sower's fame,
And, as we pile the sheaves on high,
   With awe we utter Dante's name.

Six centuries, since the poet's birth,
   Have come and flitted o'er our sphere:
The richest harvest reaped on earth
   Crowns the last century's closing year.

1865.

THE DEATH OF LINCOLN.

Oh, slow to smite and swift to spare,
   Gentle and merciful and just!
Who, in the fear of God, didst bear
   The sword of power, a nation's trust!

In sorrow by thy bier we stand,
   Amid the awe that hushes all,
And speak the anguish of a land
   That shook with horror at thy fall.

Thy task is done; the bond are free:
   We bear thee to an honored grave,
Whose proudest monument shall be
   The broken fetters of the slave.

Pure was thy life ; its bloody close
   Hath placed thee with the sons of light,
Among the noble host of those
   Who perished in the cause of Right.
April, 1865.

THE DEATH OF SLAVERY.

O THOU great Wrong, that, through the slow-paced years,
   Didst hold thy millions fettered, and didst wield
   The scourge that drove the laborer to the field,
And turn a stony gaze on human tears,
      Thy cruel reign is o'er ;
      Thy bondmen crouch no more
In terror at the menace of thine eye ;
   For He who marks the bounds of guilty power,
Long-suffering, hath heard the captive's cry,
   And touched his shackles at the appointed hour,
And lo ! they fall, and he whose limbs they galled
Stands in his native manhood, disenthralled.

A shout of joy from the redeemed is sent ;
   Ten thousand hamlets swell the hymn of thanks ;
   Our rivers roll exulting, and their banks
Send up hosannas to the firmament !
      Fields where the bondman's toil
      No more shall trench the soil,
Seem now to bask in a serener day ;
   The meadow-birds sing sweeter, and the airs
Of heaven with more caressing softness play,
   Welcoming man to liberty like theirs.
A glory clothes the land from sea to sea,
For the great land and all its coasts are free.

Within that land wert thou enthroned of late,
   And they by whom the nation's laws were made,
   And they who filled its judgment-seats obeyed
Thy mandate, rigid as the will of Fate.

Fierce men at thy right hand,
With gesture of command,
Gave forth the word that none might dare gainsay ;
And grave and reverend ones, who loved thee not,
Shrank from thy presence, and in blank dismay
Choked down, unuttered, the rebellious thought ;
While meaner cowards, mingling with thy train,
Proved, from the book of God, thy right to reign.

Great as thou wert, and feared from shore to shore,
The wrath of Heaven o'ertook thee in thy pride ;
Thou sitt'st a ghastly shadow ; by thy side
Thy once strong arms hang nerveless evermore.
And they who quailed but now
Before thy lowering brow,
Devote thy memory to scorn and shame,
And scoff at the pale, powerless thing thou art.
And they who ruled in thine imperial name,
Subdued, and standing sullenly apart,
Scowl at the hands that overthrew thy reign,
And shattered at a blow the prisoner's chain.

Well was thy doom deserved ; thou didst not spare
Life's tenderest ties, but cruelly didst part
Husband and wife, and from the mother's heart
Didst wrest her children, deaf to shriek and prayer ;
Thy inner lair became
The haunt of guilty shame ;
Thy lash dropped blood ; the murderer, at thy side,
Showed his red hands, nor feared the vengeance due.
Thou didst sow earth with crimes, and, far and wide,
A harvest of uncounted miseries grew,
Until the measure of thy sins at last
Was full, and then the avenging bolt was cast !

Go now, accursed of God, and take thy place
With hateful memories of the elder time,
With many a wasting plague, and nameless crime,
And bloody war that thinned the human race ;

With the Black Death, whose way
Through wailing cities lay,
Worship of Moloch, tyrannies that built
The Pyramids, and cruel creeds that taught
To avenge a fancied guilt by deeper guilt—
Death at the stake to those that held them not.
Lo ! the foul phantoms, silent in the gloom
Of the flown ages, part to yield thee room.

I see the better years that hasten by
Carry thee back into that shadowy past,
Where, in the dusty spaces, void and vast,
The graves of those whom thou hast murdered lie.
The slave-pen, through whose door
Thy victims pass no more,
Is there, and there shall the grim block remain
At which the slave was sold ; while at thy feet
Scourges and engines of restraint and pain
Moulder and rust by thine eternal seat.
There, mid the symbols that proclaim thy crimes,
Dwell thou, a warning to the coming times.

May, 1866.

"RECEIVE THY SIGHT."

When the blind suppliant in the way,
By friendly hands to Jesus led,
Prayed to behold the light of day,
"Receive thy sight," the Saviour said.

At once he saw the pleasant rays
That lit the glorious firmament ;
And, with firm step and words of praise,
He followed where the Master went.

Look down in pity, Lord, we pray,
On eyes oppressed by moral night,
And touch the darkened lids and say
The gracious words, " Receive thy sight."

Then, in clear daylight, shall we see
Where walked the sinless Son of God ,
And, aided by new strength from Thee,
Press onward in the path He trod.

A BRIGHTER DAY.

FROM THE SPANISH.

HARNESS the impatient Years,
O Time ! and yoke them to the imperial car ;
For, through a mist of tears,
The brighter day appears,
Whose early blushes tinge the hills afar.

A brighter day for thee,
O realm ! whose glorious fields are spread between
The dark-blue Midland Sea
And that immensity
Of Western waters which once hailed thee queen !

The fiery coursers fling
Their necks aloft, and snuff the morning wind,
Till the fleet moments bring
The expected sign to spring
Along their path, and leave these glooms behind.

Yoke them, and yield the reins
To Spain, and lead her to the lofty seat ;
But, ere she mount, the chains
Whose cruel strength constrains
Her limbs must fall in fragments at her feet.

A tyrant brood have wound
About her helpless limbs the steely braid,
And toward a gulf profound
They drag her, gagged and bound,
Down among dead men's bones, and frost and shade.

O Spain ! thou wert of yore
The wonder of the realms ; in prouder years
    Thy haughty forehead wore,
    What it shall wear no more,
The diadem of both the hemispheres.

    To thee the ancient Deep
Revealed his pleasant, undiscovered lands ;
    From mines where jewels sleep,
    Tilled plain and vine-clad steep,
Earth's richest spoil was offered to thy hands.

    Yet thou, when land and sea
Sent thee their tribute with each rolling wave,
    And kingdoms crouched to thee,
    Wert false to Liberty,
And therefore art thou now a shackled slave.

    Wilt thou not, yet again,
Put forth the sleeping strength that in thee lies,
    And snap the shameful chain,
    And force that tyrant train
To flee before the anger in thine eyes ?

    Then shall the harnessed Years
Sweep onward with thee to that glorious height
    Which even now appears
    Bright through the mist of tears,
The dwelling-place of Liberty and Light.

October, 1867.

AMONG THE TREES.

OH ye who love to overhang the springs,
And stand by running waters, ye whose boughs
Make beautiful the rocks o'er which they play,
Who pile with foliage the great hills, and rear
A paradise upon the lonely plain,
Trees of the forest, and the open field !

Have ye no sense of being ?   Does the air,
The pure air, which I breathe with gladness, pass
In gushes o'er your delicate lungs, your leaves,
All unenjoyed ?   When on your winter's sleep
The sun shines warm, have ye no dreams of spring?
And when the glorious spring-time comes at last,
Have ye no joy of all your bursting buds,
And fragrant blooms, and melody of birds
To which your young leaves shiver ?   Do ye strive
And wrestle with the wind, yet know it not ?
Feel ye no glory in your strength when he,
The exhausted Blusterer, flies beyond the hills,
And leaves you stronger yet ?   Or have ye not
A sense of loss when he has stripped your leaves,
Yet tender, and has splintered your fair boughs ?
Does the loud bolt that smites you from the cloud
And rends you, fall unfelt ?   Do there not run
Strange shudderings through your fibres when the axe
Is raised against you, and the shining blade
Deals blow on blow, until, with all their boughs,
Your summits waver and ye fall to earth ?
Know ye no sadness when the hurricane
Has swept the wood and snapped its sturdy stems
Asunder, or has wrenched, from out the soil,
The mightiest with their circles of strong roots,
And piled the ruin all along his path ?

   Nay, doubt we not that under the rough rind,
In the green veins of these fair growths of earth,
There dwells a nature that receives delight
From all the gentle processes of life,
And shrinks from loss of being.   Dim and faint
May be the sense of pleasure and of pain,
As in our dreams ; but, haply, real still.

   Our sorrows touch you not.   We watch beside
The beds of those who languish or who die,
And minister in sadness, while our hearts
Offer perpetual prayer for life and ease

"... Do there not run
Strange shudderings through your fibres when the axe
Is raised against you, and the shining blade
Deals blow on blow?"

And health to the belovèd sufferers.
But ye, while anxious fear and fainting hope
Are in our chambers, ye rejoice without.
The funeral goes forth ; a silent train
Moves slowly from the desolate home ; our hearts
Are breaking as we lay away the loved,
Whom we shall see no more, in their last rest,
Their little cells within the burial-place.
Ye have no part in this distress ; for still
The February sunshine steeps your boughs
And tints the buds and swells the leaves within ;
While the song-sparrow, warbling from her perch,
Tells you that spring is near.   The wind of May
Is sweet with breath of orchards, in whose boughs
The bees and every insect of the air
Make a perpetual murmur of delight,
And by whose flowers the humming-bird hangs poised
In air, and draws their sweets and darts away.
The linden, in the fervors of July,
Hums with a louder concert.   When the wind
Sweeps the broad forest in its summer prime,
As when some master-hand exulting sweeps
The keys of some great organ, ye give forth
The music of the woodland depths, a hymn
Of gladness and of thanks.   The hermit-thrush
Pipes his sweet note to make your arches ring ;
The faithful robin, from the wayside elm,
Carols all day to cheer his sitting mate ;
And when the autumn comes, the kings of earth,
In all their majesty, are not arrayed
As ye are, clothing the broad mountain-side
And spotting the smooth vales with red and gold ;
While, swaying to the sudden breeze, ye fling
Your nuts to earth, and the brisk squirrel comes
To gather them, and barks with childish glee,
And scampers with them to his hollow oak.

Thus, as the seasons pass, ye keep alive
The cheerfulness of Nature, till in time

The constant misery which wrings the heart
Relents, and we rejoice with you again,
And glory in your beauty ; till once more
We look with pleasure on your varnished leaves,
That gayly glance in sunshine, and can hear,
Delighted, the soft answer which your boughs
Utter in whispers to the babbling brook.

Ye have no history. I cannot know
Who, when the hillside trees were hewn away,
Haply two centuries since, bade spare this oak,
Leaning to shade, with his irregular arms,
Low-bent and long, the fount that from his roots
Slips through a bed of cresses toward the bay—
I know not who, but thank him that he left
The tree to flourish where the acorn fell,
And join these later days to that far time
While yet the Indian hunter drew the bow
In the dim woods, and the white woodman first
Opened these fields to sunshine, turned the soil
And strewed the wheat. An unremembered Past
Broods, like a presence, mid the long gray boughs
Of this old tree, which has outlived so long
The flitting generations of mankind.

Ye have no history. I ask in vain
Who planted on the slope this lofty group
Of ancient pear-trees that with spring-time burst
Into such breadth of bloom. One bears a scar
Where the quick lightning scored its trunk, yet still
It feels the breath of Spring, and every May
Is white with blossoms. Who it was that laid
Their infant roots in earth, and tenderly
Cherished the delicate sprays, I ask in vain,
Yet bless the unknown hand to which I owe
This annual festival of bees, these songs
Of birds within their leafy screen, these shouts
Of joy from children gathering up the fruit
Shaken in August from the willing boughs.

Ye that my hands have planted, or have spared,
Beside the way, or in the orchard-ground,
Or in the open meadow, ye whose boughs
With every summer spread a wider shade,
Whose herd in coming years shall lie at rest
Beneath your noontide shelter? who shall pluck
Your ripened fruit? who grave, as was the wont
Of simple pastoral ages, on the rind
Of my smooth beeches some belovèd name?
Idly I ask; yet may the eyes that look
Upon you, in your later, nobler growth,
Look also on a nobler age than ours;
An age when, in the eternal strife between
Evil and Good, the Power of Good shall win
A grander mastery; when kings no more
Shall summon millions from the plough to learn
The trade of slaughter, and of populous realms
Make camps of war; when in our younger land
The hand of ruffian Violence, that now
Is insolently raised to smite, shall fall
Unnerved before the calm rebuke of Law,
And Fraud, his sly confederate, shrink, in shame,
Back to his covert, and forego his prey.

MAY EVENING.

THE breath of Spring-time at this twilight hour
    Comes through the gathering glooms,
And bears the stolen sweets of many a flower
    Into my silent rooms.

Where hast thou wandered, gentle gale, to find
    The perfumes thou dost bring?
By brooks, that through the wakening meadows wind,
    Or brink of rushy spring?

Or woodside, where, in little companies,
 The early wild-flowers rise,
Or sheltered lawn, where, mid encircling trees,
 May's warmest sunshine lies ?

Now sleeps the humming-bird, that, in the sun,
 Wandered from bloom to bloom ;
Now, too, the weary bee, his day's work done,
 Rests in his waxen room.

Now every hovering insect to his place
 Beneath the leaves hath flown ;
And, through the long night hours, the flowery race
 Are left to thee alone.

O'er the pale blossoms of the sassafras
 And o'er the spice-bush spray,
Among the opening buds, thy breathings pass,
 And come embalmed away.

Yet there is sadness in thy soft caress,
 Wind of the blooming year !
The gentle presence, that was wont to bless
 Thy coming, is not here.

Go, then ; and yet I bid thee not repair,
 Thy gathered sweets to shed,
Where pine and willow, in the evening air,
 Sigh o'er the buried dead.

Pass on to homes where cheerful voices sound,
 And cheerful looks are cast,
And where thou wakest, in thine airy round,
 No sorrow of the past.

Refresh the languid student pausing o'er
 The learned page apart,
And he shall turn to con his task once more
 With an encouraged heart.

Bear thou a promise, from the fragrant sward,
    To him who tills the land,
Of springing harvests that shall yet reward
    The labors of his hand.

And whisper, everywhere, that Earth renews
    Her beautiful array,
Amid the darkness and the gathering dews,
    For the return of day.

OCTOBER, 1866.

'Twas when the earth in summer glory lay,
    We bore thee to thy grave ; a sudden cloud
Had shed its shower and passed, and every spray
    And tender herb with pearly moisture bowed.

How laughed the fields, and how, before our door,
    Danced the bright waters !—from his perch on high
The hang-bird sang his ditty o'er and o'er,
    And the song-sparrow from the shrubberies nigh.

Yet was the home where thou wert lying dead
    Mournfully still, save when, at times, was heard,
From room to room, some softly-moving tread,
    Or murmur of some softly-uttered word.

Feared they to break thy slumber ? As we threw
    A look on that bright bay and glorious shore,
Our hearts were wrung with anguish, for we knew
    Those sleeping eyes would look on them no more.

Autumn is here ; we cull his lingering flowers
    And bring them to the spot where thou art laid ;
The late-born offspring of his balmier hours,
    Spared by the frost, upon thy grave to fade.

The sweet calm sunshine of October, now
  Warms the low spot ; upon its grassy mould
The purple oak-leaf falls ; the birchen bough
  Drops its bright spoil like arrow-heads of gold.

And gorgeous as the morn, a tall array
  Of woodland shelters the smooth fields around ;
And guarded by its headlands, far away
  Sail-spotted, blue and lake-like, sleeps the sound

I gaze in sadness ; it delights me not
  To look on beauty which thou canst not see ;
And, wert thou by my side, the dreariest spot
  Were, oh, how far more beautiful to me !

In what fair region dost thou now abide ?
  Hath God, in the transparent deeps of space,
Through which the planets in their journey glide,
  Prepared, for souls like thine, a dwelling-place ?

Fields of unwithering bloom, to mortal eye
  Invisible, though mortal eye were near,
Musical groves, and bright streams murmuring by,
  Heard only by the spiritual ear ?

Nay, let us deem that thou dost not withdraw
  From the dear places where thy lot was cast,
And where thy heart, in love's most holy law,
  Was schooled by all the memories of the past.

Here on this earth, where once, among mankind,
  Walked God's belovèd Son, thine eyes may see
Beauty to which our dimmer sense is blind
  And glory that may make it heaven to thee.

May we not think that near us thou dost stand
  With loving ministrations, for we know
Thy heart was never happy when thy hand
  Was forced its tasks of mercy to forego !

Mayst thou not prompt, with every coming day,
  The generous aim and act, and gently win
Our restless, wandering thoughts to turn away
  From every treacherous path that ends in sin !

THE ORDER OF NATURE.

FROM BOETHIUS DE CONSOLATIONE.

THOU who wouldst read, with an undarkened eye,
  The laws by which the Thunderer bears sway,
Look at the stars that keep, in yonder sky,
  Unbroken peace from Nature's earliest day.

The great sun, as he guides his fiery car,
  Strikes not the cold moon in his rapid sweep ;
The Bear, that sees star setting after star
  In the blue brine, descends not to the deep.

The star of eve still leads the hour of dews ;
  Duly the day-star ushers in the light ;
With kindly alternations Love renews
  The eternal courses bringing day and night.

Love drives away the brawler War, and keeps
  The realm and host of stars beyond his reach ;
In one long calm the general concord steeps
  The elements, and tempers each to each.

The moist gives place benignly to the dry ;
  Heat ratifies a faithful league with cold ;
The nimble flame springs upward to the sky ;
  Down sinks by its own weight the sluggish mould.

Still sweet with blossoms is the year's fresh prime ;
  Her harvests still the ripening Summer yields ;
Fruit-laden Autumn follows in his time,
  And rainy Winter waters still the fields.

The elemental harmony brings forth
    And rears all life, and, when life's term is o'er,
It sweeps the breathing myriads from the earth,
    And whelms and hides them to be seen no more :

While the Great Founder, he who gave these laws,
    Holds the firm reins and sits amid his skies
Monarch and Master, Origin and Cause,
    And Arbiter supremely just and wise.

He guides the force he gave ; his hand restrains
    And curbs it to the circle it must trace :
Else the fair fabric which his power sustains
    Would fall to fragments in the void of space.

Love binds the parts together, gladly still
    They court the kind restraint nor would be free ;
Unless Love held them subject to the Will
    That gave them being, they would cease to be.

————

TREE–BURIAL.

NEAR our southwestern border, when a child
Dies in the cabin of an Indian wife,
She makes its funeral-couch of delicate furs,
Blankets and bark, and binds it to the bough
Of some broad branching tree with leathern thongs
And sinews of the deer. A mother once
Wrought at this tender task, and murmured thus :
  "Child of my love, I do not lay thee down
Among the chilly clods where never comes
The pleasant sunshine. There the greedy wolf
Might break into thy grave and tear thee thence,
And I should sorrow all my life. I make
Thy burial-place here, where the light of day
Shines round thee, and the airs that play among

The boughs shall rock thee. Here the morning sun,
Which woke thee once from sleep to smile on me,
Shall beam upon thy bed, and sweetly here
Shall lie the red light of the evening clouds
Which called thee once to slumber. Here the stars
Shall look upon thee—the bright stars of heaven
Which thou didst wonder at. Here too the birds,
Whose music thou didst love, shall sing to thee,
And near thee build their nests and rear their young
With none to scare them. Here the woodland flowers,
Whose opening in the spring-time thou didst greet
With shouts of joy, and which so well became
Thy pretty hands when thou didst gather them,
Shall spot tl e ground below thy little bed.
  " Yet haply thou hast fairer flowers than these,
Which, in the land of souls, thy spirit plucks
In fields that wither not, amid the throng
Of joyous children, like thyself, who went
Before thee to that brighter world and sport
Eternally beneath its cloudless skies.
Sport with them, dear, dear child, until I come
To dwell with thee, and thou, beholding me,
From far, shalt run and leap into my arms,
And I shall clasp thee as I clasped thee here
While living, oh most beautiful and sweet
Of children, now more passing beautiful,
If that can be, with eyes like summer stars—
A light that death can never quench again.
  " And now, oh wind, that here among the leaves
Dost softly rustle, breathe thou ever thus
Gently, and put not forth thy strength to tear
The branches and let fall their precious load,
A prey to foxes. Thou, too, ancient sun,
Beneath whose eye the seasons come and go,
And generations rise and pass away,
While thou dost never change—oh, call not up,
With thy strong heats, the dark, grim thunder-cloud,
To smite this tree with bolts of fire, and rend
Its trunk and strew the earth with splintered boughs.
  30

Ye rains, fall softly on the couch that holds
My darling. There the panther's spotted hide
Shall turn aside the shower ; and be it long,
Long after thou and I have met again,
Ere summer wind or winter rain shall waste
This couch and all that now remains of thee,
To me thy mother. Meantime, while I live,
With each returning sunrise I shall seem
To see thy waking smile, and I shall weep ;
And when the sun is setting I shall think
How, as I watched thee, o'er thy sleepy eyes
Drooped the smooth lids, and laid on the round cheek
Their lashes, and my tears will flow again ;
And often, at those moments, I shall seem
To hear again the sweetly prattled name
Which thou didst call me by, and it will haunt
My home till I depart to be with thee."

A LEGEND OF THE DELAWARES.

THE air is dark with cloud on cloud,
    And, through the leaden-colored mass,
With thunder-crashes quick and loud,
    A thousand shafts of lightning pass.

And to and fro they glance and go,
    Or, darting downward, smite the ground.
What phantom arms are those that throw
    The shower of fiery arrows round ?

A louder crash ! a mighty oak
    Is smitten from that stormy sky.
Its stem is shattered by the stroke ;
    Around its root the branches lie.

Fresh breathes the wind ; the storm is o'er ;
    The piles of mist are swept away ;
And from the open sky, once more,
    Streams gloriously the golden day.

A dusky hunter of the wild
　　Is passing near, and stops to see
The wreck of splintered branches piled
　　About the roots of that huge tree.

Lo, quaintly shaped and fairly strung,
　　Wrought by what hand he cannot know,
On that drenched pile of boughs, among
　　The splinters, lies a polished bow.

He lifts it up ; the drops that hang
　　On the smooth surface glide away :
He tries the string, no sharper twang
　　Was ever heard on battle-day.

Homeward Onetho bears the prize :
　　Who meets him as he turns to go ?
An aged chief, with quick, keen eyes,
　　And bending frame, and locks of snow.

" See, what I bring, my father, see
　　This goodly bow which I have found
Beneath a thunder-riven tree,
　　Dropped with the lightning to the ground."

" Beware, my son ; it is not well "—
　　The white-haired chieftain makes reply—
" That we who in the forest dwell
　　Should wield the weapons of the sky.

" Lay back that weapon in its place ;
　　Let those who bore it bear it still,
Lest thou displease the ghostly race
　　That float in mist from hill to hill."

"My father, I will only try
　　How well it sends a shaft, and then,
Be sure, this goodly bow shall lie
　　Among the splintered boughs again."

So to the hunting-ground he hies,
   To chase till eve the forest-game,
And not a single arrow flies,
   From that good bow, with erring aim.

And then he deems that they, who swim
   In trains of cloud the middle air,
Perchance had kindly thoughts of him
   And dropped the bow for him to bear.

He bears it from that day, and soon
   Becomes the mark of every eye,
And wins renown with every moon
   That fills its circle in the sky.

None strike so surely in the chase ;
   None bring such trophies from the fight ;
And, at the council-fire, his place
   Is with the wise and men of might.

And far across the land is spread,
   Among the hunter tribes, his fame ;
Men name the bowyer-chief with dread
   Whose arrows never miss their aim.

See next his broad-roofed cabin rise
   On a smooth river's pleasant side,
And she who has the brightest eyes
   Of all the tribe becomes his bride.

A year has passed ; the forest sleeps
   In early autumn's sultry glow ;
Onetho, on the mountain-steeps,
   Is hunting with that trusty bow.

But they, who by the river dwell,
   See the dim vapors thickening o'er
Long mountain-range and severing dell
   And hear the thunder's sullen roar.

Still darker grows the spreading cloud
　From which the booming thunders sound,
And stoops and hangs a shadowy shroud
　Above Onetho's hunting-ground.

Then they who, from the river-vale,
　Are gazing on the distant storm,
See in the mists that ride the gale
　Dim shadows of the human form—

Tall warriors, plumed, with streaming hair
　And lifted arms that bear the bow,
And send athwart the murky air
　The arrowy lightnings to and fro.

Loud is the tumult of an hour—
　Crash of torn boughs and howl of blast,
And thunder-peal and pelting shower,
　And then the storm is overpast.

Where is Onetho? what delays
　His coming? why should he remain
Among the plashy woodland ways,
　Swoln brooks and boughs that drip with rain?

He comes not, and the younger men
　Go forth to search the forest round.
They track him to a mountain-glen,
　And find him lifeless on the ground.

The goodly bow that was his pride
　Is gone, but there the arrows lie;
And now they know the death he died,
　Slain by the lightnings of the sky.

They bear him thence in awe and fear
　Back to the vale with stealthy tread;
There silently, from far and near,
　The warriors gather round the dead.

But in their homes the women bide ;
    Unseen they sit and weep apart,
And, in her bower, Onetho's bride
    Is sobbing with a broken heart.

They lay in earth their bowyer-chief,
    And at his side their hands bestow
His dreaded battle-axe and sheaf
    Of arrows, but without a bow.

"Too soon he died ; it is not well "—
    The old men murmured, standing nigh—
"That we, who in the forest dwell,
    Should wield the weapons of the sky."

A LIFETIME.

I sit in the early twilight,
    And, through the gathering shade,
I look on the fields around me
    Where yet a child I played.

And I peer into the shadows,
    Till they seem to pass away,
And the fields and their tiny brooklet
    Lie clear in the light of day.

A delicate child and slender,
    With lock of light-brown hair,
From knoll to knoll is leaping
    In the breezy summer air.

He stoops to gather blossoms
    Where the running waters shine ;
And I look on him with wonder,
    His eyes are so like mine.

I look till the fields and brooklet
    Swim like a vision by,
And a room in a lowly dwelling
    Lies clear before my eye.

There stand, in the clean-swept fireplace,
    Fresh boughs from the wood in bloom,
And the birch-tree's fragrant branches
    Perfume the humble room.

And there the child is standing
    By a stately lady's knee,
And reading of ancient peoples
    And realms beyond the sea :

Of the cruel King of Egypt
    Who made God's people slaves,
And perished, with all his army,
    Drowned in the Red Sea waves ;

Of Deborah who mustered
    Her brethren long oppressed,
And routed the heathen army,
    And gave her people rest ;

And the sadder, gentler story
    How Christ, the crucified,
With a prayer for those who slew him,
    Forgave them as he died.

I look again, and there rises
    A forest wide and wild,
And in it the boy is wandering,
    No longer a little child.

He murmurs his own rude verses
    As he roams the woods alone ;
And again I gaze with wonder,
    His eyes are so like my own.

I see him next in his chamber,
  Where he sits him down to write
The rhymes he framed in his ramble,
  And he cons them with delight.

A kindly figure enters,
  A man of middle age,
And points to a line just written,
  And 'tis blotted from the page.

And next, in a hall of justice,
  Scarce grown to manly years,
Mid the hoary-headed wranglers
  The slender youth appears.

With a beating heart he rises,
  And with a burning cheek,
And the judges kindly listen
  To hear the young man speak.

Another change, and I see him
  Approach his dwelling-place,
Where a fair-haired woman meets him,
  With a smile on her young face—

A smile that spreads a sunshine
  On lip and cheek and brow ;
So sweet a smile there is not
  In all the wide earth now.

She leads by the hand their first-born,
  A fair-haired little one,
And their eyes as they meet him sparkle
  Like brooks in the morning sun.

Another change, and I see him
  Where the city's ceaseless coil
Sends up a mighty murmur
  From a thousand modes of toil.

And there, mid the clash of presses,
  He plies the rapid pen
In the battles of opinion,
  That divide the sons of men.

I look, and the clashing presses
  And the town are seen no more,
But there is the poet wandering
  A strange and foreign shore.

He has crossed the mighty ocean
  To realms that lie afar,
In the region of ancient story,
  Beneath the morning star.

And now he stands in wonder
  On an icy Alpine height ;
Now pitches his tent in the desert
  Where the jackal yells at night ;

Now, far on the North Sea islands,
  Sees day on the midnight sky,
Now gathers the fair strange fruitage
  Where the isles of the Southland lie.

I see him again at his dwelling,
  Where, over the little lake,
The rose-trees droop in their beauty
  To meet the image they make.

Though years have whitened his temples,
  His eyes have the first look still,
Save a shade of settled sadness,
  A forecast of coming ill.

For in that pleasant dwelling,
  On the rack of ceaseless pain,
Lies she who smiled so sweetly,
  And prays for ease in vain.

And I know that his heart is breaking,
　　When, over those dear eyes,
The darkness slowly gathers,
　　And the loved and loving dies.

A grave is scooped on the hillside
　　Where often, at eve or morn,
He lays the blooms of the garden—
　　He, and his youngest born.

And well I know that a brightness
　　From his life has passed away,
And a smile from the green earth's beauty,
　　And a glory from the day.

But I behold, above him,
　　In the far blue deeps of air,
Dim battlements shining faintly,
　　And a throng of faces there ;

See over crystal barrier
　　The airy figures bend,
Like those who are watching and waiting
　　The coming of a friend.

And one there is among them,
　　With a star upon her brow,
In her life a lovely woman,
　　A sinless seraph now.

I know the sweet calm features ;
　　The peerless smile I know,
And I stretch my arms with transport
　　From where I stand below.

And the quick tears drown my eyelids,
　　But the airy figures fade,
And the shining battlements darken
　　And blend with the evening shade.

I am gazing into the twilight
  Where the dim-seen meadows lie,
And the wind of night is swaying
  The trees with a heavy sigh.

THE TWO TRAVELLERS.

'Twas evening, and before my eyes
  There lay a landscape gray and dim—
Fields faintly seen and twilight skies,
  And clouds that hid the horizon's brim.

I saw—or was it that I dreamed?
  A waking dream?—I cannot say,
For every shape as real seemed
  As those which meet my eyes to-day.

Through leafless shrubs the cold wind hissed ;
  The air was thick with falling snow,
And onward, through the frozen mist,
  I saw a weary traveller go.

Driven o'er the landscape, bare and bleak,
  Before the whirling gusts of air,
The snow-flakes smote his withered cheek,
  And gathered on his silver hair.

Yet on he fared through blinding snows,
  And murmuring to himself he said :
"The night is near ; the darkness grows,
  And higher rise the drifts I tread.

"Deep, deep, each autumn flower they hide ;
  Each tuft of green they whelm from sight ;
And they who journeyed by my side,
  Are lost in the surrounding night.

"I loved them ; oh, no words can tell
  The love that to my friends I bore
They left me with the sad farewell
  Of those who part to meet no more.

"And I, who face this bitter wind
  And o'er these snowy hillocks creep,
Must end my journey soon, and find
  A frosty couch, a frozen sleep."

As thus he spoke, a thrill of pain
  Shot to my heart—I closed my eyes ;
But when I opened them again,
  I started with a glad surprise.

'Twas evening still, and in the west
  A flush of glowing crimson lay ;
I saw the morrow there, and blest
  That promise of a glorious day.

The waters, in their glassy sleep,
  Shone with the hues that tinged the sky,
And rugged cliff and barren steep
  Gleamed with the brightness from on high.

And one was there whose journey lay
  Into the slowly-gathering night ;
With steady step he held his way,
  O'er shadowy vale and gleaming height.

I marked his firm though weary tread,
  The lifted eye and brow serene ;
And saw no shade of doubt or dread
  Pass o'er that traveller's placid mien.

And others came, their journey o'er,
  And bade good-night, with words of cheer :
"To-morrow we shall meet once more ;
  'Tis but the night that parts us here."

"And I," he said, "shall sleep ere long ;
   These fading gleams will soon be gone ;
Shall sleep to rise refreshed and strong
   In the bright day that yet will dawn."

I heard ; I watched him as he went,
   A lessening form, until the light
Of evening from the firmament
   Had passed, and he was lost to sight.

CHRISTMAS IN 1875.

SUPPOSED TO BE WRITTEN BY A SPANIARD.

No trumpet-blast profaned
The hour in which the Prince of Peace was born ;
   No bloody streamlet stained
Earth's silver rivers on that sacred morn ;
   But, o'er the peaceful plain,
The war-horse drew the peasant's loaded wain.

   The soldier had laid by
The sword and stripped the corselet from his breast,
   And hung his helm on high—
The sparrow's winter home and summer nest ;
   And, with the same strong hand
That flung the barbèd spear, he tilled the land.

   Oh, time for which we yearn ;
Oh, sabbath of the nations long foretold !
   Season of peace, return,
Like a late summer when the year grows old,
   When the sweet sunny days
Steeped mead and mountain-side in golden haze.

   For now two rival kings
Flaunt, o'er our bleeding land, their hostile flags,
   And every sunrise brings

The hovering vulture from his mountain-crags
    To where the battle-plain
Is strewn with dead, the youth and flower of Spain.

    Christ is not come, while yet
O'er half the earth the threat of battle lowers,
    And our own fields are wet,
Beneath the battle-cloud, with crimson showers—
    The life-blood of the slain,
Poured out where thousands die that one may reign.

    Soon, over half the earth,
In every temple crowds shall kneel again
    To celebrate His birth
Who brought the message of good-will to men,
    And bursts of joyous song
Shall shake the roof above the prostrate throng.

    Christ is not come, while there
The men of blood whose crimes affront the skies
    Kneel down in act of prayer,
Amid the joyous strains, and when they rise
    Go forth, with sword and flame,
To waste the land in His most holy name.

    Oh, when the day shall break
O'er realms unlearned in warfare's cruel arts,
    And all their millions wake
To peaceful tasks performed with loving hearts.
    On such a blessed morn,
Well may the nations say that Christ is born.

THE FLOOD OF YEARS.

A MIGHTY Hand, from an exhaustless Urn,
Pours forth the never-ending Flood of Years,
Among the nations. How the rushing waves
Bear all before them ! On their foremost edge,

And there alone, is Life. The Present there
Tosses and foams, and fills the air with roar
Of mingled noises. There are they who toil,
And they who strive, and they who feast, and they
Who hurry to and fro. The sturdy swain—
Woodman and delver with the spade—is there,
And busy artisan beside his bench,
And pallid student with his written roll.
A moment on the mounting billow seen,
The flood sweeps over them and they are gone.
There groups of revellers whose brows are twined
With roses, ride the topmost swell awhile,
And as they raise their flowing cups and touch
The clinking brim to brim, are whirled beneath
The waves and disappear. I hear the jar
Of beaten drums, and thunders that break forth
From cannon, where the advancing billow sends
Up to the sight long files of armèd men,
That hurry to the charge through flame and smoke.
The torrent bears them under, whelmed and hid
Slayer and slain, in heaps of bloody foam.
Down go the steed and rider, the plumed chief
Sinks with his followers ; the head that wears
The imperial diadem goes down beside
The felon's with cropped ear and branded cheek.
A funeral-train—the torrent sweeps away
Bearers and bier and mourners. By the bed
Of one who dies men gather sorrowing,
And women weep aloud ; the flood rolls on ;
The wail is stifled and the sobbing group
Borne under. Hark to that shrill, sudden shout,
The cry of an applauding multitude,
Swayed by some loud-voiced orator who wields
The living mass as if he were its soul !
The waters choke the shout and all is still.
Lo ! next a kneeling crowd, and one who spreads
The hands in prayer—the engulfing wave o'ertakes
And swallows them and him. A sculptor wields
The chisel, and the stricken marble grows

To beauty ; at his easel, eager-eyed,
A painter stands, and sunshine at his touch
Gathers upon his canvas, and life glows ;
A poet, as he paces to and fro,
Murmurs his sounding lines. Awhile they ride
The advancing billow, till its tossing crest
Strikes them and flings them under, while their tasks
Are yet unfinished. See a mother smile
On her young babe that smiles to her again ;
The torrent wrests it from her arms ; she shrieks
And weeps, and midst her tears is carried down.
A beam like that of moonlight turns the spray
To glistening pearls ; two lovers, hand in hand,
Rise on the billowy swell and fondly look
Into each other's eyes. The rushing flood
Flings them apart : the youth goes down ; the maid
With hands outstretched in vain, and streaming eyes,
Waits for the next high wave to follow him.
An aged man succeeds ; his bending form
Sinks slowly. Mingling with the sullen stream
Gleam the white locks, and then are seen no more.
    Lo ! wider grows the stream—a sea-like flood
Saps earth's walled cities ; massive palaces
Crumble before it ; fortresses and towers
Dissolve in the swift waters ; populous realms
Swept by the torrent see their ancient tribes
Engulfed and lost ; their very languages
Stifled, and never to be uttered more.
    I pause and turn my eyes, and looking back
Where that tumultuous flood has been, I see
The silent ocean of the Past, a waste
Of waters weltering over graves, its shores
Strewn with the wreck of fleets where mast and hull
Drop away piecemeal ; battlemented walls
Frown idly, green with moss, and temples stand
Unroofed, forsaken by the worshipper.
There lie memorial stones, whence time has gnawed
The graven legends, thrones of kings o'erturned,
The broken altars of forgotten gods,

Foundations of old cities and long streets
Where never fall of human foot is heard,
On all the desolate pavement.   I behold
Dim glimmerings of lost jewels, far within
The sleeping waters, diamond, sardonyx,
Ruby and topaz, pearl and chrysolite,
Once glittering at the banquet on fair brows
That long ago were dust, and all around
Strewn on the surface of that silent sea
Are withering bridal wreaths, and glossy locks
Shorn from dear brows, by loving hands, and scrolls
O'er written, haply with fond words of love
And vows of friendship, and fair pages flung
Fresh from the printer's engine.   There they lie
A moment, and then sink away from sight.
   I look, and the quick tears are in my eyes,
For I behold in every one of these
A blighted hope, a separate history
Of human sorrows, telling of dear ties
Suddenly broken, dreams of happiness
Dissolved in air, and happy days too brief
That sorrowfully ended, and I think
How painfully must the poor heart have beat
In bosoms without number, as the blow
Was struck that slew their hope and broke their peace.
   Sadly I turn and look before, where yet
The Flood must pass, and I behold a mist
Where swarm dissolving forms, the brood of Hope,
Divinely fair, that rest on banks of flowers,
Or wander among rainbows, fading soon
And reappearing, haply giving place
To forms of grisly aspect such as Fear
Shapes from the idle air—where serpents lift
The head to strike, and skeletons stretch forth
The bony arm in menace.   Further on
A belt of darkness seems to bar the way
Long, low, and distant, where the Life to come
Touches the Life that is.   The Flood of Years
Rolls toward it near and nearer   It must pass
31

That dismal barrier.   What is there beyond ?
Hear what the wise and good have said.   Beyond
That belt of darkness, still the Years roll on
More gently, but with not less mighty sweep.
They gather up again and softly bear
All the sweet lives that late were overwhelmed
And lost to sight, all that in them was good,
Noble, and truly great, and worthy of love—
The lives of infants and ingenuous youths,
Sages and saintly women who have made
Their households happy ; all are raised and borne
By that great current in its onward sweep,
Wandering and rippling with caressing waves
Around green islands with the breath
Of flowers that never wither.   So they pass
From stage to stage along the shining course
Of that bright river, broadening like a sea.
As its smooth eddies curl along their way
They bring old friends together ; hands are clasped
In joy unspeakable ; the mother's arms
Again are folded round the child she loved
And lost.   Old sorrows are forgotten now,
Or but remembered to make sweet the hour
That overpays them ; wounded hearts that bled
Or broke are healed forever.   In the room
Of this grief-shadowed present, there shall be
A Present in whose reign no grief shall gnaw
The heart, and never shall a tender tie
Be broken ; in whose reign the eternal Change
That waits on growth and action shall proceed
With everlasting Concord hand in hand.

OUR FELLOW-WORSHIPPERS.

THINK not that thou and I
Are here the only worshippers to day,
Beneath this glorious sky,
Mid the soft airs that o'er the meadows play ;

These airs, whose breathing stirs
The fresh grass, are our fellow-worshippers.

See, as they pass, they swing
The censers of a thousand flowers that bend
    O'er the young herbs of spring,
And the sweet odors like a prayer ascend,
    While, passing thence, the breeze
Wakes the grave anthem of the forest-trees.

It is as when, of yore,
The Hebrew poet called the mountain-steeps,
    The forests, and the shore
Of ocean, and the mighty mid-sea deeps,
    And stormy wind, to raise
A universal symphony of praise.

For, lo ! the hills around,
Gay in their early green, give silent thanks ;
    And, with a joyous sound,
The streamlet's huddling waters kiss their banks,
    And, from its sunny nooks,
To heaven, with grateful smiles, the valley looks.

The blossomed apple-tree,
Among its flowery tufts, on every spray,
    Offers the wandering bee
A fragrant chapel for his matin-lay ;
    And a soft bass is heard
From the quick pinions of the humming-bird.

Haply—for who can tell ?—
Aerial beings, from the world unseen,
    Haunting the sunny dell,
Or slowly floating o'er the flowery green,
    May join our worship here,
With harmonies too fine for mortal ear.

HYMNS WRITTEN AT VARIOUS TIMES.

"THE EARTH IS FULL OF THY RICHES."

ALMIGHTY! hear thy children raise
The voice of thankfulness and praise,
To Him whose wisdom deigned to plan
This fair and bright abode for man.

For when this orb of sea and land
Was moulded in thy forming hand,
Thy calm, benignant smile impressed
A beam of heaven upon its breast.

Then rose the hills, and broad and green
The vale's deep pathway sank between;
Then stretched the plains to where the sky
Stoops and shuts in the exploring eye.

Beneath that smile earth's blossoms glowed,
Her fountains gushed, her rivers flowed,
And from the shadowy wood was heard
The pleasant sound of breeze and bird.

Thy hand outspread the billowy plains
Of ocean, nurse of genial rains,
Hung high the glorious sun and set
Night's cressets in her arch of jet.

Lord, teach us, while the admiring sight
Dwells on Thy works in deep delight,
To deem the forms of beauty here
But shadows of a brighter sphere.

GREAT BARRINGTON, 1820.

"HIS TENDER MERCIES ARE OVER ALL HIS WORKS."

OUR Father! to thy love we owe
All that is fair and good below.
Life, and the health that makes life sweet,
Are blessings from thy mercy seat.

Oh Giver of the quickening rain!
Oh Ripener of the golden grain!
From Thee the cheerful day-spring flows,
Thy balmy evening brings repose.

Thy frosts arrest, thy tempests chase
The plagues that waste our helpless race,
Thy softer breath, o'er land and deep,
Wakes Nature from her winter sleep.

Yet, deem we not that thus alone
Thy bounty and thy love are shown,
For we have learned with higher praise
And holier names to speak thy ways.

In woe's dark hour our kindest stay,
Sole trust when life shall pass away,
Teacher of hopes that light the gloom
Of Death, and consecrate the tomb.

Patient with headstrong guilt to bear,
Slow to avenge and kind to spare,
Listening to prayer and reconciled
Full soon to thy repentant child.

GREAT BARRINGTON, 1820.

"A BROKEN AND A CONTRITE HEART, OH GOD, THOU WILT NOT DESPISE."

Oh God, whose dread and dazzling brow
　Love never yet forsook!
On those who seek thy presence now
　In deep compassion look.

Aid our weak steps and eyesight dim
　The paths of peace to find,
And lead us all to learn of Him
　Who died to save mankind.

For many a frail and erring heart
　Is in thy holy sight,
And feet too willing to depart
　From the plain way of right.

Yet, pleased the humble prayer to hear,
　And kind to all that live,
Thou, when thou seest the contrite tear,
　Art ready to forgive.

GREAT BARRINGTON, 1820.

————

"HOW AMIABLE ARE THY TABERNACLES!"

Thou, whose unmeasured temple stands,
　Built over earth and sea,
Accept the walls that human hands
　Have raised, oh God! to thee.

And let the Comforter and Friend,
　Thy Holy Spirit, meet
With those who here in worship bend
　Before thy mercy seat.

May they who err be guided here
　To find the better way,

And they who mourn and they who fear
  Be strengthened as they pray.

May faith grow firm, and love grow warm,
  And hallowed wishes rise,
While round these peaceful walls the storm
  Of earth-born passion dies.

GREAT BARRINGTON, 1820.

"THE LORD GIVETH WISDOM."

MIGHTY ONE, before whose face
  Wisdom had her glorious seat,
When the orbs that people space
  Sprang to birth beneath thy feet!

Source of Truth, whose beams alone
  Light the mighty world of mind!
God of Love, who, from thy throne,
  Watchest over all mankind!

Shed on those who, in Thy name,
  Teach the way of Truth and Right,
Shed that Love's undying flame,
  Shed that Wisdom's guiding light.

"THY WORD IS TRUTH."

OH thou, whose Love can ne'er forget
  Its offspring, Great Eternal Mind!
We thank thee that thy truth is yet
  A sojourner among mankind;

A light before whose brightness fall
  The feet arrayed to tread it down,
A voice whose strong and solemn call
  The cry of nations cannot drown.

Thy servants, at this sacred hour,
  With humble prayer thy throne surround,
That here, in glory and in power,
  That light may shine, that voice may sound;

Till Error's shades shall flee away,
  And Faith, descending from above,
Amid the pure and perfect day,
  Shall bring her fairer sister Love.

"I WILL SEND THEM PROPHETS AND APOSTLES."

ALL that in this wide world we see,
Almighty Father! speaks of Thee;
And in the darkness, or the day,
Thy monitors surround our way.

The fearful storms that sweep the sky,
The maladies by which we die,
The pangs that make the guilty groan,
Are angels from thy awful throne.

Each mercy sent when sorrows lower,
Each blessing of the wingèd hour,
All we enjoy, and all we love,
Bring with them lessons from above.

Nor thus content, thy gracious hand,
From midst the children of the land,
Hath raised, to stand before our race,
Thy living messengers of grace.

We thank thee that so clear a ray
Shines on thy straight, thy chosen way,
And pray that passion, sloth, or pride,
May never lure our steps aside.

"EXCEPT THE LORD BUILD THE HOUSE."

ANCIENT OF DAYS! except thou deign
  Upon the finished task to smile,
The workman's hand hath toiled in vain,
  To hew the rock and rear the pile.

Oh, let thy peace, the peace that tames
  The wayward heart, inhabit here,
That quenches passion's fiercest flames,
  And thaws the deadly frost of fear.

And send thy love, the love that bears
  Meekly with hate, and scorn, and wrong,
And loads itself with generous cares,
  And toils, and hopes, and watches long.

Here may bold tongues thy truth proclaim,
  Unmingled with the dreams of men,
As from His holy lips it came
  Who died for us and rose again.

"THE TRUTH SHALL MAKE YOU FREE."

LORD, from whose glorious presence came
  The truth that made our fathers free,
And kindled in their hearts the flame
  Of love to man and love to thee.

Bow the great heavens, thy throne of light,
  And fill these walls, as once, of yore,
Thy spirit rested in its might
  Upon the ark that Israel bore.

Here, let thy love be strong to draw
  Our wavering hearts to do thy will,

And hush them with the holy awe
　　That makes the rebel passions still.

And while thy children, frail and blind,
　　Here bend in humble prayer to thee,
Oh, shed abroad, on every mind,
　　The truth that made our fathers free.

"OTHER SHEEP I HAVE, WHICH ARE NOT OF THIS FOLD."

Look from the sphere of endless day,
　　Oh, God of mercy and of might!
In pity look on those who stray,
　　Benighted, in this land of light.

In peopled vale, in lonely glen,
　　In crowded mart by stream or sea,
How many of the sons of men
　　Hear not the message sent from thee.

Send forth thy heralds, Lord, to call
　　The thoughtless young, the hardened old,
A wandering flock, and bring them all
　　To the Good Shepherd's peaceful fold.

Send them thy mighty word to speak
　　Till faith shall dawn and doubt depart,—
To awe the bold, to stay the weak,
　　And bind and heal the broken heart.

Then all these wastes, a dreary scene,
　　On which, with sorrowing eyes, we gaze,
Shall grow with living waters green,
　　And lift to heaven the voice of praise.

NEW YORK, 1859.

"THOU, GOD, SEEST ME."

WHEN this song of praise shall cease,
  Let thy children, Lord, depart
With the blessing of thy peace
  And thy love in every heart.

Oh, where'er our path may lie,
  Father, let us not forget
That we walk beneath thine eye,
  That thy care upholds us yet.

Blind are we, and weak, and frail;
  Be thine aid forever near ;
May the fear to sin prevail
  Over every other fear.

"HIS MOTHER KEPT ALL THESE SAYINGS IN HER HEART."

As o'er the cradle of her Son
  The blessèd Mary hung,
And chanted to the Anointed One
  The psalms that David sung,

What joy her bosom must have known,
  As, with a sweet surprise,
She marked the boundless love that shone
  Within his infant eyes.

But deeper was her joy to hear,
  Even in his ripening youth,
And treasure up, from year to year,
  His words of grace and truth.

Oh, may we keep his words like her
  In all their life and power,
And to the law of love refer
  The acts of every hour.

"WHATSOEVER HE SAITH UNTO YOU, DO IT."

"WHATE'ER he bids, observe and do;"
Such were the words that Mary said,
What time the Holy One and True
Sat where the marriage feast was spread.

Then, at his word, the servants sought
The streams from Cana's fountains poured,
And lo! the crystal water brought
Was ruddy wine upon the board.

Whate'er he bids observe and do;
Such be the law that we obey,
And greater wonders men shall view
Than that of Cana's bridal day.

The flinty heart with love shall beat,
The chains shall fall from passion's slave,
The proud shall sit at Jesus' feet
And learn the truths that bless and save.

"PROCLAIM LIBERTY THROUGHOUT THE LAND."

Go forth, oh Word of Christ! go forth,
Oh Truth of God supremely strong!
To banish, from the groaning earth,
All forms of tyranny and wrong.

For where the Word of Christ prevails
To touch a nation's mighty heart,
The oppressor's pride before it quails,
The links of bondage fall apart.

When the pure faith by Jesus taught
Its conquering course on earth began,

Where'er the blessed news was brought
    The fettered slave stood up a man.

Still may thy heralds, Lord, proclaim
    The gracious message published then,
And teach the world, in Jesus' name,
    How love makes free the sons of men.

"THIS DO IN REMEMBRANCE OF ME."

ALL praise to Him of Nazareth,
    The Holy One who came,
For love of man, to die a death
    Of agony and shame.

Dark was the grave; but since he lay
    Within its dreary cell,
The beams of heaven's eternal day
    Upon its threshold dwell.

He grasped the iron veil, he drew
    Its gloomy folds aside,
And opened, to his followers' view,
    The glorious world they hide.

In tender memory of his grave
    The mystic bread we take,
And muse upon the life he gave
    So freely for our sake.

A boundless love he bore mankind;
    Oh, may at least a part
Of that strong love descend and find
    A place in every heart.

"THOU HAST PUT ALL THINGS UNDER HIS FEET."

Oh North, with all thy vales of green!
  Oh South, with all thy palms!
From peopled towns and fields between,
  Uplift the voice of psalms.
Raise, ancient East! the anthem high,
And let the youthful West reply.

Lo! in the clouds of Heaven appears
  God's well-belovèd Son;
He brings a train of brighter years;
  His kingdom is begun;
He comes a guilty world to bless
With mercy, truth, and righteousness.

Oh, Father! haste the promised hour,
  When at His feet shall lie
All rule, authority, and power,
  Beneath the ample sky:
When He shall reign from pole to pole,
The Lord of every human soul.

When all shall heed the words He said,
  Amid their daily cares,
And, by the loving life He led,
  Shall strive to pattern theirs;
And He who conquered Death shall win
The mightier conquest over Sin.

THE FREEMAN'S HYMN.

In eastern lands a servile race
  May bow to thrones and diadems;
And hide in dust the abject face,
  Before the glare of gold and gems.

For us, we kneel to One alone;
  And freemen worship only Him
Before the brightness of whose throne
  The proudest pomps of earth are dim.

And therefore to his children here
  This bright and blooming land He gave,
Where famine never blasts the year,
  Nor plagues, nor earthquakes glut the grave;

A land where all the gifts unite
  That Heaven bestows to make life sweet;
A land of peace, a land of light,
  A land where truth and mercy meet.

CUMMINGTON, 1822.

THE DEATH OF CHANNING.

WHILE yet the harvest-fields are white,
  And few the toiling reapers stand,
Called from his task before the night,
  We miss the mightiest of the band.

Oh, thou of strong and gentle mind,
  Thy thrilling voice shall plead no more
For Truth, for Freedom, and Mankind—
  The lesson of thy life is o'er.

But thou in brightness, far above
  The fairest dream of human thought,
Before the seat of Power and Love,
  Art with the Truth that thou hast sought.

NEW YORK, 1842.

THE AGED PASTOR.

THY love, O God! from year to year,
Has watched thy faithful pastor here,
Till fifty years of toil have now
Engraved their tokens on his brow.

Fast have the seasons rolled away;
A moment in thy sight were they,
Yet while their rapid course was run,
What mighty works thy hand has done!

What empires rose, and, at thy frown,
In sudden weakness crumbled down!
What barriers, reared by earth and hell,
Against thy truth, gave way and fell!

Meanwhile, beneath thy gracious sight
This flock has dwelt in peace and light,
By living waters gently led,
And in perennial pastures fed.

Oh, when before thy judgment seat
The pastor and his flock shall meet,
May thy benignant voice attest
Their welcome to thine endless rest.

ROSLYN, *June, 1848.*

IN MEMORIAM.

Two hundred times has June renewed
    Her roses since the day
When here, amid the lonely wood,
    Our fathers met to pray.

Beside this gentle stream that strayed
    Through pathless deserts then,
The calm, heroic women prayed,
    And grave, undaunted men.

Hymns on the ancient silence broke
From hearts that faltered not,
And undissembling lips that spoke
The free and guileless thought.

They prayed, and thanked the Almighty One
Who made their hearts so strong,
And led them, towards the setting sun,
Beyond the reach of wrong.

He made for them that desert place
A pleasant heritage,
The cradle of a free-born race,
From peaceful age to age.

The plant they set—a little vine—
Has stretched its boughs afar,
To distant hills and streams that shine
Beneath the evening star.

Their fields are ours—these fields that smile
With summer's early flowers ;
Oh, let their fearless scorn of guile,
And love of truth, be ours.

ROSLYN, *May 15, 1856.*

"RECEIVE THY SIGHT."

WHEN the blind suppliant in the way,
By friendly hands to Jesus led,
Prayed to behold the light of day,
" Receive thy sight," the Saviour said.

At once he saw the pleasant rays
That lit the glorious firmament;
And, with firm step and words of praise,
He followed where the Master went.

32

Look down in pity, Lord, we pray,
  On eyes oppressed by moral night,
And touch the darkened lids and say
  The gracious words, " Receive thy sight."

Then, in clear daylight, shall we see
  Where walked the sinless Son of God;
And, aided by new strength from Thee,
  Press onward in the path He trod.

NEW YORK, 1866.

THE PASTOR'S RETURN.

FROM ancient realms, from many a seat
  Of art and power beyond the sea;
From fields o'er which the blessed feet
  Of Jesus walked in Galilee;

From snow-capped peak and glorious vale,
  That listen to the cataract's voice,
Led by the hand of God, we hail,
  Once more, the pastor of our choice.

The reaper takes his place again,
  Where the white harvest skirts the way,
With sinews strengthened to sustain
  The heat and burden of the day.

And while our hearts, with one accord,
  Welcome him to his cherished home;
As Thou hast blessed his wanderings, Lord,
  Oh, bless his labors yet to come !

NEW YORK, 1868.

THE STAR OF BETHLEHEM.

As shadows cast by cloud and sun
　　Flit o'er the summer grass,
So, in thy sight, Almighty One!
　　Earth's generations pass.

And while the years, an endless host,
　　Come pressing swiftly on,
The brightest names that earth can boast
　　Just glisten and are gone.

Yet doth the Star of Bethlehem shed
　　A lustre pure and sweet;
And still it leads, as once it led,
　　To the Messiah's feet.

And deeply, at this later day,
　　Our hearts rejoice to see
How children, guided by its ray,
　　Come to the Saviour's knee.

O Father, may that holy Star
　　Grow every year more bright,
And send its glorious beam afar
　　To fill the world with light.

NEW YORK, 1875.

THE CENTENNIAL HYMN.

THROUGH calm and storm the years have led
　　Our nation on, from stage to stage—
A century's space—until we tread
　　The threshold of another age.

We see where o'er our pathway swept
　　A torrent-stream of blood and fire,
And thank the Guardian Power who kept
　　Our sacred League of States entire.

Oh, chequered train of years, farewell!
  With all thy strifes and hopes and fears!
Yet with us let thy memories dwell,
  To warn and teach the coming years.

And thou, the new-beginning age,
  Warned by the past, and not in vain,
Write on a fairer, whiter page,
  The record of thy happier reign.

ROSLYN, 1876.

THE CAPTIVE LOOSED.

WHEN, doomed to death, the Apostle lay,
  At night, in Herod's dungeon-cell,
A light shone round him like the day,
  And from his limbs the fetters fell.

A messenger from God was there,
  To loose his chain and bid him rise,
And lo, the Saint, as free as air,
  Walked forth beneath the open skies.

Chains yet more strong and cruel bind
  The victims of that deadly thirst
Which drowns the soul, and from the mind
  Blots the bright image stamped at first.

Oh, God of Love and Mercy, deign
  To look on those, with pitying eye,
Who struggle with that fatal chain,
  And send them succor from on high.

Send down, in its resistless might,
  Thy gracious Spirit, we implore,
And lead the captive forth to light,
  A rescued soul, a slave no more.

NEW YORK, 1877.

UNPUBLISHED OR UNCOLLECTED POEMS OF VARIOUS DATA.

LOVE'S POWER.

FROM THE LATIN.

THUS all that live—swift fishes—painted birds—
The desert's ravenous tribes—the harmless herds—
And prouder man—obey the powerful call,—
And Love's almighty frenzy masters all!
The lioness, to wilder fury stung,
Then terribly walks forth, and leaves her young;—
With bloodier ravages the shapeless bear
Pollutes his woods;—the tiger leaves his lair,
In fury stalks;—fiercer rushes forth the boar;—
Woe, then, to him that walks the Lybian shore!—
Mark how the well-known gales the steed inflame,
And shoot a shivering thrill through all his frame.
Him, as with sudden bound he bursts away,
Nor curb nor lash, ravines nor rocks delay,
Nor rivers interposed, whose torrents sweep
The uprooted mountains downward to the deep.

GREAT BARRINGTON, 1817.

SPAIN.

AYE, wear the chain—ye who for once have known
The sweets of freedom—yet could crouch again
In blind and trembling worship of a throne;
Aye wear—for ye are worthy—wear the chain
And bow, till ye are weary, to the yoke
      Your patriot fathers broke.

367

Degenerate Spaniards ! let the priestly band
Possess your realm again ; and let them wake
The fires of pious murder in your land,
And drag your best and bravest to the stake,
And tread down truth, and in the dungeon bind
          The dreaded strength of mind.

Give up the promise of bright days that cast
A glory on your nation from afar ;
Call back the darkness of the ages past
To quench that holy dawn's new-risen star ;
Let only tyrants and their slaves be found
          Alive on Spanish ground.

Yet mark ! ye cast the gift of heaven away,
And your best blood for this shall yet be shed ;
The fire shall waste your borders, and the way
Be covered with its heaps of festering dead,
And vultures of the cliff on every plain
          Feast high upon the slain.

The spirit that of yore had slept so long,
Then woke, and drove the Moors to Afric's shore,
Lives, and repressed, shall rise one day more strong—
Rise and redeem your shackled race once more,
And crush, mid showers of blood and shrieks and groans,
          Mitres and stars and thrones.

GREAT BARRINGTON, 1822.

THE SHARPENING OF THE SABRE.

FROM THE GERMAN.   AUTHOR UNKNOWN.

BURNING thoughts within me call
    For the good old brand I wore ;
Hand the sabre from the wall—
    Let me try its weight once more.
Bring the sharpening-stone to me,
Sharp must now my sabre be.

Sabre, thou didst look so dull,
    Under dust and spider-net!
Ah, thou shalt be beautiful,
    With the blood of foemen wet!
Turn, boy, turn the stone for me,
Sharper must my sabre be.

Come and fill this faithful hand,
    Be again my own true sword,
Till the lost, lost Fatherland
    Shall be rescued and restored.
Turn, boy, turn the stone for me,
Sharper must my sabre be.

For the sacred German realm,
    For our honor trodden low,
Sabre! strike, through shield and helm,
    One good blow, a mighty blow.
Turn, boy, turn the stone for me,
Sharper must my sabre be.

Brothers, win the banner back!
    We must earn the death of men;
Brothers, win the banner back!
    I shall die contented then.
Turn, boy, turn the stone for me,
Sharper must my sabre be.

Heard I not, before the door,
    Peal the trumpet's thrilling blast?
Heard I not the cannon's roar?
    Ah, 'twas but the storm that passed!
Turn, boy, turn the stone for me,
Sharp must now my sabre be.

NEW YORK, 1836.   Evening Post, *July, 1836*.

I THINK OF THEE.

FROM THE GERMAN OF GOETHE.

I THINK of thee when the strong rays of noon
    Flash from the sea;
When the clear fountains glimmer in the moon,
    I think of thee.

I see thee when along the distant way
    The dust-clouds creep,
And in the night, when trembling travellers stray
    By chasm and steep.

I hear thee when the tides go murmuring soft
    To the calm air;
In lone and stilly woods I listen oft,
    And hear thee there.

I am with thee—I know thou art afar,
    Yet dream thee near;
The sun goes down; star brightens after star;
    Would thou wert here!

NEW YORK, 1840.   Godey's Lady's Book, *January, 1844.*

THE SAW-MILL.

FROM THE GERMAN OF KERNER.

IN yonder mill I rested,
    And sat me down to look
Upon the wheel's quick glimmer,
    And on the flowing brook.

As in a dream before me,
    The saw, with restless play,
Was cleaving through a fire-tree
    Its long and steady way.

The tree through all its fibres
  With living motion stirred,
And, in a dirge-like murmur,
  These solemn words I heard:

Oh, thou who wanderest hither,
  A timely guest thou art!
For thee, this cruel engine
  Is passing through my heart.

When soon, in earth's still bosom,
  Thy hours of rest begin,
This wood shall form the chamber
  Whose walls shall close thee in.

Four planks—I saw and shuddered—
  Dropped in that busy mill;
Then, as I tried to answer,
  At once the wheel was still.

Graham's Magazine, *February, 1850.*

THE SWALLOW.

FROM THE ITALIAN OF F. GROSSÈ.

SWALLOW from beyond the sea!
  That, with every dawn again,
Sitting on the balcony,
  Utterest that plaintive strain!
What is that thou tellest me?
Swallow from beyond the sea.

Haply thou, for him who went
  From thee, and forgot his mate,
Dost lament to my lament,
  Widowed, lonely, desolate.
Ever, then, lament with me,
Swallow from beyond the sea.

Happier yet art thou than I.
　Thee thy trusty wings may bear,
Over lake and cliff to fly,
　Filling with thy cries the air,
Calling him continually,
Swallow from beyond the sea.

Could I, too!—but I must pine
　In this narrow vault and low;
Where the sun can never shine,
　Where the breeze can never blow;
Where my voice scarce reaches thee,
Swallow from beyond the sea.

Now September days are near,
　Thou to distant shores wilt fly;
In another hemisphere.
　Other streams shall hear thy cry;
Other hills shall answer thee,
Swallow from beyond the sea.

Then shall I, when daylight glows,
　Waking to the sense of pain,
Midst the wintry frosts and snows,
　Think I hear thy notes again,—
Notes that seem to grieve for me,
Swallow from beyond the sea.

Planted here, upon the ground,
　Thou shalt find a cross in spring.
There, as evening gathers round,
　Swallow, come and rest thy wing.
Chant a strain of peace to me,
Swallow from beyond the sea.

NAPLES, *February 8, 1858.*

THE OLD-WORLD SPARROW.

WE hear the note of a stranger bird
That ne'er till now in our land was heard;
A wingèd settler has taken his place
With Teutons and men of the Celtic race;
He has followed their path to our hemisphere—
The Old-World sparrow at last is here.

He meets not here, as beyond the main,
The fowler's snare and the poisoned grain,
But snug-built homes on the friendly tree;
And crumbs for his chirping family
Are strewn when the winter fields are drear,
For the Old-World sparrow is welcome here.

The insect legions that sting our fruit,
And strip the leaves from the growing shoot—
A swarming, skulking, ravenous tribe,
Which Harris and Flint so well describe
But cannot destroy—may quail with fear,
For the Old-World sparrow, their bane, is here.

The apricot, in the summer ray,
May ripen now on the loaded spray,
And the nectarine, by the garden walk,
Keep firm its hold on the parent stalk,
And the plum its fragrant fruitage rear,
For the Old-World sparrow, their friend, is here.

That pest of gardens, the little Turk
Who signs, with the crescent, his wicked work,
And causes the half-grown fruit to fall,
Shall be seized and swallowed, in spite of all
His sly devices of cunning and fear,
For the Old-World sparrow, his foe, is here.

And the army-worm, and the Hessian fly,
And the dreaded canker-worm shall die,

And the thrip and slug and fruit-moth seek,
In vain, to escape that busy beak,
And fairer harvests shall crown the year,
For the Old-World sparrow at last is here.

ROSLYN, 1859.

CIVIL WAR.

FROM HORACE, EPODE VII.

HA! whither rush ye? to what deeds of guilt?
　　Why lift the sword again?
Has not enough of Latian blood been spilt
　　To purple land and main?

Not with proud Carthage war ye now, to set
　　Her turrets in a blaze;
Nor fight to lead the Briton, tameless yet,
　　Chained on the public ways.

But that our country, at the Parthian's prayer,
　　May perish self-o'erthrown.
The wolf and lion war not thus; they spare
　　Their kindred each his own.

What moves ye thus? blind fury, heaven's decree,
　　Or restless guilt?   Reply!—
They answer not; upon their faces, see,
　　Paleness and horror lie!

Fate and the wrong against a brother wrought
　　Have caused that deadly rage.
The blood of unoffending Remus brought
　　This curse upon our age.

NEW YORK, 1861.

THE SONG SPARROW.

BIRD of the door-side, warbling clear,
In the sprouting or fading year!
Well art thou named from thy own sweet lay,
Piped from paling or naked spray,
As the smile of the sun breaks through
Chill gray clouds that curtain the blue.

Even when February bleak
Smites with his sleet the traveller's cheek,
While the air has no touch of spring,
Bird of promise! we hear thee sing.
Long ere the first blossom wakes,
Long ere the earliest leaf-bud breaks.

April passes and May steals by;
June leads in the sultry July;
Sweet are the wood-notes, loud and sweet,
Poured from the robin's and hang-bird's seat;
Thou, as the green months glide away,
Singest with them as gayly as they.

August comes, and the melon and maize
Bask and swell in a fiery blaze;
Swallows gather, and, southward bound,
Wheel, like a whirl-blast, round and round;
Thrush and robin their songs forget;
Thou art cheerfully warbling yet.

Later still, when the sumach spray
Reddens to crimson, day by day;
When in the orchard, one by one,
Apples drop in the ripening sun,
They who pile them beneath the trees
Hear thy lay in the autumn breeze.

Comes November, sullen and grim,
Spangling with frost the rivulet's brin,

Harsh, hoarse winds from the woodlands tear
Each brown leaf that is clinging there.
Still thou singest, amid the blast,
" Soon is the dreariest season past."

Only when Christmas snow-storms make
Smooth white levels of river and lake,
Sifting the light flakes all day long,
Only then do we miss thy song;
Sure to hear it again when soon
Climbs the sun to a higher noon.

Now, when tidings that make men pale—
Tidings of slaughter—load the gale;
While, from the distant camp, there come
Boom of cannon and roll of drum,
Still thou singest, beside my door,
" Soon is the stormiest season o'er."

Ever thus sing cheerfully on,
Bird of Hope! as in ages gone;
Sing of spring-time and summer-shades,
Autumn's pomp when the summer fades,
Storms that fly from the conquering sun,
Peace by enduring valor won.

ROSLYN, *August, 1861.*   The William's Magazine

THE BETTER AGE.

WHEN, after days of dreary rain, a space
Of clear, soft blue, between the parting clouds,
Opens on the drenched fields and dripping woods,
The tillers of the soil are glad, and say
The storm is overpast.   For well they know
That in this clear blue spot begins the reign
Of sunshine.   Broader shall the opening grow,
As through the throng of clouds the western wind
Goes forth, a conqueror, and scatters them
And sweeps them from the glorious cope of heaven.

Thus in the works of mercy that engage
The minds and hands of thousands, we behold
Signs of a blessed future. They who watch
Beside the sick-beds of the poor, who seek
And lead the erring back to the right way,
And heal the wounded spirit with the balm
Of pity, and hold back the cruel hand
That smites the helpless; they whose labors win
The outcast hater of his kind to feel
The power of goodness and shed penitent tears,
Are God's elected agents to bring in
The better age. With gladness and with thanks
We number mercy's triumphs, and our hopes
Go forward to the train of glorious years,
When all the clouds of strife, that darken earth
And hide the face of heaven, shall roll away,
And, like a calm, sweet sunshine, love and peace
Shall light the dreariest walks of human life.

ROSLYN, 1862.

A TALE OF CLOUDLAND.

A FRAGMENT.

IF thou art one who in thy early years
Wert wont to gaze delighted on the clouds,
High-piled and floating on the silent wind,—
If then the wish arose within thy heart
To sit on those white banks of down, and thence
To look on the green earth and glittering streams,—
If thou didst wonder who they were that walked
Those shining hills of heaven and dwelt within
The palaces that flamed so gloriously
With gold and crimson in the setting sun,—
To thee, and such as thou, may I not tell
This tale of cloudland in our father's time.

Beneath the soft rays of the westering sun
A matron and a damsel sat and watched

The trains of cloud that touched the neighboring steeps
And slid from cliff to cliff.   The elder dame
Was of majestic mien, with calm, dark eyes,
That seemed to read the inmost thoughts of those
On whom they looked.   " It should not be," she said.
" I grieve that Hubert thus should leave the walks
Of daily duty for these wanderings
Among the mountain mists.   Plead as thou wilt,
Life has its cares, my daughter, graver cares,
That may not be put by."   Then Mary spoke—
A budding beauty, with soft hazel eyes,
And glossy chestnut hair whose wandering curls
The sunshine turned to gold.   " Nay, blame him not,
For not in vain he walks the mountain height,
Where the clouds cling and linger.   Pleasant 'tis
To hear him, sitting in our porch at eve,
When all the meadow grounds within this vale
Twinkle with fire-flies, tell what he has seen
From his high perch—I know not how—the march
Of armies, and their meeting in the shock
Of battle, and the couriers posting forth
To the four winds with news of victory,
Won by the yeoman's arm."
                              " Yet seest thou not,"
Rejoined the stately lady Isabel,
" That Hubert's fitter place were in the ranks
Of those brave men, that, led by Washington,
Defy the hosts of Britain ? "   " It were well,"
Said Mary, " that he too should bear his part
In this great war of freedom ; yet, I pray,
Think what he is—a dreamer from his birth.
Ever, apart from the resorts of men,
He roamed the pathless woods, and hearkened long
To winds that brought into their silent depths
The nearness of the mountain water-falls.
What should he do in battle ? "   Then she said,
Gathering fresh boldness in her brother's cause,
" Think how, since he began to wander forth
Among the mountain-peaks, the region round
Has had the kindest seasons.   Never drought

Embrowns the grassy fields, nor jagged hail
Tears tender leaf and flower; cloud-shadows make
A screen against the burning sunshine poured
Too freely from the August sky, and showers
Drop gently at due times. All summer long
Sleep the luxuriant meadows, and keep full
The clear fresh springs and gurgling rivulets;
The early and late frosts surprise not here
The husbandman, but when the air grows sharp,
Soft vapors rise, beneath whose friendly veil
The green blood of the herbage curdles not
To ice; the winds of winter toss no more
The deep snow into heaps, but softly fall
The flakes, a kindly covering for the earth
With all its sleeping germs, till April suns
Melt it to crystal for the merry brooks.
Mother, the herdsmen of our vale owe thanks
To Hubert for the wealth that crowns the year,
And I have seen—"
                    The maiden checked her speech,
For the calm eyes of Isabel were turned
Full on her own; that grave look startled her.
"Speak on," the matron said. "What hast thou seen?"

  "It was but yesterday," the maid replied,
"A white low-lying cloud swam gently in,
Touching our mountain pastures where they meet
The rocky woods above them. Hubert stepped
From its thick folds, and as they rolled away
I plainly saw a chariot cushioned deep
With sides that seemed of down, and skirt-like wings
On which they nestled. One fair form within
Was seated, flinging from the finger tips
Of her white hands a thousand kind adieus
To Hubert where he stood. It was as though
A pearly cloud had taken human shape;
I saw the round white arms; a coronet
Of twinkling points, like sparks of sunshine, bound
Her forehead, and a gauzy scarf, whose tint
Was of the spring heaven's softest, tenderest blue,
    33

Streamed from her shoulder.   As I looked, the form
Took fainter outlines, and the twinkling points
Around her brow grew paler, till at length
I only saw a cloud-wreath, floating off
On the slow wind; yet must I now believe
That Hubert holds communion in strange sort
With creatures of the upper element,
Whose dwelling is the cloud, who guide the shower
From vale to vale, and shed the snows, and fling
The lightnings?   Therefore, said I, that our vale
Owes thanks to Hubert for its genial skies."

Here spake the matron.   "Art thou then become,"
She said, "a dreamer as thy brother is?
Think not that he who moulded in his hand
The globe, and filled the chambers of the sky
With the ever-flowing air, hath need to use
The ministries thou speakest of.   He looks
Upon these vapory curtains of the earth,
And so they darken into drifts of rain
Or whiten into snow.   His thunders, launched
From the remotest West, ere thou canst speak
Are quivering at the portals of the East.
The winds blow softly where he bids, or rise
In fury, tearing from their hold in earth
The helpless oaks and twisting the huge pines
In twain, and flinging them among the clouds.
Nay, speak more reverently, and leave to God
His thunders."
                              "Reverently," the maid replied,
"I ever speak of him whose hand I see
In all the motions of the elements.
Yet hath he living agents, so our faith
Hath taught us: messengers that do his will
Among the unconscious nations—such as led
The Hebrew from the Cities of the Plain,
When heaven rained fire upon their guilty roofs;
And haply is there blame if we should deem
That in the middle air abides a race
Thoughtful and kind who at His bidding roll

The clouds together, measuring out to man
The rains and dews, and tempering the hot noon,
With shadow chasing shadow o'er the vale?"

The matron pondered as the maiden urged
Her plea, and then was silent for a while.
But Mary spoke again. "Look, mother, look!
How gloriously about the sinking sun
The flamy clouds are gathered! Lofty towers
Rise from those purple streets. Who looks abroad
From their high battlements? Behold where moves
A long procession of the shining ones,
Tall kings and stately queens with sweeping trains,
Warriors in glittering mail, and cardinals
In scarlet robes, and bearded counsellors,
Thin-haired with age, and light-limbed followers,
And mingled with the diadems I see
Helm, mitre, and tiara, while above
Rise spear, and mace, and crosses, and broad sheets
Of banner floating in the rosy air.
Oh, never was on earth a pageant seen
So gorgeous, furnished from her richest ores,
And beds of jewels, and the subtlest looms
That weave the silk-worm's thread in lustrous webs.
For all are pale beside the glory born
Of these bright vapors round the setting sun.
There is no sight so fair this side of heaven."

The stately matron heard, and looked, and smiled.
"Thus doth thy fancy cheat thy willing eye,"
She said. "The freakish wind among the mists
Moulds them as sculptors mould the yielding clay,
Fashioning them to thousand antic shapes
Beneath the evening blaze. Thy ready thought
Couples their outline, and bestows the forms
That rise in thine own mind. Thou shouldst have lived
When, on his canvas, Paul the Veronese
Laid his magnificent throngs of goodly men
And glorious ladies in their rich attire.
Thou shouldst have been his pupil. Yet behold,

Even while we speak the sunset glory fades,
And the clouds settle into purple bars
Athwart the depths of that transparent sky
Through which the day withdraws.   A chilly breath
Comes up from the moist meadows.   Let us hence."

Then rose the pair and took the homeward path;
And from the windows of their dwelling saw
The night come down upon their vale, and heard
The heavy rushing of her wind among
The neighboring maples, mingled with the brawl
Of mountain-brooks, while from the thicket near
The whippoorwill sent forth his liquid note,
Piercing that steady murmur.   As the shades
Grew deeper, Isabel and Mary knelt
To say their evening prayer, and by their side
Knelt Hubert, for the simple reverence taught
In childhood kept its hold upon his heart.
They prayed the Merciful to guide and shield
And pardon—then withdrew, with kindly words
Of parting, each to rest.   A rising mist
Meantime had quenched the stars, and o'er the earth
Shower after shower, with gentle beating, ran,
As if a fairy chase were in the air,
And myriads of little footsteps tapped
The roof above the household.   Mary slept
To the soft sounds, and dreamed.   The glorious throng
Which her quick fancy pictured in the clouds
Of sunset had laid by their bright attire—
Such was her dream—and now in trailing robes,
Sad colored, and in hoods of sober gray,
Went drifting through the air and beckoning up
The troops of mist from lake and rivulet,
And leading through mid-sky the shadowy train,
And pointing where to halt in deep array
Above the expectant fields and shed the rain.
So wore the night away.   The murmuring showers
Lengthened the slumbers in that mountain lodge,
Until, as morn drew near, the parting clouds
Opened a field in the clear eastern sky,

In which the day-star glittered, and the dawn
Glowed on the horizon's edge.   On either side
They ranged themselves to catch the earliest beams
Scarlet or golden, of the approaching sun ;
As when within a city's crowded streets
The gathered multitude divide and leave
Large space to let some glorious monarch pass.

ROSLYN, 1862.

CASTLES IN THE AIR.

FROM AN UNPUBLISHED POEM.

" BUT there is yet a region of the clouds
Unseen from the low earth.   Beyond the veil
Of these dark volumes rolling through the sky,
Its mountain summits glisten in the sun,—
The realm of Castles in the Air.   The foot
Of man hath never trod those shining streets ;
But there his spirit, leaving the dull load
Of bodily organs, wanders with delight,
And builds its structures of the impalpable mist,
Glorious beyond the dream of architect,
And populous with forms of nobler mould
Than ever walked the earth."
                         So said my guide,
And led me, wondering, to a headland height
That overlooked a fair broad vale shut in
By the great hills of Cloudland.   " Now behold
The Castle-builders ! "   Then I looked ; and, lo !
The vale was filled with shadowy forms, that bore
Each a white wand, with which they touched the banks
Of mist beside them, and at once arose,
Obedient to their wish, the walls and domes
Of stately palaces, Gothic or Greek,
Or such as in the land of Mohammed
Uplift the crescent, or, in forms more strange,
Border the ancient Indus, or behold

Their gilded friezes mirrored in the lakes
Of China—yet of ampler majesty,
And gorgeously adorned. Tall porticos
Sprang from the ground; the eye pursued afar
Their colonnades, that lessened to a point
In the faint distance. Portals that swung back
On musical hinges showed the eye within
Vast halls with golden floors, and bright alcoves,
And walls of pearl, and sapphire vault besprent
With silver stars. Within the spacious rooms
Were banquets spread; and menials, beautiful
As wood-nymphs or as stripling Mercuries,
Ran to and fro, and laid the chalices,
And brought the brimming wine-jars. Enters now
The happy architect, and wanders on
From room to room, and glories in his work.

   Not long his glorying: for a chill north wind
Breathes through the structure, and the massive walls
Are folded up; the proud domes roll away
In mist-wreaths; pinnacle and turret lean
Forward, like birds prepared for flight, and stream,
In trains of vapor, through the empty air.
Meantime the astonished builder, dispossessed,
Stands 'mid the drifting rack. A brief despair
Seizes him; but the wand is in his hand,
And soon he turns him to his task again.
" Behold," said the fair being at my side,
" How one has made himself a diadem
Out of the bright skirts of a cloud that lay
Steeped in the golden sunshine, and has bound
The bauble on his forehead! See, again,
How from these vapors he calls up a host
With arms and banners! A great multitude
Gather and bow before him with bare heads.
To the four winds his messengers go forth,
And bring him back earth's homage. From the ground
Another calls a wingèd image, such
As poets give to Fame, who, to her mouth
Putting a silver trumpet, blows abroad

A loud, harmonious summons to the world,
And all the listening nations shout his name.
Another yet, apart from all the rest,
Casting a fearful glance from side to side,
Touches the ground by stealth.   Beneath his wand
A glittering pile grows up, ingots and bars
Of massive gold, and coins on which earth's kings
Have stamped their symbols." As these words were said,
The north wind blew again across the vale,
And, lo ! the beamy crown flew off in mist ;
The host of armèd men became a scud
Torn by the angry blast ; the form of Fame
Tossed its long arms in air, and rode the wind,
A jagged cloud ; the glittering pile of gold
Grew pale and flowed in a gray reek away.
Then there were sobs and tears from those whose work
The wind had scattered ; some had flung themselves
Upon the ground in grief ; and some stood fixed
In blank bewilderment ; and some looked on
Unmoved, as at a pageant of the stage
Suddenly hidden by the curtain's fall.

" Take thou this wand," my bright companion said.
I took it from her hand, and with it touched
The knolls of snow-white mist, and they grew green
With soft, thick herbage.   At another touch
A brook leaped forth, and dashed and sparkled by ;
And shady walks through shrubberies cool and close
Wandered ; and where, upon the open grounds,
The peaceful sunshine lay, a vineyard nursed
Its pouting clusters ; and from boughs that drooped
Beneath their load an orchard shed its fruit ;
And gardens, set with many a pleasant herb
And many a glorious flower, made sweet the air.
    I looked, and I exulted ; yet I longed
For Nature's grander aspects, and I plied
The slender rod again ; and then arose
Woods tall and wide, of odorous pine and fir,
And every noble tree that casts the leaf
In autumn.   Paths that wound between their stems

Led through the solemn shade to twilight glens,
To thundering torrents and white waterfalls,
And edge of lonely lakes, and chasms between
The mountain-cliffs. Above the trees were seen
Gray pinnacles and walls of splintered rock.

But near the forest margin, in the vale,
Nestled a dwelling half embowered by trees,
Where, through the open window, shelves were seen
Filled with old volumes, and a glimpse was given
Of canvas, here and there along the walls,
On which the hands of mighty men of art
Had flung their fancies. On the portico
Old friends, with smiling faces and frank eyes,
Talked with each other : some had passed from life
Long since, yet dearly were remembered still.
My heart yearned toward them, and the quick, warm tears
Stood in my eyes. Forward I sprang to grasp
The hands that once so kindly met my own,—
I sprang, but met them not : the withering wind
Was there before me. Dwelling, field, and brook,
Dark wood, and flowery garden, and blue lake,
And beetling cliff, and noble human forms,
All, all had melted into that pale sea
Of billowy vapor rolling round my feet.

ROSLYN, 1862.   Atlantic Monthly, *January, 1866.*

FIFTY YEARS.*

LONG since a gallant youthful company
Went from these learned shades. The hand of Time
Hath scored, upon the perishing works of man,
The years of half a century since that day.
Forth to the world they went in hope, but some

---

* For the fiftieth anniversary of the class of Williams College which
was graduated in 1813.

Fell at the threshold, some in mid-career
Sank down, and some who bring their frosty brows,
A living register of change, are here,
And from the spot where once they conned the words
Written by sages of the elder time
Look back on fifty years.
                              Large space are they
Of man's brief life, those fifty years; they join
Its ruddy morning to the paler light
Of its declining hours.   In fifty years
As many generations of earth's flowers
Have sweetened the soft air of spring, and died.
As many harvests have, in turn, made green
The hills, and ripened into gold, and fallen
Before the sickle's edge.   The sapling tree
Which then was planted stands a shaggy trunk,
Moss-grown, the centre of a mighty shade.
In fifty years the pasture grounds have oft
Renewed their herds and flocks, and from the stalls
New races of the generous steed have neighed
Or pranced in the smooth roads.
                              In fifty years
Ancestral crowns have dropped from kingly brows
For clownish heels to crush; new dynasties
Have climbed to empire, and new commonwealths
Have formed and fallen again to wreck, like clouds
Which the wind tears and scatters.   Mighty names
Have blazed upon the world and passed away,
Their lustre lessening, like the faded train
Of a receding comet.   Fifty years
Have given the mariner to outstrip the wind
With engines churning the black deep to foam,
And tamed the nimble lightnings, sending them
On messages for man, and forced the sun
To limn for man upon the snowy sheet
Whate'er he shines upon, and taught the art
To vex the pale dull clay beneath our feet
With chemic tortures, till the sullen mass
Flows in bright torrents from the furnace-mouth,
A shining metal, to be clay no more.

Oh, were our growth in goodness like our growth
In art, the thousand years of innocence
And peace, foretold by ancient prophecy,
Were here already, and the reign of Sin
Were ended o'er the earth on which we dwell.

In fifty years, the little commonwealth,
Our league of States, that, in its early day,
Skirted the long Atlantic coast, has grown
To a vast empire, filled with populous towns
Beside its midland rivers, and beyond
The snowy peaks that bound its midland plains
To where its rivulets, over sands of gold,
Seek the Pacific—till at length it stood
Great 'mid the greatest of the Powers of Earth,
And they who sat upon Earth's ancient thrones
Beheld its growth in wonder and in awe.
In fifty years, a deadlier foe than they—
The Wrong that scoffs at human brotherhood
And holds the lash o'er millions—has become
So mighty and so insolent in its might
That now it springs to fix on Liberty
The death-gripe, and o'erturn the glorious realm
Her children founded here.   Fierce is the strife,
As when of old the sinning angels strove
To whelm, beneath the uprooted hills of heaven,
The warriors of the Lord.   Yet now, as then,
God and the Right shall give the victory.

For us, who fifty years ago went forth
Upon the world's great theatre, may we
Yet see the day of triumph, which the hours
On steady wing waft hither from the depths
Of a serener future; may we yet,
Beneath the reign of a new peace, behold
The shaken pillars of our commonwealth
Stand readjusted in their ancient poise,
And the great crime of which our strife was born
Perish with its accursèd progeny.

Roslyn, 1863.

TO THE NIGHTINGALE.

FROM LAS AURORAS DE DIANA.   BY PEDRO DE CASTROY AÑAYA.

BIRD of the joyous season!
  That, from thy flowery seat,
Dost teach the forest singers
  Thy music to repeat.

Thou wooer of the morning,
  That, to this wood withdrawn,
Dost serenade the daybreak,
  Dost celebrate the dawn.

Soul of this lonely region,
  That hearest me lament,
My days in sighing wasted,
  My nights in weeping spent.

Chief lyrist of the woodland,
  And poet of the spring!
That well art skilled in sorrow,
  And well of love canst sing.

Go where my lady loosens
  Her bright hair to the wind,
Held in a single fillet,
  Or floating unconfined.

The beautiful and cruel,
  Whose steps, where'er they pass,
Tread down more hearts of lovers
  Than lilies in the grass.

Sweet nightingale, accost her,
  And, in thy tenderest strain,
Say Silvio loves thee : Cruel!
  Why lov'st thou not again?

Then tell of all I suffer,
  How well have loved and long,

And counsel her to pity,
And tax her scorn with wrong.

My gentle Secretary!
If harshly then she speak,
Rebuke her anger, striking
Her red lips with thy beak.

Drink from her breath the fragrance
Of all the blooming year,
And bring me back the answer
For which I linger here.

February, 1864.

A LEGEND OF ST. MARTIN.

SHREWD was the good St. Martin; he was famed
For sly expedients and devices quaint;
And autumn's latest sunny days are named
St. Martin's summer from the genial saint.
Large were his charities; one winter day
He saw a half-clad beggar in the way,
And stopped and said: " Well met, my friend, well met;
That nose of thine, I see, is quite too blue."
With that his trenchant sword he drew—
For he was in the service yet—
And cut his military cloak in two;
And with a pleasant laugh
He bade the shivering rogue take half.

On one of the great roads of France
Two travellers were journeying on a day.
The saint drew near, as if by chance,
And joined them, walking the same way.
A shabby pair in truth were they,
For one was meanly covetous, and one
An envious wretch—so doth the legend run.
Yet courteously they greeted him, and talked
Of current topics; for example, whether

There would be war, and what to-morrow's weather,
Cheating the weary furlongs as they walked.
   And when the eventide drew near
Thus spoke the saint : " We part to-night ;
   I am St. Martin, and I give you here
The means to make your fortunes, used aright ;
   Let one of you think what will please him best,
And freely ask what I will freely give.
And he who asks not shall from me receive
   Twice what the other gains by his request ;
   And now I take my leave."
He spoke, and left the astonished men
Delighted with his words ; but then
The question rose, which of that lucky pair
Should speak the wish and take the smaller share.
   Each begged the other not to heed
   The promptings of a selfish greed,
But frame at once, since he so well knew how,
The amplest, fullest wish that words allow.
   " Dear comrade, act a princely part ;
Lay every sordid thought aside ;
   Show thyself generous as thou art ;
   Take counsel of thy own large heart,
And nobly for our common good provide."
   But neither prayers nor flatteries availed ;
   They passed from these to threats, and threats too failed.
Thus went the pleadings on, until at last
   The covetous man, his very blood on fire,
Flew at his fellow's throat and clenched it fast,
   And shrieked : " Die, then, or do what I require ;
Die, strangled like a dog."   That taunt awoke
   A fierce anger in his envious mate,
   And merged the thirst of gain in bitter hate ;
And with a half-choked voice he spoke,
   Dissembling his malign intent,
   " Take off thy hand and I consent."
The grasp was loosened, and he raised a shout,
   " I wish that one of my own eyes were out."
The wish was gratified as soon as heard.
St. Martin punctually kept his word.

The envious man was one-eyed from that day,
    The other blind for his whole life remained.
    And this was all the good that either gained
From the saint's offer in the public way.

ROSLYN, 1865.

THE WORDS OF THE KORAN.

FROM THE GERMAN OF ZEDLITZ.

EMIR HASSAN, of the prophet's race,
Asked with folded hands the Almighty's grace.
Then within the banquet-hall he sat
At his meal upon the embroidered mat.

There a slave before him placed the food,
Spilling from the charger, as he stood,
Awkwardly, upon the Emir's breast,
Drops that foully stained the silken vest.

To the floor, in great remorse and dread,
Fell the slave, and thus beseeching said:
"Master! they who hasten to restrain
Rising wrath, in Paradise shall reign."

Gentle was the answer Hassan gave:
"I'm not angry."   "Yet," pursued the slave,
"Yet doth higher recompense belong
To the injured who forgives a wrong."

"I forgive," said Hassan.   "Yet we read,"
Thus the prostrate slave went on to plead,
"That a higher place in glory still
Waits the man who renders good for ill."

"Slave, receive thy freedom, and behold
In thy hands I lay a purse of gold;
Let me never fail to heed in aught
What the prophet of our God hath taught."

November, 1865.

THE POET'S FIRST SONG.

FROM THE GERMAN OF HOUWALD.

ALREADY had I travelled,
  O'er half the globe alone;
The tongues of other nations,
  I knew them like my own.

And great men called me brother
  In many a distant land,
And many a mighty monarch
  In greeting gave his hand.

Amid Pompeii's ruins,
  Amid the Switzer's snows,
And by the mounds of Egypt,
  And where La Plata flows,

I stood and sang my verses;
  And what the poet said
Thrilled through the hearts of thousands,
  By eager thousands read.

A star upon my bosom,
  A heaven within, I came
All conscious of the glory
  That gathered round my name—

Came from afar to visit
  The little mound of earth
Where stood my father's cottage,
  The vale that saw my birth.

And now from the last hill-top,
  The boundary-stone beside,
O'er that small shady valley
  I cast a look of pride.

And, glorying in my fortunes,
  I said, I thank thee, Fate,
I who went forth so humble,
  That I come back so great.

Then up the hill came toiling
  A woman faint and pale,
And with two lovely children
  Sat looking down the vale.

And soon I heard her singing
  A simple little lay—
A strain that moved me strangely,
  Though why I could not say.

So timidly I asked her
  Whence came that simple rhyme;
" From happy days," she answered,
  " A long-remembered time."

" On parting with the maiden,
  A youth composed the song."—
Ah, then I knew the verses,—
  My first—forgotten long.

And eagerly I questioned,
  " Who gave the song to thee ? "
She blushed. " No mortal knoweth,"
  She said, " save only me."

" Thou art the poet's Mary ? "
  Her silence owned it true.
" But whither went the poet ? "
  " Ah, that I never knew."

" Hast heard of him no further ? "
  " No, never since that day."
" Wrote he no other verses ? "
  " In truth, I cannot say."

" His name ? " " Nay, gentle stranger,
  Ask not the name he bore ;

Perhaps I, too, may know him,
But me he knows no more."

" Yet once again, I pray thee,
Sing that sweet melody."
" Not now.   My husband yonder
Waits for my babes and me."

She spoke, and then descended
To join him where he stood;
Upon his arm he took her,
And led the little brood.

Here stood a mighty poet,
His name by thousands known;
But in his native valley
To one and one alone.

And lost in sadder musings
Than when he went away,
Surrendered all his honors
To that forgotten lay.

ROSLYN, *November, 1873.*   The Mayflower, *April, 1876.*

THE ASCENSION.

FROM THE SPANISH OF LUIS PONCE DE LEON.

GOOD Shepherd, wilt thou leave
In this low vale the flock that was thy care
Alone to pine and grieve,
While through the purer air
Thou risest up to fields forever fair?

They who, supremely blest,
Until the dawn of this unhappy day
Leaned on thy loving breast,
To whom on earth shall they
Hearken or look when thou art far away?

34

What comeliness or grace
Can they whose eyes beheld thy beauty see
In other form or face?
What music will not be
Harsh to the ears that hearkened once to thee?

Who now upon the deep
Shall look, and curb its fury? Who shall lay
The stormy winds asleep?
What lode-star's friendly ray,
When thine is hid, shall guide the vessel's way?

Why change our happy state,
O envious cloud! to helplessness and fear?
How proud of their rich freight
Thy shining folds appear!
How blind and wretched thou dost leave us here!

NEW YORK, *December, 1875.*   Independent, 1875.

THE MYSTERY OF FLOWERS.

NOT idly do I stray
At prime, where far the mountain ridges run,
And note, along my way,
Each flower that opens in the early sun;
Or gather blossoms by the valley's spring,
When the sun sets and dancing insects sing.

Each has her moral rede,
Each of the gentle family of flowers;
And I with patient heed,
Oft spell their lessons in my graver hours.
The faintest streak that on a petal lies,
May speak instruction to initiate eyes.

CUMMINGTON, 1840.

And well do poets teach
Each blossom's charming mystery; declare,

In clear melodious speech,
The silent admonitions pencilled there;
And from the Love of Beauty, aptly taught,
Lead to a higher good, the willing thought.

ROSLYN, 1875.

THE DEAD PATRIARCH.

OLD Tree! thy branches, fifty years ago,
    Thick set with spray and leaf, and widely spread,
Made a faint twilight on the ground below,
    And never-ending murmurs overhead.

But now unheard the winds go wandering by;
    From thy dead stem the boughs have dropped away;
And on its summit, perched in middle sky,
    The clear-eyed hawk sits watching for his prey.

Henceforth, the softening rain and rending blast.
    Summer's fierce heat, and winter's splintering cold,
Shall slowly waste thee, till thou lie at last
    On the damp earth, a heap of yellow mould.

Thou wert a sapling once, with delicate sprays,
    And from that mould another sapling tree
May rise and flourish, in the coming days,
    When none who dwell on earth remember thee.

ROSLYN, *April, 1876.*

A SONNET.

TO ———.

YOUTH, whose ingenuous nature, just and kind,
    Looks from that gentle eye, that open brow,
Wilt thou be ever thus, in heart and mind,
    As guileless and as merciful as now?

Behold this streamlet, whose sweet waters wind
  Among green knolls unbroken by the plough,
Where wild-flowers woo the bee and wild-birds find
  Safe nests and secret in the cedar bough.
This stream must reach the sea, and then no more
  Its purity and peaceful mood shall keep,
But change to bitter brine, and madly roar
  Among the breakers there, and toss and leap,
And dash the helpless bark against the shore,
  And whelm the drowning seamen in the deep.

ROSLYN, *November, 1876.*

THE BATTLE OF BENNINGTON.*

ON this fair valley's grassy breast
The calm, sweet rays of summer rest,
And dove-like peace divinely broods
On its smooth lawns and solemn woods.

A century since, in flame and smoke,
The storm of battle o'er it broke ;
And ere the invader turned and fled,
These pleasant fields were strown with dead.

Stark, quick to act and bold to dare,
And Warner's mountain band were there;
And Allen, who had flung the pen
Aside to lead the Berkshire men.

With fiery onset—blow on blow—
They rushed upon the embattled foe,
And swept his squadrons from the vale,
Like leaves before the autumn gale.

Oh! never may the purple stain
Of combat blot these fields again,

---

* Written for the hundredth anniversary of the battle of Bennington,
August 16, 1877.

Nor this fair valley ever cease
To wear the placid smile of peace.

But we, beside this battle-field,
Will plight the vow that ere we yield
The right for which our fathers bled,
Our blood shall steep the ground we tread.

And men shall hold the memory dear
Of those who fought for freedom here,
And guard the heritage they won
While these green hill-sides feel the sun.

August, 1877.

IN MEMORY OF JOHN LOTHROP MOTLEY.

SLEEP, Motley! with the great of ancient days,
    Who wrote for all the years that yet shall be;
Sleep with Herodotus, whose name and praise
    Have reached the isles of earth's remotest sea;
Sleep, while, defiant of the slow decays
    Of time, thy glorious writings speak for thee,
And in the answering heart of millions raise
    The generous zeal for Right and Liberty.
And should the day o'ertake us when, at last,
    The silence that, ere yet a human pen
Had traced the slenderest record of the past—
    Hushed the primeval languages of men—
Upon our English tongue its spell shall cast,
    Thy memory shall perish only then.

NEW YORK, *September, 1877.*   International Review, *September, 1877.*

THE TWENTY-SECOND OF FEBRUARY.

PALE is the February sky,
    And brief the mid-day's sunny hours;
The wind-swept forest seems to sigh
    For the sweet time of leaves and flowers.

Yet has no month a prouder day,
   Not even when the summer broods
O'er meadows in their fresh array,
   Or autumn tints the glowing woods.

For this chill season now again
   Brings, in its annual round, the morn
When, greatest of the sons of men,
   Our glorious Washington was born.

Lo, where, beneath an icy shield,
   Calmly the mighty Hudson flows!
By snow-clad fell and frozen field,
   Broadening, the lordly river goes.

The wildest storm that sweeps through space,
   And rends the oak with sudden force,
Can raise no ripple on his face,
   Or slacken his majestic course.

Thus, 'mid the wreck of thrones, shall live
   Unmarred, undimmed, our hero's fame,
And years succeeding years shall give
   Increase of honors to his name.

NEW YORK, *February, 1878.*   Sunday School Times

CERVANTES.*

As o'er the laughter-moving page
   Thy readers, oh, Cervantes, bend,
What shouts of mirth, through age on age,
   From every clime of earth ascend!

For not in thy fair Spain alone,
   But in the sunny tropic isles,

---

* Written for a celebration by the Spanish residents of New York, in honor of Cervantes, April 23, 1878, the anniversary of his death.

And far, to either frozen zone,
　Thy memory lives embalmed in smiles.

Dark woods, when thou didst hold the pen,
　Clothed this great land from sea to sea,
Where millions of the sons of men
　Now take delight in honoring thee.

To thy renown the centuries bring
　No shadow of a coming night.
The keen, bright shafts which thou didst fling
　At folly still are keen and bright.

FABLES.

FROM THE SPANISH OF JOSÉ ROSAS, A MEXICAN POET.

THE ELM AND THE VINE.

" UPHOLD my feeble branches
　By thy strong arms, I pray."
Thus to the Elm her neighbor
　The Vine was heard to say.
" Else, lying low and helpless,
　A wretched lot is mine,
Crawled o'er by every reptile,
　And browsed by hungry kine."
The Elm was moved to pity.
　Then spoke the generous tree:
" My hapless friend, come hither,
　And find support in me."
The kindly Elm, receiving
　The grateful Vine's embrace,
Became, with that adornment,
　The garden's pride and grace;
Became the chosen covert
　In which the wild-bird's sing,
Became the love of shepherds,
　And glory of the spring.

Oh, beautiful example
  For youthful minds to heed!
The good we do to others
  Shall never miss its meed.
The love of those whose sorrows
  We lighten shall be ours;
And o'er the path we walk in
  That love shall scatter flowers.

THE DONKEY AND THE MOCKING-BIRD.

A MOCK-BIRD in a village
  Had somehow gained the skill
To imitate the voices
  Of animals at will.

And, singing in his prison
  Once at the close of day,
He gave with great precision
  The donkey's heavy bray.

Well pleased, the mock-bird's master
  Sent to the neighbors round,
And bade them come together
  To hear that curious sound.

They came, and all were talking
  In praise of what they heard,
And one delighted lady
  Would fain have bought the bird.

A donkey listened sadly,
  And said: " Confess I must,
That these are stupid people,
  And terribly unjust.

" I'm bigger than the mock-bird,
  And better bray than he,
Yet not a soul has uttered
  A word in praise of me."

THE CATERPILLAR AND THE BUTTERFLY.

SELECTED.

"GOOD-MORROW, friend." So spoke, upon a day,
  A caterpillar to a butterfly.
The winged creature looked another way,
  And made this proud reply:
  "No friend of worms am I."
The insulted caterpillar heard,
And answered thus the taunting word:
  "And what wert thou, I pray,
Ere God bestowed on thee that brave array?
Why treat the caterpillar tribe with scorn?
  Art thou, then, nobly born?
What art thou, madam, at the best?
A caterpillar elegantly dressed."

THE SPIDER'S WEB.

A DEXTROUS spider chose
The delicate blossom of a garden rose
  Whereon to plant and bind
The net he framed to take the insect kind.
  And when his task was done,
Proud of the cunning lines his art had spun,
  He said: "I take my stand
Close by my work, and watch what I have planned.
  And now, if Heaven should bless
My labors with but moderate success,
  No fly shall pass this way,
Nor gnat, but they shall fall an easy prey."
  He spoke, when from the sky
A strong wind swooped, and whirling, hurried by,
  And, far before the blast,
Rose, leaf, and web, and plans and hopes were cast.

THE DIAL AND THE SUN.

A DIAL, looking from a stately tower,
  While from his cloudless path in heaven the Sun

Shone on its disk, as hour succeeded hour,
  Faithfully marked their flight till day was done.

Fair was that gilded disk, but when at last
  Night brought the shadowy hours 'twixt eve and prime,
No longer that fair disk, for those who passed,
  Measured and marked the silent flight of time.

The human mind, on which no hallowed light
  Shines from the sphere beyond the starry train,
Is like the Dial's gilded disk at night,
  Whose cunning tracery exists in vain.

THE WOODMAN AND SANDAL-TREE.

BESIDE a sandal-tree a woodman stood
  And swung the axe, and while its blows were laid
Upon the fragrant trunk, the generous wood
  With its own sweet perfumed the cruel blade.
Go, then, and do the like.   A soul endued
  With light from heaven, a nature pure and great,
Will place its highest bliss in doing good,
  And good for evil give, and love for hate.

THE HIDDEN RILL.

ACROSS a pleasant field a rill unseen
  Glides from a fountain, nor does aught betray
Its presence, save a tint of lovelier green,
  And flowers that scent the air along its way.
Thus silently should charity attend
  Those who in want's drear chambers pine and grieve;
No token should reveal the aid we lend,
  Save the glad looks our welcome visits leave.

THE EAGLE AND THE SERPENT.

A SERPENT watched an eagle gain
  On soaring wings, a mountain height,
And envied him, and crawled with pain
  To where he saw the bird alight.

So fickle fortune oftentimes
  Befriends the cunning and the base,
And many a grovelling reptile climbs
  Up to the eagle's lofty place.

THE COST OF A PLEASURE.

UPON the valley's lap
  The liberal morning throws
A thousand drops of dew
  To wake a single rose.

Thus often, in the course
  Of life's few fleeting years,
A single pleasure costs
  The soul a thousand tears.

NOTES.

Page 11.

POEM OF THE AGES.

In this poem, written and first printed in the year 1821, the author has endeavored, from a survey of the past ages of the world, and of the successive advances of mankind in knowledge, virtue, and happiness, to justify and confirm the hopes of the philanthropist for the future destinies of the human race.

Page 34.

THE BURIAL-PLACE.

The first half of this fragment may seem to the reader borrowed from the essay on Rural Funerals in the fourth number of "The Sketch-book." The lines were, however, written more than a year before that number appeared. The poem, unfinished as it is, would hardly have been admitted into this collection, had not the author been unwilling to lose what had the honor of resembling so beautiful a composition.

Page 43.

THE MASSACRE AT SCIO.

This poem, written about the time of the horrible butchery of the Sciotes by the Turks, in 1824, has been more fortunate than most poetical predictions. The independence of the Greek nation which it foretold, has come to pass, and the massacre, by inspiring a deeper detestation of their oppressors, did much to promote that event.

Page 44.

Her maiden veil, her own black hair, etc.

"The unmarried females have a modest falling down of the hair over the eyes."—ELIOT.

406

Page 63.

MONUMENT MOUNTAIN.

The mountain called by this name is a remarkable precipice in Great Barring-ton, overlooking the rich and picturesque valley of the Housatonic, in the western part of Massachusetts. At the southern extremity is, or was a few years since, a conical pile of small stones, erected, according to the tradition of the surrounding country, by the Indians, in memory of a woman of the Stockbridge tribe who killed herself by leaping from the edge of the precipice. Until within a few years past, small parties of that tribe used to arrive from their settlement in the western part of the State of New York, on visits to Stockbridge, the place of their nativity and former residence. A young woman belonging to one of these parties related, to a friend of the author, the story on which the poem of Monument Mountain is founded. An Indian girl had formed an attachment for her cousin, which, accord-ing to the customs of the tribe, was unlawful. She was, in consequence, seized with a deep melancholy, and resolved to destroy herself. In company with a female friend, she repaired to the mountain, decked out for the occasion in all her ornaments, and, after passing the day on the summit in singing with her compan-ion the traditional songs of her nation, she threw herself headlong from the rock, and was killed.

Page 73.

THE MURDERED TRAVELLER.

Some years since, in the month of May, the remains of a human body, partly devoured by wild animals, were found in a woody ravine, near a solitary road passing between the mountains west of the village of Stockbridge. It was sup-posed that the person came to his death by violence, but no traces could be dis-covered of his murderers. It was only recollected that one evening, in the course of the previous winter, a traveller had stopped at an inn in the village of West Stockbridge; that he had inquired the way to Stockbridge; and that, in paying the innkeeper for something he had ordered, it appeared that he had a consider-able sum of money in his possession. Two ill-looking men were present, and went out about the same time that the traveller proceeded on his journey. During the winter, also, two men of shabby appearance, but plentifully supplied with money, had lingered for a while about the village of Stockbridge. Several years afterward, a criminal, about to be executed for a capital offence in Canada, con-fessed that he had been concerned in murdering a traveller in Stockbridge for the sake of his money. Nothing was ever discovered respecting the name or resi-dence of the person murdered.

Page 101.

Chained in the market-place he stood, etc.

The story of the African chief, related in this ballad, may be found in the *African Repository* for April, 1825. The subject of it was a warrior of majestic stature, the brother of Yarradee, king of the Solima nation. He had been taken m battle, and was brought in chains for sale to the Rio Pongas, where he was exhibited in the market-place, his ankles still adorned with massy rings of gold which he wore when captured. The refusal of his captors to listen to his offers of ransom drove him mad, and he died a maniac.

Page 111.

THE CONJUNCTION OF JUPITER AND VENUS.

This conjunction was said in the common calendars to have taken place on the 2d of August, 1826. This, I believe, was an error, but the apparent approach of the planets was sufficiently near for poetical purposes.

Page 116.

THE HURRICANE.

This poem is nearly a translation from one by José Maria de Heredia, a native of the island of Cuba, who published at New York, about the year 1825, a volume of poems in the Spanish language.

Page 118.

WILLIAM TELL.

Neither this, nor any of the other sonnets in the collection, with the exception of the one from the Portuguese, is framed according to the legitimate Italian model, which, in the author's opinion, possesses no peculiar beauty for an ear accustomed only to the metrical forms of our own language. The sonnets in this collection are rather poems in fourteen lines than sonnets.

Page 119.

The slim papaya ripens, etc.

Papaya—papaw, custard-apple. Flint, in his excellent work on the Geography and History of the Western States, thus describes this tree and its fruit:

" A papaw-shrub hanging full of fruits, of a size and weight so disproportioned to the stem, and from under long and rich-looking leaves, of the same yellow with the ripened fruit, and of an African luxuriance of growth, is to us one of the richest spectacles that we have ever contemplated in the array of the woods. The fruit contains from two to six seeds like those of the tamarind, except that they are double the size. The pulp of the fruit resembles egg-custard in consistence and appearance. It has the same creamy feeling in the mouth, and unites the taste of eggs, cream, sugar, and spice. It is a natural custard, too luscious for the relish of most people."

Chateaubriand, in his Travels, speaks disparagingly of the fruit of the papaw; but on the authority of Mr. Flint, who must know more of the matter, I have ventured to make my Western lover enumerate it among the delicacies of the wilderness.

Page 130.

The surface rolls and fluctuates to the eye.

The prairies of the West, with an undulating surface, *rolling prairies,* as they are called, present to the unaccustomed eye a singular spectacle when the shadows of the clouds are passing rapidly over them. The face of the ground seems to fluctuate and toss like billows of the sea.

Page 131.

The prairie-hawk that, poised on high,
Flaps his broad wings, yet moves not.

I have seen the prairie-hawk balancing himself in the air for hours together, apparently over the same spot; probably watching his prey.

Page 131.

These ample fields
Nourished their harvests.

The size and extent of the mounds in the valley of the Mississippi indicate the existence, at a remote period, of a nation at once populous and laborious, and therefore probably subsisting by agriculture.

Page 132.

The rude conquerors
Seated the captive with their chiefs.

Instances are not wanting of generosity like this among the North American Indians toward a captive or survivor of a hostile tribe on which the greatest cruelties had been exercised.

Page 134.

SONG OF MARION'S MEN.

The exploits of General Francis Marion, the famous partisan warrior of South Carolina, form an interesting chapter in the annals of the American Revolution. The British troops were so harassed by the irregular and successful warfare which he kept up at the head of a few daring followers, that they sent an officer to remonstrate with him for not coming into the open field and fighting " like a gentleman and a Christian."

Page 139.

MARY MAGDALEN.

Several learned divines, with much appearance of reason, in particular Dr. Lardner, have maintained that the common notion respecting the dissolute life of Mary Magdalen is erroneous, and that she was always a person of excellent character Charles Taylor, the editor of "Calmet's Dictionary of the Bible," takes the same view of the subject.

The verses of the Spanish poet here translated refer to the "woman who had been a sinner," mentioned in the seventh chapter of St. Luke's Gospel, and who is commonly confounded with Mary Magdalen.

Page 142.

FATIMA AND RADUAN.

This and the following poems belong to that class of ancient Spanish ballads, by unknown authors, called *Romances Moriscos*—Moriscan Romances or ballads. They were composed in the fourteenth century, some of them, probably, by the Moors, who then lived intermingled with the Christians; and they relate the loves and achievements of the knights of Granada.

Page 143.

LOVE AND FOLLY.—(FROM LA FONTAINE.)

This is rather an imitation than a translation of the poem of the graceful French fabulist.

Page 146.

These eyes shall not recall thee, etc.

This is the very expression of the original—*No te llamarán mis ojos*, etc. The Spanish poets early adopted the practice of calling a lady by the name of the most expressive feature of her countenance, her eyes. The lover styled his mistress "ojos bellos," beautiful eyes; "ojos serenos," serene eyes. Green eyes seem to have been anciently thought a great beauty in Spain, and there is a very pretty ballad by an absent lover, in which he addressed his lady by the title of "green eyes;" supplicating that he may remain in her remembrance:

> "¡Ay ojuelos verdes!
> Ay los mis ojuelos!
> Ay, hagan los cielos
> Que de mi te acuerdes!"

Page 147.

Say, Love—for didst thou see her tears, etc.

The stanza beginning with this line stands thus in the original:

> "Dilo tu, amor, si lo viste;
> ¡Mas ay! que de lastimado
> Diste otro nudo á la venda,
> Para no ver lo que ha pasado."

I am sorry to find so poor a conceit deforming so spirited a composition as this old ballad, but I have preserved it in the version.   It is one of those extravagances which afterward became so common in Spanish poetry, when Gongora introduced the *estilo culto*, as it was called.

Page 148.

LOVE IN THE AGE OF CHIVALRY.

This personification of the passion of Love, by Peyre Vidal, has been referred to as a proof of how little the Provençal poets were indebted to the authors of Greece and Rome for the imagery of their poems.

Page 149.

THE LOVE OF GOD.—(FROM THE PROVENÇAL OF BERNARD RASCAS.)

The original of these lines is thus given by John of Nostradamus, in his **Lives** of the Troubadours, in a barbarous Frenchified orthography:

" Touta kausa mortala una fes perirá,
Fors que l'amour de Dieu, que touiours durará.
Tous nostres cors vendran essuchs, come fa l'eska,
Lous Aubres leyssaran lour verdour tendra e fresca,
Lous Ausselets del bosc perdran lour kant subtyeu,
E non s'auzira plus lou Rossignol gentyeu.
Lous Buols al Pastourgage, e las blankas fedettas
Sent'ran lous agulhons de las mortals Sagettas,
Lous crestas d'Arles fiers, Renards, e Loups espars
Kabrols, Cervys, Chamous, Senglars de toutes pars,
Lous Ours hardys e forts, seran poudra, e Arena.
Lou Daulphin en la Mar, lou Ton, e la Balena,
Monstres impetuous, Ryaumes, e Comtas,
Lous Princes, e lous Reys, seran per mort domtas.
E nota ben eysso káscun : la Terra granda,
(Ou l'Escritura ment) lou fermament que branda,
Prendra autra figura.   Enfin tout perirá,
Fors que l'Amour de Dieu, que touiours durará."

Page 150.

FROM THE SPANISH OF PEDRO DE CASTRO Y AÑAYA.

Las Auroras de Diana, in which the original of these lines is contained, is, notwithstanding it was praised by Lope de Vega, one of the worst of the old Spanish Romances, being a tissue of riddles and affectations, with now and then a little poem of considerable beauty.

Page 160.

EARTH.

The author began this poem in rhyme.   The following is the first draught of it as far as he proceeded, in a stanza which he found it convenient to abandon:

35

A midnight black with clouds is on the sky;
　A shadow like the first original night
Folds in, and seems to press me as I lie;
　No image meets the vainly wandering sight,
And shot through rolling mists no starlight gleam
Glances on glassy pool or rippling stream.

No ruddy blaze, from dwellings bright within,
　Tinges the flowering summits of the grass;
No sound of life is heard, no village 'din,
　Wings rustling overhead or steps that pass,
While, on the breast of Earth at random thrown,
I listen to her mighty voice alone.

A voice of many tones: deep murmurs sent
　From waters that in darkness glide away,
From woods unseen by sweeping breezes bent,
　From rocky chasms where darkness dwells all day,
And hollows of the invisible hills around,
Blent in one ceaseless, melancholy sound.

O Earth! dost thou, too, sorrow for the past?
　Mourn'st thou thy childhood's unreturning hours,
Thy springs, that briefly bloomed and faded fast,
　The gentle generations of thy flowers,
Thy forests of the elder time, decayed
And gone with all the tribes that loved their shade?

Mourn'st thou that first fair time so early lost,
　The golden age that lives in poets' strains,
Ere hail or lightning, whirlwind, flood, or frost
　Scathed thy green breast, or earthquakes whelmed thy plains,
Ere blood upon the shuddering ground was spilt,
Or night was haunted by disease and guilt?

Or haply dost thou grieve for those who die?
　For living things that trod a while thy face,
The love of thee and heaven, and now they lie
　Mixed with the shapeless dust the wild winds chase?
I, too, must grieve, for never on thy sphere
Shall those bright forms and faces reappear.

Ha! with a deeper and more thrilling tone,
　Rises that voice around me: 'tis the cry
Of Earth for guilt and wrong, the eternal moan
　Sent to the listening and long-suffering sky,
I hear and tremble, and my heart grows faint,
As midst the night goes up that great complaint.

Page 174.

Where Isar's clay-white rivulets run
Through the dark woods like frighted deer.

Close to the city of Munich, in Bavaria, lies the spacious and beautiful pleas-
ure-ground, called the English Garden, in which these lines were written, originally
projected and laid out by our countryman, Count Rumford, under the auspices of

one of the sovereigns of the country. Winding walks, of great extent, pass through close thickets and groves interspersed with lawns; and streams, diverted from the river Isar, traverse the grounds swiftly in various directions, the water of which, stained with the clay of the soil it has corroded in its descent from the upper country, is frequently of a turbid-white color.

Page 178.

THE GREEN MOUNTAIN BOYS.

This song refers to the expedition of the Vermonters, commanded by Ethan Allen, by whom the British fort of Ticonderoga, on Lake Champlain, was surprised and taken, in May, 1775.

Page 180.

THE CHILD'S FUNERAL.

The incident on which this poem is founded was related to the author while in Europe, in a letter from an English lady. A child died in the south of Italy, and when they went to bury it they found it revived and playing with the flowers which, after the manner of that country, had been brought to grace his funeral.

Page 184.

'Tis said, when Schiller's death drew nigh,
The wish possessed his mighty mind,
To wander forth wherever lie
The homes and haunts of humankind.

Shortly before the death of Schiller, he was seized with a strong desire to travel in foreign countries, as if his spirit had a presentiment of its approaching enlargement, and already longed to expatiate in a wider and more varied sphere of existence.

Page 185.

The flower
Of sanguinaria, from whose brittle stem
The red drops fell like blood.

The *Sanguinaria Canadensis*, or blood-root, as it is commonly called, bears a delicate white flower of a musky scent, the stem of which breaks easily, and distils a juice of a bright-red color.

Page 191.

The shad-bush, white with flowers,
Brightened the glens.

The small tree, named by the botanists *Aronia Botyrapium*, is called, in some parts of our country, the shad-bush, from the circumstance that it flowers about the time that the shad ascend the rivers in early spring. Its delicate sprays, covered with white blossoms before the trees are yet in leaf, have a singularly beautiful appearance in the woods.

Page 192.

" There hast thou," said my friend, " a fitting type
Of human life."

I remember hearing an aged man, in the country, compare the slow movement of time in early life, and its swift flight as it approaches old age, to the drumming of a partridge or ruffed grouse in the woods—the strokes falling slow and distinct at first, and following each other more and more rapidly, till they end at last in a whirring sound.

Page 194.

AN EVENING REVERY.—FROM AN UNFINISHED POEM.

This poem and that entitled "The Fountain," with one or two others in blank verse, were intended by the author as portions of a larger poem.

Page 196.

The fresh savannas of the Sangamon
Here rise in gentle swells, and the long grass
Is mixed with rustling hazels.   Scarlet tufts
Are glowing in the green, like flakes of fire.

The Painted Cup, *Euchroma coccinea*, or *Bartsia coccinea*, grows in great abundance in the hazel prairies of the Western States, where its scarlet tufts make a brilliant appearance in the midst of the verdure.   The Sangamon is a beautiful river, tributary to the Illinois, bordered with rich prairies.

Page 204.

The long wave rolling from the southern pole
To break upon Japan.

"Breaks the long wave that at the pole began."—TENNENT'S *Anster Fair.*

Page 205.

At noon the Hebrew bowed the knee
And worshipped.

"Evening and morning, and at noon, will I pray and cry aloud, and he shall hear my voice."— *Psalm* lv. 17.

Page 208.

THE WHITE-FOOTED DEER.

"During the stay of Long's Expedition at Engineer Cantonment, three specimens of a variety of the common deer were brought in, having all the feet white near the hoofs, and extending to those on the hind-feet from a little above the spurious hoofs.   This white extremity was divided, upon the sides of the foot, by the general color of the leg, which extends down near to the hoofs, leaving a white triangle in front, of which the point was elevated rather higher than the spurious hoofs."—GODMAN'S *Natural History*, vol. ii., p. 314.

Page 236.

THE LOST BIRD.

Readers who are acquainted with the Spanish language, may not be displeased at seeing the original of this little poem:

EL PAJARO PERDIDO.

Huyó con vuelo incierto,
  Y de mis ojos ha desparecido.
Mirad, si, á vuestro huerto,
  Mi pajaro querido,
  Niñas hermosas, por acaso ha huido.

Sus ojos relucientes
  Son como los del aguila orgullosa;
Plumas resplandecientes,
  En la cabeza airosa,
  Lleva; y su voz es tierna y armoniosa.

Mirad, si cuidadoso
  Junto á las flores se escondió en la grama.
Ese laurel frondoso
  Mirad, rama por rama,
  Que él los laureles y los flores ama.

Si le hallais, por ventura,
  No os enamore su amoroso acento;
No os prende su hermosura;
  Volvedmele al momento;
  O dejadle, si no, libre en el viento.

Por que su pico de oro
  Solo en mi mano toma la semilla;
Y no enjugaré el lloro
  Que veis en mi mejilla,
  Hasta encontrar mi profugo avecilla.

Mi vista se oscurece,
  Si sus ojos no vé, que son mi dia
Mi ánima desfallece
  Con la melancolia
  De no escucharle ya su melodia.

The literature of Spain at the present day has this peculiarity, that female writers have, in considerable number, entered into competition with the other sex. One of the most remarkable of these, as a writer of both prose and poetry, is Ca- rolina Coronado de Perry, the author of the little poem here given. The poetical literature of Spain has felt the influence of the female mind in the infusion of a certain delicacy and tenderness, and the more frequent choice of subjects which

interest the domestic affections. Concerning the verses of the lady already men-
tioned, Don Juan Eugenio Hartzenbusch, one of the most accomplished Spanish
critics of the present day, and himself a successful dramatic writer, says:

"If Carolina Coronado had, through modesty, sent her productions from Es-
tremadura to Madrid under the name of a person of the other sex, it would still
have been difficult for intelligent readers to persuade themselves that they were
written by a man, or at least, considering their graceful sweetness, purity of tone,
simplicity of conception, brevity of development, and delicate and particular choice
of subject, we should be constrained to attribute them to one yet in his early
youth, whom the imagination would represent as ingenuous, innocent, and gay, who
had scarce ever wandered beyond the flowery grove or pleasant valley where his
cradle was rocked, and where he has been lulled to sleep by the sweetest songs of
Francisca de la Torre, Garcilaso, and Melendez."

The author of the *Pajaro Perdido*, according to a memoir of her by Angel
Fernandez de los Rios, was born at Almendralejo, in Estremadura, in 1823. At
the age of nine years she began to steal from sleep, after a day passed in various
lessons, and in domestic occupations, several hours every night to read the poets
of her country, and other books belonging to the library of the household, among
which are mentioned, as a proof of her vehement love of reading, the "Critical
History of Spain," by the Abbé Masuden, "and other works equally dry and pro-
lix." She was afterward sent to Badajoz, where she received the best education
which the state of the country, then on fire with a civil war, would admit. Here
the intensity of her application to her studies caused a severe malady, which has
frequently recurred in after-life. At the age of thirteen years she wrote a poem
entitled *La Palma*, which the author of her biography declares to be worthy of
Herrera, and which led Espronceda, a poet of Estremadura, a man of genius, and
the author of several translations from Byron, whom he resembled both in mental
and personal characteristics, to address her an eulogistic sonnet. In 1843, when
she was but twenty years old, a volume of her poems was published at Madrid, in
which were included both that entitled *La Palma* and the one I have given in this
note. To this volume Hartzenbusch, in his admiration for her genius, prefaced an
introduction.

The task of writing verses in Spanish is not difficult. Rhymes are readily
found, and the language is easily moulded into metrical forms. Those who have
distinguished themselves in this literature have generally made their first essays
in verse. What is remarkable enough, the men who afterward figured in political
life mostly began their career as the authors of madrigals. A poem introduces the
future statesman to the public, as a speech at a popular meeting introduces the
candidate for political distinctions in this country. I have heard of but one of the
eminent Spanish politicians of the present time, who made a boast that he was in-
nocent of poetry; and if all that his enemies say of him be true, it would have
been well both for his country and his own fame, if he had been equally innocent
of corrupt practices. The compositions of Carolina Coronado, even her earliest, do
not deserve to be classed with the productions of which I have spoken, and which
are simply the effect of inclination and facility. They possess the *mens divinior*.

In 1852 a collection of poems of Carolina Coronado was brought out at
Madrid, including those which were first published. The subjects are of larger

variety than those which prompted her earlier productions; some of them are of a religious cast, others refer to political matters. One of them, which appears among the "Improvisations," is an energetic protest against erecting a new amphitheatre for bull-fights. The spirit in all her poetry is humane and friendly to the best interests of mankind.

Her writings in prose must not be overlooked. Among them is a novel entitled *Sigea*, founded on the adventures of Camoëns; another entitled *Jarilla*, a beautiful story, full of pictures of rural life in Estremadura, which deserves, if it could find a competent translator, to be transferred to our language. Besides these there are two other novels from her pen, *Paquita* and *La Luz del Tejo*. A few years since appeared, in a Madrid periodical, the *Semanario*, a series of letters written by her, giving an account of the impressions received in a journey from the Tagus to the Rhine, including a visit to England. Among the subjects on which she has written, is the idea, still warmly cherished in Spain, of uniting the entire peninsula under one government. In an ably-conducted journal of Madrid, she has given accounts of the poetesses of Spain, her contemporaries, with extracts from their writings, and a kindly estimate of their respective merits.

Her biographer speaks of her activity and efficiency in charitable enterprises, her interest in the cause of education, her visits to the primary schools of Madrid, encouraging and rewarding the pupils, and her patronage of the *escuela de par-vulos*, or infant school at Badajoz, established by a society of that city, with the design of improving the education of the laboring class.

It must have been not long after the publication of her poems, in 1852, that Carolina Coronado became the wife of an American gentleman, Mr. Horatio J. Perry, at one time our Secretary of Legation at the Court of Madrid, afterward our *Chargé d'Affaires*, and now, in 1863, again Secretary of Legation. Amid the duties of a wife and mother, which she fulfils with exemplary fidelity and grace, she has neither forgotten nor forsaken the literary pursuits which have given her so high a reputation.

Page 257
THE RUINS OF ITALICA.

The poems of the Spanish author, Francisco de Rioja, who lived in the first half of the seventeenth century, are few in number, but much esteemed. His ode on the Ruins of Italica is one of the most admired of these, but in the only collection of his poems which I have seen, it is said that the concluding stanza, in the original copy, was deemed so little worthy of the rest that it was purposely omitted in the publication. Italica was a city founded by the Romans in the south of Spain, the remains of which are still an object of interest.

Page 268.
SELLA.

Sella is the name given by the Vulgate to one of the wives of Lamech, mentioned in the fourth chapter of the Book of Genesis, and called Zillah in the common English version of the Bible.

Page 282.

HOMER'S ODYSSEY, BOOK V., TRANSLATED.

It may be esteemed presumptuous in the author of this volume to attempt a translation of any part of Homer in blank verse after that of Cowper. It has always seemed to him, however, that Cowper's version had very great defects. The style of Homer is simple, and he has been praised for fire and rapidity of narrative. Does anybody find these qualities in Cowper's Homer? If Cowper had rendered him into such English as he employed in his "Task," there would be no reason to complain; but in translating Homer he seems to have thought it necessary to use a different style from that of his original work. Almost every sentence is stiffened by some clumsy inversion; stately phrases are used when simpler ones were at hand, and would have rendered the meaning of the original better. The entire version has the appearance of being hammered out with great labor, and as a whole it is cold and constrained; scarce any thing seems spontaneous; it is only now and then that the translator has caught the fervor of his author. Homer, of course, wrote in idiomatic Greek, and, in order to produce either a true copy of the original, or an agreeable poem, should have been translated into idiomatic English.

I am almost ashamed, after this censure of an author whom, in the main, I admire as much as I do Cowper, to refer to my own translation of the Fifth Book of the Odyssey. I desire barely to say that I have endeavored to give the verses of the old Greek poet at least a simpler presentation in English, and one more conformable to the genius of our language.

Page 315.

The mock-grape's blood-red banner, etc.

Ampelopis, mock-grape. I have here literally translated the botanical name of the Virginia creeper—an appellation too cumbrous for verse.

Page 320.

A BRIGHTER DAY.

This poem was written shortly after the author's return from a visit to Spain, and more than a twelvemonth before the overthrow of the tyrannical government of Queen Isabella and the expulsion of the Bourbons. It is not "from the Spanish" in the ordinary sense of the phrase, but is an attempt to put into a poetic form sentiments and hopes which the author frequently heard, during his visit to Spain, from the lips of the natives. We are yet to see whether these expectations of an enlightened government and national liberty are to become a reality under the new order of things.

THE END. (10)